D1576668

CREATE IT
yourself

CREATE IT
yourself

Hundreds of ideas for all kinds
of things to make yourself

Published by the Reader's Digest Association Limited
London • New York • Sydney • Montreal

CREATE IT YOURSELF was published by
The Reader's Digest Association Limited, London

First edition Copyright © 2000 The Reader's Digest Association
Limited, 11 Westferry Circus, Canary Wharf, London E14 4HE

www.readersdigest.co.uk

If you have any comments or suggestions about this book, e-mail us at:
gbeditorial@readersdigest.co.uk

Copyright © 2000 Reader's Digest Association Far East Limited.
Philippines Copyright © 2000 Reader's Digest Association
Far East Limited.

Printed in Belgium

ISBN 0 276 42437 9

CREATE IT YOURSELF was adapted from *Home Made Best Made*,
published by Reader's Digest (Australia) Pty Limited, Sydney.
First edition copyright © 1997
Some projects were adapted from *Home Made Best Made*, published by
Reader's Digest Association Inc., New York.
First edition copyright © 1998.

READER'S DIGEST, GENERAL BOOKS, LONDON
Editorial Director: Cortina Butler
Art Director: Nick Clark
Executive Editor: Julian Browne
Publishing Projects Manager: Alastair Holmes
Development Editor: Ruth Binney
Picture Research Editor: Martin Smith
Style Editor: Ron Pankhurst

For *Create It Yourself* (UK)
Project Editor: Helen Spence
Assistant Editors: Caroline Boucher, Jill Steed
Art Editors: Kate Harris, Louise Turpin
Proofreader: Barry Gage

For *Home Made Best Made* (Australia)
Editors: Phil Rodwell, Michael Wall
Designers: Barbara Beckett, Cathy Campbell

For *Home Made Best Made* (USA)
Project Editor: Nancy Shuker
Project Art Editor: Virginia Wells Blaker
Editor: Judith Cressy
Associate Editor: Alexis Lipsitz
Associate Designers: Barbara Lapic, Ed Jacobus, Wendy Wong
Assistant Editor: Andrew Boorstyn

CONSULTANTS AND CONTRIBUTORS

All About Art
Catherine Alston
Susan Avery
Keran Barrett
Jennifer Bennell
Ginger Kean Berk
Jan Berry
Sophie Blackall
Virginia Wells Blaker
Jacqueline Kinghorn Brown
David Carroll
Tom Christopher
Craft Plus
Ara DerMarderosian
Kim Erickson
Brad Farrell
Mark D. Feirer
Kate Finnie
Sandra Flannery
Kim Fletcher
Kay Francis

Jackie French
Clinton Gay
Gina Grant
John Hall
Jeni Harris
Jennifer Harris
Susan Harris
Barbara Haynes
Linda Hetzer
John Hollingshead
Brenda Horne
Zuelia Ann Hurt
Lisa Johnson
Adam Jones
Kerry Anne Jones
Pamela Jones
Helen Taylor Jones

Maureen Klein
Eleanor Kostyk
Mike Lawrence
Linda Lehany
Michael Lehany
Sandra Levy
Tim Martin
Steven Mays
Zabel Meshigian
Les Miller
Robert Morrison
Dieter Mylius
Sue Ninham
Louise Owens
Mignon Parker
Leslie Glover Pendleton
Susan E. Piatt

T.C. Powers
Keith Scanlon
Susan B. Schoen
Megan Self
Howard G. Senior
Ray Skibinski
Thomas Sperling
Robert Stiemle
Jane Stoddart
Wendy Straume
Kevin Tenney
Kathy Tripp
Anne Marie Unwin
Paul Urquhart
Linda Venturoni
Diane Wallis
Rodney Weridland
Libby Wilkinson
Susan Converse Winslow
Ian Worpole

CONTENTS

ALL ABOUT THE GARDEN

CRAFTED WITH CARE

LOOKING GOOD, FEELING GOOD

ABOUT THIS BOOK

THERE is no doubt that the advances of modern technology have made all our lives easier, encouraging us to buy almost anything we might want or could imagine wanting – only a shortage of cash need cramp us.

But not so very long ago, most of the things that people wore and ate, many of their furnishings, and any luxuries such as gifts, all had to be made at home. In the process of accepting the ready availability of mass-produced, machine-made products we are aware of a sense of loss: perhaps what's missing is the pride we feel in achievement; perhaps, in these ecologically concerned times, it's having control over what we consume and use. Certainly the shop-bought product lacks the individual touch or the personal stamp – even if it involves a minor imperfection – of those things you create yourself.

This highly practical book proclaims its contents and objectives in positive and unambiguous terms. It encourages everyone to join the gentle revolution of those who are eagerly learning or relearning half-forgotten skills and using them to make all kinds of things themselves. Within these pages there is a simple, straightforward message to all those who have begun to miss the reassuring feeling that comes with knowing that homemade is best made.

In the five chapters of this book, we give you the opportunity to rediscover your creativity – whether it's in the kitchen or the garden, decorating the home, or making delightful items to give as presents. The projects in this book take two approaches to creativity: making things from scratch, and finding new ways of using items which are already on-hand. For example, in the chapter titled 'The Well-stocked Kitchen' there are hundreds of recipes for making everything from jams to sausages – and there are scores of suggestions for using or storing what you've made. The section on freezing will be particularly useful when you begin to harvest the bounty from the herb bed, vegetable patch or orchard you have made using techniques from the chapter titled 'All About the Garden'.

Cross-fertilisation is another element of the book: projects in the various chapters are interrelated so that skills learned in one place may be applied in a variety of others. Many of those in the craft chapter will find their usefulness as part of your home's decor, while patterns and stencils in the decorating chapter can be adapted for craft projects. Gardening ideas will provide materials for cookery or making your own toiletries.

At the start of each chapter, a 'Before you Begin' section describes special techniques that can be used in the projects on the ensuing pages. There are lots of little bonuses as well. On virtually every page of every chapter there are hints and tips for the easier making, serving, storing and displaying of your homemade items.

Most of the projects require only moderate ability, although we've included a few larger and more challenging tasks that you may wish to take on after honing your skills on more basic projects. Whatever your needs and interests, there's plenty here to meet your requirements.

Full-page, colour photographs and clear illustrations, including straightforward, step-by-step drawings, will guide and inspire you. For years to come, you'll find yourself turning to *Create It Yourself* regularly as an all-in-one reference to skills new and traditional.

THE WELL-STOCKED
kitchen

In the world of food, the word 'homemade' conjures up the heady aroma of baking bread and simmering sauces, and memories of special-occasion dishes – often vividly recalled on the palate – that come only from a warm and happy kitchen.

These days, we insist on foods that are as free of chemicals and preservatives as possible and the ideal way to achieve this is to prepare as much food as we can at home, using ingredients chosen for their freshness and purity. It doesn't take long to make a selection of your favourite dishes once you have acquired a few basic skills.

The Well-stocked Kitchen explores the full range of cookery skills and techniques, from baking to bottling, from freezing to special festive dishes. Recipes range from dips and spreads to pasta sauces and savoury pastries; from pâtés and sausages to stocks and yeast breads; from biscuits and muffins to a panoply of cakes and confectionery; from party drinks and punches to ice cream and sorbet.

Throughout the chapter, step-by-step drawings explain techniques and special boxes give you helpful hints and tips.

BEFORE YOU BEGIN...

The recipes in this chapter celebrate the diversity of cooking styles and methods available to the home cook – from baking to bottling, from freezing to special festive dishes. Here are a few general tips to help you to get started

YOU DON'T NEED a large kitchen or sophisticated equipment to cook well. Most foods can be prepared with a relatively limited range of utensils. All cooks require two or three kitchen knives of varying sizes, including a good paring knife, plus a wooden block or magnetic wall-mounted strip for storage. Never keep knives loose in a drawer. The following is a guide to what you will need to make the recipes in this chapter.

♦ Wooden and stainless-steel mixing and stirring spoons, a pair of tongs and a ladle, plus a slotted spoon for lifting solids from liquid. Make sure the handles are long enough to extend well beyond the heat source and that the handles of metal spoons are heatproof.

♦ A pair of sharp stainless-steel kitchen scissors.

♦ Kitchen scales.

♦ A heatproof glass measuring jug for liquid.

♦ Measuring spoons.

♦ Mixing bowls in various sizes.

♦ A double boiler, especially for melting chocolate and making custards. Alternatively you can improvise one at the last minute by using one large and one smaller saucepan; set the smaller into the larger, making sure the water in the lower pan doesn't touch the bottom of the upper pan.

♦ Potato peeler, grater, citrus zester, colander and sieve.

♦ For baking you will also need: a rolling pin, balloon whisk, spatulas, a range of cake and tart tins in varying sizes and shapes, and a hand-held electric mixer (more adaptable than a hand-held whisk).

♦ A jam thermometer is a useful luxury.

Read the recipe carefully

Before beginning any new recipe – no matter how simple it seems – it is important to read the recipe from beginning to end. Study the list of ingredients and make sure that you have all the items on hand before you start cooking. Read the method carefully and make sure you understand what you will be asked to do, so that you can proceed smoothly. Hints and tips are included throughout this chapter to help you to achieve the best results from the recipes.

Using fresh or dried herbs

Most of the herbs called for in these recipes are fresh. If you don't have fresh herbs on hand, you can substitute the dried variety. Dried herbs usually have a more intense flavour, so reduce the quantity given in the recipe by half. If you prefer a more pronounced flavour you can increase the quantities later.

Sealing jars and bottles

It is important that the containers you use for preserves are well sterilised (see page 278), and that they are properly sealed. The step-by-step directions given below for bottling jams and chutneys are equally valid for pickles and all other bottled items.

Jams and marmalades

It is important that sterilised jars are warmed before pouring in hot jam; if cold jars are used they may crack. Heat the jars in a low oven (110°C, 225°F, gas mark ¼), until they are warm to the touch,

---

BOTTLING JAMS AND CHUTNEYS

1 *Once the jam or chutney is fully cooked, remove from the heat and leave for about 10 minutes to settle. Stir to distribute fruit evenly and ladle into warm, sterilised jars.*

2 *Fill jars to the top to allow for shrinkage as the jam or chutney cools. To remove air bubbles (which can harbour bacteria), prod the contents with a sterile skewer.*

3 *When the jars are cool enough to handle, wipe off any drips from the top of each jar and clean the outside with a clean, moist cloth. Cover and leave until cold.*

4 *Seal with lids or cellophane covers. To get a tight seal, dip the cellophane in boiled water and centre over the jar. Smooth sides and secure with rubber bands or string.*

COOKING TERMS

DREDGE: to roll or dip food in a powder, such as flour or icing sugar, until generously covered

FOLD: to blend ingredients by gently stirring and lifting, so as not to lose any incorporated air

KNEAD: to incorporate ingredients and make dough smoother and more elastic by applying a pressing and stretching motion

SCALD: to heat milk to just below boiling point (100°C, 212°F)

WHISK: to beat ingredients such as cream or egg whites lightly and quickly to incorporate air

ZEST: the coloured part of citrus peel, containing flavouring oils

Home cooking is never out of fashion. A basic collection of kitchen implements will yield wonderful culinary results.

before filling them with the hot jam or marmalade. As soon as you have poured the jam into the jar, seal it using a screw-top or spring-clamp lid. Alternatively, put a waxed paper disc, waxed side down, on the surface of the jam and smooth it with your finger to remove any air pockets. Then cover with a moistened cellophane cover (available from kitchenware shops) and secure with a rubber band. Do this while the jam is still hot, otherwise moisture will collect inside the lid and the jam will go mouldy. Store in a cool, dark place.

Cooking with yeast

Yeast is the raising agent for many breads, for pizza dough and for some cakes. It is composed of live cells that react with the sugars contained in flours. Both compressed live yeast and powdered varieties, sold in convenient sachets or tubs, are available. For speed and ease of use, many cooks choose dried yeast granules, sold as easy blend yeast, that can simply be added dry to the flour.

Other varieties of yeast must first be activated by dissolving the granules in warm water until frothy. This reaction usually takes about 5 minutes. The liquid in which you dissolve the yeast should be at about body temperature; any higher and you risk killing the yeast, any lower and the yeast cells won't activate. A pinch of sugar added to the warm liquid 'feeds' the yeast and helps activate it more readily.

Preparing and freezing ice creams

The best method for making ice cream is to use either an electric or manual ice-cream churn. These incorporate air into the mix, adding volume. An alternative method to using a churn involves pouring the ice-cream mixture into freezer trays and allowing it to freeze partially. You then remove the mixture to a bowl and beat it with an electric mixer to break up the ice crystals, then return it to the freezer tray. Repeat this once or twice more before allowing the ice cream to harden. You won't get the perfect, creamy ice cream that churning produces, but it is the next best thing.

When adding fruit pieces or nuts to ice creams, add them part way into the freezing process. Most fruits freeze more quickly than the custard/cream base and, if added too soon, will turn into ice before the cream has frozen. Allow ice creams to ripen in the freezer for several hours, or as the recipe indicates, before serving.

Oven temperatures

Each oven varies in temperature slightly. The following ranges are standard: very low: below 120°C (250°F, gas mark ½); low: 140-150°C (275-300°F, gas mark 1-2); medium: 175-190°C (350-375°F, gas mark 4-5); hot: 200°C (400°F, gas mark 6); very hot: 240-260°C (475-500°F, gas mark 9-10).

Pickled Preserves

Preserving fruits and vegetables in brine or vinegar is a time-honoured method of bottling. Pickles add colour and flavour to any snack or meal

Mixed vegetable pickle

Almost any vegetable can be used as a part of this spicy pickle. It will brighten cold chicken or sliced ham, and add spice to a simple salad.

INGREDIENTS

makes two 1 litre (1¾ pint) jars
- 4 small cucumbers, halved, seeded and cut into strips
- 1 small cauliflower, cut into florets
- 8 shallots, trimmed
- 2 green peppers, deseeded and cut into strips
- 2 red peppers, deseeded and cut into strips
- 500g (1lb 2oz) green beans, trimmed
- 850g (1lb 14oz) carrots, peeled and cut into strips
- 2 tablespoons salt
- 1.5 litres (2¾ pints) white malt vinegar
- 50g (1¾oz) granulated sugar
- 50g (1¾oz) piece fresh ginger, peeled and halved
- 1 teaspoon turmeric
- 1 tablespoon each mustard seeds, peppercorns, allspice berries and mustard powder

1 Place all the prepared vegetables in a ceramic or glass bowl. Sprinkle with the salt, cover and leave for 24 hours.
2 Rinse the vegetables with cold water and then drain well.
3 Place the vinegar in a stainless-steel saucepan with the sugar, ginger and spices. Bring to the boil, then add the vegetables and cook for 2 minutes.
4 Lift the vegetables out with a slotted spoon and arrange them attractively in sterilised wide-mouthed jars.

5 Discard the ginger, strain the vinegar and pour it over the vegetables. Seal the jars. The pickle can be stored in a cool, dark place for up to 6 months. Ready to eat in 4 weeks. Refrigerate once opened.

Pickled cauliflower florets

A welcome addition to an antipasto platter, these crisp florets are also the perfect accompaniment to spicy sliced meats for a tasty picnic lunch.

INGREDIENTS

makes two 1 litre (1¾ pint) jars
- 1 large cauliflower, cut into florets
- white malt vinegar, sufficient to cover cauliflower
- 1 tablespoon salt
- 1 tablespoon white peppercorns
- 1 tablespoon muscovado sugar
- 1 medium red pepper, deseeded and finely sliced
- 6 small dried red chillies

1 Place the cauliflower florets in a stainless-steel saucepan and cover with the white vinegar. Add the salt, peppercorns and muscovado sugar to the pan.
2 Bring to the boil, add the pepper strips and boil for 1 minute. Remove the vegetables with a slotted spoon and place in two sterilised wide-mouthed jars. Pack them in snugly, distributing the pepper strips evenly, then tuck three chillies in among the cauliflower florets in each jar.
3 Pour in the hot vinegar, making sure the liquid covers the cauliflower. Seal the jars. The pickle can be stored in a cool, dark place for up to 6 months. Ready to eat in 2 weeks. Refrigerate once opened.

Pickled onions

A chunk of Cheddar, a slice or two of crusty bread and a couple of these spicy onions are all you need for a simple and delicious lunch.

INGREDIENTS

makes two 500ml (18fl oz) jars

- 2kg (4lb 8oz) small white pickling onions
- 300g (10½oz) salt
- 10 black peppercorns
- 4 fresh red chillies
- 4 bay leaves
- 2 litres (3½ pints) cider vinegar

1 Place the unpeeled onions in a bowl; cover with boiling water and leave to stand for 5 minutes, then drain. This procedure helps to make the onions easier to peel.

2 Remove the outer skins and trim the roots and crowns. Avoid removing too many of the onion layers because this area can become soggy during the pickling process. Cover the onions with cold water, add the salt and mix well. Leave to soak for 12 hours, or overnight.

3 Drain the onions and pack in sterilised wide-mouthed jars with the peppercorns, chillies and bay leaves.

4 Bring the vinegar to the boil in a stainless-steel saucepan and pour it over the onions to cover them. Seal the jars and store in a cool, dark place for up to 6 months. Ready to eat in 4 weeks. Refrigerate once opened.

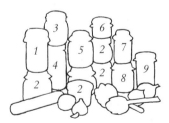

A range of pickles is a wonderful stand-by to have handy in the larder: (1) Globe Artichokes in Olive Oil, see page 23, (2) Marinated Pickled Olives, (3) Pickled Red Cabbage, (4) Mixed Vegetable Pickle, (5) Pickled Onions, (6) Pickled Quail's Eggs, (7) Pickled Spiced Plums, (8) Pickled Hen's Eggs, (9) Pickled Cauliflower Florets.

Spicy Lime Pickle. Thick and hot, this Indian pickle is delicious served with curries or cooked meat. You might also try it with chilled prawns and crusty bread.

Spicy lime pickle

If you prefer a pickle with less heat, reduce the number of fresh chillies given in the recipe.

INGREDIENTS

makes three 250ml (9fl oz) jars

- 1kg (2lb 4oz) limes, washed
- 8 fresh red chillies, chopped
- 4 cloves garlic, chopped
- 2 tablespoons fresh ginger, chopped
- 1 tablespoon ground coriander
- 1 tablespoon ground cumin
- 2 teaspoons ground cardamom
- 2 teaspoons mustard seeds
- 1 teaspoon freshly ground black pepper
- 1 teaspoon salt
- 1 teaspoon turmeric
- 375ml (13fl oz) white wine vinegar
- 125ml (4fl oz) vegetable oil

1 Cut each lime lengthways into 6 wedges and place in a stainless-steel saucepan with all the other ingredients.
2 Bring to the boil over a medium heat, reduce the heat and simmer until the fruit is tender and the pickle thick, about 50 minutes.
3 When cool enough to handle, ladle into warm, sterilised jars and seal. Store in a cool, dark place for up to a year. Ready to eat after 2 weeks but the flavour improves with longer keeping. Refrigerate once opened.

Pickled hen's eggs

Perfect for a picnic, these eggs give cold chicken and a tossed green salad a flavourful lift.

INGREDIENTS

makes two 500ml (18fl oz) jars

- 8-12 medium eggs
- 1 litre (1¾ pints) malt vinegar
- 10 black peppercorns
- 2 small dried red chillies

Pickled red cabbage

The sharp mustard flavour of this pickle makes it a complementary side dish for roast pork.

INGREDIENTS

makes two 500ml (18fl oz) jars

- 1 red cabbage
- 3 tablespoons sea salt
- 1 litre (1¾ pints) white malt vinegar
- 1 teaspoon mustard seeds
- 1 teaspoon black peppercorns
- 2cm (¾in) piece fresh ginger, peeled and bruised
- 2 bay leaves

1 Remove the outer cabbage leaves and wash the remainder well. Cut the cabbage into quarters and shred. Place in a bowl and sprinkle with the salt. Cover and leave for 12 hours, or overnight.
2 Rinse the cabbage in a colander and drain.
3 Place the vinegar, mustard seeds, peppercorns and ginger in a stainless-steel saucepan and bring to the boil. Cool and strain, retaining the liquid.
4 Pack the cabbage into two sterilised jars and cover with the spiced vinegar. Tuck a bay leaf into each jar. Seal and store in a cool, dark place for up to 6 months. Ready to eat in 2 weeks. Refrigerate once opened.

1 Hard-boil the eggs in barely simmering water for 10 minutes. Drain, then plunge into cold water and leave for 10 minutes.
2 Meanwhile, in a stainless-steel saucepan, boil the vinegar with the peppercorns.
3 Crack the shells all over, peel the eggs and pack them in sterilised wide-mouthed jars. Cover with the hot vinegar. Place a chilli in each jar and seal. Store in a cool, dark place for up to 6 months. Ready to eat in 4 weeks. Refrigerate once opened.

Pickled quail's eggs

Quail's eggs are a little tedious to peel but they make an attractive addition to an antipasto platter. Presented in attractive jars with coloured ribbon tied round the top, these dainty and unusual pickled eggs make a good Christmas present. They taste superb with ham and cold meats as well as cheese.

INGREDIENTS

makes one 500ml (18fl oz) jar
- 1 teaspoon whole mixed peppercorns
- 2 dried red chillies
- 5cm (2in) piece fresh ginger, peeled and finely chopped
- 1 blade mace
- a pared strip of orange zest
- 1 teaspoon yellow mustard seeds
- 1 teaspoon salt
- 600ml (1 pint) white wine vinegar
- 24 fresh quail's eggs

1 Put all the ingredients except the eggs into a saucepan. Bring to the boil, then remove from the heat and leave for 2 hours, or until cold.
2 Hard-boil the eggs for 3 minutes, plunge them into cold water, and set aside for 10 minutes, or until cool. Peel the eggs and pack them into a sterilised jar.
3 Strain the spiced vinegar through muslin, then pour it over the eggs so that it covers them completely.
4 Seal and store in a cool, dark place for a week before using. Refrigerate once opened. Although best used within a month, they will keep for up to 6 months.

Pickled spiced plums

These aromatic plums bring the spices of the Orient to a traditional roast of pork or lamb.

INGREDIENTS

makes two 500ml (18fl oz) jars
- 300g (10½oz) granulated sugar
- 625ml (1 pint 1fl oz) water
- 250ml (9fl oz) white malt vinegar
- 4 sticks cinnamon, broken
- 1 tablespoon each whole cloves and whole black peppercorns
- 2-3 strips orange zest
- 1kg (2lb 4oz) small, firm, ripe red Victoria plums

1 Place the sugar and water in a saucepan and bring to the boil, stirring to dissolve the sugar. Reduce the heat and simmer for 10 minutes.
2 Add the vinegar, cinnamon sticks, cloves, peppercorns and orange zest, cover the pan and simmer gently for 15 minutes.
3 Meanwhile, wash the plums, then prick in several places with a skewer or darning needle. Place in sterilised wide-mouthed jars and add the hot spiced syrup to cover.
4 Seal the jars and store in a cool, dark place for up to 6 months. Ready to serve in 4 weeks. Refrigerate once opened.

Marinated pickled olives

A Mediterranean marinade gives a rich flavour to pitted black olives. These are available in jars from delicatessen counters or in tins from supermarkets.

INGREDIENTS

makes three 500ml (18fl oz) jars
- 500ml (18fl oz) olive oil
- 250ml (9fl oz) water
- 125ml (4fl oz) dry white wine
- 4 large cloves garlic
- 4 dried whole red chillies
- 1 teaspoon dried oregano
- 1 teaspoon cracked black pepper
- 4 bay leaves
- 6 thick slices lemon
- 1kg (2lb 4oz) stoned black olives in brine, drained
- 3 sprigs fresh thyme

1 In a saucepan combine the oil, water and wine and bring to the boil. Remove from the heat, add the garlic, chillies, oregano, pepper and bay leaves. Leave to stand for 30 minutes. Strain, reserving the marinade; pick out and reserve the garlic, chillies and bay leaves.
2 Place a lemon slice in each of three sterilised 500ml (18fl oz) jars and add the olives. Arrange the garlic, bay leaves, chillies, remaining lemon slices and thyme sprigs attractively in the jars. Cover with the marinade and seal. (If the marinade does not quite cover the olives, add sufficient olive oil.) Store in a cool, dark place for up to 6 months. Leave for at least 2 weeks before eating to allow the flavours to develop. Refrigerate once opened.

Cucumber pickle

Crushed ice helps keep the cucumbers crisp during the salting process for this sweet and sour pickle.

INGREDIENTS

makes six 250ml (9fl oz) jars
- 4 small cucumbers, sliced
- 600g (1lb 5oz) onions, halved and sliced
- 2 cloves garlic, quartered
- 3-4 tablespoons sea salt
- 750ml (1lb 10oz) crushed ice
- 500g (1lb 2oz) light, soft brown sugar
- 500ml (18fl oz) cider vinegar
- 1 tablespoon mustard seeds
- 1 teaspoon celery seeds
- ½ teaspoon turmeric

1 Place the cucumber slices, onions, garlic and salt in a large glass or ceramic bowl and mix well. Stir in the ice and leave for 3 hours.
2 Drain the vegetables well. Discard the garlic.
3 Place all the remaining ingredients in a large stainless-steel saucepan. Bring to the boil, stirring to dissolve the sugar. Stir in the vegetables and, as soon as the liquid returns to the boil, remove from the heat.
4 Using a slotted spoon, transfer the pickles to sterilised glass jars. Cover the pickles in each jar with the cooking liquid. Seal and store in a cool, dark place for at least 1 week before eating. Refrigerate once opened.

◆ Chutneys for Your Table ◆

*Chutneys originated in India and are redolent with the spices of Asia. Virtually any vegetable
and many fruits can be employed in chutney-making, so you might like to vary these recipes. After
long, slow cooking, each preserve should be smooth and pulpy with a mellow flavour*

Mango chutney

*With its strong ginger flavour, this chutney
enhances a spicy, home-made vindaloo.*

INGREDIENTS

makes six 250g (9oz) jars
- 2kg (4lb 8oz) green mangoes,
  peeled and diced
- 1 teaspoon sea salt
- 300ml (10fl oz) malt vinegar
- 300ml (10fl oz) apple cider
- 1 tablespoon chopped ginger
- 2 teaspoons cayenne pepper
- 240g (8½oz) onions, chopped
- 100g soft, light brown sugar

1 Sprinkle the mangoes with the salt and leave
for 24 hours. Rinse and drain.
2 Place the mango pieces and remaining
ingredients in a stainless-steel saucepan and
simmer over a low heat for 30-40 minutes.
3 Ladle the chutney into warm, sterilised
jars, cover with a cloth and leave until cold.
4 Seal the jars and store in a cool, dark place
for up to 6 months. Ready to serve in 4
weeks. Refrigerate once opened.

Rhubarb chutney

*The tang of lemon permeates this quick-to-make
mild chutney. Serve with any cold meat.*

INGREDIENTS

makes three 250g (9oz) jars

- 1kg (2lb 4oz) rhubarb
- 250g (9oz) sultanas
- 800g (1lb 12oz)
  granulated sugar
- 2 lemons, finely chopped
- 1 teaspoon salt
- 2 tablespoons chopped ginger
- 625ml (1 pint 1fl oz) malt
  vinegar

1 Wash and trim the rhubarb stems and cut
them into 2 cm (¾ in) lengths. Place with all
the other ingredients in a stainless-steel pan and
bring to the boil. Reduce the heat and simmer
gently, uncovered, for 1 hour, or until the
chutney has thickened, stirring occasionally.
2 Ladle the chutney into warm, sterilised jars,
cover with a cloth and leave until cold.
3 Seal the jars and store in a cool, dark place
for up to 6 months. Ready to serve in
4 weeks. Refrigerate once opened.

Green tomato chutney

*Pick unripened tomatoes from your own plants, or
order them from the local greengrocer.*

INGREDIENTS

makes four 250g (9oz) jars

- 1.5kg (3lb 5oz) green
  tomatoes
- 300g (10½oz) onions, peeled
- 1 large green apple, peeled
  and cored
- 200g (7oz) sultanas
- 1 teaspoon salt
- 1 teaspoon cayenne pepper
- 1 teaspoon ground allspice
- 1 teaspoon curry powder
- 100g (3½oz) soft brown sugar
- 625ml (1 pint 1fl oz) malt
  vinegar

1 Coarsely chop tomatoes, onions and apple.
2 Place in a stainless-steel pan with the other
ingredients. Simmer gently for 20 minutes, or
until the chutney has thickened, stirring occasionally. Stop cooking if it begins to dry out.
3 Ladle the chutney into warm, sterilised jars,
cover with a cloth and leave until cold.
4 Seal the jars and store in a cool, dark place
for up to 6 months. Ready to serve in 4 weeks.
Refrigerate once opened.

Dried-apricot chutney

*Because dried apricots are available year-round, you
can make this versatile and delicious chutney in any
season to complement everything from cold ham to
hot roast chicken. Using dried apricots rather than
fresh also gives a much more intense flavour.*

INGREDIENTS

makes four 250g (9oz) jars
- 250g (9oz) dried apricots
- 3 medium green apples,
  peeled, cored and chopped
- 100g (3½oz) raisins, chopped
- 450g (1lb) onions, chopped
- 2 cloves garlic, finely chopped
- zest and juice of 1 lemon
- 1 teaspoon salt
- 1 teaspoon mustard seeds
- 1 teaspoon ground allspice
- ½ teaspoon cayenne
  pepper
- ½ teaspoon ground cloves
- 625ml (1 pint 1fl oz) malt
  vinegar
- 400g (14oz) soft brown
  sugar

1 Roughly chop the apricots, place in a bowl
and cover with cold water. Cover and leave to
soak for 12 hours, or overnight.
2 Drain the apricots. Place in a stainless-steel
saucepan with the remaining ingredients,
except the sugar. Simmer gently on a low heat
for about 30 minutes.
3 Add the brown sugar to the simmering
mixture and bring slowly to the boil. Reduce
the heat to a fast simmer and continue to cook
until the chutney has thickened.
4 Ladle the chutney into warm, sterilised jars,
cover with a clean cloth and leave until cold.
5 Seal the jars and store in a cool, dark place
for up to 6 months. Ready to serve in 4 weeks.
Refrigerate once opened.

Winter chutney

Both fresh and dried ingredients are combined to make this simple but delicious chutney.

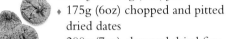

INGREDIENTS

makes four 250g (9oz) jars

- 175g (6oz) chopped and pitted dried dates
- 200g (7oz) chopped dried figs
- 1 large green pepper, deseeded and finely chopped
- 240g (8½oz) onions, finely chopped
- 4 medium green apples, peeled, cored and chopped
- 375ml (13fl oz) white malt vinegar
- 200g (7oz) soft brown sugar
- 2 teaspoons salt
- ½ teaspoon cayenne pepper
- ½ teaspoon mustard powder

1 Place all ingredients in a large stainless-steel saucepan and bring to the boil. Reduce the heat and simmer gently for 1 hour.

2 Ladle the chutney into warm, sterilised jars. Cover with a cloth and leave until cold.

3 Seal the jars and store in a cool, dark place for up to 6 months. Ready to serve in 4 weeks. Refrigerate once opened.

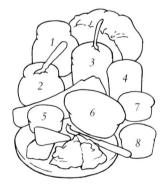

*Almost any fruit or vegetable can be transformed into a delectable chutney for summer or winter eating.
(1) Spicy Tomato Chutney, (2) Mango Chutney, (3) Lemon and Lime Chutney, (4) Green Tomato Chutney, (5) Winter Chutney, (6) Courgette Chutney, (7) Rhubarb Chutney, (8) Dried-apricot Chutney.*

Courgette chutney

Serve this mild and very versatile chutney in sandwiches or with cold or barbecued meats.

INGREDIENTS

makes two-three 250g (9oz) jars

- 1kg (2lb 4oz) courgettes
- 1 tablespoon salt
- 1 teaspoon mustard seeds, 6 allspice berries, 6 peppercorns and 6 cloves, tied in muslin bag
- 1 red pepper, chopped
- 750g (1lb 10oz) onions, chopped
- 2 cloves garlic, finely chopped
- 1 teaspoon turmeric
- ½ teaspoon ground cloves
- 200g (7oz) brown sugar
- 1 litre (1¾ pints) white wine vinegar

1 Slice the courgettes, sprinkle with the salt and drain in a colander over a bowl overnight.
2 Place the courgettes, muslin bag and all the remaining ingredients in a stainless-steel saucepan and bring to the boil. Reduce the heat and simmer gently for 1 hour.
3 Remove and discard the muslin bag. Stir the chutney and ladle into warm, sterilised jars Cover with a cloth and leave until cold.
4 Seal the jars and store in a cool, dark place for up to 6 months. Ready to serve in 4 weeks. Refrigerate once opened.

Lemon and lime chutney

This tangy citrus chutney goes well with Middle Eastern lamb dishes and couscous.

INGREDIENTS

makes four 250g (9oz) jars

- 4 large lemons
- 2 limes
- 300g (10½oz) onions, chopped
- 1 teaspoon salt
- 625ml (1 pint 1fl oz) cider vinegar
- 100g (3½oz) sultanas
- 1 tablespoon mustard seeds
- 1 teaspoon ground ginger
- 1 teaspoon cayenne pepper
- 400g (14oz) sugar

1 Wash and wipe the unpeeled lemons and limes. Chop finely, removing any pips. Place the lemons, limes and chopped onions in a bowl, sprinkle with the salt and leave for 12 hours, or overnight.
2 Place the undrained contents of the bowl in a stainless-steel saucepan and simmer gently until the fruit is soft. Add the vinegar, sultanas, spices and sugar. Bring to the boil and simmer for 45 minutes, or until the chutney thickens.
3 Ladle the chutney into warm, sterilised jars, cover with a clean cloth and allow to stand until it has cooled completely.
4 Seal the jars and store in a cool, dark place for up to 6 months. Ready to serve in 4 weeks. Refrigerate once opened.

Spicy tomato chutney

The flavour of a curry will be more intense if a spoonful of this aromatic chutney is stirred in while it simmers. Serve some more of the chutney at the table as a condiment with the curry.

INGREDIENTS

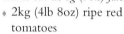

makes six 250g (9oz) jars

- 2kg (4lb 8oz) ripe red tomatoes
- 750g (1lb 10oz) onions
- 1 tablespoon salt
- 1 tablespoon chopped ginger
- 2 teaspoons turmeric
- 1 tablespoon cumin seeds
- 3 cloves garlic, finely chopped
- 2 tablespoons mustard powder
- 1 teaspoon mustard seeds
- 1 teaspoon cayenne pepper
- 300ml (10fl oz) malt vinegar

1 Cut the tomatoes into quarters and peel and roughly chop the onions.
2 Place in a stainless-steel saucepan with all the remaining ingredients and bring to the boil. Reduce the heat and simmer gently, stirring occasionally, for 50-60 minutes.
3 Ladle the chutney into warm, sterilised jars. Cover with a clean cloth and leave to stand until it has completely cooled.
4 Seal the jars and store in a cool, dark place for up to 6 months. Ready to serve in 4 weeks. Refrigerate once opened.

Apple chutney

The spice-sharp flavour that permeates this chutney makes it a delicious accompaniment to cheese. It also goes well with curries and other spicy dishes.

INGREDIENTS

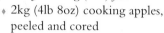

makes four 250g (9oz) jars

- 2kg (4lb 8oz) cooking apples, peeled and cored
- 600g (1lb 5oz) onions, peeled
- 200g (7oz) seedless raisins
- 2 cloves garlic
- 150g (5½oz) soft, brown sugar
- 3 tablespoons finely chopped fresh ginger
- 1 teaspoon cayenne pepper
- 2 teaspoons curry powder
- 1 teaspoon ground white pepper
- 1 teaspoon mustard seeds
- grated zest and juice of 1 lemon
- 1 litre (1¾ pints) white malt vinegar

1 Roughly dice the apples, onions, raisins and garlic; place in a food processor and process to a coarse mince. Alternatively, grate the apples and onions, and chop the raisins and garlic.
2 Place in a stainless-steel saucepan with the remaining ingredients. Bring to the boil, then simmer and cook slowly for 1 hour, or until the chutney has thickened.
3 Ladle the chutney into warm, sterilised jars, cover with a cloth and leave until cold.
4 Seal the jars and store them in a cool, dark place for up to 6 months. Ready to serve in 4 weeks. Refrigerate once opened.

PRACTICAL IDEAS

IT'S FINE TO EXPERIMENT

Recipes for chutneys are very adaptable, so don't despair if you lack a certain ingredient. For example, if you don't have the type of sugar called for in a recipe use another type. Experiment with various types of vinegar. The results may be even better than the original version. Chutney recipes are among the few where trial produces very little error.

◆ Preserving in Oil ◆

Oil is a wonderful preserving agent. As a general rule, use mildly flavoured varieties to enhance the flavour of the foods you are bottling without overpowering them. Make sure that the foods you are preserving are completely covered in oil. The longer you leave them, the better they taste

Globe artichokes in olive oil

The best time of year to make this recipe is in the spring, when small artichokes appear. Avoid using large artichokes as they can be quite woody. Good herbs to use include bay leaves, rosemary, dill or marjoram. Olive-oil-packed artichokes are delicious in salads and served with strong-flavoured cheeses, such as feta or haloumi. Artichoke hearts are great in foccacia sandwiches, toasted with cheese or prosciutto.

INGREDIENTS

makes two 1 litre (1¾ pint) jars
- 1kg (2lb 4oz) fresh young globe artichokes
- 1 large lemon, halved
- 1 litre (1¾ pints) white wine vinegar
- 1 tablespoon each sea salt, dill seeds and black peppercorns
- 2 bay leaves
- 2 sprigs fresh herbs
- 2 cloves garlic, sliced
- 2 small fresh red chillies
- 1 litre (1¾ pints) extra virgin olive oil

1 Remove the tough outer leaves of the artichokes and trim off the tips of each leaf. Cut each artichoke in half lengthways and rub with a lemon half to prevent browning. Place in a bowl of cold water with any juice remaining from the lemon halves. Leave for 1 hour.
2 In a stainless-steel saucepan, combine the vinegar, sea salt, dill seeds, peppercorns and bay leaves; bring to the boil.
3 Drain the artichokes, add to the boiling vinegar and simmer for 10 minutes.
4 Drain and dry the artichokes and place in sterilised wide-mouthed jars. Add a herb sprig, half the garlic slices and 1 chilli to each jar. Cover with the oil. Seal the jars and store in a cool, dark place for up to 6 months. Ready to eat in 4–6 weeks. Refrigerate once opened.

Roasted peppers in olive oil

Serve as part of an antipasto platter or as a snack with thick, crusty bread and feta cheese.

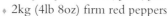

INGREDIENTS

makes four-five 250ml (9fl oz) jars
- 2kg (4lb 8oz) firm red peppers
- 2 tablespoons coriander seeds
- 1 tablespoon peppercorns
- 5 garlic cloves
- 5 bay leaves
- 1 litre (1¾ pints) virgin olive oil

1 Char-grill the capsicums on a ridged hot-plate or under the grill, or over a gas flame, until the skins begin to blacken.

The flavour of Roasted Peppers in Olive Oil is smoky and sweet, quite different from the fresh fruit. Mix red, green and yellow peppers for added colour.

2 Place in a plastic bag to sweat, then peel off the charred skin. Cut the peppers in thick slices, discarding the stalks and seeds.
3 Pack in sterilised jars, with the spices, garlic and bay leaves arranged decoratively.
4 Pour in enough olive oil to cover – use a skewer to expel any air bubbles from the oil.
5 Seal and store in the refrigerator for up to 2 months. Ready to use within a few days. Use any leftover oil for making salad dressings.

◆ A Spot of Jam ◆

*What better way to use your own seasonal fruit than by turning into jam? It's the perfect method
for keeping summer on the table year-round. Use slightly underripe fruit for
jam-making as overripe fruit loses some of its pectin and your jam may not set properly*

Strawberry jam

*Use this recipe as a guide for other berry jams, which
are all delicious on scones or muffins.*

INGREDIENTS

makes five 250g (9oz) jars
- 1kg (2lb 4oz) strawberries
- grated zest and juice of 2 lemons
- 800g (1lb 12oz) granulated
  sugar, warmed (see page 26)

1 Wash and hull the strawberries, then place
in a jam pan with the lemon zest and juice.
Simmer gently over a low heat for 5 minutes.
2 Add the warmed sugar and stir well until it
has dissolved. Bring to the boil and keep at a
gentle boil for 20 minutes, or until setting
point is reached. Use a skimmer to remove any
scum that rises to the top.
3 Remove the pan from the heat and leave to
stand for 10 minutes.
4 Stir to disperse the fruit, then ladle into
warm, sterilised jars and seal immediately. Store
in a cool, dark place for up to 6 months. Ready
to eat in 2 weeks. Refrigerate once opened.

Rhubarb and ginger jam

Lovers of ginger will really enjoy this rich red jam.

INGREDIENTS

makes ten 250g (9oz) jars
- 2kg (4lb 8oz) rhubarb stems
- 1.6kg (3lb 8oz) granulated
  sugar, warmed (see page 26)
- grated zest and juice of 3 lemons
- 4 tablespoons finely chopped
  fresh ginger

1 Wash and trim the rhubarb stems and cut
into 2cm (¾in) lengths. Place the rhubarb in
a bowl, layered with the warmed sugar. Add
the lemon zest and juice, cover with a cloth
and leave to stand overnight.

2 Place the contents of the bowl in a jam
pan and add the ginger. Bring to the boil and
continue to cook for 45 minutes, or until the
jam reaches setting point. Use a skimmer to
remove any scum that rises to the top.
3 Remove the pan from the heat and leave
to stand for 10 minutes.
4 Stir to disperse the fruit, then ladle into
warm, sterilised jars and seal immediately. Store
in a cool, dark place for up to 6 months. Ready
to eat in 2 weeks. Refrigerate once opened.

Fig and lemon jam

*Dried figs work well in this recipe. The pine nuts
are a change from the more traditional almonds.*

INGREDIENTS

makes three 250g (9oz) jars
- 500g (1lb 2oz) dried figs, washed
- 1 litre (1¾ pints) water
- 600g (1lb 5oz) granulated
  sugar, warmed (see page 26)
- grated zest and juice of 2 lemons
- 85g (3oz) lightly toasted pine nuts

1 Roughly chop the figs and place in a bowl
with the water. Leave to stand overnight.
2 Put the figs and water in a jam pan and
bring to the boil. Reduce the heat to low
and simmer for 35 minutes.
3 Add the sugar, lemon zest and juice. Stir
until the sugar dissolves. Bring to the boil,
reduce the heat and cook for 10-15 minutes,
until the jam reaches setting point. Remove
any scum that rises to the top with a skimmer.
4 Add the pine nuts and stir well. Remove
the pan from the heat and leave to stand for
about 30 minutes, stirring occasionally.
5 Ladle the jam into warm, sterilised jars and
seal immediately. Store in a cool, dark place
for up to 6 months. Ready to eat in 2 weeks.
Refrigerate once opened.

Quince jam

*Quinces are available in autumn each year. Make
this superb jam and you will have their flavour to
savour long after they have disappeared.*

INGREDIENTS

makes ten 250g (9oz) jars
- 2kg (4lb 8oz) firm quinces
- 2 litres (3½ pints) water
- juice of 3 lemons
- 1.6kg (3lb 8oz) granulated
  sugar, warmed (see page 26)

1 Wash and peel the quinces, then core and
roughly chop them.
2 Place in a jam pan with the water. Bring to
the boil and simmer gently for 20-30 minutes,
until the fruit is soft and pale pink.
3 Add the lemon juice and warmed sugar
and stir until the sugar has dissolved. Increase
the heat and boil for 10 minutes, or until the
jam reaches setting point. Use a skimmer to
remove any scum that rises to the top.
4 Remove the pan from the heat and leave
to stand for 10 minutes.
5 Stir, then ladle into warm, sterilised jars and
seal immediately. Store in a cool, dark place
for up to 6 months. Ready to eat in 2 weeks.
Refrigerate once opened.

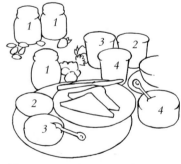

*Seasonal bounty to enjoy year-round: (1) Dried-apricot
and Almond Jam, (2) Rhubarb and Ginger Jam,
(3) Pear, Apple and Citron Jam, (4) Strawberry Jam.*

Plum and pecan jam

Red plums give this jam a rich colour, but the flavour is just as good if you use the yellow or green varieties.

INGREDIENTS

makes eight 250g (9oz) jars

- 1.5kg (3lb 5oz) plums
- 800g (1lb 12oz) granulated sugar, warmed
- zest and juice of 1 lemon
- 250ml (9fl oz) water
- 70g (2½oz) roughly chopped pecan nuts

1 Wash the plums and cut in half, discarding the stones. Place in a large bowl and sprinkle with half the sugar. Cover with a cloth and leave to stand for at least 12 hours.

2 Place the contents of the bowl in a jam pan and add the zest, juice and water. Place the pan over a medium heat and simmer for 20 minutes, or until the plums are tender.

3 Stir in the remaining sugar, bring to the boil and cook rapidly for 30–35 minutes, until the jam reaches setting point. Use a skimmer to remove any scum that rises to the top.

4 Stir in the pecan nuts. Remove the pan from the heat and leave for 15 minutes.

5 Stir to distribute the fruit and nuts, then ladle into warm, sterilised jars and seal immediately. Store in a cool, dark place for up to 6 months. Ready to eat in about 2 weeks. Refrigerate once opened.

Brandied carrot jam

Once called 'poor man's marmalade', this jam is a bright orange colour. The brandy helps it to keep.

INGREDIENTS

makes six 250g (9oz) jars

- 1kg (2lb 4oz) carrots
- sugar, 200g (7oz) for every 250ml (9fl oz) carrot pulp
- juice and zest of 1 lemon
- 3 tablespoons blanched flaked almonds
- 2 tablespoons brandy

1 Wash, peel and roughly chop the carrots. Cook in a saucepan barely covered with water for 3–4 minutes, until just soft.

SUCCESSFUL JAMS AND MARMALADES

THREE COMPONENTS are necessary for making jams and marmalades successfully: pectin, acid and sugar, which must always be in correct proportions. Pectin occurs naturally in fruits and is released when the fruit is boiled. Some fruits have more pectin than others, which is why high-pectin fruits, such as apples, are added to some jams where the pectin would otherwise be low. Other high-pectin fruits include currants and tart red plums, while fruits with moderate pectin include raspberries and apricots. Commercial setting powders – powdered pectin – are available from supermarkets and health-food stores. It is a good idea to have a packet on hand to avoid anxiety about jam not setting.

Acid helps extract pectin and aids in setting. It also improves flavour and colour in jams and marmalades. Acid is added in the form of either lemon juice or tartaric acid.

It is important to warm the sugar before it is added to the hot fruit. Cold sugar will drop the temperature of the fruit and delay proper setting. To warm sugar, put it in a shallow baking pan and place in a preheated 110°C (225°F, gas mark ¼) oven for 10 minutes, or until the sugar is warm to the touch. Stir the sugar in well to ensure it dissolves.

2 Drain the carrots and liquidise in a blender. Measure the pulp, add the appropriate amount of sugar and stir to combine.

3 Place in a jam pan and add the lemon juice. Bring to the boil, reduce the heat and cook, stirring occasionally, for 30 minutes, or until the jam has thickened. Use a skimmer to remove any scum that rises to the top.

4 Add the lemon zest, almonds and brandy; stir well. Remove the pan from the heat and leave to stand for 15 minutes.

5 Stir well to disperse the almonds, ladle into warm, sterilised jars and seal immediately. Store in a cool, dark place for up to 6 months. Ready to eat in 2 weeks. Refrigerate once opened.

Pear, apple and citron jam

Find citron peel at good delicatessens. Candied peel of another citrus fruit can be substituted.

INGREDIENTS

makes about six 250g (9oz) jars

- 6 medium apples
- 6 William pears
- juice and zest of 2 lemons
- 800g (1lb 12oz) granulated sugar, warmed
- 50g (1¾oz) blanched flaked almonds
- 2 tablespoons chopped ginger
- 50g (1¾oz) candied citron peel, thinly sliced

1 Wash, peel, core and finely chop the apples and pears and place in a bowl. Pour the lemon juice over the top, tossing thoroughly to keep the fruit from discolouring. Stir in the zest and cover the fruit with the warmed sugar. Cover and leave for at least 12 hours.

2 Place the contents of the bowl in a jam pan. Add the almonds and finely chopped ginger, then simmer for 30–35 minutes, until the mixture reaches setting point. Use a skimmer to remove any scum that rises to the top.

3 Stir in the citron peel. Remove the pan from the heat and leave to stand for 10 minutes.

4 Stir to distribute the fruit, then ladle into warm, sterilised jars and seal immediately. Store in a cool, dark place for up to 6 months. Ready to eat in 2 weeks. Refrigerate once opened.

Dried-apricot and almond jam

Use best-quality dried apricots when making this jam. The almonds give it texture.

INGREDIENTS

makes four 250g (9oz) jars
- 500g (1lb 2oz) dried apricots
- 1.5 litres (2¾ pints) water
- zest and juice of 2 lemons
- 1.2kg (2lb 10oz) granulated sugar, warmed
- 50g (1¾oz) blanched flaked almonds

1 Wash and roughly chop the apricots and soak in the water for about 8 hours.
2 Put the apricots and any remaining liquid in a jam pan with the zest and juice and bring to the boil. Reduce the heat, cover and simmer for 25 minutes, or until the apricots are soft.
3 Add the warmed sugar and bring to the boil again, stirring until the sugar has dissolved. Reduce the heat and simmer, uncovered, stirring occasionally, for 30 minutes, or until the jam reaches setting point. Use a skimmer to remove any scum that rises to the top.
4 Remove the pan from the heat and stir in the almonds. Leave to stand for 15 minutes.
5 Stir, then ladle into warm, sterilised jars and seal immediately. Store in a cool, dark place for up to 6 months. Ready to eat in 2 weeks. Refrigerate once opened.

Lime curd

Delicious as a cake filling, lime curd also makes an unusual sandwich spread, with cream cheese.

INGREDIENTS

makes two 250g (9oz) jars
- 4 limes
- 200g (7oz) sugar
- 60g (2¼oz) unsalted butter
- 2 large eggs, beaten

1 Wash and dry the limes and grate the zest. Squeeze the limes, reserving the juice.
2 Place the zest, sugar, butter and eggs in the top of a double boiler or a small heavy-based saucepan. Stir over a low heat until the butter has melted and the sugar dissolved.
3 Once the sugar has dissolved, add the lime juice. Increase the heat a little and cook, stirring, until the curd has thickened enough to coat the back of a metal spoon. If you are not using a double boiler, it is important to check constantly that the mixture does not curdle or catch and burn on the bottom of the pan.
4 Ladle the mixture into warm, sterilised jars and seal, if not using immediately. The curd can be stored unopened for 1 month in the refrigerator. Once opened, use within 2 weeks.

VARIATIONS For lemon, orange or tangerine curd, simply replace the lime juice and zest with the same quantity of the juice and zest of the fruit of your choice. For passion fruit curd, use the pulp of 6 passion fruits and the juice of 1 lemon.

Apple butter

This fresh spread makes a great filling for a sponge cake. Use ripe, tart apples for the best flavour.

INGREDIENTS

makes eight 250g (9oz) jars
- 3kg (6lb 8oz) cooking apples
- 1.2 litres (2 pints) apple juice
- 250ml (9fl oz) cider vinegar
- 800g (1lb 12oz) granulated sugar
- 2 teaspoons ground cinnamon
- ½ teaspoon ground cloves
- ½ teaspoon ground allspice

1 Quarter and core the apples. Place with the juice and vinegar in a heavy-based pan and bring to the boil. Reduce the heat, cover and simmer for 30 minutes, stirring occasionally.
2 Press through a sieve and return the purée to the pan. Stir in the sugar and spices and cook, stirring, until the sugar dissolves and the mixture boils. Reduce the heat and simmer, uncovered, for 1½-2 hours, until the mixture is very thick. Stir often to prevent sticking.
3 Ladle hot apple butter into warm, sterilised jars and seal. Ready to use immediately, but will keep, refrigerated, for a month.

MAKING JAMS AND MARMALADES

1 Place the fruit and any liquid in a jam pan (available from good cookware shops and catering suppliers) or any stainless-steel wide-mouthed pan. Bring to the boil and cook as directed in the recipe. Use a wooden spoon for stirring.

2 While the fruit is cooking, warm the sugar in a shallow baking pan in a pre-heated 110°C (225°F, gas mark ¼) oven for 10 minutes. Add the sugar to the fruit, stirring constantly until dissolved. Continue cooking, stirring occasionally, until set.

3 To check setting readiness, remove the pan from the heat and drop a teaspoonful of the jam or marmalade onto a cold saucer. The surface should wrinkle when pushed with the finger. If not, return the pan to the heat, continue to boil and test again.

4 Once set, remove from the heat and, if necessary, use a skimmer to remove stones or any scum that has risen. Let stand for a few minutes. Stir to distribute the fruit, then ladle into warm, sterilised jars and seal (see page 14 for instructions).

◆ A Wealth of Marmalades ◆

The fruity aroma of homemade marmalade permeating your kitchen is a foretaste of future delights.
Citrus comes gloriously into its own in this range of traditional spreads for the breakfast table. When
each fruit is in season you can experiment with these classic — and inventive — recipes

Three-fruit marmalade

A traditional marmalade combining the three
most popular citrus flavours.

INGREDIENTS

makes eight 250g (9oz) jars
- 1 large orange, thinly sliced
- 1 large lemon, thinly sliced
- 1 large grapefruit, thinly sliced
- 2.5 litres (4½ pints) water
- 2.4kg (5lb 6oz) granulated sugar, warmed (see page 26)

1 Place the fruit in a bowl, add the water, cover with a cloth and leave overnight.
2 Place the contents of the bowl in a jam pan and cook over a medium heat until the rind is tender. Leave to stand overnight again.
3 Re-heat the contents and add the sugar. Stir over a medium heat until the sugar dissolves. Bring to the boil and cook for 10 minutes, or until setting point is reached. Use a skimmer to remove any scum that rises to the top.
4 Remove the pan from the heat and leave to stand for 10 minutes.
5 Stir to disperse the fruit, ladle into warm, sterilised jars and seal immediately. Store in a cool, dark place for up to 6 months. Ready to eat in 2 weeks. Refrigerate once opened.

Apricot and orange marmalade

The simple addition of apricots to the traditional
citrus makes a most unusual marmalade.

INGREDIENTS

makes eight-ten 250g (9oz) jars
- 1kg (2lb 4oz) oranges
- 2 lemons
- 500g (1lb 2oz) dried apricots, finely chopped
- 4 litres (7 pints) water
- 3.2kg (7lb) granulated sugar, warmed (see page 26)

1 Wash the oranges and lemons and remove the zest with a vegetable peeler. Cut the zest into thin strips and place in a bowl. Finely chop the orange and lemon pulp, placing immediately into a jam pan. Reserve the pips and tie them in a muslin bag.
2 Place the muslin bag, apricots and water in the jam pan containing the citrus pulp. Leave for 12 hours, or overnight.
3 Over a high heat, bring the contents of the jam pan quickly to the boil, then reduce the heat and simmer gently for 1 hour.
4 Remove and discard the muslin bag. Add the warmed sugar, stirring until dissolved. Bring back to the boil and cook for 20-30 minutes until the marmalade has reached setting point. Use a skimmer to remove any scum that rises to the top.
5 Remove the pan from the heat and leave to stand for 10 minutes.
6 Stir, then ladle into warm, sterilised jars and seal immediately. Store in a cool, dark place for up to 6 months. Ready to eat in 2 weeks. Refrigerate once opened.

Pear and orange marmalade

This marmalade is ideal for those who prefer a less
bitter flavour — the sweetness of the pears tempers
the acidity of the oranges perfectly.

INGREDIENTS

makes twelve 250g (9oz) jars
- 4 medium oranges
- 1 lemon
- 750ml (1 pint 7fl oz) water
- 3kg (6lb 8oz) pears
- 2.4kg (5lb 6oz) granulated sugar

1 Wash and finely slice the oranges and lemon. Place the sliced fruit in a large bowl and add the water. Cover with a clean cloth and leave to stand overnight.

2 Peel, core and finely slice the pears and place in the bowl with the orange and lemon slices. Add the sugar, cover with a cloth and leave to stand overnight.
3 Place the contents of the bowl in a jam pan. Boil for 1 hour, or until the pears are soft and the marmalade has reached setting point. Use a skimmer to remove any scum that rises to the top.
4 Remove the pan from the heat and leave to stand for 10 minutes.
5 Stir gently to disperse the fruit, then ladle into warm, sterilised jars and seal immediately. Store in a cool, dark place for up to 6 months. The marmalade is ready to eat in 2 weeks. Refrigerate once opened.

Lime shred marmalade

Lime and lemon combine for a delectable marmalade.
Slivers of lime zest add texture and tang.

INGREDIENTS

makes six 250g (9oz) jars
- 1kg (2lb 4oz) firm limes
- 1.5 litres (2¾ pints) water
- 1.4kg (3lb 2oz) granulated sugar, warmed (see page 26)
- juice of 2 lemons

1 Remove the zest from half the limes with a vegetable peeler, cut into fine shreds and reserve. Line a medium-sized bowl with muslin. Roughly chop the limes and place in the muslin-lined bowl. Catch any juice you can in a cup and set aside. Gather the muslin corners together and tie with string to make a bag.
2 Place the zest, water and lime juice in a bowl. Add the bag, cover and leave for 12 hours, or overnight.
3 Place the contents of the bowl in a jam pan, bring to the boil, then simmer for 1 hour.

Seville Orange Marmalade, one of the great breakfast classics. The thick skin of this variety of orange gives the marmalade a bitterness that many people like.

4 Remove and discard the muslin bag. Add the warmed sugar and lemon juice. Stir over a low heat until the sugar has dissolved. Bring to the boil, reduce the heat slightly and allow to cook for 45 minutes, or until setting point is reached. Use a skimmer to remove any scum that rises to the top.
5 Remove the pan from the heat and leave to stand for 10 minutes.
6 Stir, then ladle into warm, sterilised jars and seal immediately. Store in a cool, dark place for up to 6 months. Ready to eat in 2 weeks. Refrigerate once opened.

Seville orange marmalade
Look out for Seville oranges – which have a short season – in January and February.

INGREDIENTS
makes ten 250g (9oz) jars
♦ 1kg (2lb 4oz) Seville oranges
♦ 2 litres (3½ pints) water
♦ juice of 3 lemons
♦ 1.6kg (3lb 8oz) granulated sugar, warmed (see page 26)
♦ 4 tablespoons whisky

1 Wash the oranges and slice very thinly, catching any juice and reserving any pips. Place the oranges and juice in a large bowl and add the water. Tie the pips in a small muslin bag and add to the bowl. Cover with a cloth and leave overnight.

2 Remove the muslin bag and place the rest of the contents of the bowl in a jam pan. Add the lemon juice and simmer, uncovered, for 20-30 minutes until the orange zest is tender.
3 Add the warmed sugar, stirring until it has dissolved. Bring to the boil and cook for 30-40 minutes until the marmalade reaches setting point. Use a skimmer to remove any scum that rises to the top.
4 Remove the pan from the heat and leave to stand for 20 minutes.
5 Stir to disperse the fruit, then stir in the whisky. Ladle into warm, sterilised jars and seal immediately. Store in a cool, dark place for up to 6 months. The flavour develops with time, but the marmalade is ready to eat in 2 weeks. Refrigerate once opened.

Kumquat marmalade
This marmalade is delicious on toast and also makes a pleasing accompaniment to a baked ham.

INGREDIENTS
makes four 250g (9oz) jars
♦ 500g (1lb 2oz) kumquats
♦ 1 litre (1¾ pints) water
♦ 800g (1lb 12oz) granulated sugar, warmed (see page 26)
♦ juice of 2 lemons

1 Wash and slice the kumquats, removing and reserving the seeds, and place in a large bowl. Cover with 750ml (1 pint 7fl oz) water. Place the reserved seeds in a small bowl, covered with 250ml (9fl oz) water. Allow both to stand overnight.
2 Place the kumquats and their liquid in a jam pan. Strain the liquid from the seeds and add to the pan, discarding the seeds. Bring to the boil, then lower the heat and cook for 30 minutes.
3 Add the warmed sugar and lemon juice, stirring until the sugar has dissolved. Boil for 1 hour, or until the jam has reached setting point. Use a skimmer to remove any scum that rises to the top.
4 Turn off the heat and leave for 10 minutes.
5 Stir, then ladle into warm, sterilised jars and seal immediately. Store in a cool, dark place for up to 6 months. Ready to eat in 2 weeks. Refrigerate once opened.

A Clear Case for Jellies

Served as a spread, a pastry filling or as an accompaniment to meat dishes,
these shining, jewel-like preserves will give their maker a creative glow. A jelly bag is necessary for
successful jelly-making; these bags are available from cookware and department stores

Redcurrant jelly

Try brushing over pork just before it finishes roasting.

INGREDIENTS

makes three-four 250g (9oz) jars
- 1.5kg (3lb 5oz) redcurrants
- 500ml (18fl oz) water
- granulated sugar, warmed (see page 26), 200g (7oz) for every 250ml (9fl oz) juice

1 Wash the redcurrants and place in a jam pan with the water. Cook over a medium heat until the fruit is very soft. Remove from the heat and leave until cold.
2 Strain through a jelly bag overnight.
3 Measure the resulting juice and pour it into the pan. Bring the juice to the boil. Add the appropriate amount of sugar, stirring until it has dissolved. Boil for 10 minutes, or until the jelly has reached setting point. Use a skimmer to remove any scum that rises to the top.
4 Remove the pan from the heat and leave for 10 minutes.
5 Ladle the jelly into warm, sterilised jars and seal immediately. Store in a cool, dark place for up to 6 months. Ready to eat in 2 weeks. Refrigerate once opened.

Apple and ginger jelly

Delicious with hot or cold pork and ham.

INGREDIENTS

makes eight 250g (9oz) jars
- 2kg (4lb 8oz) green apples, washed and roughly chopped
- 2cm (¾in) piece fresh ginger, peeled and lightly crushed
- 1.5 litres (2¾ pints) water
- granulated sugar, warmed (see page 26), 200g (7oz) for every 250ml (9fl oz) juice

1 Place the apples in a saucepan with the ginger and water. Simmer over a medium heat for 45 minutes, or until the fruit is very soft. Remove from the heat and leave until cold.
2 Strain through a jelly bag overnight.
3 Measure the resulting juice, pour into a jam pan and bring to the boil. Add the appropriate amount of sugar, stirring to dissolve. Gently boil for 5-10 minutes until the jelly reaches setting point. Use a skimmer to remove any scum that rises to the top.

Apple and Ginger Jelly. Apple pips are rich in pectin, so setting is never a problem. The natural acidity of apples enhances the flavour of many other fruits.

4 Remove the pan from the heat and leave the jelly to stand for about 10 minutes.
5 Ladle the jelly into warm, sterilised jars and seal at once. Store in a cool, dark place for up to 6 months. Ready to eat in 2 weeks. Refrigerate once opened.

Grape jelly

This delightfully tangy jelly goes perfectly with cold chicken or poached salmon. If you prefer, you can use green grapes, which, surprisingly, yield a jelly that is a delicate pale pink.

INGREDIENTS

makes four 250g (9oz) jars
- 2kg (4lb 8oz) slightly underripe black grapes
- 175ml (6fl oz) water
- juice of 1 lemon
- granulated sugar, warmed (see page 26), 150g (5½oz) for every 250ml (9fl oz) juice

1 Wash the grapes and remove the stems. Place the grapes in a jam pan with the water, then mash with a potato masher. Bring to the boil, cover and cook for 10 minutes. Remove from the heat and leave until cold.
2 Strain through a jelly bag overnight.
3 Measure the resulting juice and pour it into the pan. Bring the juice to the boil. Add the lemon juice and the appropriate amount of sugar, stirring until it has dissolved. Increase the heat and boil for 12 minutes, or until the jelly has reached setting point. Use a skimmer to remove any scum that rises to the top.
4 Remove the pan from the heat and leave for 10 minutes.
5 Ladle the jelly into warm, sterilised jars and seal immediately. Store in a cool, dark place for up to 6 months. Ready to eat in 2 weeks. Refrigerate once opened.

Herb jelly

Serve this flavoursome herb jelly as an accompaniment to hot or cold roast meats and poultry.

INGREDIENTS

makes three 250g (9oz) jars
- 5 medium cooking apples
- 1 bunch herb of choice, such as thyme or sage, tied with string
- zest, juice and pips of 1 lemon
- granulated sugar, warmed (see page 26), 200g (7oz) for every 300ml (10fl oz) juice

1 Wash and roughly chop the apples (do not peel or core). Place in a jam pan with your chosen herb. Add the lemon zest, juice and pips to the pan, then just cover the contents with water (about 1 litre, or 1¾ pints). Bring to the boil and simmer for 50 minutes, or until the apple is very soft. Remove from the heat and leave to stand until cold.
2 Strain through a jelly bag overnight.
3 Measure the resulting juice and pour it into the pan. Bring the juice to the boil. Add the appropriate amount of sugar and stir over a low heat until it has dissolved. Boil for 9-10 minutes, until the jelly has reached setting point. Use a skimmer to remove any scum that rises to the top.
4 Turn off the heat and leave for 10 minutes.
5 Ladle the jelly into warm, sterilised jars and seal immediately. Store in a cool, dark place for up to 6 months. Ready to eat in 2 weeks. Refrigerate once opened.

Rhubarb and mint jelly

Rhubarb is used here as a change from the more traditional apple. The combination of rhubarb and mint gives the jelly a distinctive and interesting flavour that goes well with a platter of cold meats.

INGREDIENTS

makes four 250g (9oz) jars
- 1kg (2lb 4oz) rhubarb stems
- 1 bunch fresh mint, tied with string
- 375ml (13fl oz) water
- granulated sugar, warmed (see page 26), 300g (10½oz) for every 625ml (1pint 1fl oz) juice

1 Wash the rhubarb stems and cut into 2cm (¾in) lengths. Place in a jam pan with the bunch of mint and the water. Cook over a medium heat until the rhubarb is very soft and pulpy – the mixture will seem very watery. Remove from the heat and leave until cold.
2 Strain through a jelly bag overnight.
3 Measure the resulting juice and pour it into the pan. Bring the juice to the boil. Add the appropriate amount of sugar, stirring until it has dissolved. Boil for 15 minutes, or until the jelly has reached setting point. Use a skimmer to remove any scum that rises to the top.
4 Remove the pan from the heat and leave to cool for 10 minutes.
5 Ladle the jelly into warm, sterilised jars and seal immediately. Store in a cool, dark place for up to 6 months. Ready to eat in 2 weeks. Refrigerate the jelly once opened.

MAKING JELLIES

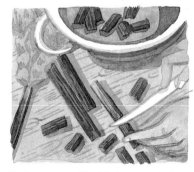

1 *Remove any blemished parts and place fruit in a pan. Just cover with water and cook for the time specified in the recipe.*

2 *Scald the jelly bag by pouring boiling water through it. Squeeze the bag well and suspend it over a large stainless-steel bowl.*

3 *Ladle the pulp into the jelly bag and leave to strain overnight. Do not squeeze the bag, as this produces a cloudy product.*

4 *Measure the strained juice and place in a clean preserving pan with the sugar. Cook to setting point (see step-by-step, page 27).*

◆ Favourite Condiments and Sauces ◆

*Keep a selection of these well-loved meal enhancers in your refrigerator or pantry.
They'll taste so much better than the store-bought variety. Be creative – spread mustard on meat
before cooking, or stir onion marmalade into rice or mashed potato for added flavour*

Presented in attractive containers, many of these condiments and sauces make welcome gifts for friends. They also add a very personal touch to the simplest meal. (1) Red Onion Marmalade, (2) Marinated Goat's Cheese, (3) Salsa Verde, (4) Oven-dried Tomatoes, (5) Bottled Tomato Sauce.

Salsa verde

This delicious combination of fresh herbs, garlic, capers and anchovies goes well with grilled seafood.

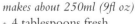

INGREDIENTS
makes about 250ml (9fl oz)

- 4 tablespoons fresh flat-leaf parsley
- 4 tablespoons fresh basil leaves
- 1 clove garlic, halved
- 60g (2¼oz) capers, drained
- 50g (1¾oz) anchovies, drained
- 1 tablespoon red wine vinegar
- 1 tablespoon extra virgin olive oil
- ½ teaspoon dijon mustard

1 Place the parsley, basil, garlic, capers and anchovies in the bowl of a food processor and process until smooth.
2 Transfer the mixture to a bowl and stir in the vinegar, olive oil and mustard. Season to taste with freshly ground black pepper. Serve at once, or refrigerate, covered, for up to 2 days.

Tomato and basil salsa

Tasty salsa makes an excellent side dish to serve with grilled fish or chilli con carne. It makes a good taco topper as well. Serve fresh for maximum flavour.

INGREDIENTS
makes 500-750ml (18fl oz-1 pint 7fl oz)

- 500g (1lb 2oz) ripe tomatoes, peeled and finely chopped
- 1 small red onion, finely chopped
- 1 clove garlic, crushed
- 1 tablespoon extra virgin olive oil
- 2 tablespoons finely chopped fresh basil

1 Toss all the ingredients together in a glass or ceramic bowl. Add salt and freshly ground black pepper to taste.
2 Cover with a lid or cling film and refrigerate for 2-4 hours to allow the flavours to develop. Will keep for 2-3 days but is best eaten on the day it is made.

Bottled tomato sauce

The fresh flavour of this delicious sauce is vastly superior to anything you can buy commercially.

INGREDIENTS

makes seven-eight 250ml (9fl oz) bottles

- 5kg (11lb) tomatoes, roughly chopped
- 500ml (18fl oz) malt vinegar
- 800g (1lb 12oz) brown sugar
- 1 teaspoon ground cloves
- ½ teaspoon cayenne pepper
- 4 cooking apples, peeled, cored and chopped
- 950g (2lb 2oz) onions, roughly chopped
- 1 tablespoon sea salt
- 1 tablespoon finely chopped garlic
- 1 tablespoon ginger powder
- 1 tablespoon ground white pepper

1 Place all ingredients in a stainless-steel pan. Cook over a medium heat until the tomatoes, apples and onions are very soft and pulpy.
2 Push the mixture through a sieve and discard the residue.
3 Return the sauce to the pan and bring to the boil; remove from the heat and pour into warm, sterilised bottles. Seal the bottles well and store in a cool, dark place for up to 6 months. Ready to use in 4 weeks. Refrigerate once opened.

Red onion marmalade

A rich and tasty condiment which you can enjoy as an accompaniment to cheese or roasted meat.

INGREDIENTS

makes two 250g (9oz) jars

- 3 tablespoons olive oil
- 1 kg (2lb 4oz) red onions, sliced
- 150g (5½oz) caster sugar, warmed (see page 26)
- 1 teaspoon sea salt
- ½ teaspoon freshly ground black pepper
- 4 tablespoons sherry vinegar
- 250ml (9fl oz) red wine

1 Heat the oil in a saucepan. Add the onion slices and cook over a medium heat for about 20 minutes, stirring occasionally.
2 Stir in the sugar, salt and pepper. Reduce the heat to the lowest possible setting, cover the saucepan and cook for 10 minutes.
3 Stir in the vinegar and wine, then cook, uncovered, for 20-30 minutes, stirring at regular intervals, until the mixture has the consistency of chutney. Use a skimmer to remove any scum that rises to the top.
4 Remove the pan from the heat. Ladle the marmalade into warm, sterilised jars, cover with a cloth and leave to cool.
5 Seal the jars and store in a cool, dark place for up to 6 months. Ready to serve in 4 weeks. Refrigerate once opened.

Oven-dried tomatoes

These homemade alternatives to purchased sun-dried tomatoes have a less intense flavour which many prefer.

INGREDIENTS

makes two 250g (9oz) jars

- 1kg (2lb 4oz) plum or large cherry tomatoes, halved; or 1kg (2lb 4oz) ripe tomatoes, quartered
- 60g (2¼oz) sea salt
- ¼ teaspoon freshly ground black pepper
- 2 tablespoons dried marjoram
- olive oil, to cover

1 Preheat the oven to 110°C (225°F, gas mark ¼). Line a baking tray with baking paper.
2 Remove and discard as many of the seeds from the tomato pieces as you can, but be careful not to remove the fibrous tissue. Place the pieces, cut side up, on the lined baking tray. Sprinkle them with the salt, freshly ground black pepper and marjoram, then place in the oven and leave for at least 12 hours. It is important to dry the tomatoes rather than cook them. If they seem to be drying out too quickly, prop the oven door open a little. The tomatoes will darken and become wrinkled. Small tomatoes should take only 12 hours but larger ones may take up to 24 hours.

3 Pack the tomatoes in warm, sterilised jars and cover with olive oil. Seal the jars and store in a cool, dark place for up to 3 months. The tomatoes are ready to eat immediately. Refrigerate once opened.

VARIATION Try drying green, red or yellow peppers in the same way as the tomatoes. Cut the peppers into quarters after seeding.

Orange and almond oil dressing

Try this light dressing on baby spinach leaves and red onion slices for a special salad treat.

INGREDIENTS

makes about 125ml (4fl oz)

- 2 tablespoons orange juice
- 4 tablespoons almond oil
- 2 tablespoons vegetable oil

1 Place the orange juice and both oils in a small bowl and whisk together until well emulsified. Add salt and freshly ground black pepper to taste, then whisk again.
2 Pour into a glass jar or bottle with a screw-top lid. Use immediately or refrigerate for up to a week. Bring to room temperature and shake well before using.

Flavoured oils

Make only small quantities of flavoured oils at a time. It is advisable to use herbs that don't contain much moisture, such as rosemary, basil or fennel fronds, or spices such as coriander seeds or chillies.

INGREDIENTS

- several sprigs of herbs or spices of your choice
- olive oil, enough to fill chosen bottle(s)

1 Lightly crush the herbs and pack them in sterilised bottle(s), then fill with the oil.
2 Seal and store in a cool, dark place for at least 2 weeks to let the herbs or spices infuse.
3 Strain into another sterilised bottle (or bottles); discard the herbs and spices. Add a fresh sprig for decoration, then seal. Store in a cool, dark place for up to 1 year. Ready to use in 3 weeks. Use within 3 weeks of opening.

Flavoured vinegars

For top results, use the best-quality vinegar you can find to make these flavoured versions.

INGREDIENTS

♦ vinegar, enough to fill chosen bottle(s)
♦ several sprigs herbs of choice (see variations below)

1 Boil the vinegar, then leave to cool.
2 Lightly bruise the fresh herbs, pack them in the warm, sterilised bottle(s), then fill the bottle(s) with the cooled vinegar.
3 Seal and place on a sunny windowsill for at least 2 weeks to infuse the flavours, giving each bottle a quarter-turn daily.
4 Strain the vinegar into another sterilised bottle (or bottles) and discard the herbs. Add a fresh sprig for decoration and seal. Store in a cool, dark place for up to 1 year. Ready to use in 3 weeks. Use within 2 weeks of opening.

VARIATIONS Good combinations with white wine vinegar include: hot chillies; lemon slices and fennel fronds; orange zest and white peppercorns; nasturtium flowers and a few nasturtium leaves. With red wine vinegar, try fresh sage leaves, or shallots and green peppercorns. With malt or cider vinegar, try infusing mashed blackberries.

An attractive selection of flavoured oils and vinegars to give to your friends or enjoy at your own table: (1) lemon zest and peppercorn-flavoured vinegar, (2) orange zest-flavoured vinegar, (3) herb-flavoured oil, (4) nasturtium-flavoured vinegar, (5) shallot and green peppercorn vinegar, (6) chilli oil.

Seed mustard

Quick to make, this mustard has a wonderful bite and freshness. In supermarkets, mustard seeds are sold only in small packets. As you need a larger amount for this recipe, it is best to buy them in bulk from your local Indian grocer.

INGREDIENTS

makes two 250g (9oz) jars
- 300g (10½oz) mustard seeds, 150g (5½oz) of which are ground
- 175–250ml (6–9fl oz) white wine vinegar
- 125ml (4½oz) clear honey
- 1 teaspoon salt

1 Mix all the ingredients together in a bowl until thoroughly combined. Leave for 2 hours.
2 Stir briskly again, then add more vinegar if the mustard has dried out.
3 Ladle into warm, sterilised jars and seal immediately. Store in a cool, dark place for up to 1 year. Ready to serve in 2 weeks.

Aïoli

Aïoli is a Mediterranean garlic mayonnaise which traditionally accompanies poached fish, seafood stews or boiled potatoes. Be aware, however, that it contains raw eggs which may contain the salmonella bacteria.

INGREDIENTS

makes about 375ml (13fl oz)
- 2 egg yolks
- 6 garlic cloves, halved
- 2 tablespoons white wine vinegar
- 300ml (10fl oz) olive oil

Place the egg yolks, garlic and vinegar in the bowl of a food processor and process until smooth. With the machine running, gradually add the oil, a drop at a time, until the mixture starts to thicken, then add the remainder in a slow, steady stream. Add salt and freshly ground black pepper to taste. Serve immediately, or refrigerate for up to 1 week. Bring to room temperature before using.

Garlic-lovers will relish the warm bite of Aïoli with any number of dishes, from a simple raw vegetable platter to grilled fish or seafood.

Marinated goat's cheese

Goat's cheese, or 'chèvre', from the delicatessen, takes on a new dimension when marinated in olive oil with fresh herbs to add flavour.

INGREDIENTS

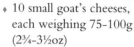

makes one 500ml (18fl oz) jar
- 10 small goat's cheeses, each weighing 75–100g (2¾–3½oz)
- 6 black peppercorns
- 6 white peppercorns
- ½ teaspoon coriander seeds
- sprigs of fresh thyme, rosemary, and fennel fronds
- 2 fresh bay leaves
- 2 small red chillies
- 2 cloves garlic
- 2 litres (3½ pints) olive oil

1 Pack the cheeses in a sterilised wide-mouthed jar and distribute the spices, herbs, chillies and garlic attractively among them.
2 Top up with the oil and seal the jar well. Store in a cool, dark place for up to 3 months for the flavours to develop. Ready to eat in 4 weeks. Refrigerate once opened.

VARIATIONS A range of Mediterranean-style cheeses can be marinated in the same way. Try haloumi or fresh baby mozzarella, or cubes of feta. It is best to make small amounts at a time. Cheeses treated in this way are delicious when eaten as part of a mezze platter, served with pitta bread, Marinated Pickled Olives (see page 19), Hummous (see page 40), and Baba Ghanoush (see page 41). Use the leftover flavoured oil for cooking and salad dressings.

♦ A Touch of Spice ♦

There's a world of flavour in these condiments from Asia, Africa and the Caribbean.
Making them yourself lends the authentic touch because you can use the freshest ingredients and
control the amount of herbs and spices that you find pleasing to the palate

Vindaloo paste

Indian curry pastes may be available commercially these days but once you've made this one you'll see both how easy it is to prepare your own and how much more flavour and life it has over a commercially made paste. This recipe is enough to curry 500g (1lb 2oz) meat. If you wish, make extra to keep in the refrigerator for future use.

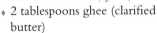

INGREDIENTS
makes about 125ml (4fl oz)
- 2 tablespoons ghee (clarified butter)
- 2 tablespoons dried coriander seeds
- 2 teaspoons turmeric
- 1 teaspoon each cumin, mustard and fenugreek seeds, and white peppercorns
- 2 teaspoons freshly chopped ginger
- 1 teaspoon freshly chopped red chillies
- 240g (8½oz) onions, chopped
- 3 cloves garlic, chopped
- 2-3 tablespoons malt vinegar
- 1 tablespoon thick tamarind pulp

1 In a small frying pan over a gentle flame, melt the ghee and stir in the coriander, turmeric, cumin, mustard and fenugreek seeds and the peppercorns. Continue to cook, stirring with a wooden spoon, for 5 minutes, or until all the spices release their aroma and start to 'jump' in the frying pan.
2 Add the ginger, chillies, onions and garlic to the spice mixture, again stirring continuously until thoroughly softened and brown. Do not allow any ingredients to start to burn. Remove from the heat and cool slightly.
3 Pulse the vinegar and tamarind in a food processor, then add the cooled curry paste

ingredients and process to a chunky paste. You may need to stop processing from time to time to scrape down the sides of the bowl so that the ingredients are well blended.
4 Store in a sterilised jar with a tight-fitting lid in a cool, dry place until required.

Spicy peanut sauce

Every South-east Asian country has a version of peanut sauce and the following one, from Malaysia, is particularly good with satay beef.

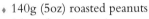
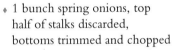

INGREDIENTS
makes about 500ml (18fl oz)
- 140g (5oz) roasted peanuts
- 1 bunch spring onions, top half of stalks discarded, bottoms trimmed and chopped
- 1 tablespoon groundnut oil
- 1 teaspoon shrimp paste
- 2 cloves garlic, quartered
- 2 teaspoons freshly chopped ginger
- 10cm (4in) piece fresh lemongrass, inner stalk chopped
- 2-3 fresh red chillies, stemmed but not deseeded
- juice and zest of 2 limes
- 1 teaspoon each ground cumin, ground coriander seeds, turmeric and ground cinnamon
- 250ml (9fl oz) coconut cream
- 2 teaspoons soy sauce

1 In the workbowl of a food processor, process the peanuts with the spring onions. Heat the oil in a frying pan and add the onion/nut mixture, stirring over a medium heat for 2-3 minutes. Stir in the shrimp paste and fry for a further minute.

2 Process the garlic, ginger, lemongrass and chillies with the lime juice, or grind in a pestle and mortar, then stir into the frying pan and cook for 2-3 minutes.
3 Add the lime zest and remaining spices to the pan and stir over a medium heat for 5 minutes, or until the spices release their aroma and the mixture forms a thick paste.
4 Add the coconut cream and soy sauce, mix in thoroughly, then cook for 5 minutes over a low heat. If the mixture is too thick, stir in a tablespoon of hot water at a time while cooking until the desired consistency is reached. Use immediately.

Chilli sauce

This pungent sauce is definitely for chilli aficionados. Use alongside beefburgers or to spice up grilled chicken.

INGREDIENTS
makes two 250g (9oz) bottles
- 2-3 tablespoons chilli powder, or to taste
- 600g (1lb 5oz) sugar
- 750ml (1 pint 7fl oz) white malt vinegar
- 3 tablespoons salt
- 375g (13oz) sultanas
- 2 tablespoons chopped garlic
- 2 tablespoons chopped fresh ginger

1 Place all the ingredients in a stainless-steel saucepan and bring to the boil, stirring constantly. Reduce the heat and simmer for 15 minutes. Remove the mixture from the heat and cool slightly.
2 Process in a blender and pour into warm, sterilised bottles. Seal well and store in a cool, dark place for up to 6 months. Ready to use in 4 weeks. Refrigerate once opened.

Plum sauce

Serve this flavoursome sauce with pork or chicken. It is also delicious drizzled over a rack of lamb 5 minutes before the end of cooking time.

INGREDIENTS

makes eight 250ml (9fl oz) bottles
- 3kg (6lb 8oz) ripe red plums
- 1kg (2lb 4oz) demerara sugar
- 1.7 litres (3 pints) white malt vinegar
- 2 teaspoons salt
- 2 cloves garlic, finely chopped
- 4 tablespoons finely chopped fresh ginger
- 1 teaspoon cayenne pepper
- ½ teaspoon ground cloves
- ½ teaspoon mustard powder

1 Remove and discard the plum stones, then chop the fruit roughly. Place in a stainless-steel saucepan with the remaining ingredients and cook, over a very low heat, for 1½ hours.
2 Push the mixture through a sieve. Discard the residue, return the sauce to the pan and bring to the boil.
3 Remove the pan from the heat and pour the sauce into warm, sterilised bottles. Seal the bottles well and store in a cool, dark place for up to 6 months. Ready to serve in 4 weeks. Refrigerate once opened.

PLEASE TAKE NOTE

HEAT CONTROL

When barbecuing meat that has been left for some time in a marinade with a high sugar content (such as the Texas Barbecue Sauce, this page), you must watch the meat carefully to ensure that it does not burn. The sugar will caramelise rapidly, long before the meat is cooked. Make sure the coals are far enough away from the items being cooked to control temperature, and turn food often.

If you want the flavour of chillies without undue heat, remove the seeds and use only the flesh. You will still get some heat, but not as much as if you use the seeds as well. Always wear gloves when handling fresh chillies and avoid touching your face.

Texas barbecue sauce

Ask your butcher for 2kg (4lb 8oz) pork spare ribs, cut in a slab of 6-8 ribs with virtually all the fat removed. Marinate them in all but 250ml (9fl oz) of this sauce overnight. On a barbecue, cook the ribs until the juices run clear, basting constantly with the marinade. Serve with the reserved barbecue sauce.

INGREDIENTS

makes 1 litre (1¾ pints)
- 375ml (13fl oz) tomato ketchup
- 250ml (9fl oz) cider vinegar
- 167ml (5½fl oz) vegetable oil, preferably groundnut or sunflower
- 85ml (3fl oz) Worcestershire sauce
- 100g (3½oz) soft brown sugar
- 3 tablespoons Dijon mustard
- 1 teaspoon freshly ground black pepper
- 2 fresh red chillies, very finely chopped
- juice of 1 lemon, plus ½ lemon

1 Combine all the ingredients (including the lemon half) in a medium-sized saucepan and bring to the boil. Immediately reduce the heat to a simmer, cover and cook for 20 minutes, or until the sugar has completely dissolved and the mixture has thickened slightly.
2 Use as directed for barbecued spare ribs, or as a barbecue sauce for meat or poultry.

Preserved lemons

Choose small, firm, thin-skinned lemons for preserving. To use, rinse one lemon and remove the peel. Cut the peel into fine strips and use in Middle Eastern stews, Indian curries or your favourite casserole. Use the juice in sauces and dressings.

INGREDIENTS

makes two 1 litre (1¾ pint) jars
- 10 lemons
- 4 tablespoons sea salt
- 500ml (18fl oz) lemon juice
- 2 cinnamon sticks
- 2 bay leaves
- 20 whole black peppercorns

1 Scrub the lemons to remove any scale. Place in a large bowl and cover with water. Leave to stand for 3 days, making sure you change the water each day.
2 Drain the lemons and cut lengthways as if to quarter, but leave them intact at the base. Sprinkle the flesh with a little salt.
3 Pack the lemons in sterilised wide-mouthed jars. Divide the remaining salt and the lemon juice evenly among the jars. Top up the jars with boiling water. Add a cinnamon stick, a bay leaf and half the peppercorns to each jar. Seal the jars and store in a cool, dark place for up to 6 months. Ready to use in 3 weeks. Refrigerate once opened.

Green curry paste

One of the favourite Thai cooking sauces, this paste goes well with more delicately flavoured meats, poultry and vegetables. To release the flavours of the crushed spices and herbs, it is imperative that the paste be fried in a little vegetable oil on its own before stirring in with a dish's main ingredients.

INGREDIENTS

makes about 250ml (9fl oz)
- 4 shallots, chopped
- 1 teaspoon shrimp paste
- 3 cloves garlic, quartered
- 2 kaffir lime leaves, finely sliced
- 10cm (4in) piece fresh lemongrass, inner stalk chopped
- 1 tablespoon coriander seeds
- 1 tablespoon freshly sliced ginger
- 1 teaspoon each freshly grated nutmeg, cumin seeds and white peppercorns
- 6 green chillies, seeded and quartered
- 3-4 tablespoons coconut cream

Place all the ingredients in the workbowl of a food processor and process until smooth. A mortar and pestle can be used if preferred. Use the curry paste at once or keep, covered with vegetable oil, in a small, airtight container in the refrigerator for up to 4 days. Alternatively you can freeze the paste in ice-cube trays, pack the cubes in a freezer bag, and use the cubes as required in recipes.

Red Curry Paste, as made in Thailand, would be ground for a long time by hand, using a mortar and pestle, but a food processor cuts the preparation time to a fraction and produces similar results.

Red curry paste

Part of the pleasure of a Thai curry is making the paste yourself – it will be far more flavoursome than the bottled variety. This popular red curry paste is quite hot, so adjust the chilli content to suit your taste. As with the Green Curry Paste, always remember to fry the paste in a little vegetable oil before adding it to the rest of the recipe.

INGREDIENTS

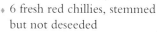

makes about 250ml (9fl oz)

- 6 fresh red chillies, stemmed but not deseeded
- 4 shallots, quartered
- 1 red onion, cut into eighths
- 4 cloves garlic, quartered
- 10cm (4in) piece fresh lemongrass, inner stalk chopped
- 4 tablespoons fresh coriander leaves, stalks removed
- 2 kaffir lime leaves, finely sliced, plus zest of 2 limes
- 1 tablespoon coriander seeds
- 1 teaspoon each cumin seeds, freshly grated nutmeg and white peppercorns
- 2 teaspoons shrimp paste
- 2 tablespoons vegetable oil

1 Heat a small, heavy-based frying pan over a medium heat. Add the coriander seeds and dry-fry them for 1 minute, or until they release their aromas.

2 Place the coriander seeds and all the ingredients, except the shrimp paste and oil, in a food processor and process until smooth. A mortar and pestle can be used, if preferred.

3 Dry roast the shrimp paste for 2–3 minutes, stirring. Add to the curry paste and process to blend in. Use the curry paste at once or place in a small, airtight container, cover with the 2 tablespoons of oil and store in the refrigerator. It will keep for up to 2 weeks.

Caribbean spicy meat mixture

Massage this blend of spices into large meat cuts the night before grilling, and leave in the refrigerator overnight to allow the flavours to be absorbed.

INGREDIENTS

makes 200ml (7fl oz)

- 2½ tablespoons soft brown sugar
- 2 tablespoons hot paprika
- 2 teaspoons mustard powder
- 2 teaspoons garlic salt
- 1½ teaspoons dried basil
- 1 teaspoon each crushed bay leaves, ground coriander, ground cumin, dried thyme and freshly ground black pepper

1 In a medium-sized bowl, combine all the ingredients, stirring well until it becomes a well-blended powder. Spoon the powdery spice mixture into a glass jar with a tight-fitting lid. Screw the lid on firmly and use the powder as required. It can be kept in a cupboard as there is no need to refrigerate it.

2 If you are using the spicy meat mixture as an ingredient in a stew or a braising sauce, add 4 tablespoons of the mixture to 2 tablespoons butter and fry them until the aromas of the spices are released, then stir the mixture into the other sauce ingredients.

VARIATION This mixture can also be used as a flavoursome ingredient in a sauce for stews or tougher cuts of meat, such as topside or brisket.

◆ Dips and Spreads ◆

Having a party is easy when you serve a selection of foods made from these recipes.
Most of them can be made several days ahead, so you can prepare and store them. On the day,
buy fresh breads and other dipping agents and you're ready for any celebration

Guacamole

Its buttery consistency and typically Mexican flavour (fresh green coriander coupled with red-hot chilli) has made guacamole a universally popular dip. A traditional guacamole contains no garlic nor should it be processed to a smooth, creamy paste.

INGREDIENTS
serves 6-8
- 2 large, very ripe avocados
- juice of 2 limes
- 2 plum tomatoes, peeled, finely chopped and drained
- 1 tablespoon freshly chopped coriander leaves, plus a few extra to garnish, if desired
- 3 tablespoons finely chopped red onion
- 1 tablespoon extra virgin olive oil
- 1 red chilli, deseeded and chopped, to garnish, optional

1 Peel and halve the avocados. Place the avocado flesh in a mortar or small bowl and cover immediately with all the lime juice. Mash the avocado and lime together with a pestle or the back of a spoon until the avocado has an even, rough-textured consistency.
2 Ensuring that the tomato pieces are as free of juice and seeds as possible, blend them and

all remaining ingredients into the mashed avocado as gently as possible.
3 Cover tightly with cling film and refrigerate until about 30 minutes before required. Leave, covered, outside the refrigerator to come to room temperature before serving. Serve garnished with chopped chilli or a few coriander leaves, if desired.

Hummous

There are faster ways of making hummous by using canned chickpeas or not bothering to skin the fresh ones once softened, but if you take the extra time you will see why this dish is loved by everyone from Afghanistan through the Middle East and all across North Africa. It's a good idea to cook and skin a large quantity of chickpeas at once. Use what you need then freeze the rest in plastic bags, ready to be thawed and used later at a moment's notice.

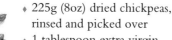

INGREDIENTS
serves 6-8
- 225g (8oz) dried chickpeas, rinsed and picked over
- 1 tablespoon extra virgin olive oil
- 2 cloves garlic, peeled and quartered
- ½ teaspoon ground cumin
- 4 tablespoons tahini (sesame paste)
- 75-125ml (2½-4fl oz) freshly squeezed lemon juice

1 Soak the chickpeas in a large pan of cold water overnight. Early next day, drain, rinse again, and return the chickpeas to the same pan. Cover with cold water and bring to a boil. Reduce the heat to low and simmer the chickpeas very gently for 3-4 hours, until quite soft but not mushy.
2 Drain the chickpeas in a colander and run cold water vigorously over them; in most

instances, the skins will float to the surface to be skimmed away and discarded. Any remaining skins can be peeled off by hand, or the chickpeas can be rubbed gently together in a clean tea towel until the skins come away. Leave the peeled chickpeas to cool completely.
3 Place the chickpeas in a food processor with the olive oil, garlic, cumin and tahini; process to a rough-textured paste.
4 With the motor running, pour in the lemon juice through the feedtube, a little at a time. Turn off the food processor once the desired consistency is reached. Season to taste with salt and freshly ground black pepper. Cover and refrigerate for at least 2 hours before serving, to allow the flavours to meld. If desired, a little chopped parsley or ground paprika can be sprinkled over the top just before serving.

Tapenade

Spread tapenade on warm bruschetta (oven-crisped Italian bread slices that have been drizzled with olive oil), or on hot pasta with fresh tomato chunks, chopped basil and olive oil.

INGREDIENTS
serves 3-4
- 200g (7oz) stoned black olives
- 6-8 anchovy fillets, drained (one standard tin contains 10 fillets)
- 50g (1¾oz) capers, drained
- 4 cloves garlic, peeled and halved
- 1 hard-boiled egg, quartered
- 75ml (2½fl oz) extra virgin olive oil

1 Place all the ingredients, except the oil, in a food processor and process until combined.
2 With the machine running, gradually add the olive oil. Season to taste with ground black pepper. Serve immediately. Keeps for 2-3 days refrigerated in a covered container.

INSPIRING IDEAS

A NEW LOOK AT DIPS

Be inventive in the way you serve your dips. Use crisp vegetables, along with bread, as dippers for Hummous. Stuff cherry tomatoes with Tapenade or spread Guacamole on ham or chicken sandwiches. Try a little Baba Ghanoush on a baked potato.

Baba ghanoush

The smoky flavour that charring imparts to the aubergine in this much-loved Middle Eastern dip is what makes it so delicious. Adding a little more lemon juice to the recipe will allow your baba to be served as a spread rather than a dip. Alternatively, add a few drops of best-quality olive oil to the baba and whisk it to a thinner consistency, which you can use as a topping for grilled meats.

INGREDIENTS

serves 6-8
- 2kg (4lb 8oz) aubergines
- 1 tablespoon extra virgin olive oil
- 2 cloves garlic, peeled and quartered
- 4 tablespoons tahini (sesame paste)
- 75-125ml (2½-4fl oz) freshly squeezed lemon juice

1 Pierce through each unpeeled aubergine just once with a skewer (this ensures the vegetable will not burst when being charred). Roast until the skins are blackened and bubbled, whatever way is easiest – under your stove's grill, in a very hot oven, directly on a cooktop, or on a barbecue plate. Keep turning the aubergine until all sides are charred and the flesh inside is very soft when squeezed with a pair of tongs.

2 When cool enough to handle, peel the aubergine and put the flesh in a food processor with the olive oil, garlic and tahini. Process until just combined; do not overprocess.

3 With the motor running, pour the lemon juice in through the feedtube, a little at a time. Turn off the food processor once the desired consistency is reached. Season to taste with salt and black pepper.

4 Cover and refrigerate the Baba Ghanoush for at least two hours before serving, to allow the flavours to meld. If desired, a little chopped parsley or ground paprika can be sprinkled over the top just before serving. Season with some freshly ground black pepper.

A trio of exotic dips, clockwise from top left: Hummous, Baba Ghanoush and Guacamole. These classics are now enjoyed world-wide.

41

◆ Pasta Sauces ◆

This quartet of recipes will let you make any number of Italian-style dishes. The basis for many of these recipes is fresh tomato pasta sauce. We show you how to combine it with all manner of foods to achieve a stunning amount of mealtime diversity

Spaghetti topped with Fresh Tomato Pasta Sauce and garnished with black olives and a generous amount of finely shredded basil leaves.

Fresh tomato pasta sauce

Use fully ripe tomatoes for this succulent topping for pasta. Always check with your greengrocer to see if there are any overripe or damaged tomatoes about – you will be able to buy a large quantity for half the price as well as make a wonderfully rich tomato sauce. To peel tomatoes, stand them in boiling water for 1 minute to loosen the skins, then place in cold water. If you use canned tomatoes, buy the best-quality chopped variety and use the juice as well.

INGREDIENTS
serves 4

- 1.2kg (2lb 10oz) ripe fresh tomatoes, or two 400g (14oz) cans tomatoes
- 2 tablespoons olive oil
- 2 cloves garlic
- 2-3 tablespoons chopped fresh basil leaves, or 2 teaspoons crushed dried leaves
- ½ teaspoon sugar

1 If using fresh tomatoes, peel and crush them with your hands over a sieve or place them in a food processor and process briefly.
2 Heat the oil in a large, heavy-based saucepan over a medium heat and cook the garlic for 1 minute. Add the tomatoes, basil and sugar and bring to the boil, stirring constantly. Reduce the heat and simmer for 8-10 minutes, until the sauce thickens.
3 Add salt and freshly ground black pepper to taste. Spoon over hot, drained pasta, toss lightly and serve sprinkled with grated Parmesan, if desired. Will make enough for four servings with 125g (4½oz) pasta each.

SAUCE VARIATIONS

All the following variations serve 4, using 125g (4½oz) cooked pasta per person

AMATRICIANA Heat 2 tablespoons each olive oil and butter in a frying pan and fry 3 tablespoons finely chopped onion and 125g (4½oz) chopped pancetta until the meat is just brown but not crisp. Drain, then stir into the warm fresh tomato sauce. Toss with the pasta and 50g (1¾oz) freshly grated pecorino or Parmesan cheese just before serving.

RADICCHIO Shred 500g (1lb 2oz) fresh radicchio (washed, dried and stems discarded). Gently fry 125g (4½oz) finely chopped bacon pieces (rind and fat removed) in 25g (1oz) butter until almost cooked. Add the radicchio and, when the bacon is brown and the radicchio just wilted, add 2 tablespoons freshly chopped parsley and 250ml (9fl oz) cream. Heat through, then stir into the warm fresh tomato sauce. Toss with the pasta and serve.

CHICKEN LIVERS Heat 2 tablespoons each olive oil and butter in a frying pan and fry 250g (9oz) cleaned and diced chicken livers, 2 tablespoons chopped spring onions, 60g (2¼oz) chopped pancetta and 1 teaspoon fresh sage over a medium heat for 4-5 minutes, stirring constantly. Remove with a slotted spoon, drain, then stir into the fresh tomato sauce. Pour 75ml (2½fl oz) vermouth into the frying pan and warm briefly, scraping the pan with a spatula to stir in any browned bits that remain. Stir the vermouth into the warm fresh tomato sauce. Toss with the pasta and serve.

COURGETTES Cut 250g (9oz) courgettes into matchsticks and fry briefly in 1 tablespoon olive oil. When just tender, add 2 tablespoons freshly chopped mint. Stir the courgettes and mint immediately into the warm fresh tomato sauce. Toss with the pasta and serve.

BAKED MACARONI Finely slice and fry 1 large aubergine in 2 tablespoons olive oil; remove from the pan, drain and reserve. Stir 375ml (13fl oz) fresh tomato sauce into the pasta. Put half of it in a buttered ovenproof dish. Layer aubergine slices on top of the pasta in the dish along with 50g (1¾oz) equal parts grated Parmesan and fresh mozzarella. Cover the cheeses with the remaining pasta, then shake another 25g (1oz) grated mozzarella over

the top. Bake at 200°C (400°F, gas mark 6) for 15-20 minutes, until firm and the top just browned; leave 10 minutes before serving.

SALMON AND CREAM Skin and dice 250g (9oz) fresh salmon steak, then gently fry in 25g (1oz) butter over a medium heat until the outside of the fish is just crisp and the middle still quite rare. Stir 250ml (9fl oz) fresh cream, 2 tablespoons diced red onion and 1 teaspoon capers into the pan with the fish. When just warmed through, stir into the warm fresh tomato sauce. Toss with the pasta and serve.

PRAWN AND FENNEL Clean, finely slice and lightly fry 250g (9oz) fennel in 2 tablepoons each olive oil and butter. When just golden-brown, add 3 tablespoons water, cover and cook for 15 minutes. Add 350g (12oz) raw peeled and deveined prawns to the fresh tomato sauce; warm for 2 minutes, stir in 1 teaspoon fresh marjoram and the fennel. Toss with the pasta and serve.

Basic pesto

Pesto is traditionally made using a pestle and mortar, with each ingredient pounded separately, in the order given here. But the flavour will still be wonderful if you use your food processor.

INGREDIENTS

serves 4

- 150g (5½oz) fresh basil leaves
- 3 cloves garlic, halved
- 150g (5½oz) pine nuts, lightly toasted
- ½ teaspoon sea salt
- 125ml (4fl oz) extra virgin olive oil
- 4 heaped tablespoons freshly grated Parmesan cheese

1 Place the basil, garlic, pine nuts and salt in a food processor and process until smooth. Gradually add the olive oil.
2 Spoon the mixture into a bowl, mix in the Parmesan and add salt and freshly ground pepper to taste, if necessary. Serve immediately or place in a glass jar, cover the surface with olive oil and seal tightly. Toss with 500g (1lb 2oz) cooked pasta just before serving. Can be refrigerated for up to a week before serving.

Sun-dried tomato pesto

Sun-dried tomatoes and walnuts make a delightful variation on the usual pesto recipe.

INGREDIENTS

serves 4

- 150g (5½oz) fresh basil leaves
- 100g (3½oz) sun-dried tomatoes in oil, undrained
- 150g (5½oz) chopped walnuts
- 1½ small red chillies, deseeded and chopped
- 4 heaped tablespoons freshly grated Parmesan cheese
- 125ml (4fl oz) olive oil

1 Process all ingredients, except the Parmesan and olive oil, in a food processor until smooth. Gradually add the olive oil.
2 Spoon the mixture into a bowl and mix in the Parmesan. Toss with 500g (5½oz) cooked pasta and serve immediately. To store, place in a glass jar, cover the surface with olive oil and refrigerate for up to a week.

Puttanesca sauce

The flavours of anchovy, capers and olives permeate this rich tomato sauce for homemade pasta.

INGREDIENTS

serves 4

- 2-3 tablespoons olive oil
- 2 cloves garlic, chopped
- 3 ripe fresh tomatoes, peeled and chopped
- 8 stoned black olives
- ½ red chilli
- 1 tablespoon capers, drained
- ½ teaspoon dried oregano leaves
- 2 tablespoons chopped parsley
- 4 flat anchovy fillets, drained and chopped

1 Heat the oil in a frying pan over a medium heat and add all the ingredients, except the parsley and anchovies; season to taste. Cook, stirring, for 15 minutes until the sauce thickens.
2 Add the parsley and anchovies and cook, stirring, for 2 minutes more. Remove and discard the chilli. Serve the sauce at once over 500g (1lb 2oz) hot drained pasta.

◆ Savoury Pastries ◆

*Make shortcrust pastry ahead of time and keep tart shells on hand in your freezer, along
with commercial puff and flaky pastry. Then you can create a simple, delicious main course or snack
at short notice. Choux pastry is quick to make – and the results can be stored for days*

Shortcrust pastry

*The measurements given here will make a double
crust pie. If you are making one tart, simply wrap
the other half in foil and freeze.*

INGREDIENTS

makes two 23cm (9in) tart shells
- 275g (9½oz) plain flour
- pinch salt
- ¼ teaspoon baking powder
- 125g (4½oz) butter, diced
- 1 egg yolk
- 2 teaspoons iced water
- squeeze of lemon juice

1 Preheat the oven to 200°C (400°F, gas
mark 6). In a large bowl, sift the flour, salt and
baking powder together, then rub in the butter
until the mixture resembles breadcrumbs.
2 Mix the egg yolk, water and lemon juice
and stir in quickly with a knife to form a
dough. Shape into a ball, wrap in cling film
and chill for 20 minutes before rolling and
shaping. (Divide in half if you need only one
quantity and freeze the other half.)
3 Roll out pastry and line two 23cm (9 in)
pie dishes or flan tins. Chill for 20 minutes.
4 Bake blind (see box, page 46) in the
pre-heated oven for 10 minutes. Remove the
paper and beans.

SPECIALITY PASTRIES

*Flamiche is one of the traditional dishes of the
French region of Burgundy. Either a pastry crust
or one made from brioche can be used.*

*Large choux puffs may still retain shreds of moist
dough in the centre after baking. Simply make a
small slit in the side and remove this with a finger.*

Tomato herb tart

*This recipe gives directions for making one large tart.
To make the small tarts pictured, cut four discs from
the sheet of pastry with a large round cutter. Proceed
with the given directions for the filling, for a perfect
and quick-to-make light lunch.*

INGREDIENTS

serves 4
- 1 sheet frozen puff pastry
- 50g (1¾oz) finely grated
  Cheddar cheese
- 2 tablespoons grated
  Parmesan cheese
- 375g (13oz) tomatoes,
  peeled and sliced
- 2 tablespoons each chopped
  parsley, basil and thyme
- 1 tablespoon virgin olive oil
- freshly ground black pepper

1 Preheat the oven to 200°C (400°F, gas
mark 6). Cut the frozen pastry as desired, and
place on a baking tray.
2 Bake the pastry in the oven for 10 minutes.
3 Sprinkle the pastry with the cheeses, leaving
a clear 1cm (½in) border around the edge.
4 Layer the tomato slices on the cheese,
sprinkling each layer with herbs and freshly
ground black pepper. Drizzle with the olive oil
and return to the oven for 5 minutes, or until
the tomatoes are hot and glistening. Turn the
oven off and leave the tart to cool for a few
minutes before removing.
5 Cut the tart into squares and serve just
warm or at room temperature.

VARIATION You can use a variety of toppings
in this way. Try thinly sliced sautéed
courgettes with sliced tomato and black olives;
or tomato paste with coarsely chopped salami
and thin slices of roasted green or red peppers;
or your favourite pizza combination.

Quiche Lorraine

*The traditional quiche from Lorraine is made
with rich cream, the bacon of the district and no
cheese. It is delicious, but these days we often
include cheese. Serve with a crisp green salad.*

INGREDIENTS

serves 6
- 1 quantity shortcrust pastry
  (see left)
- 3 rashers bacon, cut into small
  pieces and lightly fried
- 300ml (10fl oz) double cream
- 3 eggs
- ½ teaspoon salt
- small pinch each cayenne
  pepper and nutmeg
- 90g (3¼oz) Gruyère cheese
- 1 tablespoon Parmesan cheese,
  optional

1 Preheat the oven to 200°C (400°F, gas
mark 6) while you make the shortcrust pastry.
2 Line a 23cm (9in) pie dish or flan tin with
the prepared pastry. Chill for 20 minutes.
Bake blind (see page 46) for 10 minutes.
Remove the beans and paper.
3 Sprinkle the cooked bacon over the base
of the pie shell. Beat the cream well with the
eggs, salt, cayenne pepper and nutmeg. Slice
the cheese and layer it over the bacon and
gently pour in the cream mixture. Sprinkle
with Parmesan cheese, if using.
4 Reduce the oven temperature to 180°C
(350°F, gas mark 4) and bake for 30 minutes,
or until the filling is set in the centre. Leave
to stand for 10 minutes before serving.

VARIATION To make an onion quiche,
follow the method above, substituting 450g
(1lb) onions, sliced, for the bacon. Fry the
onion in a little oil or butter until soft and
proceed as if you were using bacon.

Leek and ham flamiche

This recipe uses a brioche dough for the base.

INGREDIENTS

serves 6

- 1 quantity brioche dough (see Flowerpot Brioche, page 56), risen and chilled
- 600g (1lb 5oz) leeks
- 60g (2¼oz) butter
- 125g (4½oz) ham, cut into fine strips
- 300ml (10fl oz) double cream
- 2 eggs and 1 yolk, plus a little beaten egg for brushing
- a little grated nutmeg

1 Preheat the oven to 190°C (375°F, gas mark 5). Butter a 32cm × 25cm (12½in × 10in) tin, preferably with a loose base.

2 Take two-thirds of the dough and press it into the prepared pan. Cover and leave to rise in a warm place for 15 minutes.

3 Trim the tops of the leeks, slit each from top to base and wash well under cold running water. Cut across into 1.25cm (⅝in) slices.

4 In a heavy frying pan, melt the butter and add the leeks with salt and freshly ground pepper to taste. Cover and cook gently for 20 minutes, without colouring, or until soft.

5 Remove from the pan to a bowl and fold the ham lightly through. Spread the slightly cooled leeks and ham over the dough.

6 In a bowl, lightly whisk the cream with the eggs and yolk, adding seasonings to taste. Pour the custard carefully over the leeks.

7 Take the last third of the dough and roll out to a rectangle. Cut into strips and lay over the flamiche in a lattice, pressing down at the ends. Trim edges and brush strips with beaten egg.

8 Leave the flamiche, lightly covered, to rise in a warm place for 30 minutes. Bake for 45 minutes or longer, until the crust is golden and the filling has set.

From left, Leek and Ham Flamiche, Tomato Herb Tarts, Quiche Lorraine. In France, the ingredients used in quiches vary from region to region.

BAKING BLIND

THE TERM baking blind refers to the practice of baking an unfilled pastry case, to which the filling is added later. This is done when the filling doesn't require the same amount of baking time as the crust, or where the filling requires no baking at all.

To bake blind, simply make your pastry as you would normally. Roll it out and use it to line the pastry tin. Then, instead of adding the filling, line the crust with a layer of grease-proof paper or aluminium foil, bringing the paper up the sides of the tin.

Fill the paper-lined crust to the top with dried beans (such as kidney or broad beans). Some kitchenware shops sell bags of metallic 'beans' specifically for this purpose.

Place the pastry in an oven preheated to 220°C (425°F, gas mark 7) and bake for 15 minutes. Remove the beans and paper and return the tin to the oven. Bake for 3-4 more minutes. When the bottom of the crust has lost its doughy look, you can add the filling.

Spanakopitakia

These pastries are a variation on the Greek pie, Spanakopita. They make great canapés to serve with drinks. To prepare ahead, follow the recipe to the end of step 8, wrap the triangles in foil or cling film and freeze. When ready to bake them, place the frozen pastries on oven trays, brush with oil and bake until golden.

INGREDIENTS

makes 40-50
- 375g (13oz) filo pastry
- vegetable oil

FILLING
- 350g (12oz) spinach
- 60g (2¼oz) butter
- 6 spring onions, chopped
- 2 tablespoons plain flour
- ¼ teaspoon nutmeg
- 187ml (6½fl oz) milk
- 125g (4½oz) feta cheese, crumbled

1 Make the filling first. Wash the spinach, remove the stalks and chop the leaves coarsely. Place in a pan with 25g (1oz) butter and the spring onions and cook, covered, over a medium heat for 10 minutes, until the spinach wilts and the spring onions have softened.
2 Remove from the pan, squeeze out as much water as possible and chop.
3 In another pan, melt the remaining butter and stir in the flour and nutmeg. Cook, stirring, for about a minute.
4 Warm the milk slightly and add it to the flour mixture, stirring until the sauce begins to boil and thicken. Remove from the heat.
5 Stir the spinach and feta into the sauce.
6 Place the filo pastry on a sheet of grease-proof paper and cover with a damp tea towel to prevent the pastry from drying out. Work with one sheet of pastry at a time.
7 Cut 1 sheet in half lengthways. Brush each half with oil on both sides and fold each in half lengthways.
8 Place a scant teaspoonful of the spinach filling at one end of each folded pastry strip and fold the pastry over it to form a triangle. Continue to fold the triangle over until the whole pastry strip is wrapped around the triangle. Repeat this process with the remaining pastry strips and filling.
9 Place the triangles on a baking tray and brush with oil. Bake in a 200°C (400°F, gas mark 6) oven for 15 minutes, or until the pastries are golden brown.

Pissaladière

This pizza-like dish comes from the south of France. It makes a good light lunch served with a salad, or can be sliced and served as part of a canapé platter with drinks.

INGREDIENTS

serves 6
- 1 sheet puff pastry
- 5-6 anchovy fillets, drained (one standard tin contains 10 fillets)
- 125ml (4fl oz) milk
- 1 tablespoon olive oil
- 300g (10½oz) onions, sliced
- ½ teaspoon dried thyme
- 2 tomatoes, sliced
- 8-10 stoned black olives, sliced
- 1 egg, beaten lightly

1 Preheat the oven to 180°C (350°F, gas mark 4). Oil a baking tray and place the pastry sheet on the tray. Soak the anchovy fillets in the milk for 10 minutes to remove the excess salt.
2 Heat the olive oil in a frying pan and cook the onion slices over a medium heat for 10 minutes, or until the onion is translucent. Sprinkle the thyme over the onion.
3 Spread the onion over the top of the pastry, leaving a border of 1.5-2cm (⅝-¾in). Arrange the tomato slices over the onion.
4 Drain the milk from the anchovies and remove the backbones by sliding a finger between the bone and fillet. Cut each fillet in half lengthways.
5 Arrange the anchovy fillets in a lattice pattern over the onion/tomato filling. Brush the edges of the pastry with a little beaten egg to encourage browning. Bake for 25 minutes, or until golden. Serve warm.

VARIATION Try a topping of drizzled olive oil, sliced tuna chunks, pitted olives, sliced onions, fresh oregano and grated Cheddar cheese.

Choux pastry

Choux puffs will keep several days in an airtight tin. Fill them with savoury fillings such as cream cheese with herbs, or with seafood for hors d'oeuvres. Fill with whipped cream, custard or fruit as a dessert.

INGREDIENTS

makes 12 large or about 36 small puffs
- 250ml (9fl oz) water
- 125g (4½oz) butter
- ¼ teaspoon salt
- 140g (5oz) plain flour
- 4 medium eggs

1 Preheat the oven to 200°C (400°F, gas mark 6), and sift the flour.
2 Place the water, butter and salt in a large saucepan and bring the mixture to a full boil.
3 Add the flour all at once. Stir vigorously with a wooden spoon for a minute, or until the mixture forms a smooth ball, leaving the sides of the pan clean.
4 Remove from the heat, and add 1 egg. Beat the mixture well until it becomes smooth and very shiny. Repeat this process with the remaining eggs, adding one at a time. With the addition of each egg, the paste will separate, but with continued beating becomes smooth.
5 Shape the pastry using a pastry bag or two spoons, piling small mounds onto an ungreased baking tray. The puffs will treble in size during baking, so only use a teaspoonful of mixture for each mound. Space the mounds about 2cm (¾in) apart to give them room to expand.

6 Bake for 40 minutes without opening the oven door. After turning the oven off, leave the puffs in the oven with the door slightly ajar for 5 minutes more. This allows the puffs to dry internally, ensuring a crisper product.

VARIATIONS Add a teaspoonful of sugar to the water, butter and salt mixture in step 2 if making cream puffs or éclairs. Use about twice the amount of this mixture to make large puffs.

Gougère

This delightful cheese pastry is based on choux paste, to which cheese and flavourings are added. Served with a salad, it makes a lovely light lunch.

INGREDIENTS

serves 6
- 375ml (13fl oz) water (or part water, part milk)
- 125g (4½oz) butter
- 175g (6oz) plain flour
- ⅓ teaspoon salt
- ¼ teaspoon each cayenne pepper, white pepper and ground nutmeg, or to taste
- 6 medium eggs
- 150g (5½oz) Gruyère cheese, diced
- 1 tablespoon Dijon mustard
- milk for brushing and a tablespoon of grated cheese, if desired

1 Preheat the oven to 200°C (400°F, gas mark 6). Lightly oil a large baking tray.
2 Bring the water and butter to the boil in a large saucepan. Remove from the heat and add the flour, salt, peppers and nutmeg all at once. Stir vigorously with a wooden spoon for a minute, or until the mixture forms a smooth ball, leaving the sides of the pan clean.
3 Remove from the heat and add 1 egg. Beat the mixture well until it becomes smooth and very shiny. Repeat this process with the rest of the eggs, adding one at a time. With the addition of each egg, the paste will separate, but with continued beating becomes smooth.
4 Add the diced cheese and the mustard, continuing to beat until the mixture becomes shiny. Adjust the seasoning. It should be quite highly seasoned; if not, add more pepper and perhaps a little more nutmeg.
5 Pile the mixture onto the tray, forming a ring 27cm (10¾in) in diameter – leave a 5cm (2in) circular space in the centre of the ring. Smooth the top with a spatula.
6 Brush the top of the ring with a little milk and sprinkle with a little grated cheese, if desired, to help it brown nicely.
7 Bake the gougère for 45 minutes without opening the oven door. At the end of the baking time, turn off the oven, open the door slightly and leave the gougère in the oven for 5 more minutes to dry out a little. Once baked, the gougère will be firm to the touch, although it may fall and settle a little on being removed from the oven. Serve immediately.

MAKING CHOUX PASTRY

1 *Place the water, butter and salt in a large saucepan and bring the mixture to a full boil. Add the flour all at once and stir vigorously with a wooden spoon.*

2 *Continue to stir for about a minute, or until the mixture forms a smooth ball and comes cleanly away from the sides of the pan. It should start to look 'dry'.*

3 *Add 1 egg and beat in well until the mixture looks smooth and shiny. As each egg is added, the mixture will separate and then come together again as you beat it in.*

4 *Once all the eggs are incorporated, the pastry is ready to be piped or spooned onto a buttered oven tray, in the form you wish, and baked. Allow room for expansion.*

◆ Pâtés and Sausages ◆

You can adjust the seasonings in these recipes to suit your preference, adding more or less garlic, chilli or any of the herbs. Terrines and pâtés regularly appear as party fare, and home-made sausages are special enough to take their place alongside these more exotic offerings

Chicken liver pâté

Serve this pâté with fingers of thin toast or crisp-bread. Pâtés must be refrigerated and are better made a day or two before serving to allow the flavours to meld and the texture to become firm.

INGREDIENTS
serves about 6
- 250g (9oz) fresh chicken livers
- 50g (1¾oz) unsalted butter
- 1 teaspoon fresh thyme
- 2 tablespoons brandy
- 60g (2¼oz) unsalted butter, 1 teaspoon of which at room temperature
- 125ml (4fl oz) double cream
- shelled pistachio nuts, to garnish

1 Trim any sinew or membrane from the chicken livers, rinse well under cold water, wipe dry, then chop roughly.
2 Melt 50g (1¾oz) unsalted butter in a frying pan. Add the chicken livers and cook, stirring constantly, over a low heat for 10 minutes, or until the livers are cooked through. Season with salt, freshly ground pepper and thyme, then add the brandy. Stir well to combine.
3 Remove the livers from the heat and leave to cool for 15 minutes.
4 Place the cooked livers in the workbowl of a food processor with the softened butter and purée for 10 seconds, or until smooth. Place the processor bowl in the refrigerator and chill the pâté for 15 minutes.
5 Place the cream in a large bowl and carefully whisk in the pâté with a balloon whisk until well combined. Season to taste with salt and freshly ground pepper. Spoon the pâté into a 500ml (18fl oz) pot or ramekin, cover with a lid or cling film, and chill in the refrigerator until ready to serve. Garnish with pistachio nuts before serving.

Ham, pork and veal terrine

A simple, classic baked pâté for a summer picnic.

INGREDIENTS
serves 10-12
- 500g (1lb 2oz) diced ham
- 500g (1lb 2oz) minced pork
- 500g (1lb 2oz) minced veal
- 1 clove garlic, chopped
- 6 juniper berries
- ½ teaspoon dried thyme
- ½ teaspoon dried marjoram
- ½ teaspoon ground nutmeg
- 125ml (4fl oz) dry white wine
- 2 tablespoons brandy
- 4 small bay leaves
- 4 thin, rindless bacon rashers
- 90g (3¼oz) chicken livers, cleaned, trimmed and halved

1 Combine the ham, pork and veal in a stainless-steel bowl. Add the garlic, berries, herbs and spices and salt and pepper to taste. Mix with your hands until combined. Mix in the wine and brandy, cover and leave in a cool place for 1 hour, or refrigerate overnight.
2 Arrange the bay leaves on the bottom of a shallow 1.5 litre (2¾ pint) rectangular loaf tin (or terrine) and line with some of the bacon rashers. Pack half the marinated mixture into the loaf tin. Arrange the chicken livers along the centre of the mixture, then cover with the remaining mixture. Cover with the remaining bacon, tucking in the ends and folding the ends of the bottom rashers over the top.
3 Preheat the oven to 150°C (300°F, gas mark 2). Place the loaf tin in a baking dish and fill the baking dish with enough warm water to come halfway up the sides of the loaf tin. Bake for 2-2½ hours, or until the terrine pulls away from the sides of the loaf tin and the juices run clear when the terrine is pierced with a clean skewer.

4 Leave the terrine to cool, in the tin, on a wire rack. Pour off any liquid. Turn out on a plate and cover with plastic wrap. Refrigerate overnight before slicing.

Country pork sausages

No casings are needed for these home-made sausages. Choose streaky bacon with plenty of fat to give the sausages succulence.

INGREDIENTS
makes 10-12
- 1kg (2lb 4oz) lean pork, trimmed
- 200g (7oz) streaky bacon
- 1½ teaspoons coarse salt
- 1½ teaspoons dried sage
- ½ teaspoon dried thyme
- ¼ teaspoon black peppercorns
- 60g (2¼oz) onions, finely chopped

1 Cut the pork and bacon into 1cm (½in) cubes, place in a bowl, cover and chill.
2 Place the salt, herbs and peppercorns in a pestle and mortar or spice mill and grind to a powder. Sprinkle the mixture over the meat, add the onion and mix with your hands.
3 Process half the mixture in a food processor to a medium-coarse texture. Repeat with the remaining mixture. Cover and refrigerate overnight, to firm and to develop flavour.
4 Divide the mixture into 10-12 balls. With damp hands, form the balls into small sausage shapes or patties. Freeze between sheets of greaseproof paper overwrapped in cling film. Can be refrigerated for up to 2 days before using, or frozen for a longer period.
5 When ready to cook, thaw the sausages or patties. Cook in a heavy-based frying pan over a medium heat, turning often, until browned on all sides. Drain off the fat as it accumulates.

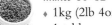

Italian pork and fennel sausages

The wonderful flavour of fennel is counter-balanced with garlic and chilli flakes in this traditional Italian sausage. This recipe gives instructions for making sausages with casings. If you prefer not to use casings, simply follow steps 4 and 5 from the Country pork sausages recipe (see page 48).

INGREDIENTS
makes 10-12
- 1kg (2lb 4oz) lean minced pork
- 1 tablespoon crushed fennel seeds
- 2 bay leaves, crushed
- 1 tablespoon dried parsley
- 3 cloves garlic, crushed
- 1 teaspoon dried red chilli flakes, optional
- 1 teaspoon salt
- ½ teaspoon freshly ground pepper
- 4 tablespoons water
- 2m (6.5ft) natural sausage casing (3cm, or 1¼in diameter), soaked in salted water for 2 hours

1 Place all the ingredients, except the casings, in a large bowl and mix well with your hands. Cover and chill for several hours, or preferably overnight, to develop flavour.
2 Fill a piping bag with sausage mixture and fit it with a large, plain nozzle. Insert the nozzle into one end of the casing. Holding the casing onto the nozzle with one hand, gently force the sausage mixture in, squeezing down into the casing as you do so. It is easiest to make 2-3 sausages, then tie them off with string and start again. There is enough extra casing for a trial run.
3 Arrange the sausages between sheets of greaseproof paper in a shallow plastic container. Cover with more paper, then with a lid. Can be refrigerated for up to 3 days before cooking, or frozen for longer storage.
4 To cook, brush the sausages lightly with olive oil, prick once or twice with a skewer, and grill or barbecue until cooked through.

Clockwise from back left, Country Pork Sausages, Italian Pork and Fennel Sausages, Ham, Pork and Veal Terrine, Chicken Liver Pâté.

◆ Super Stocks ◆

The following recipes are the basis of all home-made soups and many sauces. They can be made in large batches and stored in small containers in the refrigerator for up to four days or in the freezer for up to six months. If refrigerating, leave the fat layer as insulation, but remove before using

This Meat Stock was clarified with egg whites (see box, opposite), which makes it luminously clear. It is garnished here with sprigs of fresh chervil.

Meat stock

You can also use game or pork bones, but for a clear flavour, restrict them to one animal or bird.

INGREDIENTS

makes 1.5 litres (2 pints 15fl oz)
- ◆ 4 lamb leg bones, chopped
- ◆ 500g (1lb 2oz) onions, sliced
- ◆ 250g (9oz) carrots, chopped
- ◆ 450g (1lb) celeriac, chopped
- ◆ 1 whole head garlic, unpeeled and cut in half
- ◆ 200g (7oz) leeks, chopped
- ◆ 75g mushrooms, cut in half
- ◆ 250g (9oz) tomatoes, halved
- ◆ 3 sprigs fresh parsley
- ◆ 2 sprigs fresh thyme
- ◆ 750ml (1 pint 7fl oz) red wine
- ◆ 4 black peppercorns

1 Preheat the oven to its highest setting. Place the bones, onions, carrots, celeriac, garlic, leeks, and mushrooms in a roasting pan and roast for 30 minutes, or until the bones turn a rich brown and the vegetables golden brown.
2 Transfer the mixture to a large saucepan and add the tomatoes, parsley, thyme, wine and 4.2 litres (7 pints 7fl oz) water.
3 Bring slowly to the boil, skimming the surface with a slotted spoon to remove any scum that rises. Reduce the heat, add the peppercorns, partially cover and leave to simmer for 3 hours, skimming occasionally.
4 Clarify the stock (see box, page 51) or strain through a fine sieve lined with muslin into a large bowl and cool. Use immediately, or transfer to small containers and refrigerate for up to four days, or freeze until needed.

Fish stock

Use this fragrant stock for soups, when poaching whole fish, or when preparing sauces for seafood dishes. It is important not to oversimmer fish stock as it will lose its delicate flavour and become bitter. The scallops are not essential, but they do enrich the flavour greatly. Remove the fish and/or scallops from the finished stock with a slotted spoon, shred and use in salads, or process and use in dips or spreads, or for fish balls or rissoles.

INGREDIENTS

makes 1.5–1.7 litres (2¾–3 pints)

- 750g (1lb 10oz) whole white fish (such as snapper or bream), cleaned, scaled and filleted
- 2 stalks celery with leaves, sliced
- 60g (2¼oz) onions, sliced
- 250ml (9fl oz) white wine, or substitute juice of 1 lemon plus enough water to make up to 250ml (9fl oz)
- 3 sprigs fresh parsley
- 1 sprig fresh thyme or ½ teaspoon dried thyme
- 1 small bay leaf
- ½ teaspoon salt
- ½ teaspoon black peppercorns
- 1 allspice berry (optional)
- 1.5–1.7 litres (2¾–3 pints) cold water
- 3 or 4 fresh scallops, optional

1 Place the fish fillets, head and bones and all the remaining ingredients, except the scallops, in a large saucepan. Bring to the boil, skimming the surface with a slotted spoon to remove any scum that rises to the top.

2 Reduce the heat to medium and simmer, uncovered, for 5 minutes, or until the fillets are just cooked. Lift out the fillets with a slotted spoon, drain and set aside to use at a later date, if desired.

3 Continue simmering the liquid for 15 minutes more (add the scallops, if using, only during the last 5 minutes of cooking).

4 Remove the scallops, strain the stock through a fine sieve and cool. Transfer the fish stock to several containers, cover and refrigerate or freeze until needed.

Chicken stock

This full-flavoured stock is the ideal base for sauces, risottos and delicate soups.

INGREDIENTS

makes 2–2.5 litres (3½–4½ pints)

- 1kg (2lb 4oz) chicken bone pieces (wings or carcasses)
- 250g (9oz) chicken giblets (but not livers), trimmed, optional
- 3 stalks celery with leaves, sliced
- 140g (5oz) carrots, sliced
- 1 unpeeled onion, quartered
- 1 leek, halved lengthways, cleaned and sliced
- 6 sprigs fresh parsley
- 1 sprig fresh thyme or ½ teaspoon dried thyme
- 1 bay leaf
- 1 teaspoon salt
- ½ teaspoon black peppercorns
- 1 allspice berry

1 Place all the ingredients in a large saucepan with 2.5–3 litres (4½–5¼ pints) cold water, or just enough to cover the bones. Bring slowly to the boil, skimming the surface with a slotted spoon to remove any scum that rises.

2 Reduce the heat, partly cover and simmer gently until the stock is well flavoured, about 3 hours (the longer it simmers, the richer the flavour will be).

3 Strain the stock through a fine sieve into a large bowl and cool. Transfer to several plastic containers and refrigerate or freeze until needed. If refrigerating, discard the fat layer which lies on the top just before using.

PRACTICAL IDEAS

TO CLARIFY STOCK

Whisk 2 egg whites and crush the shells. Add both to the stock and slowly, with the lid off, bring to a simmer. When the whites begin to set, pour the contents of the pan through a muslin-lined colander or large sieve. Particles will be trapped in the egg white.

Vegetable stock

Keep all your clean vegetable peelings and off-cuts – they can be used to make a terrific soup base for meatless dining. Use this rich liquid to braise fresh vegetables, such as leeks or cabbage, and as a substitute for chicken or meat stock in most recipes.

INGREDIENTS

makes 2.5–3 litres (4½–5¼ pints)

- 60g (2¼oz) unsalted butter
- 750g (1lb 10oz) onions, chopped
- 2 leeks, halved lengthways, cleaned and sliced
- 2 whole cloves garlic
- 350g (12oz) carrots, roughly chopped
- 4 stalks celery with leaves, roughly chopped
- 8 mushrooms
- 1 small bunch fresh parsley
- 1 sprig fresh thyme or ½ teaspoon dried thyme
- 1 teaspoon salt
- ½ teaspoon ground allspice
- pinch nutmeg or mace
- 3 litres (5¼ pints) cold water
- 1 tablespoon wine vinegar
- 1 fresh red chilli, halved and deseeded

1 Melt the butter in a large saucepan over a medium heat. Add the onions, leeks and garlic and cook, stirring, for 5–8 minutes, until the onions are golden brown. Add the remaining vegetables, herbs, seasonings and water.

2 Bring slowly to the boil, skimming the surface with a slotted spoon to remove any scum that rises. Reduce the heat, partly cover and simmer for 2 hours. Add the vinegar and chilli and simmer for 30 minutes more.

3 Strain the stock through a fine sieve into a large bowl, gently pressing the liquid from the vegetables with a wooden spoon. Discard the chilli halves. This stock can be clarified in the same way as other stocks (see box, left). If clarity is not a priority and a fuller-bodied stock is preferred, purée about 8 tablespoons of the vegetables and stir into the stock. Cool. Transfer the stock to several containers, cover and refrigerate or freeze until needed.

◆ Quick Breads ◆

*Non-yeast breads are perfect for making at short
notice, since you don't have to wait for them to rise. Some savoury
breads can even be served as a light meal on their own*

Courgette and cheese bread

*You can bake this savoury bread in a loaf tin, or
make it into individual rounds for tasty bread rolls.*

INGREDIENTS

makes 1 loaf
- 2 large courgettes, grated
- 350g (12oz) self-raising flour
- 1 teaspoon baking powder
- ½ teaspoon salt
- 1 egg, beaten
- 1 tablespoon butter, melted
- 250ml (9fl oz) milk
- 50g (1¾oz) freshly grated
  Parmesan cheese
- 60g (2¼oz) onions,
  finely chopped
- 2 tablespoons finely
  chopped parsley
- 2 tablespoons snipped chives

1 Press the courgettes firmly in a folded tea
towel to extract as much moisture as possible.
2 Preheat the oven to 190°C (375°F, gas
mark 5). Grease and lightly flour a 25cm (10in)
long loaf tin.
3 Sift the flour, baking powder and salt into a
large bowl. In another smaller bowl, combine
the beaten egg, butter and milk, and add to the
dry ingredients. Mix well to combine. Add the
remaining ingredients and stir well to disperse
the courgettes throughout the dough.
4 Place the dough in the prepared tin and
bake for 45 minutes, or until a skewer comes
out clean when inserted into the bread.
5 Cool the bread on a wire rack for
15 minutes before slicing. Serve warm.

VARIATION Roll the dough into very small
balls. When baked, open and fill them with
cream cheese, smoked salmon and a few capers
to serve as an hors d'oeuvre. Shorten the
baking time appropriately.

Corn bread

*This is a lovely, wholesome yellow bread. Serve
it with hearty soups, such as leek and potato.*

INGREDIENTS

makes 1 loaf
- 250g (9oz) plain flour
- 215g (7½oz) polenta
- 2 tablespoons sugar
- 1 teaspoon sea salt
- 1 tablespoon baking powder
- 1 egg
- 250-300ml (9-10fl oz) milk
- 85ml (3fl oz) vegetable oil

1 Preheat the oven to 220°C (425°F, gas
mark 7). Grease and line a 20cm (8in) square
cake tin with baking paper.
2 Place the dry ingredients in a bowl and
mix well to combine. In another smaller bowl,
beat the egg with 250ml (9fl oz) of the milk
and the oil. Pour into the dry ingredients and
stir quickly to mix. If the mixture is too dry,
add as much of the remaining milk as required.
3 Spoon the mixture into the prepared tin,
spreading it evenly. Bake for 25 minutes,
or until golden brown.
4 When done, remove from the oven and
cool slightly. Serve while still warm.

*Some variations on the staff of life: (1) Soda Bread
Rolls, (2) Beer Bread, (3) Sesame Pumpkin
Damper, (4) Courgette and Cheese Bread, (5) Olive
and Sun-dried Tomato Bread.*

Beer bread

A versatile bread with a wonderfully malty aroma.

INGREDIENTS

makes 1 loaf

- 350g (12oz) self-raising flour
- 1 tablespoon sugar
- 375ml (13fl oz) beer
- 50g (1¾oz) butter, melted

1 Preheat the oven to 180°C (350°F, gas mark 4). Grease and line a 25cm (10in) long loaf tin with baking paper.
2 Place the flour and sugar in a bowl and mix in the beer to form a soft dough.
3 Pour the dough into the prepared tin and pour half the melted butter over it. Bake the bread for 30 minutes.
4 Remove the bread, pour the remaining butter over it and cook for 10 minutes longer.

Soda bread

Soda bread is particularly good with stews and thick country soups. Vary the topping to suit – try flax or pumpkin seeds, oatmeal, or cracked wheat. Break the bread at the table as cutting will toughen it.

INGREDIENTS

makes 2 loaves

- 400g (14oz) wholemeal flour
- 400g (14oz) plain flour
- 100g (3½oz) coarse oats
- 1 teaspoon sea salt
- 2 teaspoons bicarbonate of soda
- 700ml (1¼ pint) buttermilk
- topping of choice

1 Preheat the oven to 200°C (400°F, gas mark 6). Grease and line a large baking tray with baking paper.
2 Combine all the dry ingredients in a large bowl. Make a well in the centre and gradually stir in enough buttermilk until the dough is soft but not sticky.
3 Halve the mixture. Shape each half into a 23cm (9in) round and place on the tray. Cut a cross into each round. Add the topping of your choice. Bake in the oven for 30 minutes, or until the dough has risen and is brown.
4 When done, turn the bread out on a wire rack. Serve while still warm.

Sesame pumpkin damper

The amount of liquid used in this tasty Australian recipe depends on how moist the cooked pumpkin is. Slice and serve warm with butter and golden syrup.

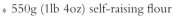

INGREDIENTS

makes 1 loaf

- 550g (1lb 4oz) self-raising flour
- 2 tablespoons caster sugar
- 1 teaspoon salt
- 25g (1oz) butter
- 1 cup cooked, mashed pumpkin
- 125-187ml (4-7fl oz) milk or water
- 1 tablespoon sesame seeds

1 Preheat the oven to 200°C (400°F, gas mark 6). Grease and flour a baking tray.
2 Sift the flour, sugar and salt into a mixing bowl. Rub in the butter with your fingertips until the mixture resembles fine breadcrumbs.
3 Make a well in the centre and add the pumpkin. Mix lightly with a knife, adding just enough milk or water to make a firm dough.
4 Turn out on a lightly floured surface; knead until smooth. Shape into a 20cm (8in) diameter round and place on the tray. Slash a cross in the top, brush lightly with a little extra milk or water and sprinkle with sesame seeds.
5 Bake for 25 minutes, then reduce the oven temperature to 180°C (350°F, gas mark 4) and bake for 20 minutes longer, or until it sounds hollow when the base is tapped. Serve warm.

Pecan damper

A modern variation on a timeless classic. Delicious as part of a cheese tray with dried fruit and soft cheeses.

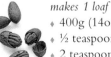

INGREDIENTS

makes 1 loaf

- 400g (14oz) self-raising flour
- ½ teaspoon sea salt
- 2 teaspoons sugar
- 1 tablespoon butter, softened to room temperature
- 140g (5oz) roughly chopped pecan nuts
- 250ml (9fl oz) milk

1 Preheat the oven to 200°C (400°F, gas mark 6). Combine the flour, salt and sugar in a bowl and mix well. Rub in the butter with your fingertips until the mixture resembles fine breadcrumbs. Add the pecan nuts and milk, then mix to form a soft dough.
2 Turn the dough out on a lightly floured surface and knead until smooth. Shape it into a round, about 23cm (9in) in diameter. Place the round on a floured baking tray and bake for 25-30 minutes.
3 When done, turn the damper out on a wire rack and cover with a tea towel. Serve warm.

Olive and sun-dried tomato bread

A great accompaniment to soup, this tasty bread is easy to prepare at short notice.

INGREDIENTS

makes 1 loaf

- 2 eggs
- 175ml (6fl oz) milk
- 275g (9½oz) plain flour
- 1 heaped teaspoon baking powder
- 1 teaspoon sea salt
- 3 tablespoons oil drained from sun-dried tomatoes, or olive oil
- 125g (4½oz) stoned black olives in oil, drained and slivered
- 125g (4½oz) sun-dried tomatoes, drained and sliced
- 1 tablespoon freshly chopped marjoram

1 Preheat the oven to 200°C (400°F, gas mark 6). Grease a 23cm (9in) cake tin.
2 Place the eggs and milk in the bowl of an electric mixer or food processor. Beat lightly, just to combine. Sift the flour and baking powder together and add to the egg mixture. Beat for 2 minutes, add the salt and oil and beat for 1 minute more. Stir in the olives, sun-dried tomatoes and marjoram with a spoon.
3 Pour the batter into the prepared tin and bake for 30 minutes, or until a skewer comes out clean when inserted into the bread.
4 Cool slightly on a wire rack. Serve warm.

VARIATIONS Try replacing the olives and sun-dried tomatoes with walnuts and tapenade (see page 40), or simply a mixture of fresh herbs and a little crushed fresh garlic.

Yeast-risen Breads

Breads that use yeast as the rising agent delight the senses with their scent and texture.
The home cook derives enormous satisfaction from kneading and shaping loaves and rolls, which
are so much more wholesome than most of the breads you can buy

Pizza dough

Use this dough for a family-size pizza or make it into small rounds for individual 'pizzette'.

INGREDIENTS

makes one 30cm (12in) pizza base
- 7g sachet dry yeast
- 185ml (6½fl oz) warm water
- 300g (10½oz) plain flour
- 1 teaspoon sea salt
- 1½ teaspoons extra virgin olive oil

1 Place the yeast in a small bowl and add the warm water. Mix quickly with a fork. Cover the bowl with cling film and leave to stand in a warm place for 20 minutes, or until frothy.
2 Place the flour and salt in a food processor, add the yeast mixture and olive oil and process until the dough holds together.
3 Turn the dough out on a lightly floured surface and knead for 2 minutes. Shape into a ball. Roll the dough around in a lightly oiled bowl to coat it with oil, cover with lightly oiled cling film and put in a warm place to rise for 1 hour, or until it has doubled in size.
4 Remove the dough from the bowl and press into a pizza shape. Place on a lightly oiled 30cm (12in) pizza tray and add toppings of choice. Bake in an oven preheated to 220°C (425°F, gas mark 7) for 20-25 minutes.

Country white bread

Shape this good basic bread into loaves or dinner rolls. For olive rolls, add sliced black olives.

INGREDIENTS

makes 2 loaves or 16 rolls
- two 7g sachets dry yeast
- 2 teaspoons caster sugar
- 300-450ml (10-16fl oz) warm water
- 1.6kg (3lb 8oz) bread flour
- 1½ teaspoons sea salt

1 Place the yeast in a small bowl with the sugar. Add 300ml (10fl oz) of the warm water and mix quickly with a fork. Cover the bowl with cling film and leave in a warm place for 20 minutes, or until the mixture is frothy.
2 Sift the flour and salt into a large bowl, make a well in the centre and add the yeast mixture. Mix well to combine, adding a little more warm water if the mixture is too dry. Mix to a firm dough.
3 Grease and line two bread tins with baking paper if making loaves, or a baking tray if making rolls. Divide the dough in two if making loaves or into 16 pieces for rolls. Place the dough in the tins or shape into rounds and place on the tray. Cover with a damp tea towel and leave in a warm place for 1 hour, or until the dough has doubled in size.
4 Preheat the oven to 220°C (425°F, gas mark 7). Remove the tea towel and place the tins or tray in the oven. Bake loaves for 30 minutes, and rolls for 15 minutes, or until golden brown.
5 When done, turn the loaves or rolls out on a wire rack and leave to cool.

BREAD BOXES

1 *For novel sandwich presentation boxes, choose dense sandwich loaves with soft crusts. With an electric knife, slice off the top crust about 2cm thick (this will be the box lid). With a serrated knife, cut around inside the crusts 1cm in from the sides.*

2 *To release the block of bread from the base, turn the loaf on its side and make an incision along one side only, 1cm from the base. Work the knife along both ways until the centre block of bread is detached. Cut the block into thin, neat slices.*

3 *Make the slices into sandwiches with fillings of your choice (avoid fillings that are too bulky and difficult to cut). Using a very sharp knife, trim all overhanging fillings from the sides and cut the sandwiches into squares, triangles or fingers, as desired.*

4 *Fit the sandwiches back into the box. Replace the lid and secure it with wide strips of ribbon, taped together at the bottom of the box. Alternatively, for a novel presentation, wrap a napkin around the box and knot it at the top.*

Herb sourdough

Sourdough requires a starter, which is a fermented paste of flour, yeast and water. This gives the bread its unique flavour. The starter needs to be prepared several days before it is used in baking.

STARTER INGREDIENTS

makes 2 loaves

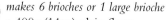

- 1 teaspoon dry yeast
- 250ml (9fl oz) tepid water
- 140g (5oz) wholemeal flour

DOUGH INGREDIENTS

- 250g (9oz) wholemeal flour
- 250ml (9fl oz) boiling water
- 7g sachet dry yeast
- 1 teaspoon caster sugar
- 1 teaspoon salt
- 250ml (9fl oz) tepid water
- 125g (4fl oz) sourdough starter (above)
- 550g (1lb 4oz) bread flour
- 1 tablespoon fresh chopped herbs of choice

1 To make the starter, place the yeast in a small bowl and add the tepid water. Mix quickly with a fork. Cover the bowl with cling film and allow the mixture to stand for 20 minutes, or until frothy, to activate.

2 Add the wholemeal flour and stir to a paste. Cover the bowl with lightly oiled cling film and leave at room temperature for 3-7 days.

3 To make the dough, mix the wholemeal flour with the boiling water and let cool.

4 Dissolve the yeast, sugar and salt in the tepid water, add the starter and mix to combine. Blend this mixture into the wholemeal paste, then add the bread flour and the fresh herbs.

5 Turn the dough out on a lightly floured surface and knead for 10 minutes. Roll the dough around in a lightly oiled bowl to coat it with oil, cover with lightly oiled cling film and leave in a warm place to rise for 1 hour at room temperature. Grease and line a large baking tray with baking paper.

6 Halve the dough. Punch each half down and knead into shape (either an oval or a round). Place the loaves on the prepared baking tray, cover with lightly oiled cling film and leave in a warm place for 1 hour, or until the dough has doubled in size.

7 Preheat the oven to 200°C (400°F, gas mark 6). Remove the cling film and bake for 30 minutes, or until golden and cooked.

8 Cool the bread on a wire rack.

Flowerpot brioche

Traditionally, brioche is made in a special fluted tin that is wider at the top than the base. For a change, try making individual brioches in small terracotta flowerpots, greased and lined.

INGREDIENTS

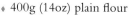

makes 6 brioches or 1 large brioche

- 400g (14oz) plain flour
- 7g sachet dry yeast
- 1 tablespoon caster sugar
- 1 teaspoon salt
- 140g (5oz) unsalted butter
- 4 tablespoons water
- 4 eggs

1 Grease and line six 9cm (3½in) terracotta pots with baking paper.

2 Place the flour, yeast, sugar and salt in a food processor and pulse a few times to blend.

3 Place the butter and water in a small saucepan and heat until the butter has melted. Pour the liquid into the flour mixture and process until the dough comes together as a ball. Add the eggs, one at a time, and process again, 10 seconds for each egg.

4 Oil a bowl and scrape the dough into it. Cover with lightly oiled cling film and leave in a warm place for 1 hour, or until the dough has doubled in size.

5 Punch down the dough and divide it among the prepared pots. Place the pots on a baking tray and cover with lightly oiled cling film. Leave in a warm place for 30 minutes, or until the dough is well risen.

6 Preheat the oven to 190°C (375°F, gas mark 5). Remove the cling film. Place the tray in the oven and bake the brioche for 15-20 minutes, until light and golden.

7 When done, turn the brioche out on a wire rack and leave to cool.

VARIATION Shape the dough into one large loaf in a brioche tin and bake for 45 minutes, or until the base sounds hollow when tapped.

Wholemeal seed bread

Any seeds can be substituted for sunflower in this recipe, or a combination can be used. Try sesame, pumpkin, sunflower or poppy.

INGREDIENTS
makes 2 loaves
- 550g (1lb 4oz) wholemeal plain flour
- 6 tablespoons sunflower seeds
- 1 tablespoon sea salt
- 7g sachet dry yeast
- 1 tablespoon olive oil
- 300ml (10fl oz) warm water
- extra olive oil, for dough
- 65ml (2¼fl oz) milk

1 Place the flour, 4 tablespoons sunflower seeds, salt and yeast in a large bowl. Add the oil and warm water and mix to a dough.
2 Turn the dough out on a lightly floured surface and knead for 5 minutes, or until smooth and elastic. Rub a little oil over the dough, return it to the bowl and cover with a damp tea towel. Leave in a warm place for 1 hour, or until doubled in size.
3 Punch the dough down and halve it. Knead each half again for 3 minutes and form into a round. Place the rounds on a greased and lined baking tray and cover with a cloth. Leave in a warm place to rise for a further 30 minutes.
4 Preheat the oven to 220°C (425°F, gas mark 7). Brush the loaves with milk and sprinkle with the remaining sunflower seeds. Bake in the centre of the oven for 30 minutes.
5 When they are cooked, turn the loaves out on a wire rack and leave to cool.

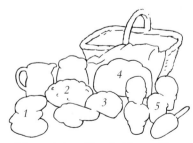

A few of the varieties of breads it's possible to create with yeast: (1) Individual pizzette (Pizza Dough), (2) Olive Flat Bread, (3) Pear and Walnut Bread, (4) Country White Bread, (5) Flowerpot Brioche.

Olive flat bread

A perfect bread for a snack with drinks or to hand around at a barbecue or picnic party.

INGREDIENTS

makes 1 loaf
- 325g (11½oz) plain flour
- 1 teaspoon salt
- 1 teaspoon sugar
- 7g sachet dried yeast
- 175ml (6fl oz) lukewarm milk
- 1 large egg
- 75ml (2½fl oz) extra virgin olive oil (including 1 tablespoon for brushing)
- 200g (7oz) roughly chopped black olives
- 15 stoned black olives

1 Sift the flour into a large bowl with the salt and stir in the sugar and yeast.
2 Make a well in the centre and add the milk, egg, 65ml (2¼fl oz) olive oil and chopped olives. Mix to a dough, then turn out on a well-floured board.

PRACTICAL IDEAS

FOR THE BEST RESULTS

Lightly oil your hands before mixing or kneading dough so the dough doesn't stick to them.

For a rich, crisp, golden crust on bread, lightly mist the dough with water before baking.

Bread can be made by hand or with a dough hook on an electric mixer. Both methods are satisfactory. Try a combination: begin by using a mixer and knead by hand in the later stages.

Bread is cooked at a high heat, so use heavy-gauge tins and baking trays to avoid warping. A porous, unglazed baking stone is ideal for flatbreads and pizzas. It distributes the heat very evenly and produces a crisp crust. Place the baking stone on the bottom shelf of the oven and pre-heat the oven for 30 minutes before baking. Unglazed quarry tiles make a good substitute.

3 Knead lightly for 4-5 minutes until smooth and elastic. Roll the dough around in a lightly oiled bowl to coat it with oil, cover with lightly oiled cling film and leave in a warm place to rise for about 1 hour.
4 Turn the dough out on a floured board and shape it into a large disc or oblong about 8mm (⅜in) thick. Place on a baking tray. Cover and leave to rise in a warm place for 15 minutes.
5 Preheat the oven to 200°C (400°F, gas mark 6). Stud the surface of the dough with olives, brush with the remaining olive oil and bake for 25 minutes, or until the crust is golden. Serve warm or cold.

Pear and walnut bread

Try this tasty bread drizzled with a mixture of honey and yoghurt. It goes well with a cheese platter.

INGREDIENTS

makes 2 loaves
- 200g (7oz) ready-to-eat dried pears, rehydrated for 1 hour in warm water to cover
- 60g (2¼oz) chopped walnuts
- 700g (1lb 9oz) bread flour or plain flour
- 2 teaspoons sea salt
- 7g sachet dry yeast
- 375-450ml (13-16fl oz) warm water
- 3 tablespoons oil

1 Drain then roughly chop the pears. Place them with the walnut pieces in a bowl and mix with the flour, sea salt and yeast.
2 Make a well in the centre and add 375ml (13fl oz) of the water and the oil. Mix well to form a soft dough, adding more water if the mixture is too dry.
3 Turn the dough out on a floured surface and knead for 10 minutes, or until smooth and elastic. Halve the dough and shape each piece into an oval. Place each oval on a greased and lined baking tray and cover loosely with lightly oiled cling film. Leave in a warm place for 40 minutes to rise, or until the dough has doubled in size.
4 Preheat the oven to 220°C (425°F, gas mark 7). Remove the cling film and cross-slash

the top of each loaf. Bake for 10 minutes, then reduce the temperature to 180°C (350°F, gas mark 4) and bake for 25 minutes, or until the loaves have browned on the top.
5 When they are done, turn the loaves out on a wire rack and allow to cool.

Focaccia

Focaccia is delicious toasted and garnished with Italian-style toppings, such as grilled or marinated vegetables and mozzarella.

INGREDIENTS

makes 2 loaves
- 7g sachet dry yeast
- 500ml (18fl oz) warm water
- ¼ teaspoon sugar
- 750g (1lb 10oz) bread flour or plain flour
- 4 tablespoons olive oil, plus extra, for drizzling
- 1 tablespoon salt
- tiny sprigs rosemary
- sea salt

1 Place the yeast in a small bowl, add the warm water and sugar and mix quickly with a fork. Cover the bowl with cling film and leave in a warm place for 20 minutes, or until activated and frothy.
2 Place the flour in a large bowl and make a well in the centre. Add the yeast mixture, oil and salt, then mix well. Knead the dough for 10 minutes, or until smooth. Place in an oiled bowl, cover with a damp tea towel and leave to rise in a warm place for 1 hour.
3 Grease and line two baking trays with baking paper. Halve the dough. Spread each half on a baking tray, pressing the dough out with your fingers to about 1.5cm (⅝in) thickness. Cover the trays with a damp cloth and leave for 15 minutes.
4 Press out the dough with your fingers again, cover and leave for 30 minutes.
5 Preheat the oven to 200°C (400°F, gas mark 6). Indent the dough all over with your fingers, press in tiny sprigs of rosemary, drizzle with olive oil and sprinkle with sea salt. Bake for 25 minutes, or until firm and golden. Serve warm or at room temperature.

CROÛTES AND CROÛTONS

YOU CAN TREAT baked or grilled slices of baguette as if they were mini pizza bases (croûtes) and invent your own toppings. Drizzle with olive oil and spread with Bottled Tomato Sauce (see page 34). Top with prosciutto, Gruyère cheese, black olive halves and a sprinkling of Parmesan cheese. Season with salt and freshly ground black pepper, add another drizzle of olive oil and bake in a preheated 200°C (400°F, gas mark 6) oven for 8 minutes.

To make croûtes, trim the crusts from sliced bread and brush with olive oil or melted butter. Toast the slices briefly, in a preheated 120°C (250°F, gas mark ½) oven, turning once, until pale golden on both sides. Use large croûtes as bases for juicy steaks or grilled quail. Small shapes can be spread with Tapenade (see page 40), or used as dippers for pâtés or for the dips on pages 40–41. Use your imagination to vary the toppings.

For garlic croûtons, trim the crusts from bread slices and cut the bread into 1cm (½in) cubes. Slice 2 cloves of garlic and fry in olive oil until golden, taking care not to burn it. Lift out and discard the garlic. Add the bread cubes to the flavoured oil and stir-fry until well coated, golden and crisp. Drain on paper towels. Use to garnish soups and salads, or to add texture to creamed or sauced vegetable and meat dishes.

Pitta bread

Thin, flat pitta is delicious eaten warm with a dip and a pre-dinner drink, or you can stretch the dough into an oval and sprinkle with sesame and poppy seeds to make Turkish bread.

INGREDIENTS

makes 4 pitta breads

- 300ml (10fl oz) warm water
- 1 teaspoon dry yeast
- 1 teaspoon sugar
- 400g (14oz) bread flour or plain flour
- 1 heaped teaspoon salt
- 4½ tablespoons olive oil
- 1 tablespoon snipped fresh herbs, such as thyme or rosemary

1 Pour the warm water into the bowl of an electric mixer or food processor and sprinkle in the yeast. Mix quickly with a fork. Add the sugar and half the flour and blend, using the mixer's paddle attachment. Cover the bowl with lightly oiled cling film and set aside in a warm place for 2 hours, or until the dough has doubled in size.

2 Return the bowl to the mixer, add the salt, ½ tablespoon olive oil and the remaining flour. Blend for 5–10 minutes, until the dough is smooth and elastic.

3 Turn the dough out on a lightly floured surface and knead for 10–12 minutes, or until smooth and elastic. Roll the dough around in a lightly oiled bowl to coat it with oil, cover with lightly oiled cling film and leave in a warm place to rise for 1½ hours.

4 Preheat the oven to 220°C (425°F, gas mark 7). Line a baking tray with baking paper.

5 Turn the dough out on a lightly floured surface and divide into four balls. While working on the first ball, cover the others with a slightly damp tea towel to prevent them from drying out. Roll each ball into a round about 13cm (5in) in diameter and 5mm (¼in) thick and place on the prepared tray. Brush the dough balls lightly with oil and sprinkle with the herbs. Bake for about 8 minutes, or until golden.

6 Turn the pitta breads out on a wire rack and leave to cool before serving.

◆ Cakes for All Occasions ◆

From this selection you can choose a cake to suit the moment: sponges filled with fruit and cream are perfect for afternoon tea, while denser cakes that slice well are good to pack for school lunches and picnic treats. They can be iced or not – the choice is yours

Chocolate fudge cake

A rich dessert cake with a crisp crust and soft centre, this is the ultimate treat for chocolate lovers. There's no need to ice it, simply decorate the top with leaf silhouettes in icing sugar and cocoa as directed.

INGREDIENTS

serves 8

- 250g (9oz) unsalted butter
- 250g (9oz) best-quality dark chocolate, roughly chopped
- 150g (5½oz) caster sugar
- 70g (2½oz) soft brown sugar
- 6 eggs, separated
- 3 tablespoons plain flour
- 3 tablespoons ground almonds
- ½ teaspoon cream of tartar
- 1 tablespoon each sifted cocoa powder and icing sugar, to dust

1 Preheat the oven to 180°C (350°F, gas mark 4). Butter the sides and base of a 25cm (10in) springform tin, line the base with baking paper and lightly flour the tin.
2 Melt the butter in a heavy saucepan, add the chocolate and stir constantly over a low heat until just melted and smooth. It should not get much hotter than 50°C (122°F). Set aside.
3 Beat the sugars into the egg yolks until just mixed. While the chocolate is still warm, pour it into a large bowl (if the chocolate mixture has cooled, warm it over a low heat, stirring constantly, until just warm). Whisk in the egg mixture, then stir in the flour and almonds.
4 Warm the egg whites slightly by swirling them in a bowl over hot water. Add the cream of tartar and beat until rounded peaks form. Gently fold the whites into the base mixture.
5 Pour into the prepared tin and bake for 35-45 minutes, until the cake is completely set around the sides but is soft and creamy in the centre. The centre should tremble just slightly when you shake the tin gently.
6 Cool thoroughly in the tin. Remove the cake carefully to a flat plate and dust with

A tempting selection for afternoon tea: clockwise from back left, Lemon Madeleines, Strawberry Cream Cake, French Apple Cake, Chocolate Fudge Cake.

cocoa powder. Arrange garden leaves, such as sycamore or lupin, in a decorative pattern on the cake, dust lightly with icing sugar and remove the leaves. Serve with softly whipped cream, if desired. This cake keeps well in its baking tin, covered with foil, for 4 days. Do not refrigerate or freeze.

Strawberry cream cake

This light sponge relies on beaten egg whites for its height, rather than a rising agent as the classic Victorian sponge does. The long cooking time and low temperature produce a cake that retains its height when removed from the oven.

INGREDIENTS

serves 8

- 200g (7oz) caster sugar
- 7 eggs, separated
- 2 teaspoons vanilla essence
- 140g (5oz) plain flour
- 100g (3½oz) potato flour (from health-food stores)
- 175ml (6fl oz) sweetened whipped cream, to serve
- 6-8 sliced strawberries, to serve
- sifted icing sugar, to dust

1 Preheat oven to 160°C (325°F, gas mark 3). Butter the sides and base of a 23cm (9in) springform tin, line the base with baking paper and lightly flour the tin.
2 Using an electric mixer, beat the sugar, egg yolks and vanilla at high speed until the mixture is pale and tripled in bulk.
3 Sift the plain flour and potato flour together and fold in gently.
4 Beat the egg whites until stiff but not dry. Stir a spoonful into the batter then quickly and lightly fold in the rest. Turn the batter into the prepared tin and bake for 65 minutes, or until the cake is light golden and a skewer inserted in the centre comes out clean. Turn off the heat and leave the cake to rest in the oven, with the door open, for 10 minutes.
5 Cool on a wire rack. To serve, split the cake and fill with the whipped cream and sliced strawberries. Dust with icing sugar before serving and scatter with crystallised pink rose petals, if desired (see box, page 73).

Lemon madeleines

These tangy, shell-shaped sponge cakes are a traditional French indulgence.

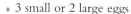

INGREDIENTS

makes 20

- 3 small or 2 large eggs
- 70g (2½oz) caster sugar
- 100g (3½oz) plain flour
- ½ teaspoon baking powder
- ¼ teaspoon salt
- 100g (3½oz) butter, melted
- finely grated zest of 1 lemon
- 1 tablespoon lemon juice
- sifted icing sugar, to dust

1 Preheat the oven to 180°C (350°F, gas mark 4). Grease and flour a madeleine tray. (If you cannot find one, use a small-bun tin.)
2 Place the eggs and sugar in a bowl and beat with an electric mixer until light and thick. In another bowl, sift the flour, baking powder and salt together, then add to the egg and sugar mixture. Fold in gently. Add the butter, lemon zest and juice and fold in until combined.
3 Spoon the mixture into the moulds and bake for 20-25 minutes, until golden.
4 Remove from the oven. Leave the madeleines in the moulds for 5 minutes, then turn out on a wire rack. When cold, dust the madeleines with icing sugar. Can be stored in an airtight container for up to 3 days.

VARIATION For a really delectable tea-time treat, serve the madeleines with lime curd (see page 27) and whipped cream.

FOR THE BEST RESULTS

Use medium-weight metal cake tins if you want a thin, evenly browned crust on your cake. For a heavier, browner crust, use toughened glass pans.

Chocolate or very rich cakes may depress slightly when pressed with a finger and still be done, but most cakes, such as sponges and butter cakes, will spring back when tested in this way.

Lemon and almond cake

Give this delicately flavoured cake an attractive shape and even brown crust by baking it in a traditional German bundt tin. This type of tin has swirled fluting on the outside, and a tube in the centre that allows for even cooking throughout. Serve warm, with a dollop of cream, for dessert, or with fresh berries for afternoon tea.

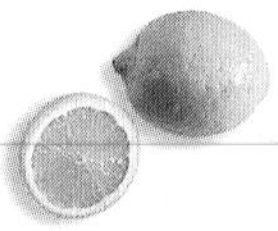

CAKE INGREDIENTS

serves 8-10

- 280g (10oz) plain flour
- 1 teaspoon baking powder
- 250g (9oz) unsalted butter, at room temperature
- 200g (7oz) caster sugar
- finely grated zest of 2 lemons
- 250ml (9fl oz) buttermilk
- 1 teaspoon vanilla essence
- 6 egg whites
- ¼ teaspoon salt
- 150g (5½oz) finely chopped blanched almonds

TOPPING INGREDIENTS

- 100g (3½oz) caster sugar
- 3 tablespoons lemon juice

1 Preheat the oven to 180°C (350°F, gas mark 4). Grease and flour a 1.5-litre (2¾-pint) bundt tin or 24cm (9½in) springform tin. Sift the flour with the baking powder twice to aerate thoroughly.
2 Beat the butter, 100g (3½oz) of the sugar and the lemon zest in the large bowl of an electric mixer until thick and creamy.
3 Add the flour mixture alternately with the buttermilk. Add the vanilla essence and beat until well mixed.
4 With clean beaters, beat the egg whites and salt in a bowl until stiff peaks form. Gradually add the remaining 100g (3½oz) of sugar, beating until the peaks are glossy.
5 Fold in a large spoonful of the meringue to the creamed butter mixture and combine. Lightly fold in the remaining meringue until no streaks remain. Fold in the almonds.
6 Spoon the mixture into the prepared tin and smooth the surface. Bake for 55-60 minutes, or until a skewer inserted in the centre comes out clean and the cake begins to pull away from the sides of the tin.
7 For the topping, combine the sugar and lemon juice in a saucepan and stir over a low heat until the sugar dissolves and forms a syrup.
8 Place the cake, still in the tin, on a wire rack and pierce the top all over with a fine skewer. Pour the hot syrup over the hot cake. Serve warm or cool completely in the tin before unmoulding. Can be stored in an airtight container for 3-4 days.

Apricot and pecan loaf

This delicious fruit-and-nut loaf is best eaten warm from the oven. Serve it sliced and thinly spread with butter, cottage cheese or cream cheese.

INGREDIENTS

serves 8

- 150g (5½oz) roughly chopped dried apricots
- 65ml (2¼fl oz) boiling water
- 125g (4½oz) unsalted butter, at room temperature
- 200g (7oz) caster sugar
- 1 egg
- 280g (10oz) strong white flour
- 1 teaspoon baking powder
- 1 teaspoon bicarbonate of soda
- ¼ teaspoon salt
- 250ml (9fl oz) milk
- 1 teaspoon vanilla essence
- 140g (5oz) chopped pecan nuts
- 150g (5½oz) apricot jam

1 Preheat the oven to 180°C (350°F, gas mark 4). Grease a 25cm × 12cm × 6cm (10in × 4½in × 2½in) loaf tin and line it with baking paper.
2 Place the apricots in a bowl, cover with the boiling water and leave for 10 minutes.
3 In a large bowl, beat the butter and sugar until creamy. Beat in the egg. Sift the flour, baking powder, bicarbonate of soda and salt into a bowl. In a smaller bowl, combine the milk and vanilla essence.
4 Add the flour and milk mixtures alternately to the creamed butter and sugar, beginning and ending with flour. Fold in the pecan nuts and apricots with their soaking liquid.
5 Spoon the mixture into the prepared tin and bake for 40-45 minutes, or until a skewer comes out clean when inserted in the loaf.
6 Remove from the oven and leave to stand for 5 minutes. Turn out on a wire rack.
7 Heat the apricot jam in a small saucepan with a few drops of water, stirring constantly. Brush the jam over the top of the warm loaf with a pastry brush for a shiny, glazed finish.

French apple cake

Choose either Golden Delicious or Granny Smith apples to make this lovely cake.

INGREDIENTS

serves 6

- 60g (2¼oz) butter
- 140g (5oz) caster sugar
- 1 egg
- 140g (5oz) self-raising flour, sifted
- 65ml (2¼fl oz) milk
- 3 apples, peeled, quartered and cored
- juice of 1 lemon
- 3 tablespoons caster sugar, for a topping
- 2 tablespoons ground cinnamon, for a topping

1 Preheat the oven to 180°C (350°F, gas mark 4). Butter a 23cm (9in) springform tin.
2 Using an electric mixer or a wooden spoon, cream the butter and caster sugar until light and fluffy.
3 Add the egg and beat well. Add half the flour and fold through. Add the milk and the remaining flour, alternately. The resulting batter will be quite thick.
4 Spread the mixture over the base of the prepared cake tin.
5 Cut the quartered apples into thin slices, cutting from the peeled side towards the cored side, but do not cut all the way through. As the apples are prepared, place them in a bowl of cold water into which you have squeezed the lemon juice. This will prevent discoloration of the apples.
6 When all the apples are sliced, drain them and place, cored side down and fanning the slices a little, on the batter. Bake for 1 hour. While still warm, sprinkle liberally with the combined sugar and cinnamon.

Portuguese nut cake

Quick and easy to make, this flourless cake with a rich, nutty flavour will become a favourite.

INGREDIENTS

serves 8-10

- ◆ 200g (7oz) caster sugar
- ◆ 4 eggs, separated
- ◆ 350g (12oz) ground almonds
- ◆ 100g (3½oz) dark chocolate
- ◆ 1 tablespoon double cream
- ◆ 50g (1¾oz) flaked blanched almonds, to decorate
- ◆ 70g (2½oz) pecan nut halves, to decorate

1 Preheat the oven to 180°C (350°F, gas mark 4). Grease the sides and base of an 18cm (7in) springform tin. Line the base with baking paper.
2 Place the sugar and egg yolks in a large bowl and beat until creamy and frothy. Stir in the ground almonds. In another bowl, beat the egg whites until stiff peaks form, then gently fold into the egg-yolk mixture.
3 Spoon the mixture into the prepared tin and bake for 30-35 minutes, until a skewer inserted in the cake comes out clean. Remove from the oven and transfer to a wire rack. When the cake is cool, peel off the baking paper.
4 Place the chocolate in a double boiler over a low heat and stir until melted. Stir in the cream and mix well to combine. Remove from the heat and spread the chocolate mixture thinly over the cake with a spatula.

5 Decorate the cake with nuts before serving. Serve cut into wedges. Can be stored in an airtight container for up to 5 days.

Passion fruit sponge

If you wish, split this sponge and fill it with whipped cream before topping with the passion fruit.

SPONGE INGREDIENTS

serves 8-10

- ◆ 250g (9oz) butter, at room temperature
- ◆ 200g (7oz) caster sugar
- ◆ 3 eggs
- ◆ 280g (10oz) self-raising flour, sifted

ICING INGREDIENTS

- ◆ 140g (5oz) icing sugar, sifted
- ◆ pulp of 2 passion fruit

1 Preheat the oven to 190°C (375°F, gas mark 5). Grease a deep 20cm (8in) round cake tin and line the base with baking paper.
2 Place the butter and sugar in a large mixing bowl and beat with an electric mixer until thick and creamy. Beat in the eggs, one at a time, until combined. Fold in the sifted flour, then lightly fold in 2 tablespoons hot water.
3 Spoon the batter into the prepared tin and smooth the surface. Bake for 35-40 minutes, or until a skewer inserted in the centre comes out clean and the cake begins to pull away from the sides of the tin.

4 Cool the sponge cake in the tin on a wire rack for 5 minutes, then turn out on the wire rack to cool completely.
5 To make the icing, stir the icing sugar and fruit pulp together until the mixture is smooth and spreadable. Pour the icing over the cake and carefully spread to the edges. Let stand until set. Cut the cake into wedges to serve.

Kugelhopf

A traditional cake from the Alsace region of France, this yeast cake is studded with rum-soaked fruit and is cooked in the distinctive bundt tin (see Lemon and Almond Cake, opposite page).

INGREDIENTS

serves 6

- ◆ 70g (2½oz) currants
- ◆ 60g (2¼oz) raisins
- ◆ 3 tablespoons rum
- ◆ 40g (1½oz) flaked almonds
- ◆ two 7g sachets dried yeast
- ◆ 200ml (7fl oz) lukewarm milk
- ◆ 325g (11½oz) plain flour
- ◆ pinch salt
- ◆ 1½ tablespoons caster sugar
- ◆ 3 eggs, lightly beaten
- ◆ 125g (4½oz) butter, melted
- ◆ sifted icing sugar, to dust

1 Soak the currants and raisins in the rum while you proceed with steps 2 to 4.
2 Preheat oven to 190°C (375°F, gas mark 5). Generously butter a 20cm (8in) fluted bundt tin and press the almonds into the butter. Refrigerate until needed.
3 Stir the yeast into the lukewarm milk.
4 Sift the flour and salt into a warm bowl. Make a well in the centre and add the yeast mixture, sugar, eggs and melted butter. Beat well and add the soaked fruits with rum. Pour the batter into the prepared tin (the tin should be three-quarters full).
5 Cover with a damp cloth and stand in a warm place for 20-30 minutes, until the mixture has risen to 2.5cm (1in) from the top.
6 Bake for 50-60 minutes, until a fine skewer inserted comes out clean. Stand for a few minutes, then turn out on a wire rack to cool. Dust with icing sugar and serve sliced.

TO LINE A ROUND OR SQUARE CAKE TIN

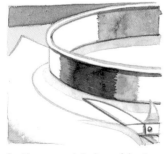

1 *Trace around the base of the tin on baking paper and cut out, cutting a little inside the line. (For fruit cakes, cut 3 thicknesses to protect the cake during the long cooking period.)*

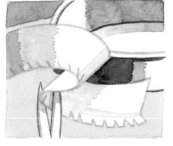

2 *Cut a strip of paper a little longer than the perimeter of the tin and a little wider than the height. Fold a 1.5cm cuff along one edge. Open cuff and slash diagonally at 2cm intervals.*

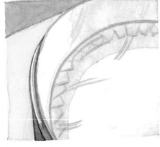

3 *Fit the long strip into the tin with the cuff flat on the bottom. Insert the paper base. For a square tin, slash only at the corners or cut out notches and mitre the corners neatly.*

Biscuits, Muffins and Scones

It takes only minutes to whip up a batch of home-made biscuits, so keep a jar filled with your favourites — they beat the store-bought variety any day. And nothing is as comforting as freshly made muffins for breakfast or piping-hot scones for tea

Macadamia biscotti

These twice-baked Italian biscuits are perfect with coffee at any time of the day. They freeze very well, so make an extra batch to have on hand.

INGREDIENTS
makes 24-30

- 90g (3¼oz) unsalted butter, chopped, at room temperature
- 150g (5½oz) caster sugar
- 2 eggs
- 1 teaspoon vanilla essence
- 2 teaspoons grated lemon zest
- 300g (10½oz) plain flour
- 1½ teaspoons baking powder
- ¼ teaspoon salt
- 100g (3½oz) coarsely chopped macadamia nuts

1 Preheat the oven to 170°C (340°F, gas mark 3½). Grease and flour a baking tray.
2 Place the butter and sugar in a large bowl and beat with an electric mixer until pale and creamy. Beat in the eggs, vanilla essence and zest. In another bowl, sift the flour, baking powder and salt. Add these to the butter/sugar mixture and stir to combine. Fold in the nuts.
3 Halve the dough and, with lightly oiled hands, roll each half into a log 4cm (1½in) thick and 30cm (12in) long. Place the logs on the tray and bake in the centre of the oven for 25 minutes, or until light golden brown.
4 Remove from the oven, place the cakes on a wire rack and cool.
5 Place the cakes on a bread board and cut slices 2.5cm (1in) thick at a 45° angle – to avoid crumbling, use firm, decisive strokes with a serrated knife. Place the slices flat on a baking tray and return to a 180°C (350°F, gas mark 4) oven for about 10 minutes, turning once, to dry them.
6 Cool on a wire rack. Will keep in an airtight container for 2-3 weeks.

Sesame Parmesan biscuits

Served warm, these easy-to-make biscuits are good as a savoury snack for afternoon tea.

INGREDIENTS
makes 24-30

- 140g (5oz) plain flour
- 1 heaped teaspoon sesame seeds
- ½ teaspoon baking powder
- 1 tablespoon butter
- 65ml (2¼fl oz) chilled water
- 25g (1oz) grated Parmesan cheese
- 2 tablespoons poppy seeds, optional

1 Preheat the oven to 170°C (340°F, gas mark 3½). Grease a baking tray.
2 Place the flour, sesame seeds and baking powder in a medium-sized bowl. Add the butter and rub it in, using your fingertips, until the mixture resembles fine breadcrumbs. Add enough chilled water to form a dough.
3 Roll the dough out thinly on a lightly floured surface. Use shaped cutters to cut out the biscuits. Place them on the tray, sprinkle with cheese and poppy seeds, if using, and bake for 15 minutes, or until golden and crisp.
4 The biscuits can be stored in an airtight container for 1 week. To serve, reheat in a 150°C (300°F, gas mark 2) oven for 5 minutes.

Coconut macaroons

Desiccated coconut may make the mixture seem dry, but it produces an excellent result.

INGREDIENTS
makes about 35

- 3 egg whites
- 150g (5½oz) caster sugar
- 500g (1lb 2oz) desiccated coconut
- 100g (3½oz) finely chopped macadamia nuts or almonds

1 Preheat the oven to 180°C (350°F, gas mark 4). Lightly oil two baking trays.
2 Whisk the egg whites with an electric mixer until soft peaks form. Gradually add the sugar, whisking well after each addition until the peaks are glossy. Fold in the coconut and nuts.
3 With wet hands, roll level tablespoons of the mixture into round or oval shapes and place on baking trays.
4 Bake for 20 minutes, or until lightly golden. Cool on wire racks and store in an airtight container. Will keep for 2-3 days.

Chocolate-almond bites

These little chocolate-almond shortbreads, dredged in icing sugar, are delicious served with coffee.

INGREDIENTS
makes 48-60

- 280g (10oz) plain flour
- 75g (2¾oz) good-quality cocoa powder
- 250g (9oz) butter, at room temperature
- 50g (1¾oz) caster sugar
- 1 teaspoon vanilla essence
- ¼ teaspoon salt
- 125g (4½oz) finely chopped toasted almonds
- sifted icing sugar, for dredging

1 Preheat the oven to 170°C (340°F, gas mark 3½). Grease a baking tray.
2 Sift the flour with the cocoa powder.
3 Place the butter, sugar, vanilla essence and salt in a large mixing bowl and beat with an electric mixer until pale and creamy.
4 Stir in the flour mixture, then fold in the almonds. Cover and refrigerate the dough for about 1 hour.
5 Shape heaped teaspoonfuls of the dough into balls and arrange on the prepared baking

tray. Bake for 20-25 minutes, until firm to the touch. Cool for a few minutes on the tray before removing to a wire rack.

6 While still slightly warm, dredge the biscuits with icing sugar. When cold, store in an airtight container. Will keep for 5 days. Lightly dust again with icing sugar before serving.

Almond tuiles

The curved roof tiles on the lovely old farmhouses of southern France inspired these curved almond biscuits. Hence the name tuiles, or tiles.

INGREDIENTS
makes about 24
♦ 90g (3¼oz) unsalted butter
♦ 70g (2½oz) caster sugar
♦ 50g (1¾oz) plain flour
♦ pinch salt
♦ 60g (2¼oz) slivered or flaked blanched almonds

1 Preheat the oven to 200°C (400°F, gas mark 6) and butter two baking trays.

2 Using an electric mixer, beat the butter and sugar until light and creamy.

3 Sift the flour with the salt and fold into the creamed mixture with the almonds. Drop teaspoonfuls of the mixture onto one of the prepared trays. Start with three at first, until you are used to removing and handling the hot biscuit quickly enough to shape it. Flatten the mixture slightly with a wet spatula or knife and leave plenty of room for spreading.

4 Bake the tuiles in the centre of the pre-heated oven for 5 minutes, or until golden. Remove from the oven and leave for a few moments to cool on the tray. While still warm and soft, carefully lift each tuile off with a spatula and drape it over a rolling pin to give the characteristic curved shape. Leave for a few seconds to harden, then carefully remove and finish cooling on wire racks. Once cooled, store in airtight containers.

Delicious picnic and party fare: clockwise from top right, Macadamia Biscotti, Almond Tuiles, Sesame Parmesan Biscuits cut in several different shapes, Chocolate-almond Bites.

Orange and date muffins

These delicious, wholesome muffins are equally good for a morning or late-afternoon snack.

INGREDIENTS

makes 15

- 240g (8½oz) plain flour
- 1 teaspoon baking powder
- 1 teaspoon bicarbonate of soda
- ½ teaspoon salt
- 90g (3¼oz) pitted and chopped dates
- 125g (4½oz) unsalted butter, at room temperature
- 150g (5½oz) caster sugar
- 1 large egg
- 125ml (4fl oz) freshly squeezed orange juice
- 1 whole orange, chopped, seeded and puréed

1 Preheat oven to 200°C (400°F, gas mark 6). Grease a muffin pan with 15 cups, each measuring 7cm (2¾in) in diameter.
2 Mix the flour, baking powder, bicarbonate of soda and salt together in a bowl. Add the dates and toss to coat. In a large bowl, beat the butter and sugar until pale and creamy. Beat in the egg, orange juice and puréed orange. Fold in the dry ingredients – do not overmix.
3 Spoon the mixture into the muffin cups. Bake in the centre of the oven for 20 minutes, or until golden on top and risen.
4 Turn the muffins out on a wire rack to cool. Serve warm or cold.

Freezer biscuits

Make rolls of this biscuit dough and freeze for a ready supply of biscuits.

INGREDIENTS

makes 24-36

- 125g (4½oz) butter
- 100g (3½oz) caster sugar
- ½ teaspoon vanilla essence
- 1 egg
- 280g (10oz) plain flour
- ¼ teaspoon salt

1 Place the butter, sugar and vanilla essence in a large bowl and beat with an electric mixer or with a wooden spoon until thick and creamy. Beat in the egg. Fold in the flour and salt.
2 Place the dough on a piece of baking paper. Shape into a sausage about 2cm (¾in) in diameter, then roll, first in foil and then in plastic wrap. Freeze for later use.
3 When required, remove the dough from the freezer, unwrap, slice into rounds with a serrated knife and decorate as desired.
4 Preheat the oven to 180°C (350°F, gas mark 4). Grease a baking tray, place the biscuits on it and bake for 12-15 minutes, until golden. Cool on a wire rack.

VARIATIONS To make jam drops, press a finger into each disc and fill the hole with a little jam before cooking. Alternatively, press a nut into each disc before cooking.

Blueberry muffins

Long a favourite in the US, these muffins are easily made now that blueberries are readily available.

INGREDIENTS

makes 12

- 200g (7oz) blueberries, fresh or frozen (if frozen, thaw first)
- 400g (14oz) plain flour
- 1 tablespoon baking powder
- 1 teaspoon salt
- 100g (3½oz) caster sugar
- 2 tablespoons butter, melted
- 2 eggs, lightly beaten
- 185ml (6½fl oz) buttermilk
- 1 teaspoon vanilla essence

1 Preheat the oven to 200°C (400°F, gas mark 6). Grease a muffin pan with 12 cups, each measuring 7cm (2¾in) in diameter.
2 If using fresh blueberries, rinse and dry them. Toss the blueberries with 2 tablespoons of the flour. Place the remaining flour and the baking powder, salt and sugar in a large bowl; stir to combine. Lightly mix in the melted butter, eggs, buttermilk and vanilla essence – do not overmix. Fold in the blueberries.
3 Spoon the mixture into the prepared muffin cups. Bake in the centre of the oven for 20 minutes, or until golden.
4 Cool on a wire rack. Serve warm.

Herb and bacon muffins

Quickly mixed for breakfast, snacks or afternoon tea, savoury muffins are always popular.

INGREDIENTS

makes 12

- 240g (8½oz) plain flour
- 2 teaspoons baking powder
- ½ teaspoon salt
- 2 tablespoons chopped herbs, such as sage
- 2 tablespoons grated Parmesan
- 1 tablespoon caster sugar
- 100g (3½oz) crumbled, crisp, cooked bacon
- 1 egg, beaten
- 185ml (6½fl oz) milk
- 60g (2¼oz) butter, melted

1 Preheat oven to 200°C (400°F, gas mark 6). Grease a muffin pan with 12 cups, each measuring 7cm (2¾in) in diameter.
2 Sift the flour, baking powder and salt into a large mixing bowl. Stir in the herbs, cheese, sugar and bacon. Make a well in the centre.
3 Combine the egg, milk and butter in a bowl and add to the dry ingredients. Mix lightly with a fork just until the dry ingredients are moistened. The mixture should be lumpy; do not overmix or the muffins will be tough.
4 Spoon the batter into the prepared tins, filling two-thirds full. Bake for 15-20 minutes, until browned. Serve the muffins warm.

MAKING AND STORING

Do not overmix muffin mixtures. Only a few light strokes are needed. Any more and the mixture will produce tough and heavy muffins.

For lighter, flakier scones, use buttermilk or soured milk in place of plain milk in most recipes.

To freeze scones or muffins, wrap individually in foil; store in freezer bags for up to 6 months. Reheat thawed, foil-wrapped scones or muffins in the oven at 180°C (350°F, gas mark 4) for 12-15 minutes.

Fruit scone fingers

A different way to present scones – cut into fingers.
Serve with jam and cream, if desired.

INGREDIENTS

makes 16

- 200g (7oz) plain flour
- 1 teaspoon cream of tartar
- ½ teaspoon bicarbonate of soda
- ¼ teaspoon salt
- 100g (3½oz) butter, chopped
- 100g (3½oz) sugar
- 100g (3½oz) currants
- 165ml (5½fl oz) buttermilk
- 1 egg, separated
- 1 tablespoon caster sugar, to dust

1 Preheat oven to 190°C (375°F, gas mark 5). Grease a 16cm (6¾in) square cake tin; line base with baking paper.
2 Sift the flour, cream of tartar, bicarbonate of soda and salt into a large bowl. Add the chopped butter to the dry ingredients and rub it in, using your fingers, until the mixture resembles fine breadcrumbs. Add the sugar and currants and mix well.
3 Beat the buttermilk and egg yolk together and mix them into the dry ingredients.
4 Spoon the mixture into the prepared tin and, using your fingertips, spread it as evenly as possible. Score the mixture into fingers with a floured knife. Brush the fingers with egg white and dust with caster sugar. Bake for 15–20 minutes, or until golden. Serve warm.

Cheese and parsley wedges

For a crusty, golden appearance, sprinkle the loaf
with a little grated cheese before baking.

INGREDIENTS

makes 8

- 280g (10oz) wholemeal self-raising flour
- 90g (3¼oz) mature cheese, roughly chopped
- 40g (1½oz) fresh parsley sprigs
- 1 teaspoon salt
- 185ml (6½fl oz) milk

1 Preheat the oven to 230°C (450°F, gas mark 8). Place the flour, cheese, parsley and salt in a food processor. Process until the cheese crumbles into the flour and the parsley is finely chopped.
2 Add the milk, all at once, and process just until a soft dough forms, about 5 seconds.
3 Turn the dough out on a floured surface and knead gently. Shape the dough into a round on a lightly floured baking tray. Cut almost through the dough with a sharp knife into eight wedge-shaped pieces.
4 Bake the dough in the centre of the oven for 20–25 minutes, until puffed and brown. Remove the loaf from the oven, wrap in a tea towel and cool slightly. Cut through the marked wedges and serve buttered.

Ginger and pecan scones

Make these as individual scones or in a round loaf,
scored into segments, as in the previous recipe.

INGREDIENTS

makes 16

- 280g (10oz) plain flour
- 1 tablespoon baking powder
- 2 tablespoons sugar
- ½ teaspoon salt
- 4 tablespoons unsalted butter, chopped
- 2 eggs, lightly beaten
- 85ml (3fl oz) double cream
- 4 tablespoons chopped crystallised ginger
- 2 tablespoons chopped pecan nuts
- 1 egg white, lightly beaten, for brushing
- 1 tablespoon caster sugar, to dust

1 Preheat the oven to 190°C (375°F, gas mark 5). Place the flour, baking powder, sugar and salt in a bowl and mix well. Add the butter and rub it into the flour, using your fingertips, until the mixture resembles coarse breadcrumbs. Add the eggs, cream, ginger and nuts, then mix until the dough comes together.
2 Turn the dough out on a lightly floured surface and roll it out gently with a floured rolling pin to 1cm (½in) thickness. Using a cutter dipped in flour, cut the dough into rounds or other fancy shapes. Place on a lightly floured baking tray, brush with the beaten egg white and dust with the sugar. Bake for 20 minutes, or until golden brown.
3 Turn the scones out on a wire rack to cool. Serve warm or cold with butter or cream cheese for spreading.

Apple and sultana muffins

The apple in these muffins provides natural sweet-
ness that reduces the need for a larger quantity of
sugar, while the nuts, sultanas and cereal give a
blend of crunchy and chewy textures.

INGREDIENTS

makes 10–12

- 280g (10oz) plain flour
- 3 teaspoons baking powder
- 1 teaspoon salt
- ½ teaspoon ground cinnamon
- ¼ teaspoon ground nutmeg
- 1 apple, peeled and shredded
- 40g (1½oz) sultanas
- 140g (5oz) soft brown sugar
- 35g (1¼oz) chopped walnuts or pecans
- 2 eggs, well beaten
- 165ml (5½fl oz) milk
- 60ml (2½fl oz) vegetable oil
- 4 tablespoons breakfast cereal (corn, bran or wheatflake)

1 Preheat the oven to 200°C (400°F, gas mark 6). Grease a muffin pan with 12 cups, each measuring 7cm (2¾in) in diameter.
2 Sift the flour into a large mixing bowl with the baking powder, salt and spices. Stir in the apple, sultanas, brown sugar and nuts, then make a well in the centre.
3 Combine the eggs, milk and oil. Add the liquid, all at once, to the dry ingredients and stir just until moistened and combined – do not overmix. Fold in the cereal.
4 Spoon the mixture into the prepared muffin pan, filling the cups two-thirds full. Bake for 15–20 minutes, until puffed and brown. Cool for 5 minutes before removing from the tins. Serve warm.

Sweet Tarts and Pies

*For a satisfying dessert, a tart or pie is hard to beat. Use our recipe for shortcrust
pastry and your choice of fillings to produce a whole range of delights. Make a change from
the old standard with a tart crust made from crushed biscuits and ground nuts*

Rich shortcrust pastry

*Use this pastry as the base for fruit flans and any
sweet tart that requires a sweet, crisp crust.*

INGREDIENTS

makes one 23cm (9in) pie crust

- 200g (7oz) plain flour
- 1 teaspoon caster sugar
- ¼ teaspoon salt
- 2 tablespoons dried milk powder
- 125g (4½oz) butter, cubed
- 1 egg

1 Mix the flour, sugar and salt in a bowl. Add
the milk powder. Make a well in the centre.
2 Place the butter and egg in the well and mix
with your fingers, rubbing the butter into the
flour until the mixture sticks together.
3 Turn the dough out on a floured surface.
With the heel of your hand rub the dough
across the board; gather and rub three or four
times more until the butter is fully worked in.
4 Flour your hands generously and roll the
mixture into a ball. Wrap this in plastic and
chill in the refrigerator for 2-3 hours.
5 Roll out as for Shortcrust Pastry (see page 44).

Key lime pie

*This pie derives its name from the Florida Keys in
the US, where it is a traditional dessert.*

INGREDIENTS

serves 6

- 4 eggs, separated
- 185ml (6½fl oz) condensed milk
- finely grated zest 4 limes
- 125ml (4fl oz) lime juice
- 1 crushed biscuit crust
  (see page 69)
- 50g (1¾oz) caster sugar

1 Beat the egg yolks in a large bowl until pale
and creamy. Add the condensed milk and

continue beating until pale and thickened.
2 Add the zest, mixing well, then gradually
beat in the lime juice.
3 Pour the egg-yolk mixture into the
prepared tart shell. Refrigerate for about
1 hour, until the filling is set.
4 Preheat the oven to 200°C (400°F, gas
mark 6). In a separate bowl, beat the egg
whites until they begin to stiffen. Add the
sugar, a bit at a time, beating continuously,
until it is incorporated. Pile the meringue on
top of the filling, using the back of a spoon to
spread the meringue around and form peaks.
Place in the oven for 5-10 minutes, until peaks
become lightly golden. Cool before serving.

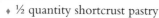

PIE AND TART SHELLS

*When making shortcrust pastry, handle the dough
as little and as lightly as possible. Overhandling will
make the pastry tough. A light (and cool) hand
produces tender, flaky pastry.*

*Make sure that the water you add to shortcrust
dough is as cold as possible – some recipes even
specify using iced water. And avoid using too much.
If you can get by with less than the maximum
recommended amount, so much the better.*

*Chilling pastry dough in the refrigerator before
rolling helps make it tender and prevents shrinkage
during baking. Several hours is ideal, but at least
30 minutes is recommended. Once removed from the
refrigerator, the dough should be allowed to come to
room temperature (about 30 minutes) to make it
easier to handle and roll.*

*To spread biscuit crumbs evenly into a pie dish, place
the mixture in the dish, then press down with another pie dish of the same diameter.*

Custard tart

*A perennial dessert favourite. If you prefer a richer
custard, use half cream and half milk.*

INGREDIENTS

serves 6

- ½ quantity shortcrust pastry
- 500ml (18fl oz) milk
- 1 teaspoon vanilla essence
- 3 eggs, lightly beaten
- 2 tablespoons sugar, or
  to taste
- pinch salt
- pinch ground nutmeg

1 Preheat the oven to 200°C (400°F, gas
mark 6). Make the pastry according to the
directions on page 44. Bake blind (see box,
page 46) for 10-15 minutes to set the pastry.
Remove from the oven and lower the heat
to 160°C (325°F, gas mark 3).
2 Meanwhile, heat the milk in a saucepan
until scalded. Remove from the heat and add
the vanilla essence.
3 Place the eggs, sugar, salt and nutmeg in
a bowl and whisk lightly to combine. Stir in
about a third of the hot milk, then return this
egg mixture to the remaining milk in the
saucepan and mix well.
4 Strain the mixture into a measuring cup,
then pour into the partially baked pastry shell.
Place the tart on a baking tray to catch any
drips and place in the oven.
5 Bake at 160°C (325°F, gas mark 3) for
30-40 minutes, until a knife inserted in the
centre of the custard comes out clean. Remove
the tart from the oven and leave to cool.

VARIATIONS Add a little grated orange zest
to the eggs in step 4 for a pleasing hint of
orange; or add a bay leaf or a few cardamom
pods to the scalded milk and leave to infuse for
30 minutes. Remove before proceeding.

Pumpkin Pie is an autumn treat when the pumpkin vines give up their bounty. Ring the changes with different varieties – each has its own special flavour.

Pumpkin pie

This sweet, moist pie is the ideal way to use up any flesh scooped out of your Hallowe'en lanterns.

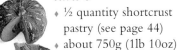

INGREDIENTS

serves 8

- ½ quantity shortcrust pastry (see page 44)
- about 750g (1lb 10oz) pumpkin
- 60g (2½oz) butter, diced
- 100g (3½oz) soft brown sugar
- 2 large eggs
- 1-2 tablespoons bourbon, whisky or vanilla essence
- 1 tablespoon grated orange zest
- ½ teaspoon ground cinnamon
- 250ml (9fl oz) milk
- pecan halves, to decorate
- whipped cream, to serve

1 Preheat the oven to 225°C (430°F, gas mark 7½). Roll out the pastry and line a 23cm (9in) pie tin or flan ring. Trim the edges. Chill for at least 15 minutes.
2 Peel the pumpkin, remove the seeds, and boil until tender. Process or mash the pumpkin to a smooth purée.
3 Beat the butter, sugar, eggs, flavourings and milk into the pumpkin and pour the filling into the pie case. Top with the pecan halves.
4 Bake in the oven for 10 minutes, then reduce the heat to 180°C (350°F, gas mark 4) and bake for 45-50 minutes longer, until browned and set. Leave to cool for 45 minutes before serving with whipped cream.

VARIATION To make a Pumpkin Chiffon Pie, soak 1 gelatin leaf in 65ml (2¼fl oz) cold water. Cook the filling ingredients over hot water until thickened, then add the dissolved gelatin. Whisk 2 egg whites and, once the mixture has begun to set, fold in. Pour into a crushed biscuit crust and chill until set.

Crushed biscuit crust

This quick-and-easy biscuit crust is particularly good to use with fillings that require little or no baking and must spend some time in the refrigerator.

INGREDIENTS

makes one 23cm (9in) pastry shell

- 185g (6½oz) plain biscuits, finely crushed
- 75-90g (2¾-3¼oz) unsalted butter, melted

1 Place the biscuit crumbs in a bowl and add the butter, a tablespoon at a time, mixing with a wooden spoon until the crumbs are well coated with butter.
2 Pour the biscuit-crumb mixture into a pie tin, spread it evenly around with your hands and press it well into the tin. Chill for 1 hour, or until set. Fill with your choice of filling.

VARIATIONS Use chocolate biscuits or replace 60g (2¼oz) of biscuit crumbs with finely ground almonds or hazelnuts.

Sweet Temptations

*Homemade confectionery and chocolates charm guests and make delightful gifts. Use
the best ingredients you can find – the superior flavour will make the extra expense worth while,
and you'll find that the sweets you make yourself will still save you money*

Candied citrus peel

*Candied peel makes a delicious decoration for
desserts and ice cream. Try dipping larger candied
strips in melted chocolate to serve with coffee.*

INGREDIENTS
makes about 115g (4oz)
- 3 firm ripe lemons
  or oranges
- 3 tablespoons caster sugar

1 Using a vegetable peeler, remove the peel
from the fruit – try to remove just the peel,
leaving the bitter white pith behind. Using a
sharp knife, cut the peel into strips. The size
of the strips will vary according to your
requirement – if you want to use the candied
peel on cakes or tartlets, cut into thin julienne
strips; if candying to dip in chocolate as a
sweet, cut the peel into larger strips.
2 Place the strips in a small saucepan and
cover with cold water. Bring to the boil,
drain and refresh under cold running water.
Return to the saucepan, add the sugar and
8 tablespoons water and cook over a medium
heat until the liquid has evaporated and the
peel is bright and shiny.
3 Store in a sealed jar in the refrigerator.
Keeps for up to 6 months.

Chocolate fruit clusters

*For a gift, present these rich fruity treats in mini
cake cases made of brightly coloured foil. These are
readily available from kitchen shops.*

INGREDIENTS
makes about 30
- 250g (9oz) chocolate
- 140g (5oz) chopped
  hazelnuts
- 200g (7oz) preserved stem
  ginger in syrup, drained
- 50g (1¾oz) sultanas

1 Line a baking tray with baking paper or
greaseproof paper.
2 Place the chocolate in a double boiler over
a low heat and stir until melted. Remove from
the heat and stir in the hazelnuts, ginger and
sultanas. Mix to coat.
3 Place heaped teaspoons of the mixture on
the prepared baking tray. Refrigerate until set.
Can be stored in an airtight container in the
refrigerator for 1-2 months.

Coconut ice

*No cooking is required to make this attractive and
delicious old-fashioned sweet, always a favourite at
fêtes. It can also be packed in tiny baskets lined
with foil as a gift, and wrapped in cling film to keep
the sweet fresh. This version is very easy to make.*

INGREDIENTS
makes 30-36
- 275g (9½oz) desiccated
  coconut
- 100g (3½oz) caster sugar
- ¼ teaspoon cream of tartar
- 5 tablespoons condensed milk
- few drops pink food
  colouring

1 Line a shallow 28cm × 18cm
(11in × 7in) tin with aluminium foil.
2 Mix the coconut, sugar and cream of tartar
in a medium-sized bowl to combine. Add the
condensed milk and mix until it forms a mass.
3 Spread half the mixture into the tin. Add a
few drops of pink colouring to the remaining
mixture, mix well to gain a uniform colour
then spread on top of the white layer. Cover
the coconut ice with foil and leave in the
refrigerator overnight to set.
4 Cut the coconut ice into bars or squares and
store in an airtight container. The bars will
keep in the refrigerator for up to 1 month.

Chocolate truffles

*An irresistible indulgence or an extravagant gift
for a special occasion, these chocolate truffles will
delight your family and friends alike.*

INGREDIENTS
makes about 30
- 250g (9oz) chocolate
- 2 tablespoons double cream
- 2 tablespoons cognac
- 250g (9oz) finely chopped
  dried apricots
- 140g (5oz) finely chopped
  hazelnuts
- ½ cup preserved ginger
  in syrup, drained and
  finely chopped
- 2 tablespoons icing
  sugar, sifted
- hazelnut halves,
  to decorate

1 Line a large baking tray with baking paper
or aluminium foil.
2 Place half the chocolate in a double boiler
and stir until melted. Remove from the heat
and beat in the cream and cognac. Stir in the
apricots, hazelnuts, ginger and icing sugar. Stir
well to combine. Cover the bowl and place
in the refrigerator for 2 hours, or until the
mixture is firm enough to handle.
3 Shape heaped teaspoons of the mixture into
balls and set aside on greaseproof paper.
4 Melt the remaining chocolate in the double
boiler. Remove from the heat and, using a
fork, dip each truffle into the chocolate,
allowing any excess chocolate to run off.
Place the truffles on the prepared baking tray.
Top each with a hazelnut half and place in the
refrigerator to chill for about an hour.
5 When the chocolate has set, the truffles
can be stored in an airtight container in the
refrigerator for up to 1 month.

Caramels

You will not be able to resist this creamy version of the traditional chewy caramel.

INGREDIENTS

makes about 64

- 4 tablespoons cream
- 6 tablespoons evaporated milk
- 350g (12oz) caster sugar
- 1 tablespoon liquid glucose
- ¼ teaspoon salt
- 2 tablespoons golden syrup
- 2 tablespoons unsalted butter
- 1 teaspoon vanilla essence

1 Line an 18cm (7in) square cake tin with foil. Place all the ingredients, except the essence, in a heavy-based saucepan over a low heat. Stir until blended and dissolved. Increase the heat and boil, stirring constantly, until the mixture reaches 124°C (255°F) on a sugar thermometer.
2 Remove the saucepan from the heat and mix in the vanilla essence. Carefully pour the mixture into the prepared cake tin and set aside to cool and harden.
3 When cold, remove the caramel from the tin, remove the foil and, using a sharp knife, cut the caramel into 2.5cm (1in) squares on a wooden board. Can be stored in an airtight container in a cool place for 1-2 months.

VARIATION Add 2 tablespoons nuts, such as chopped macadamias, pistachios or pecans to the caramel, just before pouring the cooked mixture into the prepared tin.

This selection of classic confections will satisfy every sweet tooth: (1) Turkish Delight, (2) Chocolate Truffles, (3) Chocolate Fruit Clusters, (4) Peanut Brittle, (5) Coconut Ice, (6) Marshmallows.

71

Marshmallows

These easy-to-make sweets can be eaten as they are, dipped in hot chocolate or toasted on a barbecue.

INGREDIENTS
makes about 36
- 2 tablespoons icing sugar
- 2 tablespoons cornflour
- 1½ tablespoons gelatine powder
- 100g (3½oz) sugar
- 175ml (6fl oz) liquid glucose

1 Line a 28cm × 18cm × 5cm (11in × 7in × 2in) slice tin with greaseproof paper. Combine 1 tablespoon each of the icing sugar and cornflour and sift evenly into the prepared tin. Reserve the remainder for dusting and dredging the cut pieces of marshmallow.
2 Place the gelatine and 85ml (3fl oz) water in a small bowl and stir a little. Set aside for 5 minutes, or until the gelatine has softened.
3 Sit the bowl in a larger bowl of boiling water and stir until the gelatine has dissolved. Add the sugar and continue to stir until it has dissolved. Place the liquid glucose in a large bowl, add the gelatine mixture and whisk for 15-20 minutes. By this stage, the mixture should be creamy and thick.
4 Pour the mixture into the prepared tin and gently shake to even out the top. Set aside for 20 minutes to cool and set.
5 Transfer the set mixture to a wooden board. Lightly dust with a little of the reserved icing

sugar and cornflour and cut into squares or festive shapes. Dredge the pieces in icing sugar and cornflour and store in an airtight container in a cool, dry place. Keeps for 1-2 weeks.

Peanut brittle

Packed with peanuts, this old-fashioned sweet is quick and easy to make and is always well received.

INGREDIENTS
makes about 45
- 350g (12oz) caster sugar
- 200g (7oz) soft brown sugar
- 75g (2¾oz) unsalted butter
- 200g (7oz) unsalted peanuts

1 Line a shallow 25cm × 15cm (10in × 6in) tin with foil. Place both the caster sugar and the soft brown sugar, butter and 165ml (5½fl oz) water in a heavy-based saucepan and stir with a wooden spoon until the sugars dissolve and the butter melts. Increase the heat, bring to the boil and boil until the mixture reaches 154°C (309°F), the caramel space on a sugar thermometer.
2 Immediately remove the saucepan from the heat and place on a marble slab or in cold water to stop further cooking. Stir in the nuts.
3 Pour the mixture into the prepared tin. When set, cool before breaking into bite-sized pieces. Can be stored in an airtight container in a cool, dry place for up to 1 month.

Caramel fudge

Cut into squares and wrapped in gift wrap, this creamy fudge makes a great present. For the best results, use a heavy-based saucepan of 5-6 litres (8¾-10 pints) capacity.

INGREDIENTS
makes 50-60
- 1.2kg (2lb 10oz) soft brown sugar
- 200g (7oz) unsalted butter, cubed
- 300ml (10fl oz) milk
- 165ml (5½fl oz) cream
- 1 teaspoon vanilla essence

1 Grease a 28cm × 18cm × 5cm (11in × 7in × 2in) slice tin and line it with foil.
2 Place the sugar, butter, milk and cream in a large, heavy-based saucepan over a medium heat and stir constantly with a wooden spoon until the sugar dissolves and the mixture boils.
3 Reduce the heat and boil gently, stirring occasionally to prevent sticking, until the mixture reaches the soft ball stage (116°C, or 241°F, on a sugar thermometer).
4 Transfer the saucepan to a marble slab or a larger pan of cold water and allow the fudge to cool until the bottom of the saucepan can rest comfortably on the palm of your hand, but be very careful not to burn yourself.
5 Add the vanilla essence and beat the mixture with a wooden spoon until it becomes

---

MAKING PEANUT BRITTLE

1 *Choose a heavy-based saucepan for making Peanut Brittle. Stir the sugars, butter and water together over a medium heat. Bring to a simmer – the toffee should deepen in colour.*

2 *Once the mixture begins to bubble, remove the pan to a cool surface, such as a marble slab. Stir in the peanuts. Use the same amounts and method to make praline; substitute toasted almonds for the peanuts.*

3 *Pour the mixture into a shallow, greased, foil-lined, rectangular tin and leave it to set and become cold. This should take no more than about 30 minutes, but check for hardness before proceeding to step 4.*

4 *When set and cool, break the brittle into bite-sized pieces with a knife handle. If making praline, use a rolling pin to crush the pieces finely. Store both sweets in airtight jars in a cool, dry place.*

creamy and thick. As the mixture begins to lighten in colour and lose its gloss, pour it into the prepared tin and set aside to cool.

6 Using a knife dipped in hot water, score the cooled fudge into squares, then cut it. Pieces can be stored in an airtight container in the refrigerator for up to 2 weeks.

Sweet spiced nuts

These make unusual nibbles. Store in an airtight container if you want to make ahead of time.

INGREDIENTS
makes 250g (9oz)
- 2 egg whites
- 4 tablespoons cold water
- 250g (9oz) nuts of choice
- 200g (7oz) sugar
- 70g (2½oz) cornflour
- 3 teaspoons cinnamon
- 1 teaspoon allspice
- ½ teaspoon ground ginger
- ½ teaspoon ground nutmeg

1 Preheat the oven to 180°C (350°F, gas mark 4). Beat the egg whites lightly with the water and dip the nuts in the mixture.

2 Combine the sugar and cornflour with the spices and a pinch of salt. Roll the nuts individually in the spice mixture and place, not touching, on a baking tray. Bake for 1½ hours.

Turkish delight

This appealing sweetmeat is easy to make at home. Rosewater can be obtained from delicatessens and pharmacies. When the sugar syrup boils, brush the inside of the saucepan with a brush dipped in water to prevent sugar crystals forming.

INGREDIENTS
makes about 96
- 800g (1lb 2oz) caster sugar
- 1.2 litres (2 pints) water
- 2 teaspoons lemon juice
- 175g (6oz) cornflour
- 1 teaspoon cream of tartar
- 1½ tablespoons rosewater
- red food colouring, optional
- 140g (5oz) icing sugar

CRYSTALLISED FLOWERS

F LOWERS SUCH AS violets, nasturtiums, rose petals and marigolds are the most successful for crystallising. Don't use flowers from gardens that have been sprayed with pesticides.

1 Line a baking tray with baking paper.

2 Very lightly beat some egg white with a pinch of salt just until foamy and paint it on both sides of the petals with a soft artist's brush. Don't apply too much, you need only to moisten the surface. Sift very fine caster sugar lightly all over the flowers. Repaint any parts where the sugar won't stick with egg white and resprinkle.

3 Place the flowers on the prepared tray, making sure that they don't touch each other. Place in a very low oven with the door slightly ajar for 10-15 minutes. Check from time to time that the flowers are not discolouring. Alternatively, dry in the refrigerator for 1-3 days.

4 Crystallised flowers will keep for 3-4 days if they are very well coated with sugar and stored in an airtight jar.

---

1 Oil a 28cm × 18cm × 5cm (11in × 7in × 2in) slice tin. Combine the sugar, 375ml (13fl oz) of the water and the lemon juice in a heavy-based saucepan and stir over a medium heat until the sugar dissolves and the mixture boils. Reduce the heat and simmer gently, without stirring, to the soft ball stage (116°C, or 241°F, on a sugar thermometer). Remove the pan from the heat.

2 In a separate heavy-based saucepan, stir together 140g (5oz) of the cornflour and the cream of tartar. Gradually stir in the remaining water until no lumps remain. Cook over a medium heat, stirring constantly, until the mixture boils and thickens.

3 Pour the hot syrup gradually into the cornflour mixture, stirring constantly. Bring to the boil, reduce the heat and simmer, stirring occasionally to prevent sticking, for 1 hour, or until the mixture has become a pale golden colour.

4 Stir in the rosewater and tint as desired with food colouring. Pour the mixture into the prepared tin and spread evenly. Cool to room temperature and let stand, uncovered, overnight to set firm.

5 Sift the icing sugar and remaining cornflour onto a large cutting board. Turn the Turkish delight out on a board and cut into 3cm × 2cm (1¼in × ¾in) pieces with an oiled knife. Roll the pieces in the sugar mixture to coat well. Store in an airtight container with sheets of greaseproof paper dredged with the sugar mixture between every layer.

Drinks with Dash ♦

*Whether it's a summer barbecue, holiday get-together, or simply having a few friends over
on a Saturday night, hospitality demands that drinks are festive and plentiful. These welcoming
beverages, with or without alcohol, will maintain your reputation as a perfect host*

Drinks for all seasons, from Christmas cheer to something cooling for summer picnics. Frozen grapes make great ice blocks because they don't dilute drinks as they melt. (1) Lemon Syrup drink, (2) Cranberry Punch, (3) Whisky Eggnog, (4) Fruit Cup, (5) Hot Bloody Mary, (6) Red Wine and Strawberry Cup, (7) Hot Chocolate Espresso, (8) Sangria.

Sangria

Instead of serving a variety of drinks at a group function, make up a large jug or bowl of this simple but refreshing drink. To add a real tang, garnish with long strips of citrus peel.

INGREDIENTS
makes 3 litres (5¼ pints)

- 2 oranges, sliced
- 2 lemons, sliced
- 2 cinnamon sticks
- 185ml (6½fl oz) brandy
- 750ml (1 pint 7fl oz) red wine
- 750ml (1 pint 7fl oz) sparkling lemonade, chilled
- ice blocks

1 Place the orange and lemon slices in a large jug or bowl, add the cinnamon sticks and the brandy.

2 Pour the red wine and lemonade over the ingredients in the bowl, stirring in some ice blocks at serving time.

Cranberry punch

Cranberry juice can be purchased in many supermarkets and also in health-food stores. This refreshing punch is perfect for a hot summer's day.

INGREDIENTS
makes 3 litres (5¼ pints)

- 500ml (18fl oz) cranberry juice
- 500ml (18fl oz) unsweetened pineapple juice
- 250ml (9fl oz) orange juice
- 185ml (6½fl oz) lemon cordial
- 250g (9oz) strawberries, hulled and sliced
- 1 lime, thinly sliced
- 1 litre (1¾ pints) dry ginger ale, chilled
- ice cubes, to serve

1 In a large glass container, combine the juices, lemon cordial, strawberries and lime slices. Chill thoroughly.

2 Just before serving, slowly stir in the dry ginger ale. Pour into a punch bowl or large jug and add the ice cubes.

Hot Bloody Mary

Warm the cockles of your heart with this heated version of a popular traditional recipe.

INGREDIENTS
makes 500ml (18fl oz)
- 65ml (2¼fl oz) vodka
- 435ml (15½fl oz) tomato juice
- 4 drops Tabasco sauce
- 4 drops Worcestershire sauce
- long celery or cucumber sticks, to garnish

1 Pour the vodka into a microwave-proof glass or mug and top with the tomato juice. Add the Tabasco and Worcestershire sauces. Microwave on Medium-High for 30 seconds, or gently heat the vodka, tomato juice and the sauces in a small saucepan. Pour the warm liquid into glasses with handles.
2 Sprinkle with salt and pepper to taste, and garnish with a long celery or cucumber stick.

Whisky eggnog

A warm and welcoming cold-weather drink, this is traditionally served at Christmas. For a variation, brandy can be substituted for whisky.

INGREDIENTS
makes 1.7 litres (3 pints)
- 4 eggs
- 100g (3½oz) caster sugar
- 750ml (1 pint 7fl oz) milk
- 1 teaspoon vanilla essence
- 125ml (4fl oz) whisky
- ½ teaspoon freshly grated nutmeg
- 125ml (4fl oz) double cream

1 In a saucepan, beat the eggs and sugar until creamy. In a second saucepan heat two-thirds of the milk over a low heat until hot. Slowly add to the egg mixture, stirring continuously. Cook over a low heat, stirring, for 15 minutes, or until the mixture reaches 76°C (170°F) and has thickened. Stir in the remaining milk, vanilla, whisky and half the nutmeg.
2 In a medium-sized bowl, beat the cream until soft peaks form. Fold into milk mixture.
3 Ladle the eggnog into a serving bowl and sprinkle with the remaining grated nutmeg.

Citrus vodka liqueur

This is a delicious, warming drink to sip by the fire. Because liqueur has a higher alcohol content than wine, enjoy this drink in small amounts.

INGREDIENTS
makes 1.2-1.5 litres (2-2¼ pints)
- 350ml (12fl oz) dry white wine
- 750ml (1 pint 7fl oz) vodka
- 2 lemons, sliced
- 1 orange, sliced
- 2 strips lemon zest
- 2 cinnamon sticks
- 3 allspice berries
- 3 cloves
- 1 vanilla pod
- 1 sprig rosemary
- 4 tablespoons sugar

1 Place all the ingredients in a large wide-mouthed jar and seal with a tight-fitting lid. Leave in a warm place for 4 weeks to allow the flavours to develop. Shake daily.
2 Wash some sealable bottles, then rinse with boiling water and drain.
3 Strain the liqueur through doubled muslin or a very fine sieve into a jug. Pour into the clean, dry bottles and seal. Can be stored in a cool, dry place for 6-12 months.

Red wine and strawberry cup

Strawberries steeped in port give this cooling drink a heady fragrance and ambrosial taste.

INGREDIENTS
makes 2 litres (3½ pints)

- 250g (9oz) strawberries
- 70g (2½oz) caster sugar
- few strips orange zest
- 170ml (6fl oz) port
- 750ml (1 pint 7fl oz) red wine
- soda water, chilled
- mint sprigs, to decorate

1 Wash, hull and slice the strawberries. Put in a large jar with the sugar, zest and port. Cover and chill for 24 hours.
2 When ready to serve, transfer to a punch bowl and add the red wine. Serve in glasses, topped up with chilled soda water and decorated with the sprigs of mint.

Iced tea

Why always have tea hot when this zesty version makes such a wonderful summer refresher?

INGREDIENTS
makes 1-1.2 litres (1¾-2 pints)
- 2 teaspoons tea leaves
- 1 litre (1¾ pints) freshly boiled water
- sugar (optional)
- crushed ice
- lemon slices and mint sprigs, to garnish

1 Make a pot of tea and infuse for 4 minutes.
2 Strain the tea into a jug and cool. Stir in sugar to taste, if using. Do not refrigerate or the tea will become cloudy.
3 Divide the tea among four tall glasses and fill each to the top with crushed ice. Add a slice of lemon and a mint sprig to each glass.

VARIATIONS Lime slices are equally as good as lemons in iced tea. Fresh lemon or fruit-scented tea can also be used.

Hot chocolate espresso

Not for the faint-of-heart or the worried weight watcher, this creamy drink is pure indulgence.

INGREDIENTS
makes 250ml (9fl oz)

- 125ml (4fl oz) prepared coffee (espresso or instant)
- 1 teaspoon sugar, optional
- 125ml (4fl oz) single cream, or 60ml (2¼fl oz) single cream and 60ml (2¼fl oz) milk
- 1 teaspoon cocoa powder
- whipped cream, grated chocolate and cinnamon stick, to serve

1 Pour the hot coffee into a cup and sweeten to taste with the sugar, if desired.
2 Heat the cream, or cream and milk, in a small saucepan. Add the cocoa powder and mix well to combine.
3 Add the mixture to the coffee and top with the whipped cream and grated chocolate. Serve with a cinnamon stick.

Fruit Brandy. The strongly flavoured fruit imparts a characteristic taste to the brandy. You can use both the liquid and the fruit, whether kumquats or cherries.

Fruit cup

Non-alcoholic and perfect for summer entertaining.

INGREDIENTS

makes 6 litres (10½ pints)
- 500ml (18fl oz) fresh orange juice
- 2 litres (3½ pints) grape juice
- 1 litre (1¾ pints) pineapple juice
- 2 litres (3½ pints) soda water, chilled
- mint leaves, lemon or orange slices, to decorate serving bowl
- crushed ice

1 Mix all the juices together in a serving bowl and chill in the refrigerator.
2 Just before serving, add the chilled soda water, mint leaves and lemon or orange slices. Spoon some crushed ice into each glass and ladle the fruit cup over it.

Lemon syrup

Dilute this syrup base with water, mineral water or soda water and decorate with starfruit or citrus slices. It can be chilled with frozen grapes. You can also make up a glass with hot water and a tablespoon of brandy to help ease a head cold.

INGREDIENTS

makes 6 litres (10½ pints)
- juice and zest of 6 lemons
- 1.6kg (3lb 8oz) granulated sugar
- 85ml (3fl oz) citric acid
- 70g (2½oz) Epsom salts
- 2 tablespoons tartaric acid
- 2.5 litres (4½ pints) boiling water

1 Sterilise five to six 500ml (18fl oz) sealable bottles (see method on page 278).
2 Place all the ingredients, except the boiling water, in a large bowl. Mix well to combine. Add the boiling water and stir well until the sugar has dissolved.
3 Pour the liquid into the sterilised bottles and store in a cool place for up to 6 months. Ready to use immediately.

Fruit brandy

The fruit from this brandy, which you can make with either cherries or kumquats, make a delicious dessert with ice cream if you do not leave them in the jar for more than 6 months. The brandy itself will keep for several years.

INGREDIENTS

makes 750ml (1 pint 7fl oz)
- 750g (1lb 10oz) firm kumquats or red cherries
- 200g (7oz) granulated sugar
- ½ vanilla pod
- 500ml (18fl oz) water
- 1 litre (1¾ pints) brandy

1 Carefully wash the fruit and prick the kumquats eight times each with a needle, or remove the stones from the cherries.
2 Place the sugar, vanilla pod and water in a saucepan, bring slowly to the boil over a low heat, and simmer for 15 minutes. Add the fruit, return to the boil and simmer for 5 minutes.
3 Remove the pan from the heat and ladle the fruit into a 1.5 litre (2¾ pints) capacity warm sterilised jar with a slotted spoon.
4 Over a high heat, reduce the syrup by half. When cool, pour the reduced syrup over the fruit, discarding the vanilla pod.
5 Pour in the brandy and seal. Label and store in a cool, dark place for at least 3 months.

◆ Festive Foods ◆

Preparing goodies for Christmas is a year-end tradition in most homes.
Baking a fruit cake or steaming the pudding yourself means you get the exact flavour you
want. We've included seasonal favourites from other countries to help you celebrate

Orange shortbread fingers

The tangy flavour of these mouth-watering
shortbread fingers makes a pleasant change from
traditional Christmas shortbread.

INGREDIENTS
makes 32-36

- 40g (1½oz) plain flour
- 3 tablespoons cornflour
- 50g (1¾oz) caster sugar, plus 2 tablespoons extra for dusting
- grated zest of 1 orange
- 100g (3½oz) unsalted butter, chopped

1 Preheat the oven to 150°C (300°F, gas mark 2). Grease a 28cm × 18cm × 2cm (11in × 7in × ¾in) shallow baking tin and line it with baking paper.
2 Sift the plain flour and cornflour into a medium-sized bowl. Add the sugar and orange zest. Using your fingertips, rub the butter into the dry ingredients until the mixture resembles fine breadcrumbs.
3 Knead the mixture until it forms a dough, then spread it onto the prepared pan. Score the dough into fingers and prick each finger with

a fork. Dust with the extra caster sugar. Bake in the oven for 30 minutes, or until pale golden in colour.
4 Remove the pan from the oven and leave the shortbread to cool in the pan until it holds its shape enough to remove to a wire rack.
5 When cool, separate the fingers. They can be stored, airtight, for up to a week.

Christmas mincemeat

Serve this spicy fruit mixture in little tart cases or
pies for Christmas. Prepare the mincemeat well
beforehand to ensure a full flavour. This vegetarian
version, popular today, replaces the traditional
mincemeat which used beef suet, hence its name.

INGREDIENTS
makes about 2.5kg (5lb 8oz)

- 425g (15oz) currants
- 215g (7½oz) sultanas
- 215g (7½oz) chopped raisins
- 100g (3½oz) chopped candied peel
- 500g (1lb 2oz) cooking apples, peeled, cored and finely chopped
- 500g (1lb 2oz) light or dark muscovado sugar
- 1 teaspoon ground allspice
- 1 teaspoon ground nutmeg
- 1 teaspoon cinnamon
- grated zest and juice of 2 lemons
- 185ml (6½fl oz) brandy

1 Place all the ingredients in a bowl and mix well to combine. Cover with cling film and leave overnight. Meanwhile, select some jars with tight-fitting lids and sterilise them (follow the step-by-step method on page 278).
2 Pack the mixture into the sterilised jars. Leave in the refrigerator for 4-6 weeks.
3 Stir the mixture well before using.

Kourambiedes

These delicious little almond biscuits are a
traditional treat in Greece. They can be baked
ahead of time for Christmas and frozen. They
thaw quickly, so you can take them out of the
freezer and get them ready while you are making
the coffee that usually accompanies them.

INGREDIENTS
makes about 50

- 250g (9oz) unsalted butter, at room temperature
- 70g (2½oz) caster sugar
- 1 egg, plus 2 egg yolks
- 400g (14oz) plain flour
- 100g (3½oz) finely chopped almonds
- about 50 whole cloves
- 140g (5oz) icing sugar

1 Preheat the oven to 150°C (300°F, gas mark 2). Butter two baking trays.
2 Place the butter, sugar, egg and egg yolks, flour and chopped almonds in the workbowl of a food processor. Process for 30 seconds, or until just combined.
3 Roll the mixture into balls about the size of a walnut and place a clove in each. Bake in the oven for 25-30 minutes, until golden.
4 Remove the trays from the oven and transfer the biscuits to a wire rack. Leave to cool slightly, then dredge generously with icing sugar. They can be stored in an airtight container for 1-2 weeks. If you wish to freeze the Kourambiedes, layer them, without icing sugar, in a freezer container, separating each layer with paper.

Christmas is a time for treats loved since childhood.
Clockwise from top right, Christmas Mincemeat,
Traditional Christmas Cake, Kourambiedes,
Christmas Pudding, Orange Shortbread Fingers.

PRACTICAL IDEAS

FOR SUCCESSFUL BAKING

To ensure that dried and glacé fruits don't sink to
the bottom in a Christmas cake, toss them in a little
flour before adding to the mixture.

When making biscuits, use unsalted butter to grease
the baking trays to help prevent over-browning. For
the same reason, remove biscuits from the baking
trays as soon as they are baked.

Any shortcrust pastry is suitable for mince pies.

Lebkuchen

This tasty delicacy from Germany is a cross between a cake and a biscuit. It keeps well and will suit any occasion, but is possibly best eaten in cold weather.

BASE INGREDIENTS

serves about 24

- 330ml (10½fl oz) clear honey
- 150g (5½oz) sugar
- 3 tablespoons butter
- 400g (14oz) plain flour
- 1 teaspoon baking powder
- ½ teaspoon bicarbonate of soda
- 75g (2¾oz) blanched almonds
- 35g (1¼oz) chopped candied peel
- ¼ teaspoon ground ginger
- ½ teaspoon ground cardamom
- 2 teaspoons ground cinnamon
- 1 teaspoon ground allspice

ICING INGREDIENTS

- 200g (7oz) icing sugar
- 60ml (2¼fl oz) lemon juice
- 1 tablespoon butter, softened

1 Preheat the oven to 180°C (350°F, gas mark 4). Grease a 28cm × 18cm × 2cm (11in × 7in × ¾in) shallow baking pan and line it with baking paper.
2 Place the honey and sugar in a large saucepan and stir over a gentle heat. Add the butter and stir until melted. Remove the saucepan from the heat.
3 Sift together the flour, baking powder and bicarbonate of soda in a large bowl and add to the honey mixture. Add the almonds, candied peel and spices, stirring well to combine. The mixture will be sticky.
4 Spoon the mixture into the prepared pan, level the mixture and smooth the top. Bake for 25 minutes, or until a skewer inserted in the cake comes out clean.
5 Cool the cake in the pan on a wire rack.
6 To make the lemon icing, place the sugar, lemon juice and butter in a bowl and mix until blended and smooth. Ice the lebkuchen while still warm. It can be stored in an airtight container for up to 1 week.

Christmas pudding

No Christmas dinner is complete without pudding. This delicious version can be made 2-3 months ahead and steamed again before serving.

INGREDIENTS

serves 12-16

- 175g (6oz) chopped raisins
- 115g (4oz) pitted and chopped dates
- 200g (7oz) chopped soft dried figs
- 125g (4½oz) currants
- 90g (3¼oz) sultanas
- 125ml (4fl oz) brandy
- 250g (9oz) unsalted butter
- 200g (7oz) soft brown sugar
- grated zest of 1 lemon
- grated zest of 1 orange
- 4 eggs, beaten
- 150g (5½oz) chopped blanched almonds
- 100g (3½oz) self-raising flour
- 1 teaspoon each cinnamon, ground allspice and ground ginger
- ½ teaspoon nutmeg
- 140g (5oz) white breadcrumbs

1 Grease a 2-litre (3½-pint) pudding basin.
2 Place all the fruit in a large bowl and pour the brandy over it. Stir well to disperse the brandy. Cover with a clean cloth and set aside for 12-24 hours to allow the fruit to soften.
3 Place the butter and sugar in a large bowl and beat with an electric mixer until thick and creamy. Beat in the zests and the eggs. Fold in the fruit and the almonds. Sift the flour and spices into the mixture. Stir well to combine, then fold in the breadcrumbs.
4 Spoon the mixture into the prepared basin, press down well and level the surface. Cut sheets of greaseproof paper 5cm (2in) larger than the top of the basin. Pleat the paper twice through the middle to allow for expansion as the pudding rises. Place the paper on top of the mixture in the basin and cover it with a double thickness of foil. Tie down securely with string. Place the basin in a large stockpot and fill with boiling water to come halfway up the sides. Steam for 4 hours, topping up the boiling water to the same level when necessary.

5 Remove the basin from the stockpot and leave the pudding to cool. Place fresh paper and foil on top and store the pudding in the refrigerator until ready to use.
6 Steam again for 2 hours before serving.

Traditional Christmas cake

This rich, flavoursome cake can be made at the last minute before Christmas – it does not need to mature, although it keeps well, too.

INGREDIENTS

serves about 30

- 250g (9oz) butter, at room temperature
- 300g (10½oz) soft brown sugar
- 4 eggs
- 400g (14oz) plain flour
- ¼ teaspoon salt
- 1 teaspoon ground allspice
- 1 teaspoon cinnamon
- ½ teaspoon nutmeg
- 175g (6oz) each currants, sultanas, chopped raisins
- 250g (9oz) chopped soft dried figs
- 200g (7oz) chopped pitted dried dates
- 175g (6oz) chopped stoned dried prunes
- 275g (9½oz) chopped dried apricots
- 115g (4oz) chopped blanched almonds
- 125ml (4fl oz) brandy, plus 4 tablespoons extra to drizzle
- 2 tablespoons coffee essence

1 Preheat the oven to 150°C (300°F, gas mark 2). Grease a round 24cm (9½in) cake tin and line the bottom and sides with several layers of baking paper (see page 63).
2 Place the butter and sugar in a large bowl and beat with an electric mixer until thick and creamy. Add the eggs, one at a time, beating well after each addition. Add a spoonful of the flour to prevent curdling at this stage. Sift together the remaining flour, salt and spices, then fold into the creamed mixture. Add the fruit, almonds, 125ml (4fl oz) of brandy and coffee essence, folding in well to combine.

3 Spoon the mixture into the prepared tin, making sure the surface is level. Place the pan in the centre of the oven and bake for 30 minutes, then reduce the temperature to 140°C (275°F, gas mark 1) and bake for 3½ hours longer, or until a skewer inserted in the centre of the cake comes out clean.

4 Remove the tin from the oven, cover with a tea towel and then a thick bath towel so the cake will cool slowly.

5 When the cake is cool, prick the top with a skewer and drizzle with the extra brandy. Wrap in baking paper and store in an airtight container in a cool place for up to 3 months.

Stollen

The distinctive oval shape of this traditional German Christmas cake is said to represent the Christ child wrapped in swaddling clothes.

INGREDIENTS

serves 10-12

- 550g (1lb 4oz) plain flour
- 1 teaspoon salt
- 7g sachet dry yeast
- 125ml (4fl oz) warm milk
- 70g (2½oz) caster sugar
- 250g (9oz) unsalted butter, melted
- 2 tablespoons cognac
- 150g (5½oz) chopped blanched almonds
- 175g (6oz) chopped raisins
- 40g (1½oz) mixed peel
- 1 tablespoon grated lemon zest
- 60g (2¼oz) butter, melted
- sifted icing sugar, to dust

1 Sift the flour and salt into a large bowl. In a small bowl, dissolve the yeast in half the milk. Make a well in the centre of the flour and salt mixture then add the yeast and milk mixture, sugar, remaining milk, melted unsalted butter and cognac. Mix well to combine.

2 Turn the dough out on a lightly floured surface. Knead for 3 minutes. Lightly oil a large bowl, place the dough in it, turning to coat the dough well with oil. Cover with lightly oiled cling film and leave to stand in a warm place for about 1 hour.

3 Turn the dough out on a lightly floured surface. Knead in the almonds, raisins, mixed peel and lemon zest. Return the dough to the bowl, cover with a clean cloth and allow to rise once more until it has almost doubled in bulk.

4 Remove the risen dough from the bowl and shape it into a round about 26cm (10½in) in diameter. Fold the round almost in half and flatten and shape it a little to form an oval. Place the dough on a greased baking tray, cover with lightly oiled cling film and allow to stand in a warm place for a further 30 minutes.

5 Preheat the oven to 190°C (375°F, gas mark 5). Brush the stollen with about 15g (½oz) of the melted butter. Bake, brushing every 10 minutes with melted butter, for 45-50 minutes, until a skewer comes out clean when inserted into the cake.

6 Remove from the oven and leave to cool. When cold, wrap in several layers of foil and store in the refrigerator – it will keep for 3-4 weeks. To serve, refresh by slicing thinly, wrapping the slices in foil and warming them in a moderate oven for 15 minutes. Dust thickly with icing sugar before serving.

PRACTICAL IDEAS

PUDDING PREPARATION

The Christmas pudding recipe can also be used to make four smaller puddings. Fill four 500ml (18fl oz) pudding basins with the mixture and steam for 2 hours.

Puddings can be prepared ahead of time and either stored in the refrigerator for up to 2-3 months, or frozen, wrapped in a freezer bag, for up to 12 months. When preparing to steam a frozen pudding, allow it to thaw for about 3 days in the refrigerator and then leave it outside the refrigerator for 12 hours or overnight before steaming.

A microwave is useful for heating puddings, as it takes much less time than conventional steaming. Set the microwave on medium and heat the pudding for about 15 minutes. Reheat individual servings on high for 1-2 minutes.

A Christmas pudding, still in its basin and wrapped decoratively, makes a lovely seasonal gift.

Panforte

This traditional Italian nut cake, a speciality from Siena, is best left for a day before cutting.

INGREDIENTS

serves about 36

- 113g (4oz) chopped blanched almonds, toasted
- 100g (3½oz) chopped hazelnuts, toasted
- 100g (3½oz) chopped mixed glacé fruits, including cherries and apricots
- 40g (1½oz) plain flour, sifted
- 2 tablespoons cocoa powder, sifted
- 1 teaspoon cinnamon
- 100g (3½oz) dark chocolate
- 70g (2½oz) caster sugar
- 125ml (4fl oz) honey
- sifted icing sugar, to dust

1 Preheat the oven to 150°C (300°F, gas mark 2). Grease a round 20cm (8in) cake tin and line it with baking paper (see page 63).

2 Mix the nuts and glacé fruits with the flour, cocoa powder and cinnamon in a large bowl to coat thoroughly.

3 Place the chocolate in a double boiler over a low heat and stir until melted. In a separate saucepan, dissolve the sugar and honey over a low heat. Once the sugar has dissolved, bring the syrup to the boil, reduce the heat and simmer for about 5 minutes. Add the syrup and the melted chocolate to the fruit and nut mixture and mix well to combine.

4 Spread the mixture quickly and evenly into the prepared tin. Bake for 30 minutes. The panforte will be soft and appear underdone but will harden as it cools.

5 Remove the panforte from the oven and allow it to cool in the tin. Remove from the tin, dust with icing sugar and leave wrapped in foil overnight before serving. The panforte can be stored in an airtight container in a cool place for 3-4 weeks.

VARIATION Panforte can also be made in a square tin lined with edible rice paper and topped with rice paper before baking. Cut and store the panforte in the same way as above.

Delightful Desserts

The simplest combinations of ingredients can produce the most memorable dishes.
Poached fruit from the garden, bathed in liqueur, a classic sauce lavished on homemade ice cream,
snowy meringues … components such as these make up dessert heaven

Desserts need not be heavy and rich to make a satisfying end to a meal. Today's eating style calls for light, flavoursome desserts such as these: (1) Peaches Preserved in Kirsch, (2) Brandied Figs, (3) Meringues, (4) Gratin of Brandied Figs.

Brandied figs

Dried figs can be prepared in this manner as easily as the fresh variety. Brandied figs can be served with a jug of cream or as a gratin (see below).

INGREDIENTS
makes two 500ml (18fl oz) jars

- 1kg (2lb 4oz) fresh figs or 500g (1lb 2oz) dried
- 140g (5oz) granulated sugar
- 4 star anise
- 1 cinnamon stick
- 250ml (9fl oz) brandy

1 Halve the figs lengthways and place in a saucepan with 250ml (9fl oz) of water and sugar. Bring slowly to simmering point and poach gently for 2 minutes if using fresh, 5-8 minutes if using dried figs.
2 Remove the figs with a slotted spoon and, when cool enough to handle, layer attractively with the spices in a glass storage jar.
3 Pour on the brandy, add enough cooking syrup to fill to the top and cover tightly. The flavour develops if the fruit is allowed to steep for more than a week.

Gratin of brandied figs

A speciality of many top restaurants and a lovely dinner-party dessert. You can prepare the figs yourself using the recipe above.

INGREDIENTS
serves 4

- 8 brandied fresh figs
- 2 egg yolks
- 1 tablespoon caster sugar
- 250ml (9fl oz) dry champagne
- sifted icing sugar, to decorate
- fresh mint leaves, to decorate

1 Remove the figs from their syrup and drain in a large strainer. Slice each fig in half and arrange on four heatproof serving plates.

2 Whisk the egg yolks and sugar together in a bowl over a pan of simmering water. Whisk in the champagne and continue to beat until the mixture is light, fluffy and slightly thickened. Remove from the heat and continue to whisk until cooled slightly.
3 Spoon the sauce over the brandied figs, sprinkle lightly with icing sugar and place under a very hot preheated grill for a few moments until the top is lightly coloured. Decorate with mint leaves.

VARIATION This recipe works well with any preserved fruit. See Peaches Preserved in Kirsch (below) for another way to prepare fresh fruits for this recipe.

Peaches preserved in kirsch

Poached fruits preserved in sugar syrup and spirits, such as kirsch or brandy, are the basis of many easy desserts. Serve them simply with cream or made into a gratin (see above) or compote (see page 84) for a special occasion. Plums, nectarines and apricots can be treated this way just as successfully.

INGREDIENTS
makes two 500ml (18fl oz) jars

- 2kg (4lb 8oz) peaches
- 400g (14oz) sugar
- 500ml (18fl oz) water
- 1 cinnamon stick
- 4 cloves
- 1 litre (1¾ pints) kirsch

1 Skin the peaches by scoring a cross in the base of each one. Scald them in boiling water for about a minute and then dip them in cold water. The skins then peel off easily.
2 Place the sugar, water and spices in a saucepan and bring to the boil.
3 Halve and stone the peaches. Prick each half four times through so that the syrup can penetrate. Add the peach halves to the syrup and simmer for 5 minutes.
4 Remove the fruit with a slotted spoon and pack into warm, sterilised jars with the spices.
5 Over a high heat, reduce the syrup to half. Fill the jars a third of the way up with syrup and top up with kirsch. Seal and keep for several months before opening.

Peach compote with sabayon

This beautiful compote of peaches and plums or other fruits in alcohol is a perfect hot dessert. The French use a vanilla pod, while the Italians prefer the zest of a lemon or orange to flavour the syrup.

INGREDIENTS

serves 4-6

- 250ml (9fl oz) syrup drained from preserved fruit
- 1 vanilla pod, or the pared zest of 1 lemon or orange
- 4 preserved peaches, drained
- 4 preserved plums, drained

SAUCE SABAYON

- 2 egg yolks
- 1 tablespoon caster sugar
- 125ml (4fl oz) sweet sherry

1 Place the syrup in a medium-sized saucepan and add the vanilla pod or zest. Stir over a medium heat and simmer for 5 minutes.
2 Add the fruit to the syrup and warm gently until heated through. Turn the fruit over once or twice and spoon the syrup over it frequently.
3 For the sabayon sauce, whisk the egg yolks with the caster sugar and sherry in a bowl standing in a saucepan of simmering water. Whisk briskly until the sauce becomes thick and mousse-like. Do not allow the water to boil or the sauce will curdle.
4 Pour the sauce over the warm fruit and serve immediately with a crisp dessert biscuit.

Meringues

Stored in an airtight container, meringues will last for weeks. If they soften, dry them again by placing in the oven on a low temperature for 5 minutes.

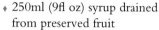

INGREDIENTS

makes 24-36

- 3 large egg whites
- scant ⅛ teaspoon cream of tartar
- 100g (3½oz) each caster and soft brown sugar
- 300ml (10fl oz) double cream

1 Preheat the oven to 120°C (250°F, gas mark ½). Brush three baking trays with oil and dust with flour, or use baking paper to line the trays.
2 Using either a freshly cleaned copper bowl and a balloon whisk, or an electric mixer, beat the egg whites, slowly at first, until frothy. Add the cream of tartar and now beat quickly by hand, or on the highest speed of the mixer, until peaks hold their shape.
3 Gradually beat in 2 tablespoons of the caster sugar and continue beating for 2-3 minutes. Mix the remaining sugars together and beat in half, beating until very thick. Sift the rest of the sugar into the bowl and fold in lightly and quickly with a large metal spoon.
4 Take up a spoonful of the meringue mixture in a dampened spoon and, with a finger or dampened spatula, smooth it quickly over, piling it in the centre and pointing the

two ends. With another spoon, slip the meringue onto one of the prepared trays. Leave at least 2cm (¾in) between each meringue.
5 Bake for 1½ hours, or until crisp, then remove from the oven. Turn each meringue over and make an indentation in each by pressing gently with your finger. Return to the oven for a little longer to dry completely. When cool, store in an airtight container.
6 Whip the cream until thick, and sweeten and flavour with a little sugar and vanilla, if desired. Fill the meringues with the cream, sandwiching them in pairs. Alternatively, use Lime Curd (see page 27) to sandwich them.

Ricotta and rum dream

A rich dessert, this is wonderful served with fresh ripe berries and Italian biscotti or almond bread.

INGREDIENTS

serves 6-8

- 500g (1lb 2oz) ricotta cheese
- 125ml (4fl oz) thick sour cream
- 70g (2½oz) caster sugar, or to taste
- 3 large eggs, separated
- 125ml (4fl oz) rum or brandy
- dark chocolate, grated

1 Place the ricotta cheese and sour cream in a bowl and beat with an electric mixer until smooth. Beat in the sugar until blended.

MAKING MERINGUES

1 *Carefully separate the whites from the yolks – even a speck of yolk prevents the whites from whipping up satisfactorily. Use either a balloon whisk and a clean copper bowl or an electric mixer for whisking.*

2 *The mixture is ready when smooth, with no undissolved sugar grains. Shape each meringue with a wet spoon and smooth the top with a finger. With another spoon, slip off onto the prepared baking trays.*

3 *Try to take the same amount of raw mixture for each meringue. Allow plenty of room around each meringue on the tray so that they don't stick together. When cooked, they should be barely coloured.*

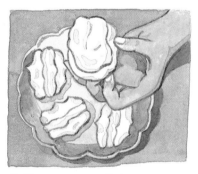

4 *If you are going to fill the meringues with cream, lift each and press gently with a finger on the bottom at the end of cooking time. To serve, sandwich pairs of meringues together with cream, jam or lime curd.*

2 Add the egg yolks, one at a time, beating well after each, until the mixture is light and creamy. Beat in the rum.

3 With clean beaters, beat the egg whites until stiff peaks form when the beaters are lifted. Fold into the cheese mixture.

4 Spoon the mixture into a bowl or individual dessert dishes or ramekin dishes. Refrigerate for several hours, or until firm.

5 Sprinkle with the chocolate before serving.

Vanilla pudding

Serve this economical family dessert with fruit or ice cream, or try the delicious chocolate variations.

INGREDIENTS

serves 4-6
- 150g (5½oz) sugar
- 1½ tablespoons cornflour
- pinch salt
- 500ml (18fl oz) milk
- 1 egg
- 2 tablespoons butter
- 1 teaspoon vanilla essence

1 Combine the sugar, cornflour and salt in a saucepan. Stir in the milk until smooth. Cook over a moderate heat, stirring constantly, until the mixture boils and thickens. Reduce the heat and simmer, stirring constantly, for 2 minutes. Remove from the heat.

2 Beat the egg in a bowl until foamy. Stir about half of the hot mixture into the egg, then stir this egg mixture back into the hot mixture. Cook over a low heat, stirring constantly, for 2 minutes more.

3 Remove from the heat, stir in the butter and vanilla essence and immediately pour into a bowl or individual dessert dishes. Cool, then refrigerate until cold before serving.

VARIATIONS To make chocolate pudding, add 60g (2¼oz) chopped good-quality dark chocolate with the milk in step 1. For a delicious chocolate mint pudding, heat the milk with several lightly crushed mint leaves until scalded. Cool to room temperature and strain. Use this milk as directed in step 1.

SERVING SUGGESTIONS

Pour hot chocolate or caramel sauce over crêpes filled with sliced bananas and serve with ice-cream or whipped cream for an elegant party dessert.

Make a pyramid of meringues by stacking and joining them with vanilla or chocolate pudding. Just before serving, pour hot chocolate sauce all over and sprinkle with toasted flaked almonds.

Orange rice custard

Serve warm or chilled, with cream or a favourite jam. Marmalade will emphasise the citrus flavour.

INGREDIENTS

serves 6
- 4 tablespoons short-grain rice
- 2 tablespoons sugar
- 2 teaspoons finely grated orange zest
- 875ml (1 pint 11fl oz) milk
- 1 tablespoon butter, cut into small pieces
- ¼ teaspoon ground nutmeg
- 2 tablespoons cream

1 Preheat the oven to 160°C (325°F, gas mark 3). Butter a 1.5-litre (2¾-pint) ovenproof dish. Place the rice, sugar, orange zest and milk in the dish and stir well to dissolve the sugar. Add the butter and sprinkle with nutmeg.

2 Bake for 1½ hours, stirring with a fork every 30 minutes.

3 Stir well, then mix in the cream. Bake for 30 minutes longer, or until the top is brown.

Raspberry coulis

Either fresh or frozen berries can be used to make this fresh-tasting dessert sauce.

INGREDIENTS

makes 250ml (9fl oz)
- 250g (9oz) raspberries
- caster sugar, to taste

---

1 Rinse the raspberries (if using fresh), drain, then place with about 2 tablespoons sugar in a food processor or blender and purée. Sieve the mixture to remove any seeds. Taste and add more sugar, if necessary.

2 Chill before serving. Can be refrigerated in a covered container for up to 2 days.

VARIATIONS Try strawberries, blackberries or loganberries, when in season; or use fresh peaches and apricots (these purée better if lightly poached first).

Hot chocolate sauce

Make this irresistible sauce at the last minute and pour it, piping hot, over rich vanilla ice cream.

INGREDIENTS

makes 250ml (9fl oz)
- 85ml (3fl oz) milk
- 125ml (4fl oz) single cream
- 1 tablespoon honey
- 200g (7oz) dark chocolate

1 Place the milk, cream and honey in a small saucepan and stir over a low heat.

2 Melt the chocolate in a double boiler and pour it into the hot cream mixture. Mix until well blended. Serve at once.

Caramel sauce

Try this versatile sauce warm, poured over steamed pudding, ice cream or a plain sponge cake.

INGREDIENTS

makes 625ml (1 pint 1fl oz)
- 100g (3½oz) unsalted butter
- 300g (10½oz) soft brown sugar
- 250ml (9fl oz) single cream
- 1 teaspoon vanilla essence

1 Melt the butter in a small saucepan over a low heat. Add the sugar and cream, stirring until the sugar has dissolved. Simmer for 8-10 minutes over a low heat, stirring constantly so the sugar does not crystallise, until the sauce has just thickened. Add the vanilla.

2 Serve warm or cool. Can be refrigerated in a covered container for up to a week.

◆ Ice-cream Variety ◆

*Making your own ice creams gives you the
scope to experiment. Let these recipes inspire you to
invent new and exciting flavour combinations*

Mango ice cream

*The most exotic of fruits gives this ice cream a rich,
tropical taste. Serve within two days of making.*

INGREDIENTS
makes 1-1.2 litres (1¾-2 pints)
- 750g (1lb 10oz) ripe mangoes
- 200g (7oz) caster sugar
- 500ml (18fl oz) single cream
- 250ml (9fl oz) milk
- 1 teaspoon vanilla essence

1 Peel the mangoes and cut all flesh from the
stones. Place the mango flesh and the sugar in
a food processor and purée.
2 Place the mango purée and all remaining
ingredients in an ice-cream maker and churn
according to the manufacturer's instructions.
3 Spoon into a container, cover with cling
film; place in the freezer overnight. Soften in
the refrigerator for 20 minutes before serving.

Lavender ice cream

*For a lovely rich flavour, use lavender honey in this
recipe. However, if it is unavailable, use any honey
with a delicate flower-like essence.*

INGREDIENTS
makes 1-1.2 litres (1¾-2 pints)
- 250ml (9fl oz) milk
- 125ml (4fl oz) lavender honey
- 750ml (1 pint 7fl oz) single
  cream
- 4 egg yolks
- 2 teaspoons fresh lavender flowers
- 1 teaspoon vanilla essence

1 Place the milk, honey and 250ml (9fl oz) of
the cream in a large saucepan. Warm over a
moderate heat, stirring constantly with a
wooden spoon until the honey dissolves.
2 In a medium-sized bowl, beat the egg yolks
together. Slowly pour half the milk mixture

into the egg yolks, stirring constantly. Return
this mixture to the saucepan. Cook over a
low heat until the mixture begins to bubble at
the edges. Stir for 2 minutes then mix in the
remaining cream, the lavender flowers and
the vanilla essence.
3 Place the mixture in the refrigerator for
1 hour to chill. Remove flowers, if desired.
4 Pour into an ice-cream maker and churn
according to the manufacturer's instructions.
5 Spoon the ice cream into a container, cover
with plastic wrap and place in the freezer.
Allow to soften in the refrigerator for 15–30
minutes before serving.

Berry ice cream

*Try this recipe with one variety of berry or a mixture
for deeper flavour – such as blackberries with currants
or blueberries. Serve with a few fresh berries.*

INGREDIENTS
*makes 750ml - 1litre
(1 pint 7fl oz - 1¾ pints)*
- 300g (10½oz) berries of choice
- 100g (3½oz) caster sugar
- white of 1 small egg
- 100ml (3½fl oz) milk
- 200ml (7fl oz) single cream
- pinch salt

1 Rinse the berries and place them in a bowl
with 50g (1¾oz) of the sugar, then mash with
a potato masher.
2 In a bowl, whisk the egg white, then mix in
the milk, cream, salt and remaining sugar. Add
the berries and stir well to combine.
3 Pour into an ice-cream maker and churn
according to the manufacturer's instructions.
4 Spoon the ice cream into a freezer-proof
container, cover with cling film and place in
the freezer. Allow to soften in the refrigerator
for 15–30 minutes before serving.

Mandarin ice cream

This ice cream can be made using canned mandarin segments. As these are sweeter than the fresh variety, reduce the sugar to 200g (7oz). Do not use less than this because, once frozen, ice cream tastes less sweet than the unfrozen mixture.

INGREDIENTS

makes 1-1.2 litres (1¾-2 pints)
- 10-12 mandarins to make about 500ml (18fl oz) juice
- juice of 1 orange
- 250g (9oz) caster sugar
- 250ml (9fl oz) double cream, plus extra cream, to serve
- extra mandarin segments or fresh berries, to decorate

1 Peel and divide the mandarins into segments. Place them in a food processor with the orange juice. Process for 1 minute then strain the mixture through a fine sieve; measure 500ml (18fl oz) juice (use the remainder for another purpose). Add the sugar and stir to dissolve.

2 Whip the cream and fold in the mandarin juice. Spoon the mixture into a stainless-steel or plastic bowl or mould, then freeze for 2-2½ hours, until soft frozen.

3 Whisk the mixture and return to the mould. Cover with cling film and place in the freezer. Leave for 3-6 hours.

4 Unmould the ice cream and decorate with extra cream and mandarin segments or fresh berries of your choice.

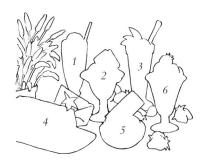

Nothing will win you more compliments than homemade ice creams and sorbets. Flavour a base mixture with anything from berries to nuts. (1) Berry Ice Cream, (2) Lavender Ice Cream, (3) Mango Ice Cream, (4) Pecan Nut Semi-freddo (page 90), (5) Lemon-mint Sorbet (page 92), (6) Strawberry Sorbet (page 90).

ICE-CREAM TOPPINGS

CHOCOLATE HONEYCOMB SAUCE Melt 100g (3½oz) dark chocolate in the microwave or in a bowl over simmering water. Stir in 125ml (4fl oz) cream and 100g (3½oz) 'honeycomb' until melted and well combined. Serve warm.

To make your own honeycomb for the sauce, see the recipe for Hokey Pokey Ice Cream (page 89) and follow steps 1-3. *Makes about 250ml (9fl oz).*

MANGO PASSION FRUIT SAUCE Peel 1 large mango and purée the pulp. Stir in the pulp of 3 large passion fruits and chill before serving. *Makes about 250ml (9fl oz).*

Banana and honey ice cream

Small servings of this ice cream with a dessert biscuit or brandy snap make a delicious finale to a meal.

INGREDIENTS

makes 1.2-1.5 litres (2-2¾ pints)
- 6 egg yolks
- 500ml (18fl oz) milk
- 4 tablespoons clear honey
- 2 teaspoons vanilla essence
- 500ml (18fl oz) single cream
- 3 medium bananas, mashed

1 Place the egg yolks and milk in a double boiler and whisk until blended. Add the honey and essence. Stir over a medium heat until the mixture coats the back of a metal spoon.

2 Pour the mixture into a bowl and allow to cool. Cover with cling film and place in the refrigerator for 1 hour to chill.

3 Stir in the cream and mashed banana. Pour into an ice-cream maker and churn according to the manufacturer's instructions.

4 Spoon the ice cream into a freezer-proof container, cover with cling film and place in the freezer. Allow to soften in the refrigerator for 15-30 minutes before serving.

Vanilla ice cream

To this plain vanilla ice cream you can add your favourite toppings, or try those in the box (left).

INGREDIENTS

makes 1.2-1.5 litres (2-2¾ pints)
- 500ml (18fl oz) milk
- 1 small vanilla bean (or pod), split
- 8 egg yolks, beaten
- 150g (5½oz) caster sugar
- ¼ teaspoon salt
- 4 tablespoons vanilla essence
- 500ml (18fl oz) double cream

1 Place the milk in a heavy-based saucepan and heat until just bubbling. Remove from the heat, add the vanilla bean, cover and set aside to cool until just warm.

2 Remove and discard the bean. Place the egg yolks, sugar, salt and vanilla essence in a bowl and beat with a balloon whisk until the mixture is thick and creamy. Gradually add the warm milk, whisking constantly.

3 Pour the mixture into a heavy-based saucepan and cook over a low heat, whisking constantly, for about 6 minutes, or until the mixture coats the back of a metal spoon.

4 Strain the mixture into a bowl and stir as it cools. Whisk in the cream, then cover the bowl with cling film and place in the refrigerator for 1 hour to chill.

5 Pour the mixture into an ice-cream maker and churn according to the manufacturer's instructions.

6 Spoon the ice cream into a freezer-proof container, cover with cling film and place in the freezer. Allow to soften in the refrigerator for 15-30 minutes before serving.

Citrus ice cream

Refreshing and tangy, this ice cream makes an ideal complement to a fresh fruit salad.

INGREDIENTS

makes 1.2-1.5 litres (2-2¾ pints)
- 250ml (9fl oz) double cream
- 1 egg
- 200g (7oz) caster sugar
- 1 tablespoon grated citrus zest of choice
- 125ml (4fl oz) citrus juice of choice
- pinch salt
- 375ml (13fl oz) milk

1 Place the cream in the large bowl of an electric mixer. Add the egg and beat for 10 seconds. Add the sugar, a few tablespoons at a time, and beat until well incorporated. Add the citrus zest, juice, salt and milk. Blend all the ingredients together thoroughly.

2 Place the mixture in the refrigerator for 1 hour to chill.

3 Pour into an ice-cream maker and churn according to the manufacturer's instructions.

4 Spoon the ice cream into a container, cover with cling film and place in the freezer. Allow to soften in the refrigerator for 15-30 minutes before serving.

PRACTICAL IDEAS

PREPARATION AND STORAGE

If mixtures that are to be frozen in the churn of an ice-cream maker are made up the day before freezing, you will get a smoother result and increase the yield.

Ice-cream makers work by using paddles that stir constantly during freezing, to incorporate air and break up ice crystals that form. Old-fashioned churns are turned by hand; as the mixture hardens, a strong arm is needed to keep the paddles turning.

If you don't have an ice-cream maker, freeze the mixture in shallow trays until it is set firm around the edges. Scrape into a bowl and beat for about 10 minutes. Refreeze in the trays. Repeat this process at least once more, then leave to freeze.

Peach ice cream

This rich, fruity ice cream is full of the flavour of summer. For an equally tasty alternative you can substitute 10-12 fresh apricots for the peaches.

INGREDIENTS
makes 1-1.2 litres (1¾-2 pints)
♦ 5 large fresh peaches
♦ 1 tablespoon lemon juice
♦ 125ml (4fl oz) clear honey
♦ 500ml (18fl oz) double cream
♦ 3 tablespoons caster sugar
♦ 1 teaspoon vanilla essence

1 Wash the peaches and cut a cross in the base of each. Drop them into boiling water for 1 minute then lift out with a slotted spoon and plunge them into cold water. Slip off the skins, chop the flesh roughly, and discard the stones.
2 Place the peaches, lemon juice and honey in a food processor. Pulse on and off to make a rough purée, about 625ml (1 pint 1fl oz).
3 In a separate large bowl, beat the cream with the sugar and vanilla essence until soft peaks form. Stir in the peach purée.
4 Pour into an ice-cream maker and churn according to the manufacturer's instructions.
5 Spoon the ice cream into a freezer-proof container, cover with cling film and place in the freezer. Allow to soften in the refrigerator for 15-30 minutes before serving.

Hawaiian ice cream

Tropical flavours permeate this tangy ice cream. Serve it simply with a dessert biscuit.

INGREDIENTS
makes 1-1.2 litres (1¾-2 pints)
♦ 300ml (10fl oz) double cream
♦ 300ml (10fl oz) vanilla custard
  (available ready-made
  in cartons or cans)
♦ 450g (1lb) can crushed
  pineapple, drained
♦ 100g (3½oz) large-flake
  desiccated coconut

1 Place all the ingredients in a bowl and blend well with a fork.
2 Pour into an ice-cream maker and churn according to the manufacturer's instructions.

3 Spoon the ice cream into a freezer-proof container, cover with cling film and place in the freezer. Allow to soften in the refrigerator for 15-30 minutes before serving.

VARIATIONS Instead of using the pineapple and coconut, try adding the following combinations to the cream and custard: 200g (7oz) chopped fruit-and-nut chocolate; 200g (7oz) each glacé fruit and preserved stem ginger; 200g (7oz) crushed sugared almonds. Or make a Christmas ice-cream pudding by adding 200g (7oz) mixed dried and glacé fruit and nuts that have been soaked for at least 8 hours in 3 tablespoons brandy.

Hokey pokey ice cream

The sweet crunch of honeycomb and the smooth taste of vanilla ice cream combine here to produce a unique texture and an irresistible flavour.

HONEYCOMB INGREDIENTS
makes 1.2-1.5 litres (2-2¾ pints)
♦ 5 tablespoons caster sugar
♦ 2 tablespoons golden syrup
♦ 1 teaspoon bicarbonate of soda

ICE CREAM INGREDIENTS
♦ 300ml (10fl oz) milk
♦ 200ml (7fl oz) double cream
♦ 1 vanilla bean (or pod), split
♦ 100g (3½oz) caster sugar
♦ 200ml (7fl oz) water
♦ 6 egg yolks

1 Line a swiss-roll tin with baking paper.
2 To make the honeycomb, place the sugar and golden syrup in a heavy saucepan and, stirring constantly, bring slowly to the boil. Reduce the heat to very low and simmer gently for 4 minutes, stirring occasionally.
3 Remove from the heat, add the bicarbonate of soda and stir briskly – the toffee will froth up dramatically. Pour into the prepared tin and leave to cool and harden.
4 Break the honeycomb into small pieces.
5 To prepare the ice cream, scald the milk and cream in a heavy saucepan, with the vanilla bean added. Remove from the heat, then cover with a lid and leave to infuse until completely cooled.

6 In a second saucepan, dissolve the sugar and water over a gentle heat, then increase heat and boil rapidly until it tests at 120°C (248°F) on a sugar thermometer, or when a little syrup dropped into cold water forms a hard ball.
7 While the syrup is boiling, beat the egg yolks in the bowl of an electric mixer until thick and creamy. With the mixer running, pour the boiling syrup slowly onto the yolks and continue beating until cold. The mixture should be thick and fluffy.
8 Strain the milk/cream infusion, add to the egg mixture and mix well. Pour into an ice-cream maker and churn according to the manufacturer's instructions. When half frozen, stir in 100g (3½oz) of the honeycomb pieces and continue to churn.
9 Spoon into a container, cover with cling film and put in the freezer for 2-6 hours.

Chocolate custard ice cream

Who can resist chocolate ice cream? This easy-to-make version adds custard for extra richness.

INGREDIENTS
makes 1-1.2 litres (1¾-2 pints)
♦ 200g (7oz) dark chocolate
♦ 250ml (9fl oz) double cream
♦ 500ml (18fl oz) vanilla custard
  (available ready-made
  in cartons or cans)

1 Place the chocolate in a double boiler over a low heat and stir until melted.
2 Place the cream in a heavy-based saucepan and heat over a low heat until just warm. Add the chocolate to the cream and stir constantly until blended. Add the custard and mix well.
3 Pour into an ice-cream maker and churn according to the manufacturer's instructions.
4 Spoon the ice cream into a container, cover with cling film and freeze. Allow to soften in the refrigerator for 20 minutes before serving.

VARIATION Give chocolate ice cream a twist by adding a hint of lemon verbena, or rose or peppermint geranium. Infuse a generous handful of leaves of your choice in the cream as it is heating in step 2. Leave 5 minutes longer, then remove and discard the leaves.

• Iced Desserts and Treats •

*Sorbets and granitas are based on a sugar syrup to which flavourings have been
added. Like ice creams, the basic recipe can be adapted to use a variety of flavouring ingredients, such
as yoghurt, to produce an assortment of healthy and tasty iced desserts*

Pecan nut semi-freddo

*Semi-freddo means 'partly frozen'. In texture it is
more like a frozen mousse than a true ice cream.*

INGREDIENTS

serves 8
- 625ml (1 pint 1fl oz) milk
- 6 egg yolks
- 2 tablespoons caster sugar
- 425ml (15fl oz) double cream
- 2 tablespoons maple syrup
- 70g (2½oz) chopped pecan nuts
- 12 sponge fingers
- grated chocolate,
  to decorate

1 Grease a loaf tin about 25cm × 12cm × 6cm
(10in × 4½in × 2½in) in size. Line the tin
carefully with cling film, leaving enough to
fold over the top of the ice-cream loaf.
2 Heat the milk until hot but not scalded.
Remove from the heat.
3 Place the egg yolks and sugar in a medium-
sized, heat-resistant bowl and whisk vigorously
with a balloon whisk. Slowly whisk in the hot
milk. Place the bowl over a saucepan of
simmering water and cook, stirring constantly,
until the mixture thickens enough to coat the
back of a metal spoon.
4 Remove the bowl from the heat and cover
with cling film to prevent a skin forming on
the top. Leave the mixture to cool completely.
5 Beat the double cream until soft peaks form.
Fold in the cold custard, maple syrup and
chopped pecan nuts.
6 Pour the mixture into the lined loaf tin.
Carefully place the sponge fingers in a row on
top of the ice cream. Fold the cling film over
the ice cream and place in the freezer for 6-8
hours, until solid. Allow the semi-freddo to
soften for about 15 minutes in the refrigerator
before serving. Turn out on a serving plate so
the sponge fingers form the base. Sprinkle with
the grated chocolate and serve immediately, or
you can refrigerate the semi-freddo until it is
ready to serve, but no longer than 30 minutes.

Strawberry sorbet

*Use ripe, best-quality fruit. For a change, try a
mixture of raspberries, blueberries and strawberries.*

INGREDIENTS

makes 1.5 litres (2¾ pints)
- 750g (1lb 10oz) strawberries
- 400g (14oz) caster sugar
- 500ml (18fl oz) fresh orange
  juice, strained
- 2 tablespoons Grand
  Marnier
- mint leaves or strawberry flowers
  and leaves, to decorate

1 Wash and hull the strawberries, then drain.
Halve them and place in a bowl with the sugar
and orange juice. Set aside for 1 hour.
2 Place the berries and juice in the workbowl
of a food processor and purée. Add the Grand
Marnier and stir to combine.
3 Pour the mixture into ice cream trays or a
shallow freezer-proof dish. Place in the freezer
and leave until almost firm but not hard.
4 Spoon the mixture back into the food
processor and pulse on and off until slushy.
5 Pour the mixture back into the trays or dish
and return to the freezer.
6 Once again, when the mixture is almost
firm, repeat the pulsing process.
7 Return the mixture to the trays or dish,
cover with cling film and allow to freeze until
solid. Leave to soften in the refrigerator for
15 minutes before serving.
8 To serve, run a fork through the sorbet to
break it up, then spoon into chilled serving
dishes or glasses. Garnish with borage or
strawberry flowers and leaves, or as desired.

Kiwi fruit sorbet

*Refreshing, light and tasty, this sorbet is ideal for
serving between courses as a palate-cleanser, or as
a light dessert after a rich main course. Serve it in
a dish that complements the pretty colour.*

INGREDIENTS

makes 1.2 litres (2 pints)
- 250ml (9fl oz) water
- 400g (14oz) caster sugar
- juice of 2 lemons
- 6 large ripe kiwi fruit
- 2 egg whites
- pinch salt
- sprigs mint,
  to decorate

1 Place the water, sugar and half the lemon
juice in a small saucepan and stir over a
moderate heat until the sugar has dissolved.
Bring the syrup to the boil and simmer
for 3 minutes. Remove from the heat and
leave until cold.
2 Peel the kiwi fruit, chop the flesh roughly
and place in the workbowl of a food processor.
Add the remaining lemon juice and process
to a purée. Add the purée to the cold syrup,
stirring well to combine.
3 Whisk the egg whites with the salt until
soft peaks form. Fold the egg whites into the
kiwi-fruit mixture, then spoon into freezer
trays or a shallow freezer-proof dish. Place the
sorbet in the freezer until it is set 1cm (½in)
around the edges.
4 Spoon the mixture into the workbowl of a
food processor and purée.
5 Return the mixture to the freezer container,
cover with cling film and freeze until set.
Leave the sorbet to soften in the refrigerator
for 15 minutes before serving.
6 Spoon the kiwi fruit sorbet into chilled
serving bowls or glasses, garnish with the
sprigs of fresh mint and serve.

Troppo ice blocks

Choose a mixture of fruits from among pineapple, papaya, passion fruit, lychee, mango, apple and orange. Work over a bowl when peeling the fruit, so as to catch any juices which you can use in the recipe.

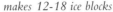

INGREDIENTS

makes 12-18 ice blocks

- 750g (1lb 10oz) finely chopped fruit, peeled and cored, if necessary, and cut into bite-sized pieces
- 750ml (1 pint 7fl oz) fresh orange juice

1 Place the fruit in the bowl with any juices. Stir well and spoon the mixture into plastic cups, or any small, shaped moulds, until almost full.

2 Cover the fruit with freshly squeezed orange juice, leaving space for expansion, and partially freeze. Insert a wooden stick in the centre and freeze overnight.

Nutty chocolate bananas

For fun, dye the wooden skewers a range of bright colours using food colourings.

INGREDIENTS

makes 8

- 8 ripe bananas
- 300g (10½oz) dark chocolate with 70 per cent cocoa solids
- 140g (5oz) chopped mixed nuts, roasted
- 8 wooden skewers, sharp ends cut off

1 Line a flat tray with cling film.

2 Push a blunt skewer into one end of each banana to halfway along its length. Place the bananas on the prepared tray, cover with cling film and freeze solid.

3 Melt the dark chocolate in the microwave, or in a heatproof bowl over simmering water. Holding a banana over the bowl, spoon chocolate over until the banana is well coated. Quickly sprinkle with the nuts before the chocolate hardens.

4 Repeat with the remaining bananas and return them to the freezer until required.

Strawberry icy poles

Natural ingredients make these a healthy choice.

INGREDIENTS

makes about 8 ice blocks

- 500g (1lb 2oz) strawberries
- 125ml (4fl oz) well-flavoured apple juice

Colourful and delicious summer treats that kids will love: clockwise from top left, Nutty Chocolate Bananas, Troppo Ice Blocks, Strawberry Icy Poles.

Roughly mash the strawberries and stir in the apple juice. Spoon into ice-block moulds, push a stick into each and freeze until required.

Lemon-mint sorbet

Served in chilled glasses, this refreshingly light dessert is just right for a hot summer evening.

INGREDIENTS

*makes 750ml-1 litre
(1 pint 7fl oz-1¾ pints)*
♦ 200g (7oz) sugar
♦ 625ml (1 pint 1fl oz) water
♦ handful fresh mint leaves
♦ 125ml (4fl oz) lemon juice

1 Place the sugar and water in a saucepan over a moderate heat and stir until the sugar has dissolved. Bring the syrup to the boil and simmer for 3 minutes. Remove from the heat, add the mint leaves and set aside for about 1 hour to allow to cool completely.
2 Strain the syrup into a large bowl and stir in the lemon juice.
3 Pour the lemon-syrup mixture into ice-cream trays or a shallow freezer-proof dish and freeze for about 4 hours.
4 Run a fork back and forth through the sorbet to break it up. Cover the trays or dish with cling film and freeze for a further 4-8 hours. Leave the sorbet to soften in the refrigerator for 15 minutes before serving.

Melon and peach sorbet

Slices of cantaloupe or honeydew melon make the perfect accompaniment to this fresh-tasting sorbet.

INGREDIENTS

makes 1 litre (1¾ pints)
♦ 1kg (2lb 4oz) melon
♦ 100g (3½oz) sugar
♦ 6 tablespoons water
♦ 2 tablespoons peach
   liqueur, such as schnapps

1 Peel and seed the melon. Chop it roughly and purée in a food processor. Pour the purée into a medium-sized bowl.
2 Place the sugar and water in a small saucepan over a moderate heat and stir until the sugar has dissolved. Bring the syrup to the boil, simmer for 3 minutes, remove from the heat and leave until cold.
3 Combine the purée, syrup and liqueur in the bowl. Refrigerate until thoroughly chilled.

4 Pour into an ice-cream maker and churn according to the manufacturer's instructions.
5 Spoon the sorbet into ice-cream trays or a shallow freezer-proof dish, cover with cling film and freeze until firm. Leave to soften in the refrigerator for 15 minutes before serving.

Frozen passion fruit yoghurt

Serve this light and pleasantly sharp-tasting dessert after a heavy meal such as a casserole or roast dinner. Substitute low-fat yoghurt, if preferred.

INGREDIENTS

makes 1.2-1.5 litres (2-2¾ pints)
♦ 750ml (1 pint 7fl oz) natural
   yoghurt
♦ pulp of 6 passion fruit
♦ 150g (5½oz) caster sugar
♦ 65ml (2¼fl oz) maple syrup

1 Place the yoghurt in a fine strainer or one lined with muslin and set over a bowl to drain for 1 hour in the refrigerator.
2 Discard the whey from the bowl. Place the passion fruit pulp, caster sugar and maple syrup in a bowl and stir until the sugar has completely dissolved. Add the drained yoghurt and mix well to combine.
3 Pour the yoghurt mixture into an ice-cream maker and churn according to the manufacturer's instructions.
4 Spoon the frozen yoghurt into a container, cover with cling film and place in the freezer.

Cappuccino granita

This Italian speciality is delightful on a hot day, garnished with chocolate-coated coffee beans.

INGREDIENTS

*makes 750m-1 litre
(1 pint 7fl oz-1¾ pints)*
♦ 300ml (10fl oz) strong black
   coffee, not instant
♦ 50g (1¾oz) caster sugar
♦ 6 tablespoons Kahlua, or
   coffee cream liqueur
♦ 315ml (10¼fl oz) double cream
♦ 1 tablespoon icing sugar
♦ cocoa powder, to dust

1 Place the coffee, caster sugar and half the Kahlua in a small bowl and mix well.
2 Pour the liquid into a shallow ice-cream tray or freezer-proof dish and place in the freezer. To make the granita icy and flaky, run a fork through the mixture three times, at half-hourly intervals. Finally, cover with cling film and freeze for at least 8 hours.
3 Whip the cream until soft peaks form. Fold through the remainder of the Kahlua and the icing sugar.
4 Before serving, leave the granita to soften in the refrigerator for 15 minutes. To serve, roughly break up with a fork, place spoonfuls in chilled serving glasses, top with the cream mixture and dust with cocoa powder.

VARIATION For a subtle almond flavour, substitute amaretto for the Kahlua.

Citrus champagne granita

You can make this refreshing iced treat with oranges, lemons, grapefruits or any combination of your favourite citrus fruits.

INGREDIENTS

makes 1.5 litres (2¾ pints)
♦ 300g (10½oz) caster sugar
♦ 250ml (9fl oz) water
♦ 500ml (18fl oz) freshly
   squeezed citrus juice
♦ 500ml (18fl oz) champagne
♦ pinch salt

1 Place the sugar and water in a saucepan over a moderate heat and stir until the sugar has dissolved. Bring the syrup to the boil, simmer for 3 minutes, remove from the heat and leave for about 1 hour to cool completely.
2 Place the syrup, juice, champagne and salt in a bowl and stir well to combine.
3 Pour the mixture into a shallow ice-cream tray or freezer-proof dish, cover with cling film and place in the freezer. To make the granita icy and flaky, run a fork through the mixture three times, at half-hourly intervals.
4 Cover with cling film and place in the freezer for 8 hours or overnight. Leave to soften in the refrigerator for 15-30 minutes before serving in chilled glasses or bowls.

Peach granita

Mangoes or nectarines can also be used for this granita. Serve alone or with chilled fresh fruit.

INGREDIENTS

makes 1 litre (1¾ pints)
- ♦ 250ml (9fl oz) water
- ♦ 100g (3½oz) sugar
- ♦ 4 ripe peaches, peeled, stoned and roughly chopped
- ♦ 1 tablespoon peach schnapps or fruit liqueur

1 Place the water and sugar in a small saucepan and stir over a moderate heat until the sugar has dissolved. Bring the syrup to the boil, simmer for 3 minutes, remove from the heat and leave to cool completely.
2 Purée the peaches in a food processor. Add the sugar syrup and schnapps or liqueur and stir to combine.
3 Pour the mixture into a shallow ice-cream tray or freezer-proof dish, cover with cling film and place in the freezer. To make the granita icy and flaky, run a fork through the mixture three times, at half-hourly intervals.
4 Cover with cling film and freeze for at least 6 hours, until solid. Leave to soften in the refrigerator for 15 minutes before serving in chilled bowls or glasses.

Frozen chocolate-nut yoghurt

This is an energising snack for any time of day.

INGREDIENTS

serves 4-6
- ♦ 200g (7oz) dark chocolate, with 70 per cent cocoa solids
- ♦ 300ml (10fl oz) double cream
- ♦ 500ml (18fl oz) natural yoghurt
- ♦ 100g (3½oz) dark chocolate chips
- ♦ 1 teaspoon vanilla essence
- ♦ 40g (1½oz) finely chopped dried apricots, softened
- ♦ 75g (2¾oz) ground almonds
- ♦ 35g (1¼oz) sultanas
- ♦ 70g (2½oz) finely chopped hazelnuts

1 Line a mould, bowl or loaf tin with cling film, leaving plenty to fold over the top.
2 Melt the chocolate in a microwave or a double boiler over a low heat, stirring from time to time. Leave until cool.
3 Whip the cream until stiff peaks form. Add the yoghurt and chocolate and mix well to combine. Fold in the remaining ingredients.
4 Spoon the mixture into the mould, then fold the cling film over the top and freeze. Soften to room temperature before cutting the frozen yoghurt into slices or wedges.

Iced zabaglione

This Italian dessert makes an impressive end to a dinner party – and is far easier to make than it looks.

INGREDIENTS

serves 6
- ♦ 6 egg yolks
- ♦ 6 tablespoons caster sugar
- ♦ 6 tablespoons Marsala
- ♦ 300ml (10fl oz) double cream
- ♦ strawberries dipped in chocolate, optional

1 Using a balloon whisk, beat the egg yolks, caster sugar and Marsala in a heatproof bowl over simmering water for about 15 minutes.
2 Remove the bowl from the heat and place in a larger bowl, quarter-filled with cold water. Rest the outer bowl on a folded tea towel to prevent it from slipping. Whisk until the mixture is cold.
3 Whip the cream with a clean whisk until soft peaks form. Spoon it onto the egg-yolk mixture and lightly fold through until no white streaks remain.
4 Spoon the zabaglione into individual glass dessert or parfait dishes, cover with cling film and freeze for 6-8 hours, until firm. Serve the dessert garnished with chocolate-dipped strawberries, if desired.

MAKING SORBETS AND GRANITAS

1 *Purée the fruit and liquid in a food processor, if necessary. (Any juicy fruits, including tomatoes, are suitable for sorbets and granitas, but be careful with added alcohol as too much will inhibit freezing.)*

2 *Pour the mixture into ice-cream trays or shallow freezer-proof dishes and freeze until grainy and partly frozen. Run a fork through the sorbet from time to time to achieve an even texture.*

3 *Return the partly frozen sorbet to the processor and pulse to break up any lumps. Repeat steps 2 and 3 at least once more. Freeze for at least 6 hours. Transfer to the refrigerator about 15 minutes before serving.*

4 *To serve, run a fork through the sorbet to break it up, then spoon into chilled serving glasses. For a special occasion, serve it from an ice bowl (see page 97), decorated to complement the sorbet's flavour.*

The Frozen Pantry

*Freezing captures the true colour, texture and flavour of fresh vegetables
and fruits, preserving them at their nutritional peak. When particular fruits are plentiful
in the shops, or your garden, preserve enough to enjoy year-round*

Vegetables

*Most vegetables can be frozen with excellent results.
The box on page 95 gives instructions for water-
blanching and steam-blanching. Prepare vegetables as
directed below, then pack snugly and expel as much
air as you can before sealing, then label and freeze.
For best results, use sturdy, moisture and vapour-
proof wrappings and containers. Once thawed,
vegetables should never be refrozen. It is good to pack
them in containers that hold serving-sized amounts.
There is no need to thaw frozen vegetables before
cooking; just place them in boiling water to cover and
cook until they are crisp and tender.*

Asparagus and French beans

Wash, trim and cut into lengths suitable for
chosen containers or into 5cm (2in) pieces.
Sort asparagus according to the thickness of
the stalks: water-blanch thin stalks for
2 minutes, thick stalks for 4 minutes. Water-
blanch French beans for 3 minutes. Cool
quickly, drain thoroughly and package.

Beetroot

Wash and trim, leaving 1cm
(½in) stems – be careful not to pierce the skin.
Sort according to size and cook in boiling
water for 25-30 minutes for small beetroot,
45-50 minutes for large, or until tender when
pierced with a fork. Drain quickly and cool,
then peel off the skins. Slice or cube the
beetroot, as desired, and package.

*Fresh vegetables from your own garden are a great
blessing, but at certain times of the year you can find
yourself with an overwhelming supply of riches. The
answer is easy – just freeze the surplus.*

Broad beans

Shell young, tender beans and discard any damaged ones. Water-blanch beans for 2 minutes. Cool quickly and drain thoroughly.

Broccoli, cauliflower

Wash and peel stalks if woody. Cut the broccoli or cauliflower into florets about 3.5cm (1¼in) thick. Steam-blanch for 5 minutes. Cool quickly and drain thoroughly.

Brussels sprouts

Trim off coarse leaves and stems and sort by size. Water-blanch for 3 minutes for small, 5 minutes for large sprouts. Cool quickly and drain thoroughly.

Carrots

Leave young carrots whole, but peel and cut larger ones into 1cm (½in) thick slices or into matchsticks, as desired. Water-blanch for 3 minutes for whole, 2 minutes for sliced carrots. Cool and drain thoroughly.

Courgettes

Trim and cut into 1cm (½in) thick slices, lengthways or across diagonally, as desired. Steam-blanch for 5 minutes. Cool quickly, drain thoroughly and package in freezer bags, expelling all air.

Leeks

Remove the outer leaves of the leeks, trim and wash well. Cut into 1cm (½in) thick slices and water-blanch for 3 minutes. Drain thoroughly and package in freezer bags. Seal, expelling as much air as possible.

Mushrooms

Wipe with a damp cloth to remove any dirt. Do not peel. Large mushrooms should be sliced and sautéed in butter. There is no need for blanching. Pack cooked mushrooms in small containers with their cooking liquid.

Button varieties can be frozen whole, raw. Spread the mushrooms on a baking tray and place in the freezer. When hard, pack into bags, label and return to the freezer.

Peas

Shell peas, discarding any damaged ones. Water-blanch for 1½ minutes. Cool quickly, drain thoroughly and package. Seal, expelling as much air as possible.

Peppers

Wipe glossy, firm peppers and cut out the stems, removing all the seeds and pithy membrane. Cut in halves, slices or rings, as desired. Blanch halves for 3 minutes, slices for 2 minutes. Cool quickly and drain thoroughly. Seal, expelling as much air as possible.

Pumpkins, squash

Wash the pumpkin or squash, peel and cut in half, and remove seeds and strings. Cut into slices or cubes. Steam-blanch until tender. Mash to a purée. Cool and pack into containers with lids, leaving 1-2cm (½-¾in) space at the top of the container.

Runner beans

'String' the beans and cut diagonally into 1cm (½in) lengths. Water-blanch for 1 minute. Cool quickly, drain thoroughly and package. Seal, expelling all air.

Spinach

Wash the leaves thoroughly and remove any thick stems and imperfect leaves. Water-blanch the tender leaves for 30-60 seconds, until just wilted. Cool quickly by running cold water over the leaves, and drain thoroughly, pressing out excess moisture. Freeze in a plastic bag and seal, expelling as much air as possible.

Sweetcorn

Use young cobs only. Remove the husks and silks and sort by size. Water-blanch for 7 minutes for small ears, 9 minutes for medium and 11 minutes for large. Cool quickly, drain well and wrap each ear individually, airtight, in freezer paper or foil, moulding to the shape of the ear of corn. Package several together.

Vegetables, mixed

Blanch the vegetables, diced or cut small, according to the directions for each individual vegetable (a shorter blanching time may be required to compensate for the smaller size). When cool, mix your choice of vegetables together and pack in polythene bags in one-meal quantities, seal, label and freeze.

PREPARING VEGETABLES FOR FREEZING

WITH THE EXCEPTION of salad greens and vegetables with high water content, such as onions, celery, cucumbers and radishes, most vegetables freeze well. All vegetables destined for the freezer must be blanched in order to retain colour and fresh flavour. Vegetables may be blanched in boiling water or by using a steam method.

TO WATER-BLANCH Bring at least 3 litres (5¼ pints) water to the boil in a large saucepan. Place 500g (1lb 2oz) prepared vegetable pieces in a wire-mesh basket and plunge into the boiling water. When the water returns to the boil, cook vegetables for the time indicated on these pages. Lift the basket and place straight into a large bowl of cold or iced water to cool (it may be necessary to change the water or add more ice). Drain thoroughly.

TO STEAM-BLANCH Place vegetables in a single layer in a steamer basket in a large saucepan over a layer of boiling water 5cm (2in) deep. Cover and steam the vegetables for the time indicated. Cool as directed for water-blanched vegetables. Drain thoroughly.

Fruit

Ensure that you have a supply of fruit for delicious crumbles, dessert toppings and pastry fillings all year round by purchasing or picking the season's best and freezing it for later use.

Sugar-packed fruit

Because there is no added liquid with this method, sugar-packed fruit is best for baking and for sauces.

INGREDIENTS

makes 500g (1lb 2oz)

- 500g (1lb 2oz) prepared fruit of choice, dipped into acidulated water (see box, right)
- 100-140g (3½-5oz) sugar

1 Drain the dipped fruit thoroughly on paper towels so it is as dry as possible.
2 Place the fruit in a bowl, add just enough sugar to coat all pieces evenly, then gently mix to dissolve the sugar.
3 Pack snugly into two 500ml (18fl oz) freezer containers or bags and expel all air. Seal tightly, label and freeze.

Syrup for frozen fruit

Use a thin, medium or heavy syrup to freeze fruit, depending on the tartness of the fruit. Sour cherries and plums will benefit from a medium or heavy syrup while fresh grapes or melon require only a thin syrup. You will need 250-375ml (9-13fl oz) syrup for each 500g (1lb 2oz) of prepared fruit. Use 1 litre (1¾ pints) water to produce the following yields for each of the three syrups.

SYRUP	SUGAR	YIELD
thin	400g (14oz)	625g (1lb 6oz)
medium	600g (1lb 5oz)	700g (1lb 9oz)
heavy	950g (2lb 2oz)	800g (1lb 12oz)

1 Bring the water to the boil in a large saucepan. Add the sugar, stir to dissolve and simmer for 2 minutes.
2 Remove the pan from the heat, cool, then chill until cold. Use as directed in recipes.

VARIATIONS Add a vanilla bean (or pod), cinnamon stick or strips of lemon peel to the syrup in step 1 while simmering to flavour it, if desired. Strain the cooled syrup before chilling.

Fruit packed in syrup

Fruits which have been packed in syrup can be drained – or not – and used just as you would any commercially canned fruit. They're delicious served with ice cream or home-made custard. Home-packed fruits are superior in flavour – nothing beats the summer-fresh taste of fruit from your own freezer.

INGREDIENTS

makes about 850g (1lb 14oz)

- 1 quantity sugar syrup (see previous recipe)
- 750g (1lb 10oz) prepared fruit of choice, dipped into acidulated water (see box, right)

1 Prepare and chill the syrup.
2 Pour 125ml (4fl oz) chilled syrup into each of three 500ml (18fl oz) freezer containers. Place the fruit pieces in the containers, pressing to remove any air bubbles.
3 Pour in enough remaining syrup to cover the fruit, leaving a 1cm (½in) space below the rim, then cover tightly, seal, label and freeze until required.

Sugar-free frozen fruit

This method is ideal for all fruit, particularly berries intended for use as garnishes. Thawed fruit can also be puréed and used as a simple sauce, or coulis, to serve over ice cream or with other desserts.

INGREDIENTS

makes 500g (1lb 2oz)

- 500g (1lb 2oz) prepared fruit of choice, dipped into acidulated water (see box, above)

1 Drain the dipped fruit thoroughly on paper towels. Arrange on a freezer tray and freeze until just firm.
2 Transfer the fruit to two 500ml (18fl oz) freezer containers or bags and expel all air. Seal tightly, label and freeze.
3 Thaw the frozen fruit in a sealed container in the refrigerator or in a bowl of cool water. Serve while still slightly icy.

PREPARING FRUITS

FRUIT BROWNS QUICKLY when handled, so prepare it as quickly as possible and do not leave exposed to the air for too long. Keep it in a bowl of acidulated water, made from 2 litres (3½ pints) water with 1-2 tablespoons lemon juice or mild vinegar added. This is known as dipping. After dipping, drain the fruit on paper towels to remove as much moisture as possible. This prevents ice forming around the pieces when they are frozen and keeps them from sticking together.

The following fruits freeze well: apples, apricots, blackberries, blackcurrants, cherries, peaches, plums, raspberries, redcurrants, rhubarb and strawberries. Peel, core and slice apples. Stem and pit cherries. Berries and currants should have stems removed; melon should be peeled and cubed or made into balls with a melon baller. Stone and slice or halve apricots, peaches and plums. To remove the stone from such tree fruits, carefully cut around the fruit following the natural groove. Gently twist the halves in opposite directions, separate and remove the stone.

General freezing

Many foods freeze well, which allows you to take advantage of sales, or to prepare baked goods ahead to have on hand for last-minute meals.

Bread

Bread should be fresh when frozen. Leave in its original packaging or pack in plastic freezer wrap or foil. Loaves will keep up to 6 months, rolls up to 3 months.

Cakes

These keep longer if frozen un-iced and unfilled. Wrap in cling film. Sponge layers should be frozen separately. Will keep for 4 months. To thaw: leave at room temperature about 2 hours (small cakes, 1 hour).

Cake mixture

Do not freeze sponge mixture. To freeze plain cake mixture, line a baking tin with foil, add the batter and freeze uncovered. Remove the frozen batter from the tin and wrap in a double layer of foil. Will keep for about 2 months. TO BAKE: remove the outer wrapping; place with the foil lining in the original baking tin and bake in a preheated oven for slightly longer than freshly made batter.

Cheese

Hard cheese (eg Cheddar, Edam, Gouda): pack tightly in a double layer of plastic wrap, forcing out air. Will keep for 6 months. To thaw: leave overnight in the refrigerator.

Cream cheese can be frozen for about 6 weeks. Cottage and ricotta cheeses are unsuitable for freezing.

Choux pastry

Line baking trays with baking paper. Form the desired shapes on the trays and freeze uncovered. When frozen, pack into plastic freezer bags or foil. Will keep for up to 3 months. Do not thaw before baking.

Eggs

Raw whole eggs and yolks: mix with a fork to break up; add ½ teaspoon salt for every 6 whole eggs or a pinch of salt for every 6 yolks. Freeze in small containers. Whites: Do not beat or add salt before freezing. Pack in small containers. Whole eggs, yolks and whites will keep for 6 months.

Fish

For maximum freshness, fish should be frozen within 24 hours of catching. Scale and wash small fish and seal them in plastic bags, excluding as much air as possible. Store large fish whole, or cut into fillets or steaks and package in the same way. Small fish, and fillets or steaks, can be cooked from frozen; large whole fish should be thawed for 24 hours in the refrigerator. White fish will keep for about 3 months, oily fish for about 2 months.

Herbs

Pack sprigs in plastic freezer bags, and chopped herbs in plastic containers or ice-cube trays, covered with water. Will keep for 2 months.

Meat

Wrap fresh meat well in cling film, expelling air. Pack in meal-sized amounts; layer chops and steaks with waxed paper. Beef will keep for 8 months; lamb, 6 months; pork, 6 months.

Poultry

Pack whole or halved birds in freezer bags, excluding as much air as possible. Pack poultry pieces in a single layer in bags. Crumbed pieces should be placed on a tray, frozen for an hour or two, then packed into freezer bags. Whole birds will keep for about 6 months, pieces for about 4 months.

Shortcrust pastry

Roll out shortcrust pastry and line baking tins. Freeze, uncovered, until hard. Remove from baking tins and pack in plastic bags, stacked in a box. Baked pastry cases can be frozen in the same way.

ICE BOWLS TO GRACE YOUR TABLE

To MAKE an ice bowl, take two glass or stainless-steel bowls of the same shape, but one small enough to fit inside the other with 10-15mm (½-⅝in) space between the two.

Arrange flowers, leaves, herb sprigs or citrus slices around the inside of the larger bowl and place the smaller bowl inside. (Choose decorations to complement the flavours of what you plan to serve in the bowl.) Tape the two bowls together so that they are flush and will not move apart. Gently pour cooled, boiled water into the gap between the bowls to 1cm (½in) from the top. (Cooled, boiled water gives a clearer, more sparkling ice bowl.) Add some more flowers or other decorations, if needed, arranging them with a skewer. Freeze overnight.

Next day, remove the bowls from the freezer and stand at room temperature, on a plate or a tea towel, for 15 minutes, or until they will separate easily – do not run them under water to speed the process, or the ice bowl may be ruined. Remove the tape, lift out the inner bowl and invert the larger bowl to release the ice bowl. Return this to the freezer until needed.

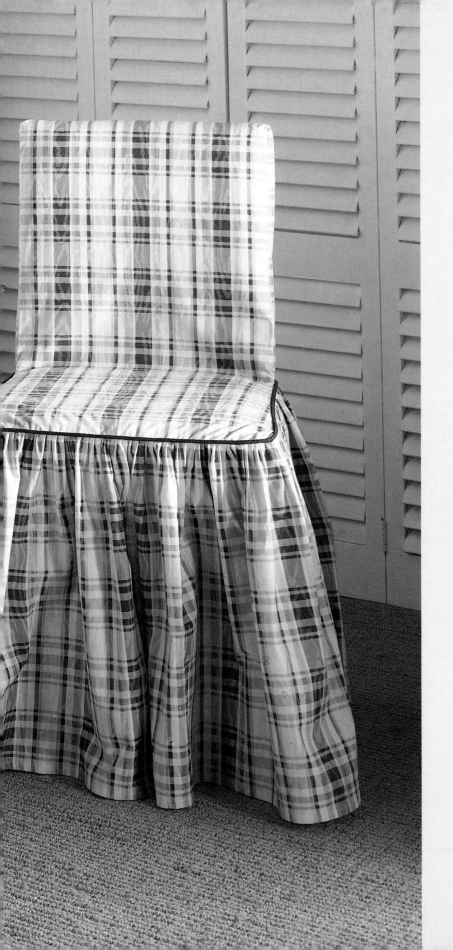

FINISHING
touches

Achieving a professional 'designer' effect in your home is not difficult – all it takes is a little time, imagination and, in most cases, a modest amount of money. In this chapter, several experts reveal some of their secrets to show you how easy it is to produce those special touches that give a distinctive appearance to a room.

You'll learn the secrets of achieving stylish wall and floor finishes quickly and inexpensively. Because you can do it all yourself, you'll save money while producing exactly the look you want.

Once you are satisfied with the walls and floors, complete your decorating with furniture and furnishings you create yourself – use clever painting techniques to rejuvenate tables, chairs and picture frames, or make cushions and tassels or chair covers.

Disguise an unused fireplace with a charming fireguard or screen. Create an attractive mosaic border for a bathroom mirror. Design your own handsome stained-glass panels for your front door. There are ideas for every room in the house, and basic tips for saving time and money while achieving stylish results.

You'll even find eco-friendly homemade cleaning and polishing products that will keep your home smelling sweet and fresh.

BEFORE YOU BEGIN...

The creative projects in this chapter offer some clever alternatives to mass-produced materials and accessories, giving you the opportunity to add a personal touch to your home. Before you begin, take time to consider the impact your project will have on the existing décor

EVERYTHING IN YOUR HOUSE contributes some element of colour, pattern and texture to the overall appearance. In order to make the most of the finishing touches presented here and achieve a professional result, always consider colour and proportion carefully before embarking on a project. At the same time, think about the consequences of introducing new colours or features to a room.

The object of interior decorating is to emphasise the good features of a room and to minimise or even disguise any less desirable aspects. If you feel that the ceiling in a room is so low you can almost touch it from the floor and that the windows seem to dominate the mid-sections of the walls, then proportionally the room has problems. Colour, pattern and texture, whether on walls, floors or in soft furnishings, do much to change the information received by the eye about a room's depth, height and width.

Playing with proportion

A ceiling can be made to appear higher – and a room airier – by painting it several shades paler than the floor and walls. You can take the illusion even further by hanging floor-length, striped curtains from a broad pelmet that covers the gap between the window and the ceiling. For maximum effect, the background colour to the curtains' stripes should match the wall colour.

Framing floor-to-ceiling patterned rectangles – either painted on or of pasted-on wallpaper – with strips of moulding will invite the eye upwards, while similar rectangular shapes applied horizontally, wall-to-wall above the skirting board, will tie a scheme to the floor.

If a ceiling appears unusually high, extending its colour down to picture rail level will make the walls appear longer and the ceiling lower. Applying horizontal stripes to the walls will produce a similar effect but only if they are not interrupted too frequently by doors and windows – broken stripes may separate the room's units rather than unify them. In a small room, any horizontal feature below waist height draws the eye down and makes the walls seem farther apart.

Colour power

Colour is the most significant element in decorating. With paint mixing services offered at many DIY stores, just about every colour and shade imaginable is readily available.

While at first glance a manufacturer's colour chart may overwhelm with its breadth of choice, colour preferences can be determined quite simply by associating colours with very basic things such as particular moods, pleasant emotional responses and fond memories. Even the colours you choose for your clothing can be starting points for the colours you choose to live with.

DESIGNING WITH COLOUR, TEXTURE AND PATTERN

Colour is a powerful decorating tool. Use it boldly but always give thought to the views from one space to another. The colour of an entrance hallway, for example, not only sets the scene for the whole house but also has a direct impact on adjoining rooms.

Texture adds an extra dimension to walls by inviting touch while also introducing subtle distinctions between light and shade – which in turn add depth and interest to colours. Texture works particularly well with an all-white or neutral colour scheme.

Patterns provide a reassuring element in any decor because of their reliance on regular repetition. Pattern can be introduced in ornaments and other accessories as well as in larger, more obvious forms such as on fabric or wallpaper.

The aim of decorating is to find a scheme that provides an attractive and comfortable backdrop for your domestic life. Here, blue and white china provides a break in the comfortable neutrality of the buttoned upholstery, wooden shelves and books.

Relatively little equipment is required to add those special finishing touches to any room, and it is generally inexpensive. Paint and the means to apply it come top of the list, followed by scissors and pens. Materials can be bought project by project.

Colour is a useful atmospheric tool on large expanses of wall, ceiling and floor. Dark rich colours intensify the areas to which they are applied and make spaces appear cosy and intimate. Light colours, on the other hand, promote a feeling of airiness and space.

While you can buy specially coordinated paint, paper, borders and fabrics which take the risk out of colour choice, rooms decorated in these combinations can have a bland, impersonal feel. A more rewarding approach is to discover colour for yourself; your inventive mixing and matching will pay dividends in terms of originality and style, and in the sense of accomplishment when you finish a project.

Pattern and texture

Pattern performs similar functions to colour but it takes more practice to use successfully. Fussy or detailed patterns can be overwhelming in a small room and using two patterns requires careful consideration. Generally, the size of the pattern used should be in proportion to the size of a room, with large patterns reserved for large spaces and small patterns applied to living areas of modest size. If you decide to apply a pattern by hand (stencilling a whole wall, for example), bear in mind that decoration involving constant repetition requires patience: you may lose interest in completing the task.

The contours of a textured surface affect not only the way we expect that surface to feel but also the colour of the surface: the most prominent parts catch the light and are brightest while the rest is, at least to some degree, in slight shadow.

The magic wand: a coat of paint

It is no overstatement to say that a fresh coat of paint can lift your spirits and even change your attitude to your immediate environment. Whether giving a drab room a cheerful, new look, or reviving an old piece of furniture, painting is one of the easiest and most satisfying jobs to be undertaken by the home decorator. The key to success is careful preparation, which makes all the difference to achieving a well-executed, well-finished job.

Make sure all surfaces are properly sanded to provide a smooth surface to receive the new paint. If the surface is pitted or uneven, you may need to fill cracks, holes or dents with a plaster or wood-filler and then sand again when this has dried. All traces of dust or grit from the sanding should be removed by wiping the surface down with a lightly dampened soft cloth for a wall, or with a tack rag, when working with wood. (A tack rag is a piece of cotton sheeting, cheesecloth or other absorbent lint-free cloth slightly dampened with boiled linseed oil, or with a thin mixture of polyurethane varnish and white spirit, that picks up the fine, often invisible particles of dust produced by sanding.)

Always use a high-gloss oil-based paint when painting chairs. Seating, particularly in a kitchen, takes a lot of knocks, and oil-based paint is harder-wearing than water-based finishes. As a general rule, the glossier the paint, the harder the finish.

There is no substitute for quality

The type and size of paintbrush you use depends on the job you are doing. For example, when applying the base colour or varnishing a picture frame, choose a brush slightly smaller than the width of the frame. Detailed work can be done with fine brushes – the better quality the brush, the better the finish. A cheap bristle brush is liable to produce a less than smooth finish and will constantly moult bristles. It's better to buy good-quality synthetic brushes unless bristle is specified in the instructions.

If you need to use a sponge to apply paint (as with some wall finishes), use a natural sea sponge rather than a synthetic kitchen or bath sponge made of foam rubber. Because of their natural irregularities, sea sponges produce a soft paint effect, while foam rubber produces harsh outlines that are difficult to disguise when a seamless appearance is being aimed for.

For ragging a wall, have a large number of clean, absorbent cloths available; once a cloth is clogged with paint it is useless and you need a fresh one. An old cotton sheet, ripped into squares, is ideal.

Decorative effects for walls and floors

If you are a beginner at stencil cutting (see also page 221), start with a simple pattern such as the leaf pattern on page 107 or the Greek key design on page 136. When making your stencil, always cut out the design segments carefully. The 'bridges', which link the various cut-out parts of the design, must be kept intact. They read as 'lines' on the completed stencil and without them the design will lack definition and could degenerate into a formless blob.

Stencil cutting is an exacting and time-consuming task that requires patience to achieve the best results. As it is likely that you will want to save stencils for further use or to freshen a design at a later time, proper cleaning and storage are important. After using the stencil, remove any masking tape. Put the stencil on a table covered with newspaper and wipe it with a soft cloth moistened with white spirit or turpentine to remove any vestiges of paint. Store stencils on a flat surface between two sheets of stiff cardboard.

Fitting and applying the design

Once you have chosen a stencil design, measure the length of the surface onto which it will be applied and divide this figure by the width of the stencil to find out how many times the outline is to be repeated. Mark the surface where each repeat has to be placed. You may need to adjust the spacing between the repeats to ensure that the pattern fits neatly into corners. Depending on the design, you may find that using just a portion of the stencil at corners gives an attractive, symmetrical result.

Traditionally, colour is applied over the surface of a stencil using a stiff stencilling brush to stipple paint over the surface. If you do not have a stencil brush (available from art supply shops), trim the bristles

DESIGN ELEMENTS FOR WALLS AND FLOORS

Create an illusion of space in a small, low-ceilinged room by choosing furniture on legs – so you can see a sweep of the floor – tall plants on low tables and tall lamps, but no ceiling-hung light fittings. Paint the walls and ceiling in pale shades.

Make the best use of space in an attic room by fitting cupboards or shelves or putting a desk where there is insufficient headroom to stand. To counter summer heat, shield the windows with blinds and ensure that there is cross-ventilation.

Panels provide a distinctive way of adding a sense of height to a room. An easy way to do this is to frame areas of patterned wallpaper, fabric or a stencilled design with a simple border of stained or painted timber moulding or beading.

Treat a plain wall as a canvas on which to display a favourite collection of ornamental odds and ends. Choose your objects – plates or hats, for example (here they are pieces of rusted ironware), hang them on the wall and enjoy the effect.

of a round paintbrush to about 1 cm in length to achieve the required stiffness. When you are stencilling, wipe the back of the stencil with a damp cloth every now and then to remove excess paint which may bleed around the edges of your image.

Nothing beats gilding for style

The ancient art of applying paper-thin metal leaf to ornamental objects produces an elegant and stylish finish rarely matched by other forms of decoration. In its most highly refined form, gilding involves the application of real gold or silver to a surface. But there are other metals, such as Dutch metal or aluminium, which are easier to apply and which will still produce a beautiful effect. Dutch metal, an alloy of copper and zinc, is an inexpensive substitute for gold leaf and is used for the gilding projects in this chapter (see pages 138 and 153). Once you have mastered Dutch metal you may like to try gold leaf, which requires special equipment and a very deft hand.

Gilding is not difficult to master as long as you maintain a lightness of touch with your raw materials. Even your breath can disturb and distort a sheet of leaf once its upper surface is exposed so breathe softly when necessary. It is important that your fingers do not come into direct contact with the leaf, as it is likely to disintegrate. Wear a pair of cotton gloves and manipulate the leaf using the rouge paper (the paper between each sheet) onto the object being gilded. Similarly, once the gilt has been applied avoid touching the object with bare fingers until it is varnished. Gilding takes practice, so you may like a few trial runs before beginning in earnest.

You will often find when you brush down the leaf at the end of the gilding process that surface cracks reveal the red paint layer below. This is quite normal and in fact adds to the beauty of the finish. Always work in an environment that is as dust-free as possible. Use a tack rag (see page 102) to ensure that all residue is removed from any items you have sanded in preparation for applying leaf.

Something different: découpage

Although a sable brush is called for in the materials list for the découpage mirror frame (page 140), imitation sable, which is less expensive, works just as well for a one-off project. Never work in circles when sanding between applications for découpage. Always use the left to right, top to bottom, cross-hatching motion adopted for varnishing. If you varnish your finished frame with satin-finish oil-based varnish and want to give it a burnished glow, wait until it is completely dry (up to a week) and, using a soft cloth (a clean cotton sock is ideal), polish the frame using light strokes.

Although it takes time, patience and some dexterity with the scissors, this traditional craft can make wonderful and very personal gifts. Try covering a wooden jewellery box with pictures of your favourite flowers, or choose family childhood photographs to decorate a box for storing precious memorabilia.

Making do: alternatives and substitutions

If certain specified materials are not readily available or if you have materials left over from another project, you can often use a substitute 'ingredient'. If, for example, you don't have a natural sponge to hand for applying a paint finish, you can make your own from a standard synthetic one (see page 118). And if you don't happen to have any masking tape in the kitchen drawer, cut off a length of ordinary sticky tape and press it against and peel it off a smooth fabric surface a few times to lose some of its stickiness.

MAKING A STENCIL FOR A CURVED BORDER

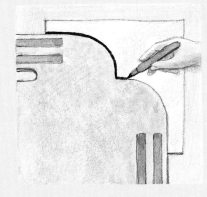

1 *Place the stencil acetate underneath the area needing a curved border. With a fine felt-tipped marker pen, trace the curved shape, stopping about 5cm beyond any adjoining straight edge. Use a trimming knife to cut the curved edge.*

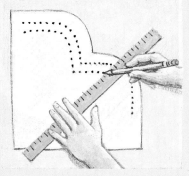

2 *To measure out curved parallel lines, use a ruler to mark two rows of dots equidistant inside the curved edge of the acetate. Follow the measurements given in particular project instructions (the fire screen, on p.136, for example) for spacings.*

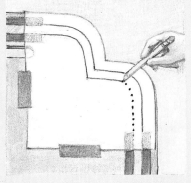

3 *Use a French curve and ruler to connect the dots into two parallel curved border lines inside the curved edge. Lay the marked acetate on the curved area of the project to check that the curved border is properly spaced to meet the side lines.*

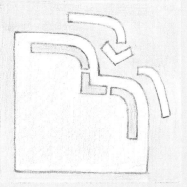

4 *Prevent the stencil falling apart by creating connecting bridges between the parallel border lines: draw lines at 10-15cm intervals, 3mm apart and be careful to leave these bridges intact when you cut out the stencil areas with a trimming knife.*

◆ Painted Wall Finishes ◆

Why settle for a plain painted wall when paint can be used in so many creative ways?
Some beautiful effects can be achieved with the easily mastered techniques given here. As you
become more confident, who knows where your creative imagination may lead?

Fresco effect

This finish gives a subtle, aged look to a surface;
the softly muted blend of shades adds a warm touch
to any surroundings. The technique is suitable for
either rustic or modern decor and complements many
styles of furnishings. It is wise to practise on a board
or small area to refine your technique before
embarking on a complete wall.

MATERIALS
- 2 large paintbrushes
- matt emulsion paints in off-white and yellow ochre
- natural sea sponge
- cleaning rag

1 Seal the surface with two coats of off-white paint and allow to dry.

2 Apply the yellow ochre (or any colour of your choice) with a paintbrush, working quickly and evenly.

3 Before this coat dries, use a second, dry paintbrush to rub the colour into the surface, achieving a mottled effect. Wipe this brush regularly on a clean rag as you progress to keep the bristles as dry as possible. Repeat this procedure if the effect is too patchy.

4 Make a mixture of 1 part off-white to 1 part water. Wet a fresh sponge with the mix and, working quickly, apply to the entire surface. Wet the sponge repeatedly in the mixture as you progress. When covering large areas, it is much easier if two people work side by side.

5 Wring all the moisture out of the sponge. Working in a circular motion over the wet wall, rub the sponge over the entire surface. Do not apply pressure to the sponge or the spread of paint will be too uneven. Work your way over the entire surface until an evenly mottled effect is achieved. Wring the sponge periodically to remove excess moisture.

Give your walls the look of aged plaster without
waiting for time to take its inevitable effect. Two
people working together can create this look in just a
couple of days. A variety of base colours look good
but the best are the earthy, ochre tones of Tuscany
and the South of France.

Ragged wall

This dappled effect is not difficult to achieve. Two paint colours are used (here, a warm grey and a mid-green). When the basecoat is dry, the second colour (or glaze) is thinned with water, painted on, and then partially removed by rolling or dabbing with twisted or crumpled pieces of cloth. For best results, use silk-finish emulsion and test the technique on a small area first. The job should be tackled by two people working together.

MATERIALS
- large paintbrush
- basecoat and a second colour in silk-finish emulsion paint
- water to dilute the second colour (or glaze)
- plenty of muslin cloth or old cotton sheets to tear into rags

1 Using the grey paint, apply two base coats allowing 4 hours drying time between coats. Let dry for 24 hours after the second coat.

2 Working on only a small area (1m²) at a time, the first person quickly applies the glaze colour, diluted 1 part paint to 1 part water, over the base coat, using a cross-hatching technique (see below).

3 The second person follows immediately and, working quickly with crumpled strips of cloth, blots off part of the glaze in an irregular pattern. Stand back regularly to check that the effect is consistent (using different textures of cloth will create different surface textures), and

Ragging gives a subtle, muted effect, rather like an unobtrusive wallpaper but without the seams. Soft pastel tones work well for this treatment.

exactly the finish you are trying to achieve. Catch paint drips immediately as these will show as lines on the finished work. For best results, rag a room from start to finish as one continuous process. If it is necessary to interrupt the application of the paint, always do so in a corner or inconspicuous place. Never rework a part of a wall because the new work will stand out as different from the rest; repainting the entire wall is the only way to achieve a satisfactory result.

4 Allow the glaze to dry.

A sponged ceiling gives a room a warm, intimate feeling. You can take breaks when doing this finish – start and stop lines are easy to disguise.

Sponging

Sponging is one of the quickest and easiest finishes to apply. It produces a stylish effect and mistakes can be rectified quite easily. We used a rich green as the base colour for our sponged finish, but choose any deep colour, observing the ratios of paint to water that are given here. An off-white works well on top of any deep shade.

MATERIALS
- paintbrush
- matt emulsion paints in a dark colour of your choice and an off-white tone
- natural sea sponges

1 Paint the wall with the dark colour. Allow to dry. It may appear far too dark at the moment, but don't worry – the final effect will be much lighter.

2 Dilute the off-white paint 1 to 1 with water. Using the sponge, rub the mixture over the entire surface.

Even a novice can achieve an excellent result with sponging. Although the look is deliberately patchy, it is not meant to disguise poorly prepared surfaces. For the best finish, prepare your walls with care.

3 Now make a mixture of 1 part dark paint to 1 part off-white. Dab the sponge in the mixture, so that the sponge is almost dry, then dab onto the wall, working with an even pressure. Make sure you vary the angles at which you lay the sponge against the wall to avoid making an obvious pattern. Take care to use a corner of the sponge to apply paint right up to the edge of the wall. Leave to dry.

4 Add more off-white to the original mix to lighten it a few shades. Using a clean sponge, apply this new shade as a second coat and allow to dry.

5 Add more off-white to the mix. Using a clean sponge, apply the new shade as a third coat and allow to dry. This shade will provide the dominant colour of the finished surface.

Stencils for Floor and Wall

In former times, stencilling was an inexpensive way to add beauty to a wall, floor or other surface and, indeed, for many people there were few alternatives. These days, such simple techniques are valued for their inherent charm and the individuality and character they give your home

Floor stencilling

A delicate border around the edge of a wooden floor is easy to apply. Use the design on this page, or choose a precut stencil at a craft shop. Stencilling will not adhere to wax or varnish; the technique is suitable for a sanded floor or one that has been painted with two or three coats of matt emulsion.

MATERIALS
- stencil design
- waxed stencil card or acetate
- trimming knife
- low-tack adhesive spray
- pencil, ruler and rubber
- stiff brush and small paintbrush
- emulsion paint
- tracing paper (if not using photocopier)
- masking tape
- polyurethane varnish

1 Enlarge the design below, or your chosen design, to the desired size on a photocopier (to enlarge without copying, see page 220).
2 Spray the back of the design with adhesive to prevent any movement during cutting, then place on the stencil material and cut out the shape using a sharp trimming knife. Take care when cutting around the narrow connecting pieces – such as the joins in the circle – as these hold the stencil together. If you cut through one of these bridges by accident, you can mend it with a tiny piece of masking tape.
3 Before you apply any paint, you must establish how to fit the stencil to the given space (see page 102). Measure the length of the stencil and measure your floor, then work out

A simple, classical border design discreetly defines the floor area while adding the perfect complementary touch to a stencilled wall border (see page 108).

how much space to leave between each repeat. For the neatest appearance, it is preferable to leave a space that allows the circle at the centre of the stencil to fall at a corner.
4 Mark the floor lightly with a pencil where each stencil will start. (See 'note', next column, for an alternative way to fit to the corners with the stencil.)

5 Tape the stencil in place and apply the paint with a stiff brush. Use very little paint and dab it on lightly with the tip of the brush: this is known as stippling. Lift the stencil carefully. Use the artist's brush to fill in the gaps in the circle. Leave to dry.
6 Repeat step 5 until you have completed the area you wish to stencil. Once it is finished and dry, erase any pencil marks.
7 Protect the floor with two or three coats of polyurethane varnish.

NOTE An alternative way of navigating around the corners of a room is to start at the centre of one wall and space the stencil at any interval you choose; when you need to fit to a corner shorten the leaf stem so that the circle will sit neatly in the corner. You do not need to cut the stencil to do this. Shorten the stem by covering several of the pairs of larger leaves (nearest to the circle) with masking tape – so that the tapering leaf pattern is maintained – and paint in only as many of the smaller leaves as are needed to fill the space.

You may find it easier to paint as many complete stencil designs as you can fit in before going back and filling in the gaps with the shortened stencils as described above.

Wall stencilling

These elegant Victorian wall-frieze designs add a formal period touch to a dining or living room. There are two to choose from; the one below is easier for beginners. For such intricate designs, it is best to use acetate for the stencil.

MATERIALS

- acetate (from art supply shops)
- stencil design
- pencil and rubber
- trimming knife
- low-tack adhesive spray
- stiff brush
- emulsion paint
- tracing paper (if not using photocopier)

1 Choose a design or image you like, or use one of the designs shown here. Photocopy and enlarge to the desired size (to enlarge without photocopying, see page 220). To make the stencil big enough, you may need to enlarge onto two pieces of paper and then join them together.

2 Before you start making the stencil, it is important to work out how the design will fit around the room, to accommodate corners and doors. To do this, take the photocopy of the design and start by placing it on an open area of wall that will take the whole design. Lightly mark on the wall where each repeat of the design will start. If the design does not fit exactly to a corner, place the paper at the end of the last complete design, fold it around the corner and then mark where it finishes.

3 To make the stencil, spray the back of the photocopy with adhesive and place it on the acetate. This will prevent the photocopy from moving while you are cutting. Using a trimming knife, cut out the design. Take care not to slice through the narrow connecting pieces that hold the stencil together – but if you do you can mend the 'bridges' with small strips of masking tape.

Achieve a subtle effect by milk-washing the stencilled wall (see 'For Stencilling Walls', right). Or leave the stencil unadorned, as pictured on page 107.

4 Spray the back of the stencil with adhesive to hold it against the wall. This will leave you with both hands free to paint.

5 Carefully place the stencil in position, adhesive side to the wall, and smooth it down.

6 Apply the paint to the stencil with the stiff brush, using a stippling technique (dabbing lightly, with very little paint). It's a good idea to practise this technique first, so you know exactly how much paint works best, and how firmly you need to dab the brush.

7 Lift the stencil carefully and allow the paint to dry. Then move to the next section.

8 Continue in this way around the wall, doing only complete stencils. If you come to a corner or door that will not allow for a complete stencil, leave it and come back to it when all the complete stencils are done.

9 Stencil the areas around corners and doors. You may be able to bend the stencil to fit, or you may have to cut it. Once finished, erase any pencil markings.

VARIATION To create a softer stencilled image with a faded look, allow the stencil to dry completely. Then, using a dry sea sponge, dab paint the same colour as the wall very lightly over the image. A light and a dark tone of the same colour for wall and stencilled border gives a pleasing coordinated effect, using either the light or dark for the wall.

FOR STENCILLING WALLS

If you wish to achieve an aged effect, use a milky wash over the entire wall as described in steps 4-5 of Fresco Effect (page 104) after the stencil is done.

When cutting out a stencil, always cut towards yourself. Turn the cutting board rather than the knife and make very clean cuts.

◆ Painted Floors ◆

*Floor coverings are among the most expensive items in home decoration. But
with a pot of paint and a little imagination you can transform a floor for a fraction of the usual cost,
and enjoy the satisfaction that comes from a job you can do and even design yourself*

Shell pattern

*In this project you paint a beautiful shell at the centre
of your floor and a quarter shell at each corner, using
a stencil for the outline of the shells. There is a
striped border around the outside in matching colours.
The finished piece shown in the picture opposite is
2.4 × 1.2m. It could be painted in the middle of a
floor, so it looks rather like a rug. Or you may choose
to adapt the design to cover a whole floor.*

MATERIALS

♦ materials to prepare surface,
  if needed (see box, p.112)
♦ matt or eggshell emulsion: yellow,
  blue, olive green
♦ paintbrush (6-8cm)
♦ stencil acetate or waxed stencil
  cardboard
♦ whiteboard marker (for acetate
  stencil) or tracing paper and carbon
  paper (for cardboard)
♦ trimming knife
♦ cutting board
♦ string, pencil
♦ 50mm and 25mm
  masking tape
♦ ruler, preferably steel
♦ 1-2cm stippling brush
♦ clean rags
♦ paint roller on a pole
♦ water-based floor varnish

1 Prepare your floor (or area on the floor that
you wish to cover) according to the type of
surface the floor is (see box, page 112).
2 Using the large brush, paint the design area
with yellow paint. Use two coats and allow
each coat about an hour to dry.

MASKING AND PAINTING THE BORDER
For this project, it is best to start with the
outside border and move on to the shells later.

1 Lay a strip of 50mm masking tape around
the outside edge of the floor. Inside that lay
another strip using the 25mm tape – make
sure the edges are butted neatly together with
no overlap or space between the two strips.
Inside that, neatly lay another strip, using a
masking tape that is 8mm wide (see 'For
a Novel Floor', facing page). Inside that, lay

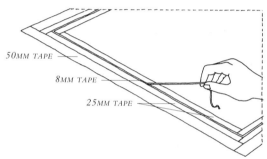

50MM TAPE
8MM TAPE
25MM TAPE

another strip of 25mm tape. See above.
2 Carefully remove the 8mm tape (above) and
then the 50mm tape. Smooth down the edges
of the two 25mm strips that are left (use a
screwdriver handle or similar). This will
prevent paint seeping under the tape.
3 Paint in green the floor exposed by the
removal of the 50mm strip. Paint in blue the
floor exposed by the removal of the 8mm strip.
Remove the outer strip of 25mm tape, but
leave the inside 25mm strip in place.

MAKING THE SHELL STENCILS
Templates for the two stencils used in this
project are drawn on the facing page.
1 Use a photocopier to enlarge both stencils
by 400 per cent (200 per cent, then 200 per
cent again; copy onto two A3 sheets and join
them together). To enlarge without
photocopying, see page 220.
2 Transfer the enlarged stencils (but not the
dotted lines) to acetate or cardboard (see page
221). Cut out with a trimming knife. The

diagram below shows the shell stencil ready to
use; note point 'A' marked at the right-angled
corner. Mark this point on your stencil.

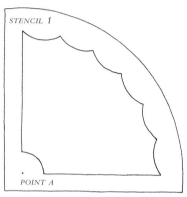

STENCIL 1

POINT A

PAINTING THE CORNER SHELLS
1 Lay stencil 1 in one corner of the design,
in line with the yellow border stripe. The edge
of the stencil (the edge of the part that will be
painted) should lie 25mm from the yellow
stripe. Point 'A' on the stencil will be 25mm
from each of the two edges of the yellow stripe
that meet in the corner.
2 Fix the stencil in place with small pieces
of masking tape.
3 Mask one segment by laying masking tape
from the indent of the first scallop across to
point 'A', as shown below.
4 To paint each segment, dip the stippling
brush in green paint, then rub the brush on a

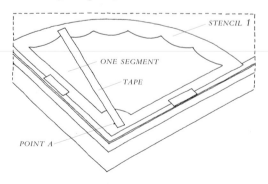

STENCIL 1
ONE SEGMENT
TAPE
POINT A

dry cloth so only a little paint is left. Apply the paint using a stippling technique. This involves lightly dabbing on the paint with the brush tip held at right angles to the floor. Start from the right side of the segment (the taped side, see below) and gradually move across to the left side of the segment, fading the paint to nothing before you reach the left side.

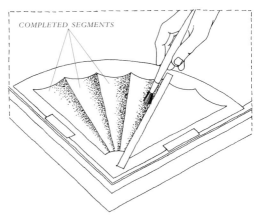

COMPLETED SEGMENTS

PRACTICAL IDEAS

FOR A NOVEL FLOOR

To make masking tape 8mm wide, lay a strip of 25mm tape on a cutting surface and lay a steel ruler along it, 8mm from one edge. Cut along the ruler line with a sharp trimming knife; remove excess tape.

There are many ways to adapt the basic shell pattern to your chosen room. You could, for instance, have more than one circular shell, or use the stencil to make half-circle shells. The border, too, can be modified to suit your own design. You can add stripes or vary the thickness and colour of the stripes.

If you learn to paint the stippling on one scalloped segment of the shell pattern you will have mastered an important step needed for this project. Take time to practise on a timber offcut before starting.

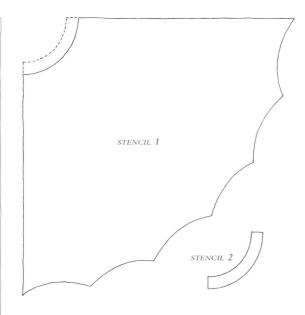

STENCIL 1

STENCIL 2

With masking tape and paint you can produce this exquisite shell pattern on your floor, either to imitate a rug, as pictured here, or to cover a whole floor.

5 You need to allow only a few minutes drying time before moving on to each new segment. Remove the tape and lay a new line of tape on the right side of the next segment. You don't need to lay tape on the left side of the new segment, as the stippling fades to nothing before you reach the left side. Stipple in the same way as for the first segment.

Repeat this process until you have painted each segment in the stencil (there is no need to tape the right side of the last one, as you can use the edge of the stencil).

6 Before removing the stencil, lightly trace in pencil along its curved scalloped edge. This will makes the final painting stage much easier. Remove the stencil.

7 Once the paint has dried, place stencil 2 at the base of the shell as shown below. (There is a dotted line in the corner of stencil 1 on the template on page 111; this line shows where stencil 2 lies in relation to stencil 1.) Stipple stencil 2 using green paint, applying it thickly so it stands out. Leave to dry.

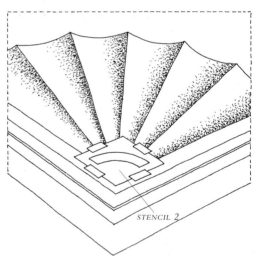

STENCIL 2

8 Repeat the whole process to paint a quarter shell in each of the other three corners.

PAINTING THE CENTRAL CIRCULAR SHELL

1 Find the central point of your design area. The easiest way to do this is to make two diagonal lines in string from corner to corner across the floor, securing the string in the corners with tape. Where the two strings cross is the centre; mark this in pencil.

2 Place stencil 1 so that the point 'A' lies on the centre point just marked. Paint the stencil in the same way as before. Paint the inside curve with stencil 2, as before.

3 Move stencil 1 around to the next quarter of the circle and repeat the process. Move it around, twice more, to complete the circle.

FINAL PAINTING AND VARNISHING

Once you have painted the border and shells, a final layer of blue paint is applied to complete the floor. Before doing this, you'll need to mask some of the stencilled areas. The painted border is already taped, because the 25mm tape stripe is still in place.

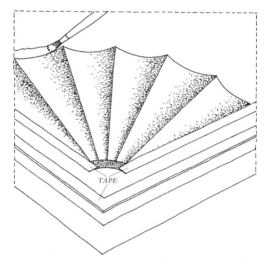

TAPE

1 Lay a strip of tape inside the straight edges of the corner shells (see above) in order to protect the stencilled area.

2 Using a large paintbrush, apply two coats of blue paint to all parts of the floor within the border that have not been stencilled (see photograph, page 111).

3 Paint the curved scallops of the shells using the smaller brush to paint carefully along the pencilled lines you drew earlier. Leave at least an hour's drying time between each coat of paint.

4 Remove all the tape and, when all the paint is completely dry, apply three coats of floor varnish to protect your work. The easiest method for applying the varnish is to use a roller on a pole. Refer to the manufacturer's instructions for drying times.

PREPARING THE SURFACE

PAINT CAN BE APPLIED to almost any surface, if a little time and effort are put into the preparation. Even if the surface of your floor has seen better days, don't despair.

Tiled floors and surfaces in bathrooms or kitchens can be repainted if a bonding medium is applied first. This medium will ensure that the paint adheres to the tiles. Make sure that you follow the manufacturer's instructions carefully when applying the bonding medium.

If you are painting over old vinyl, or wooden floorboards, sand well to obtain a slightly rough surface to which the first coat of paint will stick.

Before painting over old cork tiles, check for any patches where the original varnish has completely worn off; this is usually only a problem in the very frequently used areas of a floor. Seal these areas with a water-based sealer and let dry. Lightly sand the entire surface (a light sanding will not damage the sealer you have just applied) before applying a bonding medium.

For the very worst of floors you can paint the decorative pattern onto plywood or MDF (medium-density fibreboard) and lay this on the floor. If you intend to use this method, you will need to make sure the sub-floor is levelled first. There are a number of brands of leveller on the market which are poured as a slurry on the existing surface, then levelled and left to dry.

If you are painting over a new surface such as plywood, MDF, unsealed tiles or concrete, the surface should be first sealed with a water-based sealant.

Before painting any floor, thoroughly clean the surface of all dirt and grease using a gentle detergent. If the floor has been waxed over any length of time, you need to clean off the wax, especially in the corners. Proprietary products designed to remove wax build-up are available from supermarkets and DIY stores.

Further floor inspirations

Chequerboard floor *This traditional design is easy to draw and paint. Black and white would be a dramatic combination but it works well in most colours. Set out the border first by marking out even intervals around the perimeter and drawing lines at 45° to make the triangles. Then divide up the squares from the inner points of the triangles.*

Herringbone floor *This design is based on a common pattern for parquet floors. The different colours represent different timbers and can be varied as you wish – they do not necessarily have to be shades of brown. Mark out and paint the border first. Then mark even divisions along the longest sides and draw the connecting lines at 45°.*

Celestial floor *For this simple but cheerful design, mark and paint the border and, when dry, add the white dots and the framing lines. Add the background colour and, when it is dry, the stars and moons – stencils make this easy – placing them randomly if desired (add the shadows freehand with black paint).*

Abstract floor *This design relies for its effect on intersecting areas of colour. You can copy it or use it as inspiration for your own design. Mark out the circles using two pencils and a piece of string – tie a pencil to each end of the string, hold one steady at the centre point and describe the circle outline with the other.*

◆ Mosaic Effects ◆

*Mosaic tiling has been practised since early times, using a range of materials
such as glass, ceramics and coloured marble. With a home-made rubber stamp and a range
of coloured paints you can mimic the beauty of this ancient decorative art*

*A mosaic pattern will give a new lease of life to
a mirror or bathroom wall. You could also use the
pattern for picture frames, book covers or furniture.*

MATERIALS
- mirror with wide, flat
  timber frame
- sealer
- pieces of MDF or timber
- artist's acrylic paints: we used
  light cream for the frame; and
  grey, light blue, yellow and a
  light green for the stencil
- 70mm paintbrush
- 4 fine paintbrushes
- 3-5mm-thick, black foam
- double-sided sticky-tape
- scissors
- trimming knife
- pencil, ruler and rubber
- paint palette or old plate
- tape measure
- spirit level (optional)

1 Seal the mirror frame and let dry.
2 Paint the frame a light cream colour. Use
two coats and gently sand between coats.
3 To make the stamp, trace the pattern on
page 115 onto tracing paper, adapting it to fit
the width of your frame (ours was 10cm).
4 Cut a timber block a little larger than your
adapted pattern. Glue a smaller block onto one
side. This will create a handle that will make
the stamp easier to grip.
5 Cover the whole of the other side of the
block with the double-sided sticky tape. Cut

*The painted mosaic squares that decorate this bathroom
are applied with a home-made rubber stamp. The
colours are applied randomly, but the repetition of the
pattern gives a regularity to the randomness, for an
appealing effect. And it can be modified for any room.*

a piece of foam to the same size as the block and stick it onto the double-sided tape.

6 Make several lengths of double-sided sticky tape less sticky by pressing both sides against your clothing and peeling off a few times. Cover the whole surface of the foam with the tape, then stick the tracing paper with the mosaic design onto the foam.

7 Using the trimming knife, cut through the tracing paper and foam along the lines of the pattern. Peel away all of the short strips of foam that do not form part of the mosaic pattern. (Use the end of a screwdriver to help lift the unwanted bits of foam from the tape.) The stamp is now ready to use.

8 Using a pencil, lightly mark on the mirror frame where you will apply the stamp. Organise the design so that it covers the entire frame in an even pattern of tiles.

9 Squeeze a little of each of the grey, blue, yellow and green paints (or the colours of your choice) onto a palette. Using the fine brushes, one for each colour, paint the foam squares on the stamp pad in a varied pattern.

10 Gently stamp the frame carefully following your pencil guidelines. Reapply the paints to the stamp for each stamping to achieve an even weight, applying only a small amount of paint each time you stamp. Repeat until you have covered the entire front face of the frame.

11 When the paint is dry, erase all pencil marks from the mirror frame with a rubber.

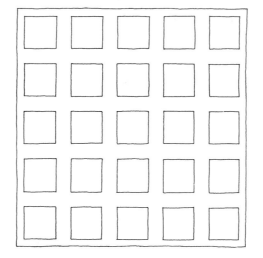

VARIATION This technique can be used on any smooth-surfaced wall. Use a spirit level and a pencil to mark a horizontal line where the pattern is to go and follow steps 9-11. Give the room a coordinated look by choosing the same colours as those you have used on the mirror.

In the example opposite, a narrow border has been worked around the bathroom but a wider border can also be effective. In a small bathroom, a good effect is achieved if you stamp a border about 90cm from the floor. This imitates the traditional dado. You could also use the mosaic print as a special trim around the bath.

In any room the mosaic pattern could be used to imitate a skirting board, or as a frame around a feature wall. In the hallway, try working a narrow border at dado rail height (90cm) in colours that harmonise with the rooms opening off the hall; this will help to unify the hall with the rooms.

You could extend the design to fill the space below dado height down to the floor – but this will take time and patience. For an even more convincing dado effect, choose one set of colours for the 'rail' band, and a different set for the area below it. This is a useful way of disguising the 'handprint zone' in a house where there are young children.

INSPIRING IDEAS

DESIGNING WITH MOSAICS

Choose colours for the stamp that will coordinate with the fabrics or wall colours that are used in the room you are decorating.

You can achieve interesting effects with only one or two colours, or by applying the colours in a definite design that will repeat. Try adapting the Greek key pattern given on page 136, for instance.

Modify the stamp design to incorporate a motif such as a fleur-de-lis, or one already in your home.

STAMPING WITH A MOSAIC BLOCK

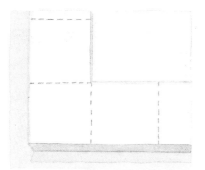

1 *Lightly mark the position of each stamp around the mirror frame. Be as accurate as possible. It's easier to do the corners first. Some areas may require only a part of the stamp, so allow for this in the spacing.*

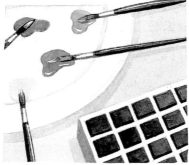

2 *Squeeze blobs of paint onto the palette or plate far enough apart to prevent mixing. Use a fresh brush for each colour. Ensure even application by mixing each colour to the same texture and consistency.*

3 *Paint the foam squares of the pad in a varied pattern. When reapplying paint during the stamping process, always paint each square with the same colour as in the previous application.*

4 *Press the stamp gently on the position you have marked on the frame. Repeat until you have covered the entire area. For best results, apply a fresh coat of paint to the stamp for each stamping.*

◆ A Wallpaper Border ◆

*Use our design, or create your own, for a unique wall border that will
give any room a stamp of individuality. Make the photocopies on a coloured paper that
matches or contrasts with the walls. Here, we simply stayed with white*

Wallpaper border

*This border pattern was photocopied onto A3 paper.
Measure your wall length to determine the number
of pattern repeats and make plenty of spare copies.*

MATERIALS

- pattern to photocopy
  (see facing page)
- wallpaper paste
- trimming knife
- sponge
- 2 paintbrushes
- ruler
- clear water–based satin varnish

1 Enlarge and photocopy the repeated pattern
opposite enough times to more than cover
the work area. It is a good idea to photocopy
about a third more than you think you will
need so that if the paper wrinkles or tears as
you work you have enough spare sheets to
finish the job. Trim away the white margins.
2 Prepare the wall as specified on the packet
of wallpaper paste.
3 Using a clean brush, paint a thin coat of
wallpaper paste on the first section of wall to
be covered with the border. Position one edge
of the first repeat and gradually roll it onto
the wall, smoothing down with the sponge
to remove air bubbles as you go. Repeat,
carefully matching the edges of the second
repeat with the first; take your time. If the
paper crinkles or tears, replace it. Continue
until you have finished the border.
4 When all paste and paper is dry, paint the
border with a coat of water–based varnish (oil-
based varnish will make the photocopies run).

*Dragonflies hover above flowers in this elegant wall
border. The theme is repeated on the table and box,
giving an attractive coordinated look.*

Decorated table

Pick up the wall theme with a table decorated using a detail from the wall border.

MATERIALS
- paint stripper
- sandpaper
- white silk-finish emulsion
- 3 paintbrushes
- patterns to photocopy
  (see top and bottom of page)
- wallpaper paste
- trimming knife
- sponge
- masking tape
- ruler
- scissors
- clear water-based satin varnish

PREPARING THE TABLE

1 If necessary, strip the table with paint stripper and sand it. If the paint is sound, a simple sanding will suffice.

2 Paint the legs and lower shelf with the white paint. Our table was already white so one coat was sufficient, but a darker colour may require another coat.

APPLYING BORDERS

1 Make some preliminary photocopies of the floral border patterns above or other patterns you wish to use, working out the approximate enlargement or reduction to fit the areas. Experiment with placement using small pieces of masking tape to hold the photocopies in place. When you are satisfied, estimate how many copies you will need to cover the intended area – increase this number by a third to allow for miscalculations and mistakes while cutting and pasting.

2 Prepare wallpaper paste according to the manufacturer's instructions – for our table, 500ml of water was plenty for the mixing.

3 Using a ruler and trimming knife, carefully cut out the narrow border strips from the photocopied pages. Trim the ends so that each strip, when aligned with the next, matches.

4 Using a clean brush, paint a thin coat of wallpaper paste on the first area to be covered with a border. Carefully position the first strip, smoothing down with the sponge to remove any lumps of paste or air bubbles.

5 Repeat, carefully matching the edges of each strip. Take your time, and if a strip tears or crinkles, replace it with a new one.

COVERING THE LOWER SHELF

The surface of the lower shelf of our table was fairly uneven due to flaking paint. Sanding removed any possibility of further flaking, but because of the thickness of paint layers a perfectly smooth finish was not possible.

While we could have stripped this surface, as we did the table top, we decided instead to camouflage the unevenness, and at the same time give it a distinctive papier-mâché texture, using torn pieces of paper.

1 Tear up plain photocopy paper into pieces approximately 10cm square. Organise the torn paper into three piles: pieces with one straight edge and three torn; pieces with one corner of straight edges and one corner torn; and pieces with all edges torn.

2 Using a clean brush, paint a thin coat of wallpaper paste on one corner of the shelf. Cover the corner using a piece of paper with a straight-edged corner. Align the straight edges to the corner and smooth down with the sponge. Repeat for the other corners. Next cover the straight edges of the shelf using the pieces of paper with one straight edge, smoothing down with the sponge as you go. Finally, cover the centre of the shelf using the pieces of paper with all edges torn. Allow all paste and paper to dry.

3 Tear out the photocopied images that are to go on the shelf (we used dragonflies from the pattern below). The torn edges will blend with the background and each other. Paste on the images and smooth with the sponge.

4 When the table is completely dry, apply a coat of water-based varnish (oil-based varnish will make the photocopies run).

Brighten with Paint

You can give new life to old furniture with a painted finish. The special effect of sponge painting is easy to achieve, even for a beginner, while simple stencils, applied over a painted finish, can customise a piece for a particular person

Sponged chest

In this sponging process we used two shades of the same colour, but you can easily use three or four. Experiment on a piece of scrap board before you begin. The possibilities are almost limitless, so keep track of the steps you take and the paints you use at each part of the process.

MATERIALS

- sandpaper
- tack rag (see p.102)
- emulsion paint in two or more shades
- paintbrush
- large and small natural sea sponges
- bucket of water
- paper plates
- rubber gloves
- clear polyurethane varnish

1 Remove the drawer knobs. Sand smooth the surfaces of the chest, including any wooden knobs, to prepare it for the new paint. Check inside the drawers – you may want to freshen them up, too. If so, sand the drawer interiors smooth before painting.

2 Wipe all the sanded surfaces clean with the tack rag. Paint the drawer interiors if desired. Leave to dry completely before proceeding to the next step.

3 Paint the exterior of the chest with the lighter of your chosen colours. Let dry. Repeat with a second, and possibly a third, coat to achieve an even colour.

4 Put on the rubber gloves for the sponging process. Soak the sponges in the water and squeeze them out so they are just damp.

5 Dip the bottom of the sponge lightly into the darker paint and blot it around on a paper plate a couple of times. This will help to disperse the paint through the sponge and remove any excess.

6 Working randomly over each surface, dab the sponge onto the furniture with a light rolling motion. It is important to work randomly because the first dabs will release more paint than subsequent ones – the less paint on the sponge the lighter the imprint.

7 Repeat steps 5 and 6 until the piece is completely covered. Use the smaller sponge in hard-to-reach areas and on small details, such as the knobs.

8 Once the paint has dried completely, apply several coats of polyurethane varnish, following the manufacturer's instructions.

Rocking chair

Personalise the top rail of a rocking chair (pictured overleaf) with a child's name where 'my chair' is seen. Letters, numbers and punctuation marks spill out over the rocker in several bright colours to make a cheerful design.

MATERIALS

- sandpaper
- tack rag (see p.102)
- 1 litre emulsion paint in a colour of your choice
- paintbrush
- artist's acrylic paints in several colours
- small stencil brushes
- palette or old plate
- paper towels
- precut stencils of letters, numbers and punctuation marks (3-5cm high)
- scissors
- masking tape
- clear polyurethane varnish

SUBSTITUTE FOR A NATURAL SPONGE

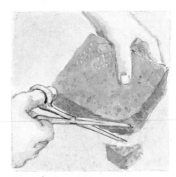

1 *If you can't find natural sponges to use in your painting, you can adapt a synthetic sponge. First cut off any sharp corners with a pair of scissors.*

2 *Cut out rounded recesses from the angular edges, then make additional irregular cuts across the flat surface. You are aiming for soft rounded edges.*

3 *Apply paint sparingly to the sponge, and use it as you would a natural sponge – dabbing and rolling the surface around in various directions.*

This new unpainted chest was transformed into a pretty bedroom unit using two tones of green paint. The technique would be just as effective on a tired old chest of drawers – and the choice of colours is yours.

1 Sand the surfaces of the chair smooth to prepare it for the new paint. Wipe all the sanded surfaces clean with the tack rag.
2 Paint the chair yellow, or the colour of your choice. Let it dry. Repeat with a second and even a third coat if necessary.
3 Cut the large stencil into smaller units (see illustration, right, and box, below right).

4 To stencil, work with one paint colour at a time and a dry brush. Apply a small amount of paint to the palette and dab the brush tip in it. Swirl the brush in a circular motion lightly over a paper towel to disperse the paint evenly.
5 Position the selected letter, number, or punctuation stencil on the rocking chair and use the same circular motion to stencil in the

colour. Use masking tape to fix the stencil flush with the surface while stencilling, so that paint doesn't seep under the stencil's edges. You may also find it helpful to block off adjacent letters with tape before stencilling the selected one.
6 Repeat steps 4 and 5 – changing to a clean, dry brush when you switch stencilling colours – until you achieve your desired effect.
7 When the stencilling is finished and the paint is completely dry, finish the rocking chair with several coats of polyurethane varnish, following the manufacturer's directions.

PRACTICAL IDEAS

WORKING WITH PRECUT STENCILS

A ready-made stencil can be cumbersome to work with, particularly in a scattered arrangement, such as this rocking chair. You'll find it awkward placing individual letters and numbers on a large sheet – especially around the posts and rails.

An easy solution is to cut the stencil into smaller, more flexible units with four to six letters or numbers on each.

Use masking tape around the edges of these mini-stencils to provide a buffer for the stencil brush. Since the tape is pliable, it allows the mini-stencil to be tucked in between slats for painting and gives you equal access to all the letters, numbers and punctuation marks.

A brightly painted rocking chair, stencilled with a youngster's name, makes an ideal present for a birthday or other special occasion.

A plain pine bedside table becomes something special when paint is applied in an unconventional fashion. This one uses dragging, stippling and stencilling.

Bedside table

An unfinished pine bedside table or cabinet can be turned into a distinctive piece of furniture with the addition of a simple blue glaze in two different finishes, and contrasting details in pink and white.

MATERIALS

- fine sandpaper
- water-based sealer
- paintbrushes
- white matt emulsion
- tack rag (see p.102)
- blue and pink glazes made by mixing 1 part matt emulsion with 1 part water or 1 part proprietary emulsion glaze
- small stippling brush
- narrow masking tape
- stencil acetate or cardboard
- marker pen or carbon paper
- trimming knife, ruler
- furniture wax, or water-based satin-finish varnish

1 Rub down the table with sandpaper, then seal with water-based sealer.

2 When dry, sand the table again to flatten the grain raised by the sealer.

3 Paint the table with two coats of white paint. Sand each coat when dry and wipe with the tack rag to remove any dust.

4 Lay a strip of masking tape around the top of the table 3-4cm in from the edge. If your table has a drawer and door, as pictured here, repeat the border on these.

5 Apply the blue glaze to the areas inside the tape and, while it is still wet, drag a small bristle brush through the glaze. This 'dragging' creates an attractive streaked effect in the glaze. Leave to dry, then remove the tape.

6 Lay a strip of tape on the dragged area so that the outside edge of the tape lies on the outside edge of the area. Lay a very narrow strip of tape (3mm wide) about 6mm outside

SURFACE EFFECTS

Glazing techniques can be varied to suit your taste. For the cabinet pictured, we used dragging for the main body of each surface, with stippling for the borders. These techniques could be reversed.

The exact effect you achieve will vary according to the pressure you apply to the brush, and the type of brush you use. If you do not have the brush specified for the job, experiment with what you have at hand. To drag paint, for example, try using steel wool or a fine-toothed comb.

Try extending the coordinated theme of the table and lamp by stippling a pale blue glaze on the walls.

this tape (see step 3, below). To make this narrow tape, lay a strip of masking tape on a cutting surface and place a ruler over the tape 3mm from one edge. Cut along the ruler edge with a trimming knife and remove excess tape.
7 Apply a very small amount of blue glaze to the stippling brush and dab the brush tip lightly onto the area outside the first tape to the edge of the table. Leave to dry and remove both strips of tape.
8 Isolate the uncovered 3mm border with two parallel strips of masking tape. Apply pink glaze with the stippling brush between the strips

of tape. Leave to dry. Remove the tape; there will be a band of blue stippling between the pink border and the edge of the dragged area (see step 4 on previous page).
9 Use the stippling brush to apply stencils in white on the areas of dragged glaze. We used a bow stencil for the top of the cabinet and door, and a star stencil for the drawer and the door. To make the stencils, enlarge the designs given on previous page and below to the desired size with a photocopier (to enlarge without a photocopier, see page 220). Transfer the designs to acetate or cardboard (see page 221) and cut out.
10 When dry, apply two coats wax or varnish.

Stencilled shade

You can transform a bedside lamp simply by using a stencil and some paint. Coordinate your lamp with the bedside chest by choosing the same motif to decorate both. The stars used on the chest work very well on a lampshade (see illustration page 101).

MATERIALS
- lamp base
- cream or white lampshade
- fine sandpaper
- tack rag (see p.102)
- emulsion paint in cream or white, and blue (or the colour of your choice)
- clear water-based varnish
- stencil
- paintbrush
- masking tape

1 Lightly rub down the lamp base with sandpaper, and wipe with a tack rag.
2 Paint the base with two coats of cream or white paint, sanding between coats.
3 When the base is dry, paint with one or two coats of varnish.
4 Fix the star stencil firmly against the lampshade using the masking tape.
5 Using a small amount of the coloured paint on a stiff brush, dab lightly to stencil the stars onto the shade. For a varied pattern, apply in a random fashion, filling in parts of the stencil only. Move the stencil when the paint is dry.

APPLYING GLAZES AND STENCILS

1 *Prepare all surfaces by painting white and sanding. Apply a strip of masking tape right around the table top, about 3-4cm in from the edge. Apply tape to sides, door and drawer in the same way.*

2 *On each table surface, apply blue glaze to the area inside the tape, and immediately drag a small bristle brush through the wet glaze to create a streaked effect. Leave to dry, then remove the masking tape.*

3 *Lay tape within the outside edge of dragged area. About 6mm outside this, lay a 3mm strip (cut down wider tape to this width). Stipple blue glaze outside the first tape. Let dry; remove all tape.*

4 *Lay two parallel strips of tape around the 3mm strip; paint with pink glaze using stippling brush; remove tape. Stipple stencils in white onto the dragged areas as desired. Let dry. Apply wax or varnish.*

◆ Painted Glass Bottles ◆

*Use glass paints to imitate the beautiful translucent qualities of traditional
stained glass. Here, a trio of plain glass bottles are given a new lease of life with striking floral
motifs outlined in gold and flooded with vibrant shades of colour*

Daisy bottles

*The large and small glass bottles have framed
daisy flowers to complement each other. The
medium-sized bottle is encircled with a band of
scattered flowers which is edged with rows of golden
squares and a random sponged effect.*

MATERIALS

- 3 clear or recycled glass bottles
- masking tape
- spirit-based glass paints in
  green, deep yellow,
  bright pink and pale pink
- old plate
- natural sponge
- gold outliner
- sharp HB pencil
- fine paintbrush
- tracing paper
- carbon paper
- kitchen paper towels

SPONGING THE PAINT

1 To create level edges on the sponged band,
fill the bottle with water, 4cm deep. Apply
masking tape around the bottle just above the
water level. Add more water until it is 11cm
deep, then apply another length of tape just
below the water level. Discard the water.

2 Working in a well-ventilated room, pour a
small amount of green paint onto an old plate.
Dip the natural sponge into the paint and dab
it lightly and randomly on the bottle, above
and below the masking tape. Leave the paint
to dry overnight, then peel off the tape.

3 Rest the bottle on a few sheets of kitchen
paper towel to keep it steady. With the
outliner, draw a row of 1.2cm squares along
the edges of the sponged bands. Work on
the upper surface and leave the paint to dry
completely before rotating the bottle.

TRANSFERRING THE DESIGNS

1 Enlarge or reduce the motif outlines to fit
the bottles using the directions on page 220.

2 Trace the motifs and position them against
the bottles. Place the large framed flower in
the centre of one bottle, the small framed
daisies vertically on another and the individual
flowers dotted between the outlined squares.

3 Place a piece of carbon paper, ink side
against the glass, under the outlines and secure
with tape (see step 1, below). Draw over the
outlines in pencil to transfer the designs, then
remove the outlines and carbon paper.

OUTLINING AND PAINTING

1 Before applying outliner or paint, rest the
bottle face up on a few sheets of kitchen paper
towel to prevent it from rolling. Experiment
with the outliner on a scrap of paper.

2 Hold the outliner almost vertically and
squeeze the tube gently as you draw it along
the transferred design. When complete, set the
bottle aside to dry. Wipe the nozzle of the
tube on a piece of kitchen paper towel and
remember to replace the lid immediately
to prevent the outliner from drying out.

*Transfer this large framed flower to tracing paper
in order to make a template for the large design.*

GLASS PAINTING

1 *Position the motif outline on
the glass bottle and place a small piece
of carbon paper, ink side down,
underneath. Secure with tape. Slowly
draw around the outline using a sharp
pencil to transfer the image.*

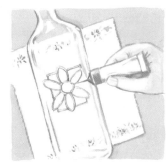

2 *Outliner paste gives a raised line
which creates a reservoir to contain the
glass paint. Draw the outliner tube
along the transferred line, squeezing
it gently. Wipe away mistakes with
kitchen paper towel before they dry.*

3 *Working in a well-ventilated room,
apply a pool of glass paint within each
outlined area. Brush the paint to the
edges for an even coverage. Always
finish painting one section before
moving on to the next.*

TO ACHIEVE PERFECT WORK

Before painting, make sure that the glass is grease-free. Any grease or dirt can be removed by wiping the glass with a soft cloth moistened with a small amount of methylated spirits.

When the outliner is dry, which will take about 12 hours, check the accuracy of the lines, bearing in mind that once painted the eye is drawn to the coloured areas rather than the outliner. However, for a professional finish, cut away any blobs of outliner along the edge of the lines using a trimming knife. Do not neaten the lines too much, or they will look as if they have been machine drawn, and will loose their hand-crafted appeal.

Air bubbles occasionally appear when you are applying glass paint. Wait for a few minutes before bursting them with the tip of a pin. A pin can also be used to remove any tiny pieces of fluff that may have landed in the wet paint.

Do not apply a second coat of paint or an additional line of colour once the original layer has dried. This will create a noticeable ridge and may cause an unsightly crackled effect. If the paint has not flooded to the edge of the motif, add more outliner to cover the unworked area.

Create a matching set of colourful bottles by decorating the glassware with a coordinating floral theme. Use recycled or hand-blown glass for a green tinge, or sponge paint over clear glass.

3 Generously apply deep yellow paint within the outlined areas of the flower centres, the squares and the rectangle frames. Use a fine paintbrush to push the paint into the corners and distribute it evenly over the surface of the glass. Occasionally hold the bottle up to the light to check that the paint is not patchy and that it has reached the edges of the outliner. Paint the leaves green.

4 To shade the petals, apply bright pink paint near the flower centres and pale pink paint at the tips. Blend the shades together where they meet in the middle using the tip of the brush. When painting the sponged bottle, work on the upper surface and allow the paint to dry overnight before rotating the glass and continuing. This will prevent the paint from running and resulting in a streaked effect.

5 Clean the brush well in white spirit when changing colours, to avoid contamination.
6 When the paint has dried, randomly dot the outliner in the centre of the large flower, and in between the flowers on the sponged bottle. Allow each bottle to dry for at least 24 hours.
7 Do not clean the bottles for a couple of weeks. After this time they may be washed gently in warm, soapy water.

Transfer these floral images to tracing paper to use as templates for outlining the designs on the small bottles. Enlarge or reduce the images to fit your glassware.

Fuchsia Stained Glass

Achieve the look of leaded-light windows by mixing artist's oil paints into varnish and painting onto plain glass. No glass-cutting or piecing together with lead is involved. You can draw the flowers freehand or trace the design and then paint it on the glass

The fuchsias used to decorate these panels should droop gracefully as they do in the garden. If you have a favourite variety, copy its colouring.

MATERIALS

- design to enlarge
  (see left, or choose your own)
- stencil acetate
- 2 pieces picture glass,
  cut to size of door panels
- glass-bonding medium
- black gloss paint
- artist's oils in transparent colours:
  (we used crimson, prussian blue,
  violet, brown madder, gold oxide)
- marker pen
- fine sandpaper
- white spirit or turpentine
- solvent-based gloss varnish
- aluminium foil or shallow lid
- no. 3 artist's paintbrush
- small square-tip bristle brush

1 Enlarge your selected design on a photocopier until it is the right size for the glass panels you want to decorate (to enlarge without a photocopier, see page 220).

2 Using the marker pen, trace the enlarged design onto acetate. This project requires you to paint two pieces of glass, each the mirror image of the other, so write the word 'front' on the front of the acetate to avoid confusion when reversing the image.

3 Lightly sandpaper around all edges of the glass, then thoroughly clean front and back.

4 Apply bonding medium to the back of the glass, following the maker's instructions. (The design is painted on the *back* of the glass.)

5 Lightly tape the design to the *front* of the glass, with the word 'front' on the acetate reading the correct way. Turn the glass over and work on the back.

6 Using the artist's brush, well-loaded with slightly thinned black gloss, paint in all the 'lead' lines. Allow to dry overnight before applying the oil colours.

7 To achieve the density of colour desired, squeeze a small amount of oil colour onto a piece of aluminium foil or a shallow lid then dilute with gloss varnish. You will not need more than 3 teaspoonfuls of varnish in all.

8 If you wish to include fine details, such as delicate leaf veins, they must be painted on

PAINTING THE GLASS

1 *Trace the design onto acetate and write 'front' on the front of the acetate. Tape to the front of the glass.*

2 *On the back of the glass (coated with bonding medium) draw in the outline (the 'lead' lines) with enamel.*

3 *Stipple in the first colour to imitate the thick-and-thin look of textured glass. Repeat for the other colours.*

first and allowed to dry before being over-painted with the main colour.

9 Using the square-tip brush, paint in all the areas of the first colour using a stippling technique (see page 101) to create the thick-and-thin look of textured glass. Where adjacent areas are the same colour, you can simply paint over the black lead lines.

10 Clean the brush in turpentine or white spirit, squeeze it as dry as possible on a paper towel and continue with the next colour. You can complete the whole panel in one session, butting up the colours to within a fine line of each other. To avoid smudging the wet paint, start in the centre and work outwards.

11 Leave to dry for at least 48 hours then clean off the bonding medium from the unpainted areas with a cloth dampened in water and detergent.

12 Repeat steps 4–11 for the second panel. In order to create a mirror-image, tape the design to the front of the prepared panel with the word 'front' on the acetate appearing in reverse. Turn over and paint.

13 To install, lay the glass over the existing door panel with the painted surface innermost. Secure with timber beading. Paint the beading to match either the door or the black lead lines.

The attractive painted panels in this door are fitted over the original plain glass, transforming a quite ordinary front door into a handsome feature.

Tassel Finishes

*If you wish to add colour and interest in a living room or bedroom, you can achieve
an attractive effect by making tassels to decorate cushions or bolsters. Tassels can also be
used as pulls for blinds, on curtain tiebacks and on lampshades*

Simple tassel

*Tassels can be made with many different threads.
These instructions are for those on the yellow
cushion pictured here. They are 8cm long.*

MATERIALS

- piece heavy cardboard,
  12 × 8cm
- 1 ball DMC Cebelia crochet
  cotton no. 5, ecru
- large-eyed tapestry needle
- scissors

Follow the basic method given on page 128,
using these specifications: in step 1, wind
cotton 150 times around the 8cm width
of cardboard. In step 2, use a 50cm length
of cotton for the tie at the top. In step 3, use
a 1 metre length of cotton to wrap the neck
about 2cm from the top of the tassel.

Four tassels can be made on one piece of
cardboard. Instead of cutting the thread when
the first tassel has been wound, take the thread
about 2cm farther along the card and wind
the next tassel and so on. Snip the connecting
threads before removing tassels from cardboard.

*A selection of elegant soft furnishings: (1) cushion
with simple tassels, (2) curtain tieback, (3) flanged
cushion with family tassel, (4) bolster with simple
tassel, (5) family tassel on pot, (6) mitred cushion
with piping and simple tassels, (7) piped cushion
with twisted cord and simple tassel.*

Family tassel

A family tassel, made up of a number of separate uncut tassels, looks wonderful, especially when, as pictured on the flowerpot on page 127, the impact comes from massing several small tassels (these ones are 4.5cm long) in a combination of colours.

MATERIALS
- piece of heavy cardboard, 12 × 4.5cm
- 1 ball red DMC Cebelia crochet cotton no. 10
- 1 ball coffee DMC Cebelia crochet cotton no. 10
- 2 skeins gold DMC cotton Perle no. 5
- 2 skeins ecru DMC cotton Perle no. 5
- large-eyed tapestry needle

Make four tassels in each colour, following steps 1 to 3 of the step-by-step method illustrated below. Each set of four tassels can be made together, as described in the instructions for the Simple Tassel on page 127.

In step 1, wind the yarn around the cardboard 80 times. In step 2, cut two 1m lengths of yarn for the tie at the top of each tassel. In step 3, cut a 50cm length of yarn for wrapping the neck of each tassel 1cm from its top. Do not cut the loops as specified in step 4;

simply fan them out a little. Knot the four ties in each colour together about 4–6cm above the top of the tassels, staggering the distance of each tassel from the knot. Then knot the four sets of ties together about 2–3cm above the first knots. Loop all the threads back on themselves and knot again.

Flanged cushion

A flange is a flat border around a cushion. This elegant cushion (page 127) is made from two coordinating fabrics, the outer one featuring a beautiful floral border for the flange. The finished size of the cushion is 50cm square. A 1cm seam allowance is used unless otherwise specified.

MATERIALS
- 60 × 115cm of fabric A
- 30 × 115cm of fabric B
- 43cm zip
- 45cm cushion pad

1 To make the front of the cushion, cut a 28cm square from fabric A. From fabric B, cut four strips 52 × 15cm.

2 With the right sides of the fabric together and the raw edges even, pin the two short ends of two strips of fabric B together and then

stitch them diagonally so as to form a mitred corner (see instructions for stitching mitred corners on page 222), leaving the first centimetre on the inner corner unstitched.

3 Repeat this process for the other two strips of fabric, then stitch the strips together to form a mitred square. Trim any fabric excess at the corners. Press the seam allowance on the inner edge to the wrong side.

4 Centring the border square on top of the inner fabric square, pin and then topstitch the two pieces together close to the fabric edge.

5 To make the back of the cushion, cut two pieces, one measuring 52 × 42cm and one 52 × 15cm, from fabric A.

6 With the right sides of the fabric together and using a 2.5cm seam, pin and then stitch the long edges of the two pieces together for a distance of 4cm at each end, leaving an opening in the centre. Pin and then stitch the zipper into the opening.

7 With the right sides of the fabric together and the zipper open, stitch the front and back pieces of the cushion together. Turn the cover right side out and then stitch a row of machining around all four sides of the cushion, 3cm from the outside edge, so as to form the flange.

8 Fit the cushion pad inside the cover.

9 Decorate, if desired, with a small family tassel, as pictured on page 127.

BASIC METHOD FOR TASSEL-MAKING

1 *Make a pattern for tassel by cutting cardboard desired width. Hold end of thread at edge of card and wind around card until tassel is desired thickness, or wind for the number of times specified in project instructions. Cut cotton from the ball.*

2 *To tie tassel, thread a length of cotton into a tapestry needle; pass needle and thread under the wound yarn. Unthread needle, pull thread to the top of the tassel and knot securely. You can use twisted cord (see page 129) to tie tassel instead of thread.*

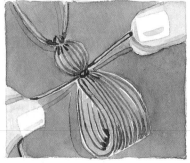

3 *Remove tassel from cardboard. Use length of thread to tie the neck with a knot. Take thread ends to opposite side and knot again. Wind half tie around neck until you near the end, then thread into needle and take behind neck and into skirt. Repeat with other half.*

4 *Cut loops at the bottom of tassel and trim to an even length. To smooth out kinks in the thread and plump up the skirt, use tongs to hold tassel over the spout of a steaming kettle for about 30 seconds. For a neat finish, use the needle to comb out the skirt.*

Bolster

The elongated shape of a bolster adds interest to a group of standard cushions. Bolsters are easier to make than they look and suit either living room or bedroom decor. This bolster is 50cm long and 55cm in circumference.

MATERIALS

♦ 70 × 60cm piece fabric
♦ 1.2m medium piping cord
♦ 2m cord for bolster ends
♦ 50cm length bolster
  cushion pad

1 Cut piping cord into two equal lengths.
2 On the right side of the fabric, measure 14cm in from each long edge. Pin then stitch a seam on each of these lines using the zipper foot, enclosing the piping cord (see below).

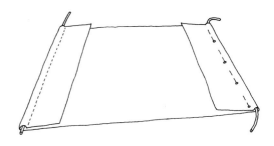

3 With right sides facing and using a 2.5cm seam, pin then stitch the two short edges together (see below).

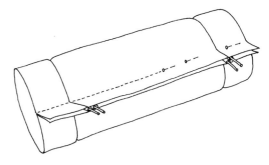

4 To make the casing for the drawstring cord at each end of the bolster, press a 1cm hem to the wrong side. Press a further hem, 4cm wide; pin and stitch close to the 1cm hem edge, leaving the last 2cm unstitched. Turn to right side and press.

TO MAKE A TWISTED CORD

A TWISTED CORD is the perfect way to finish either a single tassel or a family tassel. Made in the same colour and yarn as the tassel itself, or in contrasting colours and textures, it can be used simply to attach the tassel to a cushion or some other object, or it can become part of the decorative trim.

Cut the threads for the cord so that they are about three times the length that the finished cord is required to be. Knot all the threads together at each end. Attach one knotted end to a firm anchor, such as a cup hook or a door handle. Push a pencil between the threads at the other end. Keeping the threads taut, pinch them alongside the pencil with one hand while twisting the pencil round and round with the other. Keep twisting the pencil until the threads are very tightly wound.

Remove the pencil, then, keeping the threads taut, hold the halfway point in one hand and bring the two knotted ends together. Release the halfway point and the threads will twist back on themselves. Work along the cord with your fingers in small sections to tighten the twist as necessary and to keep the cord smooth. Knot the ends together.

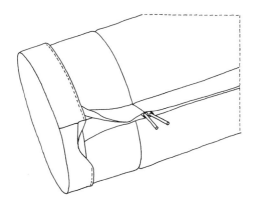

5 Cut cord in half and thread through the casing at each end. Draw up one end, tie cord in a bow, then place pad inside cover. Draw up the other end and tie cord to match.
6 Attach tassels to each end of the bolster.

Piped cushion

Piping gives a tailored finish to a simple cushion, and tassels complete the look. We give instructions here for a cushion made using two coordinating fabrics, but the look is equally attractive if a single fabric is used. The finished size of the cushion is 40cm square. A 1cm seam allowance is used unless otherwise specified.

MATERIALS

♦ 50 × 115cm fabric A
♦ 30 × 115cm fabric B
♦ 1.6m medium piping cord
♦ glue or thread for cord ends
♦ 30cm zip
♦ 40cm cushion pad

1 To make the cushion front, cut a 22cm square from fabric A. Then, from fabric B, cut four strips 42 × 11cm.
2 With the right sides together and the raw edges even, pin then stitch each strip of fabric B to the edges of the square of fabric A, leaving the final centimetre of each end unstitched. Stitch the corners together so as to form mitred corners (see page 222). Trim away excess fabric.
3 To make the piping covering, cut two strips, 66 × 4cm, from fabric A. Join them to form a length 130 × 4cm. Press in half lengthways, wrong sides together. With the cord placed inside the fabric, and using the zipper foot on the sewing machine, stitch through the fabric close to the cord.
4 With the zipper foot, and with right sides together and raw edges even, stitch the piping along the seamline of the cushion front. Glue or sew the ends of the piping cord together.
5 To make the cushion back, cut a square, 42 × 42cm, from fabric A.
6 With right sides of the back and front of the cushion together, stitch along one side 6cm from each corner, leaving the centre open. Press the seams and remaining opening flat. Stitch the zip into the opening.
7 Open the zip and, right sides together, stitch the remaining sides together along the seam line. Neaten the seams. Turn the cushion right side out and press. Attach tassels to corners. Place the cushion pad inside the cover.

• Decorative Chair Cover •

Change your chair without changing your furniture. A chair cover with a gathered
skirt will soften the effect of a formal, upright chair. Depending on the fabric chosen, the dressed
chair will fit comfortably into a bedroom, sitting room or breakfast room

Easy-fitting slip-on covers are masters of disguise, dramatically changing the complete appearance of a room setting. This chair cover has soft, fluid lines that are most appealing.

MATERIALS

- ♦ tape measure
- ♦ pattern paper
- ♦ pencil
- ♦ scissors
- ♦ approximately 2.3–3m furnishing fabric, 144cm wide, per chair
- ♦ pins
- ♦ matching thread
- ♦ 1.9m ready-made piping cord with a self seam allowance, or fabric and piping cord for making piping (see page 129)

This simple chair cover has no openings or fastenings and is slipped on and off the chair. The seat and the inside and outside chair back of the cover are made from a single piece of fabric. After the chair measurements are taken, a paper pattern is made for this single piece. Once the piece for the top of the chair has been stitched, the piping is tacked to it before the skirt is joined on. To check the exact amount of fabric to purchase, lay the pattern pieces out on a marked 144cm wide area and calculate the length of fabric required.

MEASURING THE CHAIR

1 Keep a record of the figures as you take the chair measurements with a tape measure as shown in diagram 1.
2 Measure the front edge of the chair seat (A). Next, measure across the widest part of the chair back which is usually the top edge (B). Now measure the depth of the seat (C), the height of the back from the seat (D) and the thickness of the back (E).

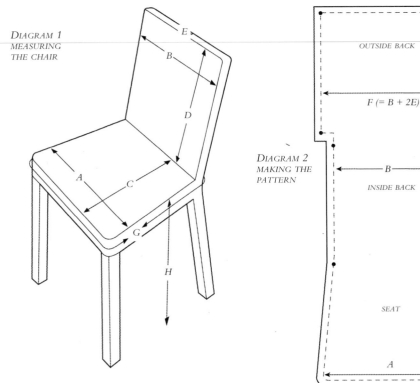

DIAGRAM 1
MEASURING
THE CHAIR

DIAGRAM 2
MAKING THE
PATTERN

OUTSIDE BACK

F (= B + 2E)

INSIDE BACK

SEAT

3 For the gathered skirt, measure around the total circumference of the chair seat (G) and from the top of the seat to the floor (H).

MAKING THE PATTERN

1 Using the measurements taken and adding approximately 5mm to each for slight ease, mark the pattern piece for the top of the chair on the pattern paper (diagram 2). Note that the outside back is wider than the inside back, since it includes extra width on each side to accommodate the thickness of the chair back.
2 Mark slightly curved corners at the front edge of the seat front to make an easier shape for joining on the gathered skirt.
3 Place large dots at the points indicated on the diagram for matching the side seam. Add a seam allowance of 1.5cm around the shape.

4 Cut out the paper pattern piece. Lay the paper pattern piece over the chair to check the size and shape, then set aside.
5 There is no need to make a pattern for the skirt piece, but calculate the size of the three skirt pieces now. A skirt approximately two-and-a-half times the width of G will provide sufficient gathers. Three widths of furnishing fabric cut across the material from selvage to selvage (144cm) and joined end-to-end is the right amount for most average-sized chairs. (If your chair is especially large or much smaller than an average chair, adjust the total fullness of the skirt.) The depth of each skirt piece is the drop (H) plus an allowance of 4cm for the seam at the top and the hem.

CUTTING OUT

1 Iron the fabric flat and place it on a cutting surface, wrong side up. Cut out the three skirt pieces following the calculations made for the size of the piece.

2 Pin the paper pattern to the remaining fabric on the straight grain. Cut out the fabric piece and transfer the dot markings to the wrong side of the fabric using a pencil. Unpin and remove the paper pattern.

SEWING THE COVER

1 Matching the dots on the inside back to those on the outside back, fold the chair top piece right sides together. Pin each seam, clipping halfway into the seam allowance at the dot at the top of the inside back to turn the corner. Machine stitch the seams starting at the fold at the top, pivoting at the top dots and ending the seam at the bottom dots without stitching into the seam allowance at the bottom (see below).

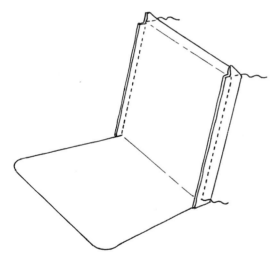

2 Pin and tack the piping to the right side of the seat piece around the edge and across the back. With right sides together, machine stitch the skirt widths together along the selvage edges, taking a 1.5cm seam allowance and forming a ring of fabric. Press the seams open.

3 Stitch two lines of gathering stitches along the top of the skirt, one 7mm from the raw edge and the other 14mm from it. Pull the ends of the threads to gather the skirt.

4 Align the raw edges, spread the gathers evenly and pin the skirt to the top over the piping with the right sides together. Machine stitch the seam (see below).

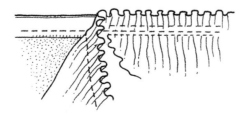

This bright fabric cover can be made for any plain dining room or kitchen chair, without arms. It will fit the chair whether it is all wood or partially padded.

5 Turn right side out and place the cover on the chair. Mark the hemline. Remove the cover and trim the hem to 2cm. Press under 1cm twice to make a double hem and machine stitch in place. Press the cover carefully, using the nose of the iron to press into the gathers around the seat.

◆ Renovating Chairs ◆

*Bold, bright fabrics and paint to match can really ring the changes for a dowdy old chair
and turn it into an eye-catching piece. New fabric can work wonders for an old drop-in chair seat, and
a colourful cushion will make a simple wooden chair both decorative and more comfortable*

Colourful cushions

*Two café or kitchen chairs present a perfect
opportunity for brilliant colour combinations.
Instead of taking the traditional path of subdued
restraint, this pair (far right) is creatively
mismatched to great effect.*

MATERIALS
- wood glue
- wood filler and filling knife
- fine sandpaper
- paintbrush
- wood primer
- undercoat
- gloss paint for each
  chair (different colours)
- tracing paper, pencil
- scissors
- 1m² medium-weight furnishing
  fabric for each chair cushion
  (different colours and patterns)
- piping cord (twice the
  circumference of each chair seat)
- 2 pieces of 40mm thick foam
  the size of the chair seats

PREPARING THE CHAIRS
1 Check the chairs to see whether any repairs
are needed to the joints or woodwork.
Strengthen the joints with wood glue as
necessary, and use a filling knife to fill any gaps
or holes with wood filler. When the filler is
dry, sand smooth any rough areas.
2 Apply wood primer and undercoat, and
allow the recommended drying time between
coats. Paint each chair a different colour to
tone with your chosen fabric and allow to dry.

*Do up a few second-hand chairs – using all your
favourite colours in one room if you wish – and
you will be surprised and pleased with the effect.*

MAKING THE CUSHIONS

1 Using tracing paper and a sharp pencil, draw around the seat of one chair. Place the traced pattern on the foam and cut out a seat cushion. Repeat for the second chair.

2 Using the pattern, cut two fabric seat pieces per cushion, adding a 1cm seam allowance.

3 To make the bias strips for the piping, fold the fabric at a 45° angle to the selvage and cut strips 4cm wide. For each chair you will need enough strips to cover the piping (that is, twice the circumference of the seat). Join the strips together to make up the required length: lay the pieces right sides together as shown in the diagram and stitch across the grain. Trim the seams and press them open.

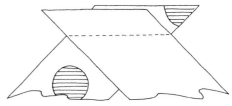

4 Fold the bias strips in half lengthways, wrong sides together. Place the piping cord inside the fold. Using a zipper foot on the sewing machine, stitch close to the cord.

5 Starting at the back of the cushion with raw edges matching, stitch a length of piping to the right side of the top cushion piece, crossing the end over the beginning to finish. Do the same with the bottom cushion piece.

6 Cut a fabric strip, 8cm wide, on the straight grain for the cushion gusset. Join two pieces, if necessary, to make a piece long enough to go around the cushion. Cut two strips 30 × 4cm wide to make the ties.

7 With right sides together, stitch the short ends of the gusset pieces together to make a loop. With right sides together and raw edges matching, pin one edge of gusset around top cushion piece. Using zipper foot, stitch along the previous line of stitching, close to the piping. Ease the gusset around curves. Cut notches at the curves, taking care not to cut the stitching, and trim seam. Repeat this process to attach gusset to the bottom piece, leaving a 20cm gap at the back through which to insert pad.

8 Turn the cover right side out and press.

9 Ease the foam pad into the cover and slipstitch (see page 222) the opening closed.

10 Fold the two 30 × 4cm strips in half lengthways with right sides together. Press flat. Allowing 1cm for seams, sew the two long sides together. Trim the seams. Turn inside out and press flat. Neatly slipstitch the open end, tucking the raw edges inside the tube. Iron flat.

11 Place the cushion on the seat and mark the positions of the back posts on it with pins.

12 Fold the ties in half and hand stitch the centre of each tie at the pin marks.

13 Repeat steps 4–12 for the second chair cushion, using the other fabric.

14 Tie the cushions to the chairs.

Drop-in seats

To brighten up your old chairs or to add new life to chairs bought at a garage sale or second-hand furniture shop, just take to them with a tin of paint and some colourful furnishing fabric.

MATERIALS

- 2 chairs with drop-in seats
- wood glue
- wood filler and filling knife
- fine sandpaper
- primer
- undercoat
- gloss paint for each chair (different colours)
- paintbrush
- 1m² upholstery-weight fabric for each chair (different colours and patterns)
- sharp scissors
- approximately 50cm square piece of felt for each chair, to coordinate with fabric
- spray adhesive
- upholstery tacks
- hammer

1 Take the seats out of the chairs. Assess the chairs for repairs to joints and woodwork and glue as necessary. Use a filling knife to fill any gaps with wood filler. When the filler is dry, sand smooth any rough areas.

2 Apply wood primer and then undercoat and paint each chair a different colour, following the manufacturer's instructions and allowing recommended drying time between coats.

3 Remove the existing upholstery fabric from one seat, pulling out the old tacks and staples, and lay it, right side down, on one of the pieces of new upholstery fabric, also placed right side down. The grain or design of the new fabric should run from the back to the front of the chair. Using the old fabric as a pattern, cut out the shape from the new fabric.

4 Spray the adhesive on the wrong side of the fabric along the back edge (the one that goes along the back of the seat). Turn the seat upside down and stick down the edge of the fabric under the back of the seat (see below). Make sure that the grain is straight. Starting at the centre, hammer in the tacks, spacing them at approximately 5cm intervals. Do not tack the corners at this stage.

5 Spray along the front edge of the fabric on the wrong side. Turn the seat right side up, pull the fabric tightly across the seat and attach the sticky edge under the front of the seat. Make sure the fabric is smooth on the top of the seat, then hammer in the tacks under the front edge.

6 Repeat the process outlined in step 5 for each side of the seat in turn.

PICTURE-PERFECT FINISH

Take a pattern of your seat to your foam retailer and have the cushion filler accurately cut to size.

For the tie-on cushions, the cushion top and bottom, gusset, ties and bias strips for the piping trim are all cut from the upholstery fabric. It's a good idea to make newspaper patterns for all these pieces and lay them out on the fabric before you start to cut into it.

Extend the life of your cushions by treating them with a spray-on moisture and dirt repellent.

7 To finish the corners, fold the fabric neatly underneath. If the corners are bulky, it will be hard to fit the seat back in. Try to make the front and back corners symmetrical, and secure each with two tacks (see below).

8 Cut a piece of felt the same shape as the underside of the seat but measuring 5mm less than the seat all round.

9 Spray the felt with adhesive and stick it neatly to the underside of the seat to cover the fabric's raw edges and the tacks.

10 Repeat steps 3–9 for the second chair.

11 Tap both re-covered seats back into position in their respective chairs.

REUPHOLSTERING DROP-IN SEATS

1 *Take out drop-in seat and turn it over – it may or may not have webbing strips, as above. Remove all the staples and tacks and take off the old upholstery fabric.*

2 *Cut out your new cover, using the old one as a pattern. Glue the edge of the new cover to the back of the seat, then, working out from the centre, tack in place.*

3 *Turn the seat over and pull cover over padding and seat, making sure it is tight and smooth. Glue and tack in place along the front edge first, then along each side.*

4 *To finish the corners, fold the fabric to get a neat, symmetrical result. Pull fabric to the underside and tack securely in place. Glue on a piece of felt to cover underside.*

Fireboard and Firescreen

A pretty fireboard is ideal for permanently concealing an unused fireplace, while the freestanding firescreen is easily removed when you want to light an open fire. We used the same découpage motif for both – and each provides an attractive focal point in a room

Fireboard

A fireboard fits neatly to cover the whole fireplace. This one has découpage flowers at its centre, and a gold border with moulded plastic rosettes.

MATERIALS

- 1 sheet MDF (medium-density fibreboard), 6mm thick, cut to fit your fireplace
- water-based sealer
- paintbrush (50-60mm)
- fine sandpaper
- emulsion paints (or artist's acrylics) in background colour and second colour (we used a pale blue and a pale green)
- scumble medium
- natural sea sponge
- giftwrapping paper of choice
- PVA adhesive
- clean cloth or rubber roller
- pattern for stencil (see bottom of p.136)
- stencil acetate
- marker pen
- scalpel or trimming knife
- small stencil brush
- gold paint
- plastic moulded rosettes, for corners (optional)
- water-based varnish
- small, sharp scissors

1 Apply a coat of water-based sealer to the board using the paintbrush. When the sealer is dry, give the surface a light sanding.
2 With the brush, apply two coats of your chosen background colour and leave to dry.

While a blazing open fire in winter is a fine sight, a cold, empty grate is not. Hide an unused fireplace behind this attractively decorated fireboard.

3 Make a glaze of 1 part paint (your second colour), 1 part scumble medium, 1 part water. Wet the sponge and squeeze until it is just damp – this gives a softer image and applies when using both oil and water-based paints. Dab the sponge in the paint mix and then remove most of it by dabbing on newspaper – there should be no 'wet' spots in the sponge.

Apply lightly over the background colour, changing direction all the time to avoid getting any sort of regular pattern. Allow some background to show through. Let dry.
4 With small, sharp scissors, carefully cut out decorative motifs from the wrapping paper. We used one large motif of a vase of flowers. Scissors were used for most of the cutting, and

a scalpel or craft knife for the areas that could not easily be reached with scissors. If your chosen image is large and difficult to handle, you can cut it into smaller pieces along the lines of the pattern and reassemble it when you glue it onto the board.

5 Position the motifs carefully in a design that pleases the eye and mark a few key points lightly with a pencil on the board.

6 Coat the backs of the motifs with glue and stick them onto the board. Press a damp cloth firmly on the motifs to get rid of any air bubbles or, if you have one, roll from the centre out with a rubber roller. Do not rub the motifs.

7 For the gold border, use a photocopier to enlarge the stencil pattern (see below) to 200% (to enlarge without copying, see page 220). Lay the acetate on the enlarged design, trace with a marker, and cut out with a scalpel.

8 With the stencil brush, apply a gold border around the board, with the outer edge of the border about 2cm from the board edge.

9 To add plastic mouldings, paint them with gold paint and allow to dry. Glue them at the corners of the gold border.

10 Coat the finished fireboard with varnish.

TIPS FROM THE EXPERTS

When cutting out paper motifs, hold scissors at an angle to give a slanted rather than a perpendicular cut to the underside of the paper edges. This makes a flatter edge, with no white paper showing.

To apply the glue to each motif, turn it face down on a pasting board and brush the glue on, working from the centre out to the edges.

For easier positioning and moving of paper motifs, dilute the PVA glue with up to 50 per cent water.

Firescreen

This handy firescreen adds a decorative touch to your fireplace but you can easily remove it when you want an open fire. It uses the same motif as the fireboard (page 135) but creates quite a different effect.

MATERIALS

- 1 sheet MDF (medium-density fibreboard), 6mm thick, 70 × 55cm
- pencil
- paper
- compasses
- ruler
- tenon saw, jigsaw, 6mm chisel
- drill with 35mm bit
- sandpaper (fine and medium grades)
- 40cm length 50 × 25mm dressed pine
- water-based sealer
- emulsion paints or artist's acrylics: background colour, second colour, and third colour (we used light pink, a pale blue and a darker blue)
- scumble medium
- paintbrush (50-60mm)
- small flat brush (10mm)
- natural sea sponge
- masking tape
- giftwrapping paper for the découpage
- small, sharp scissors
- sharp trimming knife
- clean cloth or rubber roller
- water-based varnish

MAKING THE SCREEN

1 Use the diagram on the opposite page as a guide to marking measurements for cutting the top of the screen. First, measure and mark in pencil a rectangle (100 × 75mm) at each top

corner. Cut out using a tenon saw.

2 Set your compass so it will draw a circle of 50mm radius; put the compass point at 'A' ('A' is 50mm in from the edges, see diagram) on one corner and draw the corner curve. Repeat for the other corners, placing the point of the compasses at 'A' each time. Carefully cut out each curved corner with a jigsaw.

3 For the handle, drill two 35mm holes (see diagram). Insert the jigsaw blade into one and cut out the MDF between the two holes.

4 Sand all of the cut edges to a smooth finish, first using the medium grade abrasive paper and then using the fine.

5 To make the feet for the screen, cut the length of pine in half so that you have two pieces 200mm long. To make the slots for the MDF to fit in, mark two vertical lines 6mm apart and 25mm deep at the centre of each

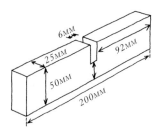

piece (for measurements, see above). With a tenon saw, cut down halfway through each piece at the marked lines. Use a chisel to remove the wood between the cuts.

6 Round off the curved ends of the feet

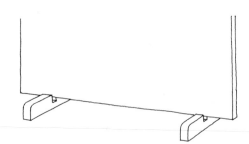

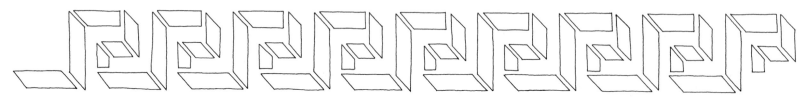

This beautiful, free-standing firescreen will make your fireplace as much a focal point in the room in summer as it is in winter with its welcoming blaze.

water and apply by dabbing lightly with the natural sponge (see step 3, page 135).

4 Leave to dry, then paint the back a single colour, or sponge in the same way.

5 To mark out the border (dark blue in picture), take a piece of paper, 2 × 6cm; make three pencil marks, 12mm apart, on one long side. Lay the paper horizontally so that the left pencil mark lines up with the screen's left edge. Put a pencil dot on the screen for each of the other two marks. Move the paper up and repeat; continue around the screen (at bottom edge, put the outer dots 40mm from the edge, see picture). Join dots with a ruler to form the 12mm border outline. For rounded corners, mark dots close together and join freehand.

6 Lay masking tape around the marked border, leaving corners unmasked. Paint the border with your third colour using the small brush. Paint corners freehand within the marked lines. Recoat if needed. Remove tape when dry.

7 Lay the screen flat on a table with the feet over table edge. To apply the floral motif, follow steps 4–6 of the fireboard. Let some flowers fall across the border, and shorten flower stems to fit the space as needed.

8 Coat the finished firescreen with varnish.

(see opposite) by marking a pleasing curve and cutting with a jigsaw. Sand to a smooth finish, again first using the medium grade abrasive paper, then the fine grade.

7 Coat the slots with glue and insert the screen (see opposite), placing each foot about 45mm in from the side. Allow to dry.

DECORATING THE SCREEN

1 Decorate the front as for the fireboard. First coat with sealer and, once dry, sand the surface.

2 Apply two coats of your chosen background colour and leave to dry thoroughly.

3 Make a glaze of 1 part of your second colour, 1 part scumble medium and 1 part

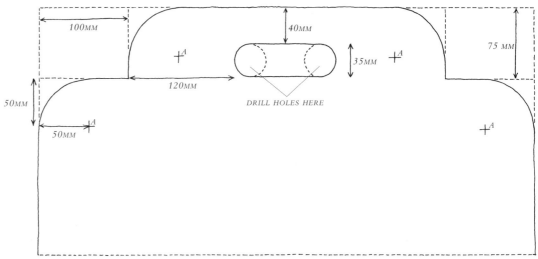

◆ Finishes for Frames ◆

*Framing pictures can be expensive. Recycling old frames that you rescue from car
boot sales or second-hand shops is a more economical option – and gives you a chance to
show your creative flair and produce some individual effects and finishes*

Gilded frame
Turn a basic frame into an instant 'antique'.

MATERIALS
- plastic moulded segments (from specialist craft shops)
- garnet red matt emulsion paint or artist's acrylic
- fine abrasive paper
- acrylic-based gold size
- nylon brush, soft-bristled brush
- cotton gloves
- book of Dutch metal leaf (see p.103)
- PVA adhesive
- water-based varnish

1 Paint the frame and the moulded segments with two coats of the deep red emulsion. Sand each coat lightly when dry.
2 Apply gilding to the segments (see gilding instructions, page 153) but not to the frame.
3 Arrange the moulded segments on the frame, working to create a pleasing symmetry.
4 Glue the segments to the frame in the

predetermined positions. Leave to set by clamping the piece, or placing it under two or three heavy books overnight.
5 Finish with water-based varnish.

Pearlised frame
Achieve the opalescent effect of mother-of-pearl.

MATERIALS
- four glazes mixed in these proportions: 1 part matt emulsion paint or artist's acrylic (red, green, blue, mother-of-pearl), 1 part scumble medium, 1 part water
- steel wool

1 Apply one coat of red glaze sparingly and unevenly to create areas of light and dark; do not fully cover the frame. Allow to dry and rub lightly with steel wool.
2 Apply one coat each of green, then blue, then mother-of-pearl in the same way.

Tortoiseshell frame
The round brushes used here are important, to imitate the patterns of real tortoiseshell.

MATERIALS
- pale yellow matt emulsion paint or artist's acrylic
- round nylon brushes, nos. 1, 3, 6
- glaze 1 (1 part burnt umber paint, 1 part scumble medium); glaze 2 (1 part burnt umber, 1 part raw umber, 1 part scumble); glaze 3 (1 part black, 1 part scumble)

1 Paint the frame with the yellow paint.
2 Apply the glazes in small diagonal strokes on the yellow. Start by applying glaze 1 with the no. 6 brush. Then apply glaze 2 with the

no. 3 brush, and then glaze 3 with the very fine no. 1 brush. Use all three glazes together (that is, do not paint all of one before starting the others; apply all three then reapply the first one and so on). Keep dipping the brushes

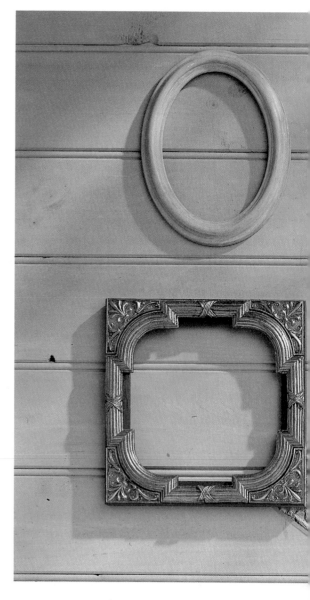

SURFACE PREPARATION

I F THE FRAME or surface you have been working on has already been painted, varnished or french polished, clean it using steel wool and methylated spirits and, when dry, rub down with fine sandpaper.

Raw surfaces should also be smoothed with sandpaper and sealed with acrylic-based sealer.

An uneven surface may be levelled with fine sandpaper or steel wool. Afterwards, wipe with a cotton duster, then a clean tack rag.

A 50ml tin of paint is plenty, or you can use leftover paint from a previous project. Try out the chosen method on a piece of card first.

---

into water to soften and move the glazes around. Choose your own balance of the three glazes. Blend some of the colours into each other and keep others separate. Allow a little background yellow to show through. As an accent, pick out fine details with glaze 3.

Spectacular finishes. Top row, from left: two distressed effects, a plaster ceiling moulding ready for transformation and a tortoiseshell finish. Bottom row, a gilded frame with plastic mouldings, a pearlised finish and a combination of distressing and gilding.

Distressed finish

Layers of paint, with sanding, produce this finish.

MATERIALS

- two or three 50mm foam brushes
- matt emulsion paints or artist's acrylics in white, green, pink and blue
- sandpaper
- tack rag (see p.102)
- wax paste

1 Apply a coat of white paint sparingly and unevenly to create areas of light and dark; do not completely cover the frame. Allow the paint to dry. Sand the surface, then wipe thoroughly with the tack rag.

2 Apply one coat each of green, pink and blue, sanding each time and allowing to dry. Do not completely cover the frame with any one colour. There are no strict rules for this finish; if desired, continue applying colours, and sanding, until satisfied with the look. The impression you want is of wear and age.

3 To finish, apply clear beeswax polish to the whole surface and buff lightly with a cotton lint-free cloth to a soft sheen.

◆ Découpage Mirror Frame ◆

The word découpage is derived from the French word 'découper', meaning 'cut out'.
Découpage became something of an art form and was traditionally worked with up to 100 layers of
varnish. This project uses far fewer layers but still achieves a beautifully finished frame

Découpage mirror frame

Transform a basic bare wood-framed mirror into an
heirloom with this traditional découpage method.

MATERIALS
- undecorated wood-framed mirror
- screwdriver

PREPARATION AND PAINTING
- fine wet-and-dry sandpaper
- 70mm and 20mm paintbrushes
- matt black emulsion paint
- scrap paper, pencil, ruler
- white chalk pencil
- 20mm masking tape
- J cloths
- artist's acrylic paint in a rich
  red-brown (pimento or sienna)
- gold acrylic paint
- size 10 shader brush
- fine artist's brush
- water-based sealer

CUTTING AND GLUEING
- sheets of plastic
- giftwrapping paper of choice
- scalpel or trimming knife
- small straight-edged scissors
- Blu-Tack
- paper paste and pva adhesive
- 100mm rubber roller
- white vinegar

VARNISHING AND SANDING
- sable varnishing brush
- clear water-based gloss varnish
- extra fine wet-and-dry sandpaper
- tack rag (see p.102)
- clear satin-finish oil-based
  varnish

PREPARATION AND PAINTING
1 Remove the screws from the mirror
backing and keep in a safe place. Remove the
mirror and store flat, protecting the back.
2 Sand all the surfaces of the wooden frame
using dry, fine sandpaper.

3 Using the larger paintbrush, apply one coat of black paint to both sides of the frame. Once dry, lightly sand with dry, fine sandpaper. Apply a second coat and let dry.

4 To mark out the gold border, take a piece of paper, about 2 × 6cm, and make three pencil marks, 1cm apart, on one long side. Lay the paper horizontally so that the left pencil mark lines up with the frame's left edge. With a chalk pencil, put a dot on the frame for each of the other two pencil marks. Move up and continue all the way around the frame. Join corresponding dots to form the outlines of a 1cm border. For straight edges, join dots using a ruler; for curves and rounded corners, make the dots close together and join freehand. This technique works whatever shape the frame.

5 Lay masking tape on each side of the marked border; leave curved areas unmasked. With the size 10 shader brush, paint the taped border with one coat of pimento. For curves, paint freehand. When dry, repeat with a coat of gold paint. Remove the tape when the paint is dry.

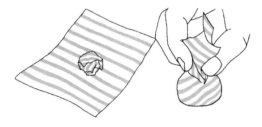

6 Make a swab by putting a small ball of J cloth into a larger piece (see above) and twisting the larger piece around the ball. Dip into a little of the red-brown artist's acrylic and wipe this around the inside bevelled edge (near mirror), the shelf edge (if your mirror frame has an integral shelf), and the side of the frame (edge between the front and the back). Allow to dry. Make another swab and repeat in gold.

7 Touch up any imperfections with the fine brush and black emulsion paint.

8 When dry, apply a coat of water-based sealer to the frame using the smaller paintbrush.

To carry through a particular theme, this elegant découpage mirror could be decorated with motifs from colour photocopies of your furnishing fabrics.

CUTTING AND GLUEING

1 Lay your chosen paper on a plastic sheet and apply water-based sealer by gently brushing over the front surface of the paper with one of the paintbrushes. Allow at least one hour drying time under normal conditions. If your paper is very thin, wait until the front dries then turn it over and seal the back as well.

2 After the paper has dried, select the sections you wish to use. Place on a cutting mat and, with a new scalpel blade or sharp trimming knife, neatly cut out the inside areas of the design that are hard to get at with scissors. For outside areas, cut out roughly with the scalpel and then finish off with the small scissors. Hold

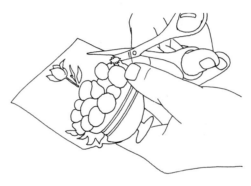

the scissors at an angle (see above) to undercut the edge at a diagonal. Then, when the paper is in place, you will see no white cut edges.

3 Lay out the motifs on the frame, trying different designs until you are happy. Use Blu-Tack to hold in place while you stand back.

4 Before proceeding, make up a mixture of 3 parts paper paste to 1 part pva adhesive.

5 Remove any Blu-Tack, and working on one motif at a time, spread the glue on the back, and on the surface of the frame where it will lie. Once it is in position, dab a little glue on the top of the motif, so you can slide your fingers over the surface to push out excess glue mixture and air bubbles. Finish off with the rubber roller, cleaning the roller after each use.

6 With a clean, damp cloth, dab up excess glue and gently wipe the area around the motif.

7 Repeat for the other motifs and wipe over the surface with a little vinegar on a cloth.

8 When the motifs are dry, prick any air bubbles lightly with the scalpel or trimming knife and apply a little more glue.

9 Using the fine artist's brush and a little diluted black paint, work gently around the outside edges of the motifs so no white areas of paper show against the black background.

10 Use a paintbrush to apply water-based sealer to the entire frame.

VARNISHING AND SANDING

1 Dip the bristles of the varnishing brush three-quarters of the way into the water-based varnish. Then, starting at the top of the frame and working downwards, apply one coat; allow to dry. Apply the next coat from side to side. Repeat, changing direction each time, until 20 coats of varnish have been applied. Allow about 30 minutes drying time between coats.

2 When thoroughly dry, rub down gently with extra fine wet-and-dry, using plenty of water. Wipe away all dust with the tack rag.

3 Continue to apply varnish as before, building up five or six coats then sanding back gently and wiping with the tack rag; repeat as needed until the surface is smooth and level.

4 After the final sanding, wipe the surface thoroughly with the tack rag and apply two coats of oil-based varnish. (Make sure the brush is completely dry before you use it for the oil-based varnish.) Allow the first coat of varnish to dry for up to 24 hours before applying the second coat. Allow the work to cure (harden) for a couple of weeks before you reassemble the mirror.

FOR THE BEST RESULTS

Use only unfolded paper; any creases, folds or other imperfections will show through the varnish. Roll up sheets of paper and store in cardboard cylinders until you need them, and keep cut-out motifs flat – between sheets of cardboard or in a flower press.

Never varnish on a wet or humid day as the varnish may go cloudy. Use a good-quality brush and work in an airy, dust-free area. Always wear a mask.

Don't sand in circles; always use a left to right and top to bottom, cross-hatching method.

On Display, or Put Away

A pair of matching shelves make a novel feature in their own right while giving you space to display your favourite knick-knacks. If you have a home office, why not consider turning your business-like filing cabinet into a display piece as well – a touch of marbling makes all the difference

Display shelves

These shelves are made of pine. The smooth planed timber pieces which you buy from the timber merchant are a little smaller than the rough timber sizes specified below. This difference is allowed for in our measurements (the actual shelf sizes are 220mm deep and 19mm thick, and 90mm deep and 19mm thick, with the front faces being 60mm high and 12mm thick).

MATERIALS

- 3m length of pine 250 × 25mm
- 3m length of pine 100 × 25mm
- two 3m lengths pine 100 × 16mm
- pencil and ruler
- try square or set square
- tenon saw
- PVA adhesive
- 30mm panel pins
- fine nail punch
- wood filler
- fine sandpaper
- steel brackets: four 100 × 90mm, four 100 × 150mm (plus screws for fixing)
- chisel (20mm or less)
- paintbrush (50mm)
- water-based primer-undercoat
- satin or gloss top coat
- spirit level
- drill with fine bit (2.5mm) for wood screws
- wall plugs and matching masonry bit for drilling wall

1 Mark the pieces of pine to the desired length (ours were 2.6m). To ensure a neat job, use a try square or set square to check that the ends are marked square. Saw both pieces to length. Mark and saw the timber for the front faces of the shelves to the length of the pine, squaring the ends.

2 Apply a smear of PVA adhesive to the front edge of one shelf, then fix a front face to this edge with the panel pins – about 450mm apart. Make sure that you centre the front face accurately so that it protrudes an equal amount above and below the shelf (see diagram, right). Repeat for the other shelf.

3 Use a fine nail punch to punch the head of each pin slightly below the surface, then use wood filler to fill the indentations. When the wood filler has dried, smooth the surface with fine sandpaper.

4 Mark the position for the brackets on the back edge of each shelf and cut rebates to match the width and depth of the brackets: carefully saw the sides then chisel out the depth. Test to make sure that the brackets fit flush to the back edge of the shelf so that the shelf will sit hard up against the wall. Drill fine pilot holes into the shelves and fix the brackets

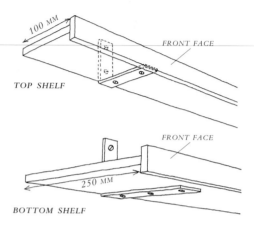

100 MM

FRONT FACE

TOP SHELF

FRONT FACE

250 MM

BOTTOM SHELF

in place with small wood screws.

5 Sandpaper all edges and faces of each shelf, and apply a coat of primer-undercoat. Leave the shelves to dry for 2 hours.

6 Lightly sand any rough spots on the shelves and apply two coats of satin or gloss paint.

7 Using a spirit level to ensure that they are even, mark the spots for all the bracket screws on the wall. Drill the wall to accept the screws,

MAKING THE SHELVES

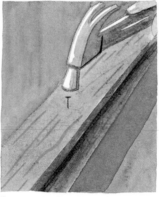

1 *Glue the front face to the shelf, then pin every 450mm. Punch the nails below the surface. Fill holes with wood filler and sand smooth.*

2 *Accurately mark the bracket positions at the back of the shelf and use as guides to cut shallow rebates for them using a tenon saw and a chisel.*

3 *Sand the shelf. Apply primer-undercoat to wood and brackets, and then two coats of satin or gloss paint allowing each coat time to dry.*

using the appropriate bit and wall plugs for
masonry walls; if the wall is plasterboard or
timber, you'll need to locate timber studs
(supporting uprights) and drill through into
these for extra strength.

8 Fix the brackets firmly to the wall.

9 To finish off, camouflage the brackets by
painting the vertical section of each (that is, the
part attached to the wall) in the wall colour.
Wait approximately two hours for the paint to
dry and the shelves are ready for use.

PRACTICAL IDEAS

FITTING TO A CUPBOARD

*If your shelves butt up to a cupboard, you need to
make sure the doors will open easily. A solution is
to cut a triangular section off the end of the shelf.
Mark and cut this section as you are sawing in
step 1. Adjust the length of the front face accordingly.*

*It is surprising what a difference a pair of simple
wall-to-wall shelves can make in a room, particularly
when one shelf is stepped back from the other to give
a sense of perspective. The shallower top shelf is ideal
for narrow objects such as picture frames or plates
while the broader bottom shelf suits bulkier items –
ornaments and plants, for example. With this design
you can make appropriate shelving for any room.*

Kitchen shelves

By adding a scalloped edge to the basic display shelves you can give them a traditional country kitchen appearance.

MATERIALS
- food tin, or similar round object to use as a template (a 440g tin or similar works best)
- tenon saw
- coping saw
- clamp

1 Lay the 'front faces' described in Display Shelves (see page 142) on a flat surface. Using a small tin as a template, draw semi-circular scallops with a pencil along the top half of each piece. The top of each scallop should just touch the edge of the wood.

2 Clamp the piece of wood to a workbench or sturdy table. Draw vertical lines from the point where the semi-circles join to the top of the wood and then saw carefully down each line to the point of each join with a tenon saw.

3 Use the coping saw to cut along the curved lines of the scallops, from the top edge of the wood down to the bottom of the vertical cut described above. The waste wood will fall away when the saw reaches the point where both of the semi-circles join.

4 Then, simply follow steps 2-9 of Display Shelves, described on pages 142-3.

Filing cabinet

The rewarding aspect of gaining expertise in the various paint finishes is that they can be used to transform even the most mundane item – such as an old metal filing cabinet – into a thing of beauty.

MATERIALS
- filing cabinet
- metal paint primer
- matt emulsion paint or artist's acrylics in the following colours: white, black, dark green, deep yellow
- scumble medium
- soft pencil, ruler
- 50mm wide low-tack masking tape
- good-quality artist's nylon brush (50mm)
- two bristle brushes (50mm)
- no. 3 round nylon brush
- large sea sponge
- clean cotton cloths
- tissue paper
- satin or gloss water-based varnish

PREPARATION
1 Use the nylon brush to paint the whole cabinet surface with primer. Let dry.
2 Paint the cabinet with two coats of white matt emulsion paint, using the nylon brush, leaving each coat of paint to dry completely.

3 Mix five different glazes in the proportions given here. Glaze 1: 1 part dark green, 1 part scumble, ½ part water; glaze 2: 1 part dark green mixed with white, 1 part scumble, ½ part water; glaze 3: 1 part black, 1 part scumble, ½ part water; glaze 4: 1 part deep yellow, 1 part scumble, ½ part water; glaze 5: 1 part deep yellow mixed with white, 1 part scumble, ½ part water.

4 With pencil and ruler, mark the cabinet with your design. Ours has a green diamond surrounded by yellow on each drawer and a diamond on sides, top and back.
Note: a band of black marbling frames the front and trims the top of each side (see right).

5 For each cabinet surface, mask around the outside edge of the diamond area (see below).

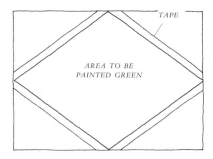

TAPE

AREA TO BE
PAINTED GREEN

PAINTING THE GREEN MARBLE
1 Paint the masked areas with matt black paint. Leave to dry.
2 Using a 50mm bristle brush, apply glaze 1 (dark green) to the black in roughly diagonal, informal drifts, as if painting clouds. Make the drifts approximately 15 × 5cm, but with irregular, blurred edges and in an uneven thickness so that some black is allowed to show through. Cover most, but not all of the surface, and check when you have finished that some haphazard black patches are visible.
3 With glaze 1 still wet, apply glaze 2 (light green) around the edges of the drifts, with a little black still showing.
4 Take a dry bristle brush and start stippling (dabbing with the brush tip) to blend the two

Introduce a cosy, country look to your kitchen with these shelves. The scalloped edge is not only decorative – it helps to keep your china safely in place.

A filing cabinet is probably the most practical piece of home-office furniture but also usually the least decorative. Work a magical transformation from cabinet to showpiece by applying some marble-finish glazes. Ours was done with green and yellow in a diamond pattern, with black around the edges.

greens together. Take light green into dark and dark green into light. Soften the edges of the light green wherever it meets the black. Use a clean cloth to remove glaze from the brush as you work, so you do not reapply glaze.

5 Wet a sponge and wring it out in a dry cotton rag. Dab on the surface to remove some of the glazes and leave a light imprint. Now pick up some of glaze 3 (black) with the sponge. Apply light drifts over the green. Use the bristle brush and stipple to blend the black into the green glazes. You may wish to remove more of the glazes with crumpled tissue. Leave to dry.

6 Repeat steps 1–5 for the other areas of the cabinet that are to be green.

PAINTING THE YELLOW MARBLE

1 Remove all masking tape. Apply masking tape along the edges of areas that are to be painted yellow (that is, lay tape inside the edges of the areas just painted green, once dried).

2 The yellow is applied in a similar way to the green. Apply glaze 4 (deep yellow) in drifts, then glaze 5 (light yellow) around the edges of glaze 4. Blend with the bristle brush, and sponge as in step 5 above. Then apply light drifts of plain white paint with the sponge.

3 Apply black emulsion paint around the front margins and along the top edge at the sides (see picture). If desired, use the round nylon brush to paint on irregular 'veins' with the white paint (see marbling, page 241).

4 Finish by coating the cabinet with varnish, being careful to work in a well-ventilated area.

VARIATION If you would like to give the filing cabinet the look and texture of aged marble, as we did for our picture, liberally sprinkle its surface with plain flour while the varnish is still wet. Once the varnish has completely dried, lightly dust off the excess flour – do not try to rub or wipe it away.

◆ Dried Flowers ◆

Drying flowers is like capturing a summer garden at its height, and in the winter months
floral displays are a wonderful reminder of sunny days. There are no secrets – it is simply a question
of growing the right plants, knowing when to pick them and using the best drying techniques

Preserving flowers

Although the summer months are the busiest, preserving flowers and foliage is a year-round activity, with a right time for picking everything. There are three main drying methods – air drying, preserving with glycerine and drying with silica gel crystals.

MATERIALS
- ◆ secateurs
- ◆ short-bladed florist's scissors
- ◆ string and elastic bands
- ◆ glycerine
- ◆ wide-necked glass jars
- ◆ food colour or dye
- ◆ plastic box with airtight lid
- ◆ silica gel crystals
- ◆ small, soft paintbrush

AIR DRYING

1 Flowers must be dried quickly to help preserve their colour. Choose a warm and well-ventilated place such as by a radiator, near a cooker or Aga, or in an airing cupboard where the air can circulate around the petals. However, keep the flowers away from direct sunlight or bright daylight – a dark room is ideal. An attic is a possibility, but never use a garage or outhouse which is too damp. The worst place is a greenhouse, where the humidity and sunlight ruins the flowers.
2 Prepare the flowers for drying as soon as they are picked, stripping off large and untidy leaves, and gathering the flowers into bunches of no more than ten stems. Secure them with an elastic band, then hang the bunches along a piece of string at 15cm intervals. Suspend the strings from coat hangers.
3 Plants with large or heavy flower-heads, such as sunflowers, should be tied individually. Feathery flowers such as astilbe and golden rod are best dried standing upright; an empty cardboard wine case with divisions is ideal.

Seedheads such as Chinese lanterns are best laid flat in a box so that they keep their shape.

PRESERVING WITH GLYCERINE

1 Using glycerine is an effective way of preserving foliage because it keeps the leaves supple and lifelike. The colour of the leaves changes, but the new colour is usually a most attractive darker tone. Refined glycerine is available from large chemists, but lower grade

---

FLOWERS TO DRY

HERBACEOUS FLOWERS dry particularly well. Lavender, delphiniums and eryngiums supply shades of blue. Alchemilla and golden rod add gold, while leek heads and ballota are silvery grey. Pink and purple flowers are bergamot, peonies and drumstick allium.

Annuals are grown each year to provide colourful material for drying, and should be grown in groups. Pick marigold, sunflower, cornflower and nigella when fully out. Other plants that work best when picked before they are fully open are helichrysum, larkspur, bells of Ireland and statice.

Flowering shrubs such as broom, roses and hydrangeas need to be dried as whole heads when they are firm and mature. Medium shades of colour work best and the flower heads must be no more than half open or they will become too fragile.

Seedheads and foliage are ideal for beginners. Poppies and honesty almost dry themselves. The best foliage are beech, oak, ivy and eucalyptus. Decorative twisted willow is also worth growing.

All types of dried flower displays can be kept fresh by an occasional spray with a special cleaner, available from a florist.

---

and less expensive glycerine can be purchased from most farm suppliers.
2 Mix one part glycerine to two parts hot water, in a wide-necked clear container. Stand the freshly picked foliage in the mixture, ensuring that the square-cut ends of the stems are below the surface. Remove lower leaves, but do not strip the bark. Place the container in a light, but shaded position. Replenish the glycerine as the level goes down.
3 Pick deciduous foliage from July onwards until the sap stops rising; this is usually when the first frosts occur. Evergreens are best picked from autumn until spring.
4 Drying times vary, depending on the season, weather and the type of plant. It could be a week or more. At first, the veins will change colour as the branch 'drinks' the glycerine, then the whole leaf will change. Do not leave the foliage in the glycerine for too long as it may go mouldy. If this happens, wash it in a mild solution of washing-up liquid and pat dry. Store inside a box.
5 Experiment by adding food colouring to the glycerine, so that the leaf takes on a colour. This can produce interesting results.

SILICA GEL CRYSTALS

1 Desiccants, or drying agents, such as silica gel are used to dry flowers that do not dry well in warm air alone. Roses picked as open buds, and astrantia, dahlias and zinnias picked when fully out, respond well to this technique, shrinking far less than with air drying, but becoming rather more brittle.
2 Sprinkle a layer of silica gel crystals into a plastic box. Carefully place the flower heads upright in the gel, then gently work more crystals between the petals with a spoon and small paintbrush. When all the flowers are in place, cover them with another layer of crystals, and place a lid on top.

3 Check the flowers after two days; they should be firm to the touch. Leave the flowers for about six days more, or until dry. Do not leave the flowers too long or they will become brittle. Use a fine hair spray to fix the colour.

4 To ensure that the flowers remain dry and keep their colour, scatter a fresh layer of silica gel on the bottom of an airtight box and place the individual flowers on top. Store them in a warm place to prevent them from going limp. The crystals can be used indefinitely, if sieved to remove broken petals.

CONTAINERS

Choosing the right container is a major part of the enjoyment of dried flower arranging, and these days anything goes. Building up a good selection of containers gives you maximum scope for creativity.

A container can be anything that will hold some florist's foam, ranging from the most delicate glass vase to an ancient distressed urn, from twiggy baskets, rustic trugs, terracotta troughs and wooden tubs to sophisticated designer pieces.

Even a tin can or jar can be transformed by being covered in moss, glossy or gilded leaves, or wheat, and for elegant occasions, containers wrapped in velvet, gauze or silk, tied with cord or ribbon, look wonderful. Plastic troughs or buckets can be covered in hay, bark or hessian tied in place with raffia; and a child's seaside bucket makes a jolly container, too.

Let the final position of the arrangement dictate the choice of container, and let the texture, colour and shape of the container guide you in choosing the right flowers. Rough textured pottery or rustic baskets suit informal country flowers, while elegant glass or metal will need a more minimalist, modern approach with the emphasis on shape.

The majority of flowers can be dried by hanging or standing them in a warm, dry, dark place, with good ventilation. This technique allows the moisture in the plant to evaporate but retains the flowers' colour.

Classic arrangement

This glorious display of dried flowers evokes the atmosphere of summer, and requires only simple techniques to achieve. The aim is to create an illusion of an armful of flowers from the garden.

MATERIALS

- a tall rustic basket
- blocks of florist's dry foam
- secateurs and scissors
- sharp knife
- stub wire and gutta percha tape (green, latex-based tape used for binding wired stems)
- glycerined and dyed eucalyptus foliage
- dyed broom or sea lavender
- purple larkspur or delphiniums
- pink peonies
- pink roses
- globe thistle heads
- poppy seedheads
- nigella seedheads

1 For a large display with heavy branches, cut blocks of dry florist's foam to fit the container. Ensure that it projects 3–4cm above the rim for stems to trail downwards. Fix wire mesh over the foam and tuck it under the rim.
2 Establish the overall height and width of the display by inserting eucalyptus foliage around the rim and trailing down.

SUPPORTING DRIED MATERIAL

1 *Cut the stems 1cm below the head and push a stub wire up through the stem, bend the end of the wire into a hook and gently pull back into the bloom. Bind with gutta percha tape, stretching it and working diagonally.*

2 *To repair or extend flower stalks, use other discarded stems. To lengthen a hollow stem, like a delphinium, just insert a thinner stem. If the flower has a solid stem, insert the stem into a wider, hollow one to lengthen it.*

3 *Glue the wire for a leaf along the back of the vein so that it will not show. Cones, nuts or fruits can be mounted onto stub wire, either pushed through or glued on using a glue gun. Twist the wire around the stem.*

A sumptuous array of flowers from the herbaceous border creates a classic display to grace a traditional interior, with the emphasis on harmonious colour.

3 Radiate the larkspur upwards and outwards, then fill in between with the broom or sea lavender, and contrasting groups of nigella.
4 At this point, the foam should not be visible. However, if it is, add more material, especially at the lower level until it is hidden. Use the peonies as large focal points, teasing out the petals, then add groups of roses.
5 Add globe thistles for contrast, then stand back to look at the display from all sides to make sure that the arrangement is well balanced. Fill any gaps with poppy seed heads.

Seeds and cones

Create a striking minimalist display for a modern interior, using just a few sculptural and exotic elements with the focus on shape.

MATERIALS

- tall terracotta pot or metal container
- gilding wax
- blocks of florist's dry foam
- secateurs, scissors and knife
- stub wire and gutta percha tape (see p.148)
- hot melt glue gun
- twisted willow branches
- reeds
- artichoke heads
- dried protea heads
- dried leuchodendron head
- poppy seedheads and peppers
- leaves, fungi and cones
- dried moss or gravel

1 If necessary, gild the container with gilding wax rubbed on with a cloth. Cut foam blocks to fit the container, levelling the blocks approximately 3cm below the rim.

2 Working against a plain background, so that the shapes are clearly visible, establish the height of the display with twisted willow branches and tall reeds. Aim for the display to be approximately one-and-a-half times the height of the container, although the final height will be partly dictated by where the arrangement is to be displayed.

3 Insert the protea or leuchodendron – the larger dried flower heads. Consider the position of each element carefully, turning the display to achieve balance from all sides.

4 Set the cones, fungi, peppers and leaves on wires (see step 1, left) and insert individual leaves or cones low in the display to cover the edge of the container.

5 Complete the display by adding a layer of dried moss or gravel to cover the foam.

In a modern arrangement, shapes and textures are important. The large blooms such as the protea and leuchodendron can be bought fresh and dried at home.

◆ Create a Warm Glow ◆

Candles commemorate birthdays, create romantic moods, and set a festive tone for any event. You can make special times even more memorable with candles you've made yourself. Complete the picture with our stunning candelabrum and gilded tray

Rolled candles

Rolled beeswax candles are easier to make than moulded candles. Sheets of pliable honeycomb-textured wax are available from craft shops.

MATERIALS

- scissors
- wick
- beeswax
- sharp trimming knife
- ruler
- butter knife

1 Heat the wax sheet on a radiator or with a hair dryer until pliable. Cut a wick 2cm longer than the length of the candle. Lay the wick along one edge of the wax; fold the wax over the wick and press tightly to seal it in.
2 Roll up the wax sheet with the wick inside, keeping top and bottom edges even.
3 When the candle is the diameter you want, cut off the excess wax using a sharp trimming knife and a metal ruler.
4 Smooth the cut end by pressing the seam with a warmed butter knife. Don't press too hard; beeswax is delicate and you might crush it. To prime the end of the wick, press a tiny bit of wax around it just before lighting it.

Moulded candles

Candle moulds come in a range of shapes, from fruits and vegetables to geometric. You can also improvise moulds — try using tin cans or flowerpots.

MATERIALS

- candle mould and wick
- double boiler
- paraffin wax
- mould seal (Blu-Tak)
- spray-on cooking oil
- wax dyes or crayons

1 Cut a length of wick 8-10cm longer than the height of the mould. In a double boiler, melt some of the wax over very low heat and soak the wick in it for 5 minutes. Lay the wick out on a piece of wax paper to dry.
2 If your mould isn't watertight, seal it with mould seal. Lightly coat the inside of the mould with spray-on cooking oil.
3 Secure the wick to the bottom of the mould with mould seal. Tie the other end to a small stick or skewer. Pull the wick taut and lay the stick across the mouth of the mould.
4 Heat the wax in a double boiler until just melted and immediately turn off the heat (hot molten wax is highly flammable so keep the temperature as low as possible).
5 Add the dye or crayon and stir until dissolved. For scented candles, add a drop or two of essential oil at this stage — try lavender, rose or jasmine. Citronella oil will make candles for outdoor use insect repellent.
6 Carefully pour the wax into the mould, stopping 1cm from the top.
7 Using oven gloves, lift the mould in a bowl of cold water. Don't let any water splash onto the wax. Leave to cool for an hour.
8 As the wax cools, a hollow will appear near the wick. Use a fork to prick small holes in the surface then fill the area with melted wax.
9 When the wax is cool and hard, use the stick to pull the candle from the mould. Trim the wick and smooth the bottom of the candle by standing it in a bowl of warm water.

MAKING ROLLED CANDLES

1 *Warm the sheet of beeswax with a hair dryer on the low setting to make it more pliable. Be careful not to melt the wax.*

2 *Lay the wick along the edge of the wax sheet. Roll against a flat surface. Keep the roll tight and even as you make each turn.*

3 *Use a metal ruler as a straightedge and put a fresh blade in your trimming knife to cut away the surplus wax from the sheet.*

4 *Press the seam closed with a butter knife warmed in hot water. The heat is more important than the pressure for fixing the seam.*

Candelabrum

With a little time, effort and patience you can fashion a graceful candle holder (see photograph, overleaf).

MATERIALS

- 1 roll each of 2mm, 1.6mm and 0.7mm-gauge steel wire
- 20 × 25cm tin sheeting, 0.23mm thick
- wire cutters
- pliers: parallel and general-purpose
- quick-drying glue
- marker pen
- electric drill with 4mm bit
- two bowls (about 12cm and 20cm in diameter)
- tin snips
- ruler
- gold spray paint

1 From the 2mm wire cut three 90cm lengths and three 55cm lengths. Loop the end of the 2mm wire around a pencil and wind the

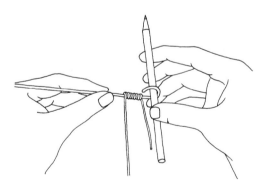

0.7mm wire around each length. Leave about 10cm of 0.7mm wire at the start, to cover the loop when you finish winding. Keep the 0.7mm wire taut so it winds tightly (hold the roll with your foot).

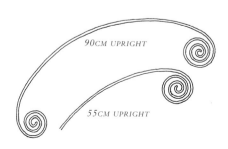

90CM UPRIGHT

55CM UPRIGHT

Warm autumnal hues were chosen for this impressive collection of rolled and moulded candles.

2 With parallel pliers, make a coil of about 5cm diameter at both ends of the 90cm wire lengths and at one end of the 55cm lengths. Then bend all six lengths with your hands, to form the uprights (see left).

3 The uprights are held together by two hoops. For the bottom hoop, take a 35cm length of 2mm wire and wind 0.7mm wire around it. Pull some of the 2mm wire out from the coil, so that it projects at one end and leaves a length of empty coil at the other. Place the wound wire around the smaller bowl to form a ring, then remove from the bowl. Place

glue in the empty coil end and insert the projecting end of wire. Hold in place until dry. Make the top hoop in the same way, using 60cm of 2mm wire and the larger bowl.

*PROJECTING
2MM WIRE*

4 Lightly mark three equidistant points around each hoop. Using short lengths of 0.7mm wire, bind the three 90cm uprights to the inside of the two hoops at the marked points so that they extend

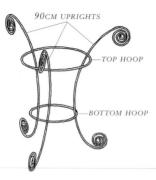

90CM UPRIGHTS

TOP HOOP

BOTTOM HOOP

about 15cm above the top hoop and about 15cm below the bottom hoop.

5 Spacing them evenly between the 90cm uprights, attach the bases of the 55cm uprights to the bottom loop and then to the top loop.

6 Using the 2mm wire, make a spiral (below) to fit just inside the top hoop. Bind the spiral in place with six radiating lengths of 0.7mm wire; start at the centre and weave the wire outwards to the edge, leaving about 6cm excess wire at each end.

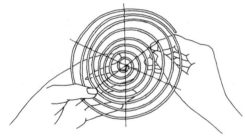

7 Use the excess wire to fix the spiral to the inside of the top hoop, at each upright.

8 Tightly twist about 3m of 1.6mm wire by looping the wire at its midpoint around a door handle and tying the two ends to a stick. Twist the stick, pulling with an even pressure. Then cut the wire into three equal lengths.

9 To form the lower diagonal struts, use a third of the wire; tie to the point where a 55cm upright meets the bottom hoop. Loop it around a foot and then up to the base of the next 55cm upright and so on back to the start.

10 Draw six 7cm circles on the tin sheet and drill a 6mm hole at the centre of each. Cut out with tin snips, and flatten edges with pliers.

11 On each circle, mark the lines shown in the diagram (top right) and cut along them. Form the circle of tin into a shallow conical shape, overlapping the right side with the left so that

the flap slips into the small slit (see below right), then fold the flap back underneath to secure the cone.

12 To attach cones to uprights, cut twelve 5cm lengths of 1.6mm wire. For each upright, clamp two lengths around the top two rings of the coil, with ends pointing up (right). Thread through the hole in the cone. Bend three ends flat, leaving one to spike the candle.

13 To form the upper diagonal struts, use a third of the twisted wire; attach where an upright meets the top hoop. Loop under the next cone, then down to where the next upright meets the top hoop. Continue back to the start and repeat with the last third of wire, starting at the next upright. Finally, spray paint the candelabrum.

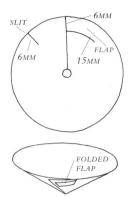

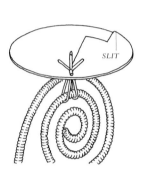

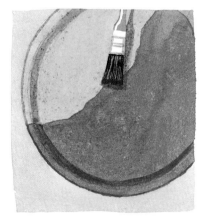

Gilded tray

Achieve the effect of gold leaf but avoid the expense and difficulty of application by using Dutch metal leaf – a combination of copper and zinc.

MATERIALS

- wooden or metal tray
- bright red emulsion paint
- soft nylon brushes, one for painting, one for sizing
- fine abrasive paper
- clean cotton rags
- tack rag (see p.102)
- acrylic-based gold size
- cotton gloves
- book of Dutch metal leaves (from art suppliers)
- sharp scissors
- soft-bristled brush, for laying leaf
- oxidant that reacts with copper (from specialist paint shops)
- rubber gloves
- water-based varnish (optional)

1 To prepare the tray for gilding, paint it with two or three coats of the red emulsion paint using a nylon brush. When the gilding is finished, some of the red will show through the leaf giving an attractive effect.

2 Allow each coat to dry thoroughly, then sand back with fine abrasive paper. After each sanding all the fine dust on the surface must be carefully cleaned away; wipe over first with a smooth, clean cotton cloth then wipe with a tack cloth to remove any remaining dust.

3 Apply the acrylic-based gold size with a soft nylon brush. Leave it for about 15 minutes. The size will remain sticky so that the Dutch metal leaf will adhere to it.

4 Wearing cotton gloves, lay the Dutch metal leaf onto the tray (see the step-by-step instructions below).

5 The next day, put on the rubber gloves and apply the oxidant to the gilded surface. Do this by dipping pieces of cotton cloth into the oxidant and randomly working across the surface of the Dutch metal leaf.

6 After about 15-30 minutes, wash off the oxidant with cold water. Some of the oxidant will still continue to react with the Dutch metal leaf overnight, producing a beautiful bluish-green aged look.

7 Varnish the tray if you wish using a water-based varnish. Varnishing will protect the surface of the tray but it will also dim some of the effects of the oxidant.

APPLYING GILDING

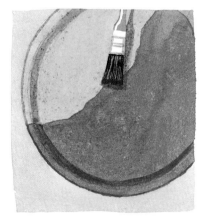

1 *Use a soft nylon brush to apply three coats of red emulsion, leaving each to dry thoroughly. Sand, then wipe with a tack rag. Apply a layer of gold size and leave for 15 minutes. It will feel sticky to the touch.*

2 *Wear cotton gloves to handle fragile Dutch leaf. Carefully cut the spine from the book of leaf, then cut the required number of sheets into quarters. Do not remove the thin layers of paper that protect the leaves.*

3 *Take one quarter. Move the top piece of paper to expose about 7mm leaf. Turn over and lay the protruding leaf on the tray. Gently slide the paper from beneath as you position the leaf, then peel off the top paper.*

4 *Overlap each sheet by about 7mm. Tamp down with a soft brush so they adhere, but avoid brushing the size. When completely covered, smooth all over. Any fragile, overlapping pieces of leaf will brush off.*

◆ Tiles in Bloom ◆

*Your favourite herbs can decorate tile markers for herbs in pots or in a bed in
the garden. Giant sunflowers, hand-painted on a white background, dramatically enhance plain
tiles on a kitchen wall or, with felt backing, become handy trivets*

Tile herb markers

*These hand-painted tiles make unusual markers
for plants. You should be able to buy the materials at
DIY stores and art shops. White paint can be mixed
with deeper shades or used to highlight leaves or flowers.*

MATERIALS
- 6 or more 15 × 5cm edging tiles
- carbon paper, pencil
- sealant for tile surface preparation and protective coating
- acrylic paints in a selection of colours (white, plus pink, lavender, blue, yellow and a couple of shades of green. Remember, too, that with a few basic colours and white you can mix myriad hues)
- small artist's brushes
- palette or old china plate
- 6 aluminum garden markers or other weatherproof stakes
- waterproof multipurpose adhesive

1 Enlarge the drawings to fit your tiles with a photocopier, or by hand, following the directions on page 220.
2 Prime the surface of each tile with the sealant; it will become dull. Use the carbon paper to transfer the drawings to the tiles.
3 Use a pencil to write the names of the herbs onto the tiles, or trace them from the drawing. Then paint the letters in using a dark green.
4 Paint leaves in pale green, and add shading and veins in a slightly darker green. On rosemary, paint a white centre vein.
5 Paint the flower petals using the lightest shade first and then adding detail such as feathery strokes or shading in a darker tone.
6 Once the paint has dried, finish by adding

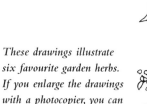

PEPPERMINT

SAGE

ROSEMARY

*These drawings illustrate
six favourite garden herbs.
If you enlarge the drawings
with a photocopier, you can
also use the enlarged labels
under each as a guide for
painting the names of the
herbs on the tiles.*

SWEET BASIL

CHIVES

THYME

another coat of the sealant to the tile.
7 Use an appropriate adhesive to attach a garden marker or stake to the back of each tile. Allow to dry thoroughly before using.

*Pretty tile markers are decorated with the herbs they
identify in this tiny kitchen garden. The same
technique could easily be adapted to make labels for
precious perennials in the herbaceous border.*

Sunflower tiles

These tiles can easily be incorporated within a wall of plain white tiles. They would also look great as a border above a dado rail in a sunny breakfast room.

MATERIALS
- square white tiles
- carbon paper, pencil
- sealant for tile surface preparation and protective coating
- acrylic paints in shades of green, yellow and brown
- artist's brushes
- palette or old china plate

1 Enlarge the sunflower (below) to fit your tiles with a photocopier, or by hand using the directions on page 220.

2 Prime the surface of each tile with the sealant. It will become dull. Use the carbon paper to transfer the sunflower drawing to the centre of each tile, as shown below.

3 Use the guidelines below to paint the sunflowers. When changing colours, wash the brushes with cold water and soap and dry with paper towels to remove all the moisture from the bristles. This will prevent the paints from becoming diluted.

4 Finish each painted tile with a coat of sealant.

Hand-painted tiles reflect the splashy colours of showy sunflowers, freshly picked from a late-summer garden.

PAINTING THE SUNFLOWER TILES

1 *Prime the surface of each tile with sealant. Place the carbon paper, carbon side down, on a tile and trace the pattern onto the tile's centre.*

2 *Fill all the leaves with your darkest green, shade with a medium green on half or parts of the leaves, and use a light green for the veins.*

3 *Paint all the petals with the lightest yellow, and then shade them with two darker yellows, letting each colour dry before adding another.*

4 *Paint the centre a light brown and shade it with two deeper browns. Finally, paint the seeds with dots of darkest brown and yellow.*

◆ Fresh and Clean ◆

Disinfectants, deodorisers and many cleaning products need not contain harsh or even toxic chemicals — there are alternative friendly mixtures for many household cleaning jobs. And you will not only help the environment but also save money by making your own cleansers

Washing-up liquid

This liquid gel will clean dishes well without creating unnecessary suds to be washed down the drain. It is unsuitable for use in dishwashers.

INGREDIENTS
- ¼ cup soap flakes
- 2 cups hot water
- ¼ cup glycerine
- ½ teaspoon lemon essential oil

1 Put the soap flakes and the hot water in a bowl and stir until the flakes have dissolved. Cool to lukewarm.
2 Stir in the glycerine and the essential oil and leave to cool. As the mixture cools it forms a loose gel. Stir with a fork to break up the gel and, using a funnel, pour into a narrow-necked plastic bottle. An old shampoo bottle would make an excellent storage container.
3 To use, squirt 2-3 teaspoons under running water into the sink.

Disinfectant glass cleaner

When cleaning windows and glass surfaces, use vertical strokes on one side and horizontal strokes on the other. It will then be easier to see which side needs more polishing after cleaning.

INGREDIENTS
- 1 tablespoon cornflour
- 1 cup vinegar
- 1 cup methylated spirits
- 1 teaspoon essential oil of rosemary

Put the cornflour into a plastic spray bottle along with the vinegar and shake to disperse the powder. Add the remaining ingredients and shake well for several minutes.

To use, shake the bottle, spray onto a window and polish with a clean cloth.

Lemon spray-on furniture polish

This polish takes less than a minute to make. It will remove dirt to give your furniture a showroom gleam.

INGREDIENTS
- 100ml (3½fl oz) liquid paraffin
- 50ml (2fl oz) turpentine or methylated spirits
- 1½ teaspoons lemon essential oil

Pour all the ingredients into a bottle with a pump-action spray top. Shake the mixture gently for several minutes to disperse the essential oil. To use, spray a fine mist of the mixture over the furniture and immediately wipe all over with a soft cloth.

Simmering potpourri deodoriser

Re-use the spices in this potpourri by straining off the liquid and putting them on a plate to dry.

INGREDIENTS
- ¼ cup dried lemon peel
- ½ cup dried orange peel
- 1 cup whole cloves
- 1 cup whole allspice
- 5 cinnamon sticks, roughly broken

Mix all the ingredients together and store in an airtight container until needed.

To use, place 2 tablespoons of the mixture in a heatproof container, cover with a cup of boiling water and leave in the room that needs deodorising. Any unpleasant odours will be replaced by the spicy fragrance released by the steaming potpourri. You can reheat the deodoriser in a saucepan or in the microwave if you need to prolong its use.

Pine floor cleaner

Washing soda, available from supermarkets, is an inexpensive yet effective cleansing agent. This mix will clean most hard floor surfaces.

INGREDIENTS
- ½ cup soap flakes
- ¼ cup washing soda
- 1 cup salt
- 2 cups water
- 2 teaspoons pine essential oil

1 Put the soap, washing soda, salt and water in a saucepan and heat gently, stirring until soap, soda and salt have dissolved.
2 Cool the mixture to lukewarm then add the essential oil. Stir well and use a funnel to transfer the mix to a screw-top plastic bottle.
3 To use, stir 2-3 tablespoons of the liquid into half a bucket of hot water.

4 After cleaning, rinse off the floor cleaner with half a bucket of clean water to which you have added a cup of vinegar.

Fabric gel wash

The old-fashioned method of washing clothing in pure soap is still one of the most reliable ways of getting them clean. This fabric gel wash, with its built-in water softener, is particularly good for hand washing clothes in hard water.

INGREDIENTS
- 2 cups pure soap flakes
- 1½ cups borax
- 1.5 litres (2¾ pints) water
- ½ cup glycerin
- 2 teaspoons essential oil of eucalyptus, lemon or lavender

1 Place soap flakes, borax and water in a saucepan, heat gently and stir until the liquid is clear. Add the glycerine and cool to lukewarm.
2 Add the essential oil and stir thoroughly.
3 Store into a wide-mouthed container and cover until needed. Ensure that the soap is fully dissolved before adding any clothes. This gel is best used with warm or hot water.

ESPECIALLY FOR CLOTHING

Hang a number of potpourri sachets in wardrobes, airing cupboards and linen cupboards to keep the contents smelling clean and fresh.

Sprinkle dried lavender among fresh linen before putting it away – but make sure the flowers are dry.

Make a large flat sachet using fine cotton material – muslin or cheesecloth are ideal. Fill with dried lavender or dried and crushed lemon verbena leaves and place on the bottom of underwear drawers. Place small sachets of potpourri in other clothing drawers.

Put a drop or two of your favourite essential oil directly onto the wood in your cupboards and drawers. The oil will be absorbed by the wood and its perfume released gradually into the surrounding air, giving your linen a pleasant aroma.

Mildew remover

Stubborn mildew on fabric often resists ordinary washing. Use this solution to remove it instead.

INGREDIENTS
- 2 parts salt
- 1 part lemon juice

Wash the fabric in warm soapy water, then mix enough salt and lemon juice to cover the mildewed area, and apply it. Place the fabric in full sun (ideally in summer), rinsing it after several hours. If the stain persists, repeat the treatment.

All-purpose disinfectant

Combined with vinegar and methylated spirits, pine essential oil makes a powerful anti-bacterial agent.

INGREDIENTS
- 200ml (7fl oz) methylated spirits
- 100ml (3½fl oz) pine essential oil
- 1 litre white vinegar

Pour the methylated spirits and essential oil into a bottle and shake to combine. Add the vinegar and shake for several minutes. Keep stoppered when not in use.

Toilet cleaner

For a clean, fresh-smelling toilet bowl, try this simple method of disinfection.

INGREDIENT
- ½ cup bicarbonate of soda or all-purpose disinfectant (see above)

Add the bicarbonate of soda or the all-purpose disinfectant to the water in the toilet bowl. Leave to stand overnight before flushing the bowl in the morning.

Septic tank activator

If persistent smells from a septic tank system suggest the absence of sufficient sewage-digesting bacteria, flush the following mixture down the toilet.

INGREDIENTS
- 1 litre (1¾ pints) hot water
- 500g (1lb 2oz) brown sugar
- 2 teaspoons dried yeast

Dissolve the brown sugar in the hot water and leave until lukewarm. Stir in the dried yeast and flush the mixture down the toilet.

Air freshener spray

This air freshener is strongly aromatic, so use a little at a time. Then you will gently scent the air in the room rather than overpower the senses.

INGREDIENTS
- 50ml (2fl oz) alcohol
- 25 drops bergamot essential oil
- 8 drops clove essential oil
- 5 drops lemon essential oil
- 200ml (7fl oz) distilled water

Put the alcohol and the essential oils into a spray bottle and shake in order to disperse the oils. Add the distilled water and shake for several minutes so as to thoroughly combine the mixture. Leave for a few days for the fragrance to mature before using.

White goods cleaner

Regular wiping with this cleaner will remove grubby fingermarks and leave the surfaces of washing machines, fridges and freezers looking like new.

INGREDIENTS
- 2 tablespoons washing-up liquid (see recipe opposite, or use a commercial product)
- 1 tablespoon cornflour
- 1 cup water
- 1 cup vinegar

1 Put all the ingredients in a plastic spray bottle and shake gently to combine.
2 Spray a fine film of the mixture over the surface and wipe clean with a soft cloth.

To deodorise the insides of refrigerators and freezers, remove all food and bottles then wipe the surfaces and shelves over with a clean cloth moistened with this cleaner and sprinkled with bicarbonate of soda. If possible, then leave the door open for an hour or two.

Before replacing food, wipe the inside surfaces with a damp cloth sprinkled with several drops of vanilla essence.

ALL ABOUT
the garden

A handful of herbs or a basket of vegetables for the kitchen, a bunch of flowers for a living-room vase, or perhaps a small fountain to decorate a shady corner, an elegant trellis to support a favourite rose or a comfortable hammock for weekend relaxation. You can produce all these things yourself – and many more – if you follow the step-by-step directions given in this chapter.

Here we provide a multitude of ideas to inspire you to make the most of your garden, not just as a place for plants but also as an outdoor room to relax in.

You'll discover how to create your own kitchen garden in a tiered terracotta-pot display right outside your back door or how to liven up your garden with a scarecrow.

Where space is limited, turn a half barrel into a garden feature as a 'mini-pond'. Find out how to construct lattice frames in such a way that they help to alter perspective and magically extend the horizons of your garden. Straightforward directions help you to master the art of wirework and make attractive stands and hangers for your pots. Add distinction to a larger garden with exciting topiary shapes and interesting pathways.

All About the Garden shows you how to turn your garden into a sunlit living room.

BEFORE YOU BEGIN...

*There is no secret to turning a nondescript patch of grass into a tranquil
retreat. Feed the soil to guarantee a backdrop of healthy plants and furnish your outdoor room with
attractive objects you have made yourself. In this chapter we show you how to do just that*

The ideal garden is one that is well suited to the maintenance and recreational routines of the owners while at the same time making the most of its site. Plants combine with paths, furniture, containers, ornaments and structures to create a garden that is attractive and easy to maintain as well as having a reassuring human scale.

With a little artifice the man-made parts of the garden can be used to introduce an element of intrigue that suggests that there might be more to the garden than meets the eye. An elegant rose-covered arbour is a subtle invitation to 'step this way' while a tall, four-sided trellis swathed in blooms acts as a majestic centrepiece that commands attention. And when you make these pieces yourself you stamp your own personality on the garden. Most of the projects in this chapter can be varied to suit your garden's dimensions or interpreted in a way that meets your individual taste.

A little planning is a good investment

A garden should have an integrated framework – usually provided by boundaries, pathways and a house – within which the 'soft' element of plants is inserted. Drawing up a plan, no matter how rough, will ensure that you successfully bring together all the elements you want in your garden. Take a hard-headed look at your requirements and the amount of space you can utilise to meet them.

Sketch in the 'hard' framework items first: walls, fences, steps and paths. Indicate changes such as a new path or hedge. A straight concrete path is the least expensive and the simplest to make but a curved path of brick or stone (see below) is far more interesting. In the same way, a square hedge may be easy to trim but a handsome piece of topiary will lift your garden out of the ordinary.

Once the solid, permanent parameters have been established it is time to prepare the soil for planting – another useful investment of time: if the soil is undernourished your vegetables, fruit and ornamental plants will not thrive and the garden will not be the welcoming place you want it to be.

Nourish the soil for healthy plants

For the successful home gardener, the secret of growing good-looking, healthy plants can be summed up in one sentence: work with nature, not against it. To begin with, observe your micro-climate: how much rain falls in each season; how long the seasons last; which areas are damp and which dry; the range of temperatures between the seasons and even between night and day.

Organic matter is essential to healthy soil so your first step before you do any planting should be to dig in a 10cm layer of compost mixed with well-rotted animal manure. Make it at least a

LAYING A PATH OF BRICKS OR PAVERS

1 *For best results, frame the path site with a removable timber edging, known as form-work. Old floorboards or similar second-hand timbers can be used for this. For a permanent edging around gravel or paving blocks use preservative-treated timber.*

2 *For a curved path, mark out the perimeter with a string line (see page 182) and pegs at 0.5m intervals. Before nailing the edging to the pegs render it flexible enough to bend by making a series of saw cuts halfway through the inside surface.*

3 *Excavate between the edging to a depth that will allow the bricks to sit level with the surface on top of a 5cm layer of base material – here, sand. Spread the base material with a rake, checking for evenness with a spirit level before tamping it down.*

4 *Starting in a corner and kneeling on a piece of flat board, pack the bricks tightly in position according to your chosen pattern. When all the bricks are laid, sweep fine sand into cracks and crevices and hose down the path with a fine spray.*

A garden provides you with more scope for creativity than any other part of the home. All that is required is some inexpensive tools and the investment of a little labour.

Providing shade when the weather gets hot is a priority, and for those gardens too small to contain a large tree or trees the projects in this chapter aim to provide a solution. A canvas awning and a hammock need not rely on trees for support, they can simply be attached to a wall of the house and a sturdy post. A simple water feature, whether a wall fountain or a 'mini-pond' in a barrel or other container, has an instantly cooling, relaxing effect.

Items of furniture you intend using outside – such as the covered director's chairs (see page 210) or the shade structure (page 209) – should be both lightweight and stackable so that they can easily be moved to a shed or garage when not required. Permanent outdoor chairs should have well-designed seats that do not retain puddles of water making them unusable after rain.

twice-yearly ritual to repeat this procedure and to mulch the soil after the compost is dug in – this will increase water and nutrient retention in sandy soil and help to open the pores of clay soil, thus allowing excess water to drain away. Time spent improving the level of organic matter in the soil in the initial stages is time well spent. It will save you money and effort in the future.

Following the sun: the aspect

Understanding the position of the sun in the seasonal sky allows you to take advantage of the best level of sun or shade, and helps you to find the best location for the garden features you make yourself as well as larger items such as patios, decks, ponds and barbecues.

In the Northern Hemisphere the south side of a house is far sunnier than the north side which is, conversely, shadier. Winds from the north are generally cooler than those from the south so plants for the northern side need to be chosen with this in mind.

Throughout most of the year, the sun shines from the south-east in the morning and the south-west in the afternoon so trees planted on the east or west of a house will help to shade and cool it in summer. The angle of the sun is lower in winter, so sunlight penetrates below the lowest branches, but it also creates longer shadows. In summer, the sun is higher in the sky and more directly overhead.

The trimmings: working with wire

Planting and landscaping make a garden, but small, decorative 'extras' – an intricate holder for a party light or a smart pot stand – can give it the finishing touch, particularly for a special occasion. Before starting on the wirework projects in this chapter, read the following information about the special materials and general skills needed. Garden wire can be bought quite cheaply in rolls at hardware stores, DIY stores or garden centres and comes in various thicknesses. Wire dimensions are given in this section as thin (approx 1mm), medium (approx 2mm) and thick (approx 3mm). Choose the thickness to suit your purpose. A pair of long-nose pliers is essential, as are sturdy leather working gloves; an engineer's vice is also very useful.

To wind a length of wire into a decorative twist use a hook held in an electric drill (see page 200). To make a wire ring or hoop, bend a length of wire around an upside-down saucepan (the diameter of your desired circle or a bit less), holding the pan handle firmly on the ground with your foot. Make hooks at each end by bending them over with pliers, then loop the hooks together; for most wirework projects you will need to close each hook firmly with the pliers.

The Kitchen Garden

It is easy to create a productive vegetable garden that is also good to look at by using the exciting foliage textures and colours of carefully chosen edible plants. With a little basic preparation and regular fertilising you have the makings of a fresh salad always to hand

A potted garden

If you have limited space, are troubled by back problems or find it inconvenient trudging down to the vegetable garden for a sprig of mint, why not grow some commonly used herbs in a sunny spot near the back door. You can use a range of different-sized pots, grouped together (as pictured below) or construct the simple three-tiered stand as described and pictured opposite. Terracotta and reconstituted stone make handsome containers; terracotta-coloured plastic pots are easy to move and inexpensive.

MATERIALS

- 3 saucer-shaped bowl planters ranging from about 40–60cm in diameter
- 2 small conical flowerpots at least 12cm high
- large bag of potting compost
- small bag of gravel
- herb and salad seedlings

1 Position the largest bowl where you want it to stand. Cover the drainage hole with insect-screen mesh and a 1cm layer of gravel. Place an upturned conical pot in the centre.

2 Fill the bowl to within 3cm of the rim with potting mix. A few handfuls of well-rotted manure and a sprinkling of slow-release fertiliser will encourage faster, stronger growth.

3 Stand the middle bowl on the upturned pot and repeat the procedure described above. Top with the smallest bowl, fill with potting mix, and you are ready to plant.

4 Plant low-growing or cascading plants in the first and second tiers; you can reserve the top bowl for a single, larger plant such as a tomato. Water regularly – compost in pots tends to dry out quickly – and apply liquid fertiliser fortnightly. Remove dead and dying leaves to stimulate the growth of new foliage.

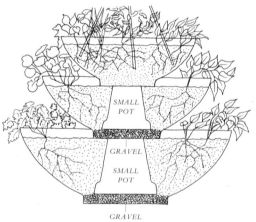

SMALL POT

GRAVEL

SMALL POT

GRAVEL

In this grouped planting, we used a collection of salad greens such as rocket, cress, lambs lettuce, mustard greens, curly endive and mixed lettuce, including a purple-leafed variety, with popular herbs – basil, parsley, chives and feathery dill. Flowering edibles including nasturtiums, marigolds and violas make a colourful addition. For more substantial crops, try some modern dwarf varieties of vegetables such as carrots, courgettes, cucumber and tomatoes.

FROM MEDIEVAL TIMES

MODERN KITCHEN gardens have their origins in the old walled gardens of medieval monasteries. In the Middle Ages, the gardens were laid out in rows with formal edged paths and ranks of espaliered fruit trees, herbs and vegetables. This almost geometric arrangement is as good a basis for an edible-plant garden today as it was then.

Now, as then, herbs are a valuable asset in the garden for practical as well as purely aesthetic reasons, so your herb plantings are a good starting point for the kitchen garden. Herbs are not only invaluable in cooking, they can define borders, deter insects and encourage the growth of other plants. They also work well in a cottage garden and make useful ground cover as an alternative to lawn.

Most herbs are informally decorative, often having simple, cloud-like masses of flowers in white, pink, blue or silver in sharp contrast to the stiffness of many ornamental plants. They help to soften formal gardens and are well suited to a position behind low hedges of box or lavender where their tendency to spread is easily controlled. They can also be grown in pots and other containers.

As a general rule, herbs need full sun (at least four hours a day) and good drainage. Many scented herbs originated from stony Mediterranean hillsides where roots sought relief from hot, dry summers in cracks under boulders. Most of these herbs are not too particular about soil fertility, but beds should be enriched before planting with a 4-5cm layer of well-rotted manure or compost.

An application of a complete fertiliser and mulching in summer is beneficial. Where summers are wet, reduce humidity with a gravel mulch or use pots and raised beds.

Tiered bowls make an attractive feature so place them where they can be admired while still receiving the maximum amount of sun. If one side is shadier than the other, grow mint or other shade-tolerant plants.

A bed of herbs

With a little preparation you can enjoy the freshness of culinary herbs picked straight from the garden.

MATERIALS
- tape measure
- string and wooden pegs
- set square, spirit level
- hardwood edging (old railway sleepers are ideal)
- galvanised bolts or brackets

1 Use a tape measure, string and wooden pegs and a set square to mark out a rectangular or square bed to the size you want. Tie string to a peg at each corner to mark the perimeter.
2 Set the hardwood edging in place. Use the spirit level to check the top edges, excavating soil from underneath if necessary. Fix the corners together with brackets or bolts.
3 Dig the bed to the depth of a spade blade, adding a 4–5cm layer of well-rotted manure.
4 Plant your herbs, putting tall varieties at the back or in the middle and groundcover herbs at the edges where they can spill onto paths.

Make use of the decorative qualities of herbs: marjoram, thyme and oregano perform handsomely in a raised bed (above). Catmint, lavender, bronze fennel and dill all mix happily with calendulas (right) while the garden at top right is ornamental by virtue of the combination of varied shapes and leaf forms — salvia and edible nasturtiums add flower colour.

A raised bed

Vegetables need a soil rich in well-rotted organic matter and with good drainage. The most effective way of achieving the latter is to raise the bed above the surrounding ground level – this also allows plenty of room for adding manure and compost to encourage your plants to grow quickly. We have made divisions within a large bed with timber shingles but you could use any attractive, natural-looking material such as old slate or terracotta tiles, brick pavers or smooth pieces of natural stone.

MATERIALS
- graph paper, pencil, ruler
- string line and hammer
- galvanised nails
- marker stakes
- hardwood or sleepers for edging
- timber shingles

1 Mark out a scale plan on paper. Include paths, beds, trellises or other features needed.
2 Translate the plan to the ground, marking out the beds with string and pegs (see step 1, page 164). Hammer marker pegs into the ground in each corner and dig out a shallow channel so the timber edging will sit firmly in place. Line the channel with 5cm coarse sand.
3 If the ground slopes, as ours did, lay the first pieces of timber on level surface sand, and add

Tightly packed timber shingles laid end to end are a handsome, hard-wearing and versatile way of preventing soil runoff. They should last for about ten years used this way. A plan for this bed is overleaf.

Surrounding a bed with raised edging makes it easy to build up the soil with the organic matter necessary to raise healthy crops such as courgettes, tomatoes, marrows, spinach, salad greens or beans. Separate beds also allow you to cater for the individual soil, nutritional and watering needs of different plants.

additional edging in a stepped or terraced fashion to follow the natural slope (see right), making sure that the top edge is level. Bolt or bracket the corners (see step 2, page 164).

4 Divide up individual planting areas within a large bed by slotting timber shingles, tiles or slates on edge in a shallow trench. Press them firmly in place and tap the edges lightly so that they fit tightly side by side.

5 Dig the soil thoroughly to spade-blade depth and add plenty of well-rotted organic matter as for herbs (see page 164).

6 If you leave the narrow access paths between beds as bare earth, you'll be able to vary bed widths easily as required – simply move the shingles and dig up the path.

EDGED AND DIVIDED BED

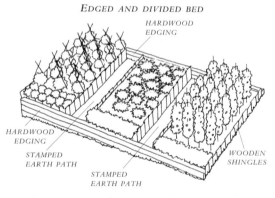

HARDWOOD EDGING

HARDWOOD EDGING

STAMPED EARTH PATH

STAMPED EARTH PATH

WOODEN SHINGLES

TERRACED BEDS

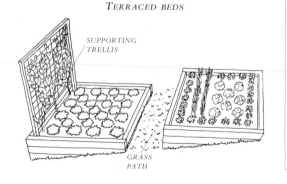

SUPPORTING TRELLIS

GRASS PATH

FAVOURITE HERBS AND VEGETABLES

BASIL, a summer-growing annual, prefers moist, rich soil conditions. It is frost tender.

BEETROOT comes in several different types. The red-leafed variety is the one most often grown but there are others available; look through catalogues from specialist mail-order nurseries and seed merchants.

CLIMBING BEANS produce a generous bounty for little labour. The tall varieties need support but dwarf beans will stand alone if planted in tight rows. Runner beans, with their scarlet flowers, always provide an attractive show.

CORIANDER, a herb of tropical Asian origin, requires warmth and plentiful water in the summer growing season. It tends to run to seed so try to buy a non-bolting variety.

CUCUMBER is invaluable for summer salads. Trailing cucumbers can be trained up a trellis or the bushier apple-shaped varieties can be planted in beds or large tubs.

LOVAGE is a strongly celery-flavoured leaf. A sprig or two chopped into salad gives an invigorating piquancy, but don't overdo it.

MARJORAM and **OREGANO** are very similar and often confused, though marjoram is the milder tasting of the two. Use in stuffings, and in dishes with a Mediterranean flavour. The leaves are good in tomato salads. Golden and variegated forms are useful ground covers.

MINT is one of the most widely used culinary herbs, whether finely chopped in mint sauce for roast lamb, or shredded in cucumber and yoghurt salad. Different varieties, such as applemint, spearmint and peppermint, have very distinctive flavours and aromas.

SAGE is a major culinary herb. Other members of the salvia family have cosmetic uses.

THYME is one of the most useful herbs in the garden. It is ornamental, attractive to bees and other pollinators, and is widely used in stuffings and Mediterranean-based cuisines.

TOMATOES are a must in the home kitchen garden. The cherry varieties are less troubled by pests than most of the large fruiting types, and can be grown easily in pots.

VARIATION Many flowers and herbs enhance the growth and taste of vegetables, as well as providing protection against certain pests and diseases. Some amiable plant combinations are: marigolds with most vegetables and herbs to confuse and deter pests with their smell and to boost the yield of beans (a bonus is the edible petals for mixed-leaf salads); roses with tomatoes, garlic and members of the onion family to encourage vigorous growth; basil near its culinary partner, tomato, to deter white fly which spreads fungal diseases.

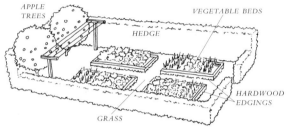

APPLE TREES

HEDGE

VEGETABLE BEDS

HARDWOOD EDGINGS

GRASS

Solid edging clearly defines a bed as well as preventing soil runoff (left). Sleepers laid in a stepped profile are best for a sloping site (below left). On the gradient's low side, where drainage is best, herbs will thrive.

PRACTICAL IDEAS

GETTING THE BEST FROM YOUR PLANTS

An open but sheltered position with at least four hours of sunshine a day is essential – for best results choose a south or south-westerly aspect.

A moisture-retentive but free-draining loam is ideal and can be made from either sandy or clay soils with the addition of plenty of well-rotted organic matter.

Regular watering during the summer is a must. Water in the cool of the day – early morning or dusk – and mulch to prevent moisture evaporating.

Remove weeds regularly – these compete with vegetables and they may harbour diseases – and check frequently for insects and leaf fungus.

Keep plantings away from large trees. They not only shade precious sunshine but their substantial root systems will compete for water and nutrients.

◆ Small Garden Fruit Trees ◆

*Few pleasures can compare with that of walking into your garden and picking
fruit from the trees or shrubs that you have planted and tended. There are many fruiting plants
that are ornamental as well as being well suited to small-scale cultivation*

*Low growing or step-over hedges are perfect for small
gardens. Train fruit trees such as apples along wires
for a decorative edible edging feature.*

its roots. Water it well, fill the hole with soil
and firm the surface. Tie the trunk of the tree
to the stake and secure the branches to the
tensing wires. Water regularly until the trees
are established, specifically during drought.

4 Prune the branches in summer in order to
encourage fruit production. Horizontal shoots
should be pruned back to between four and
six buds. In winter, prune the branches for
shape, shortening the stems to two buds.
Remove any shoots that are more vertical
than horizontal, or ones that are coming
forward from the main trunk.

An apple hedge

*Apple cultivars grafted on to dwarfing rootstocks and
trained into two-tier branch systems make attractive
and productive hedges for a kitchen garden and to
edge a lawn. Buy pre-trained trees for speedy fruiting
or purchase maiden trees that can be trained into
your required shape. Maiden trees need to be grown
for at least four years before they yield fruit.*

MATERIALS

- string, pegs and spade
- tensing tools, tensing wire and
  1m posts, available from
  garden centres
- compost and bonemeal
- 1m stakes and ties
- young espalier apple trees
  (pre-trained varieties)

1 Use the string and pegs to mark out a
straight line for the length of the hedge.
Drive in a post at each end to a depth of
25cm. Secure two rows of tensing wire to
each post. The rows of wire should be at the
height required for the two tiers of branches
to grow along. Use the tensing tool to tighten
the wire clip; refer to the manufacturer's
instructions for details.

2 Dig evenly spaced planting holes between
the two posts for the trees. Each hole must be
one-third wider than the tree's root system
and sufficiently deep for the soil mark on the
main stem to be level with the surrounding
soil. Fork well-rotted compost and a handful
of bonemeal into each of the holes.

3 Place a stake in each hole, driving it into
the soil so that 75cm shows above ground.
Place an apple tree in each hole and spread out

Fan-trained cherry

*By growing a cherry in a fan shape against a wall
you can protect the tree from harsh weather and
easily control any outbreaks of pests and disease. In
a small garden, a morello cherry, which has an acid
flavour, is the best choice. Sweet cherries need to
have additional trees to aid cross-pollination and,
therefore, will take up more space.*

MATERIALS

- vine eyes and tensing wire
- spade
- maiden or pre-trained
  cherry tree
- bonemeal
- bamboo canes
- string

1 Fix vine eyes and horizontal support wires
to the wall (refer to the manufacturer's
instructions). They should be about 15cm
apart and start 38cm from soil level.

STARS OF THE ORCHARD

PLUMS, WHICH INCLUDE gages and damsons, are good trees for small gardens because they provide ornamental attraction as well as crops of fruit. Dwarf varieties are best for growing as bushes or for training into fan shapes. When planting a fan-trained plum, try to position it against a sheltered but sunny south-facing wall; see Fan-trained Cherry, left, for information about planting and training the branches. Plant the trees in November when the soil is warm, and provide sturdy supports with stout stakes and canes.

When grown in containers, plums should be planted into a rich compost, and fed and watered regularly. They can also be grown in a lawn for eye-catching appeal with fruit-laden branches weeping down towards the grass.

Most plum varieties, along with blueberries, pears and apples, need to be cross-pollinated, so different varieties are needed for the tree to fruit. However, self-fertile plums include Denniston's Superb, Czar and Giant Prune.

All plum trees should be pruned first in the spring and again in the summer. Do not cut back the branches in winter as this may encourage disease to infect the open cuts.

2 Plant the maiden tree as for the apple hedge, in winter or early spring when the tree will be dormant. Position it about 30-45cm away from the wall, and prune the branches 40-45cm from the main stem.
3 Select any strong-growing shoots and tie them to the canes with string. Arrange them into a fan shape radiating out from the main stem and secure the canes, with branches attached, to the support wires.
4 If you decide to grow a sweet cherry tree, select only two strong shoots. Place them at a 45° angle to the main stem to initiate a fan shape and remove the central stem to promote

In a small garden, morello cherry trees are a good choice because they self-pollinate. The ripe, red fruit also adds colour to the garden – and makes good jam.

equal growth on both sides. Cut out any weak or deformed branches to encourage vigorous growth along the training canes.
5 As the tree grows, train new growth against additional canes. Prune morello cherry trees each year to encourage fruit on one-year-old wood. Sweet cherries fruit on two-year-old branches and should be pruned in the summer to remove excessive leaf growth.

Potted strawberries

Pots and tins are the perfect decorative and space-saving way to grow this favourite fruit and potting up takes only a few minutes. All you then need to do is water and feed the plants regularly to keep juicy strawberries coming all summer long. You could even make an unusual feature by hanging the tins in the wire holders described opposite.

MATERIALS
- strawberry plants
- pots or tins
- potting compost
- fine wire mesh or gravel
- slow-release fertiliser

1 If using tins, hammer three large nail holes in the base of each and cover with a layer of fine mesh or gravel to stop the mix from washing away. Fill tins to within 3-4cm of the rim; if using a herb planter (bottom right in photograph) fill it to the lowest pocket.

2 If using the herb planter, place a strawberry plant in the lowest pocket and thread the stems through the opening from the inside to the outside. Make sure the crown – the point at which roots and leaves join – is just above the level of the soil, so that it doesn't rot.

3 Fill the pot to the level of the next pocket and repeat the planting procedure. Plant two or three crowns in the top of the pot.

4 Place containers in a sunny position and turn them 180° twice a week so as to expose the plant evenly to sunlight.

5 During the summer, feed plants fortnightly with a liquid fertiliser containing a high phosphate content to encourage flowering. Water whenever the top 1-2cm of potting mix appears to have dried out; water the pockets of strawberry pots individually.

A STRAWBERRY PLOT

STRAWBERRIES ARE IDEAL for the home orchard; the fruit is delicious, they have few pests and on a space-for-yield ratio, they are practically unbeatable. Growing your own fruit means that you can choose the most vigorous and full-flavoured varieties.

For best results:

1 Dig the bed to spade-blade depth and add well-rotted manure and blood and bone.

2 Spray the bed with glyphosate then cover with black plastic sheeting to warm the soil and reduce competition from weeds – plant through slits in the plastic.

3 Buy certified disease-free plants only. Plant in low mounds about 30cm apart, cover the roots with soil and firm in gently, ensuring that the crowns stay above the surface.

4 Pinch out long, spindly runners as they form to encourage a strong central plant.

Plump strawberries are a cheerful sign of summer. Potted plants can be moved to follow the sun – and when the fruit comes it is easily harvested.

Strawberry hangers

Plant strawberries in large tins and hang them in these attractive wire hangers. Make the basic hanger first, then tackle the decorative variations – all three are pictured opposite. See the section on wirework techniques (page 161), before you begin.

MATERIALS

- large tins, tops removed (you could ask a local school for empty catering-size cans, or use old paint tins)
- wire: thin, medium, thick
- ruler or tape measure
- felt pen
- pliers, hammer, gloves
- saucepans of various sizes
- vice, drill
- piece of 50-60mm diameter pipe (for frilled hanger)
- gloss spray paint, or small tin of gloss paint and paintbrush

BASIC HANGER – CUTTING TO LENGTH

1 To make the three hoops that encircle the tin, bend a length of the thick wire around a saucepan with a diameter 1-2cm larger than that of the tin. Allowing about 8cm for an overlap, cut each piece of wire. Form the hoops and wrap two small pieces of thin wire around each overlap to secure the shape. Mark four points an equal distance apart around the circumference of each hoop.

2 Two pieces of wire in a cross shape form the hanger base. To make them, cut the thick wire to equal the hoop diameter plus 2cm.

3 For the uprights, cut four straight pieces of thick wire to match the height of the tin. Mark each upright at its midpoint.

4 For handles, cut four straight pieces of thick wire, each 40cm long. With pliers, bend 1cm at the ends of each piece around to make a hook; at one end leave the hook open.

ASSEMBLING THE BASIC HANGER

1 Form the base of the hanger by tying the two pieces of wire together with the thin wire so that they form a cross with even-lengthed segments (see above right). Hook about 1cm

of each cross-piece around a hoop at the marked points and close the hooks with pliers.

2 Attach one end of each upright to this base hoop by hooking 1cm around the outside of the hoop, next to the cross-piece joins. Turn the hooks inwards around the base hoop and close them with pliers.

3 To form the top of the hanger, hook the other ends of the uprights to the second hoop.

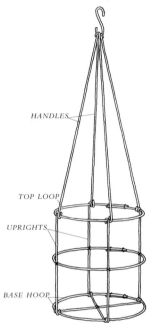

4 Insert the third hoop into the frame and tie it with the thin wire to the midpoint of the uprights (the marked points on the hoop wire and the upright wire should meet).

5 Attach the handles to the top hoop, closing the hooks with pliers.

6 Paint the wire hanger. The top of the tin planter will stand about 2cm proud of the top hoop. Bend the tops of the handles into large hooks and tie them together just below the hooks with the thin wire for easier handling. Take off the wire when taking the tin from the hanger.

VARIATION: FRILLED HANGER

1 Make the basic hanger as above, but with handles 60cm long. Use pliers to bend the tops of the handles into scrolls of about 5cm diameter (see photograph opposite).

2 To make a frill that will sit around the top hoop of the hanger, drill a hole in the pipe, about 12cm from one end. Secure one end of a 3.5m piece of medium wire in a vice. Stretch the wire out to its full length and put the free end in the hole in the pipe. Holding the pipe at each end and keeping the wire taut, slowly walk towards the vice, coiling the wire around the pipe as you go. When you reach the vice, with the wire fully coiled, cut off the

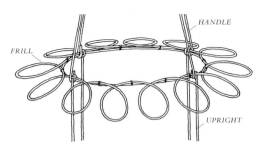

end in the small hole and release the tension; remove the other end from the vice. Spread the wire out and flatten it as it uncoils to the point where it forms a series of loops that make a frill (see above).

3 Use the thin wire to attach the frill to the top hoop at each point where the two touch.

4 Attach the handles to the top hoop, around the frill. Tie the tops of the handles together with wire just below the curls.

5 Paint the hanger, if desired.

VARIATION: FLAT-TOPPED HANGER

1 Make uprights 25cm longer than for basic hanger, marking where the extra length begins. Fix in a vice at this mark and, wearing gloves, bend the wire to a right angle; tap gently with a hammer for a neat angle. Use pliers to bend a 5cm diameter coil at the free end.

2 Make three hoops as for the basic hanger, increasing the diameter by 1cm. Attach to the shaped uprights, this time placing the uprights inside the hoops (see below).

3 Make two more hoops, one 26cm diameter and one 32cm (use larger saucepans).

4 Using the thin wire, attach these hoops to the horizontal part of the uprights (see below).

5 Attach handles as for basic hanger. Paint, or leave unpainted, as pictured opposite.

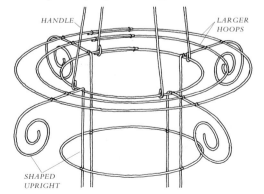

◆ Displaying the Rose ◆

*Few flowers can match the popularity of the rose and few roses can match
the spectacular beauty of a climbing rose in full bloom. A simply made arbour in metal
or timber allows the plant to display its splendour to stunning effect*

A rose arbour

*This inexpensive rose arbour allows the showy rose
to take pride of place as the main garden ornament.*

MATERIALS
- 6m reinforcing garden mesh
  (available from large garden
  centres)
- wire cutters, pliers

1 Cut mesh in half – it is usually sold in 6m
lengths. The higher the arbour the better the
display (the one in the photograph is nearly 3m
tall). The width should be at least 1.5m – any
narrower and the support is unlikely to be
strong enough to hold the weight of a fully
grown climbing rose in bloom.

2 Next, place the mesh sections on the
ground and bend them in turn to take on an
elegant curved shape similar to the one shown
in the photograph. Shape one side first and use
it as a template for bending the other. (The
curves can be as simple or as complicated as
you like, as long as the arbour is symmetrical.)

3 Our first curve was made to bend about 2m
from ground level, and can be measured as an
angle of approximately 30° from horizontal.

4 Our second curve follows the first at an
angle of between 100° and 110°. We made a
final minor bend about 40cm higher again, at
30-40° from the horizontal.

5 Form a decorative scroll or finial at the top
by cutting off the last cross-piece on each
section and bending the vertical mesh wires
outwards around a piece of pipe to form an
almost-closed circle (see photograph, right).
Wire the two sides tightly together at the top.

*Train a profusely flowering climbing rose over a
graceful arbour and the plant will provide you with a
spectacular eye-catching focal point in the garden.*

172

6 To ensure that the frame is secure enough to bear the weight of a large climber, bury the base at least 50cm and cement it in place.

VARIATIONS Arches, arbours and pergolas are much the same in principle, the main difference being the shape of the overhead support. An arch may have a flat timber beam, and the pergola, a pitched frame, while most arbours are curved. All can be used in a series to create a tunnel or to highlight an entrance.

Use robust timbers cemented well into the ground for an archway or pergola to support the vigorous growth of an old-fashioned climbing or rambling rose.

A dramatic effect can be achieved with a cordon. Attach heavy ropes or chains loosely to the tops of tall posts or along a wall to form a series of loops – or cordons – to support the rose. This is particularly effective along a path or to define a specific area.

TO TWIST OR TIE?

HOW SHOULD A climbing rose be attached to its support? While some rose growers suggest twisting shoots around the supporting structure others prefer simply to tie them flat against it. On balance, tying makes more sense as it is easier to prune a straight stem than one which has grown in a spiral.

◆ Blooms and Borders ◆

*Nothing brightens a house more than a vase brimming with fresh, home-grown flowers,
while clever use of hedging can divide the garden into a series of 'rooms', provide a lush backdrop for
flower borders, or simply define a living boundary between you and your neighbours*

Flowers for cutting

*A beautiful flower arrangement is made up of three
main elements: foliage fillers, floral fillers and focal
flowers. An ideal cutting garden should, therefore,
include a mix of shrubs and perennials as well as
seasonal annuals and bulbs. As annuals can usually
be grown readily from seed, they offer a cost-effective
way of ensuring a good supply of flowers.*

MATERIALS
- spade
- compost, manure, fertiliser
- sand
- several packets of seeds
  (long-stemmed annuals)
- bulbs (daffodils, tulips, etc)
  for spring flowers

For best results, you will need a bed devoted
to flowers for cutting. A bed of 2 × 3m will
provide flowers for several rooms, a smaller
bed will supply flowers for a couple of vases.

For the most vigorous plant growth, your
flower bed should ideally be in a sunny south
or south-west facing position. Where this is
not possible, try shade-tolerant plants such as
astilbes, foxgloves, Japanese anemones and the
tall, fragrant tobacco plant, *Nicotiana sylvestris*.

1 Prepare the soil before planting by digging
it to the depth of a spade blade. Add a 10cm
layer of well-rotted compost and animal
manure. Allow the ground to settle for about
a fortnight before planting.

2 Mark out a planting plan on the ground
by spreading a thin trail of sand around the
area where each flower variety is to grow. Put
taller varieties towards the back of the bed.

3 Water lightly with a fine spray from the
hose or watering can rose.

4 Once your plants are established, water
regularly and apply fertiliser – taking care
to follow the manufacturer's instructions.

*The flowers of a large and densely planted bed of
annuals will withstand regular thinning out to provide
flowers for the house – in fact, the action of picking
tends to encourage the formation of more blooms. In
order to have a house and garden full of flowers it
is sensible to reserve a workaday bed, similar to
the one pictured left, solely for growing cutting flowers
in your favourite varieties and colours.*

A waist-high box hedge provides a stylish division between a lawn and an area of gooseberries, redcurrants and fruiting trees.

short stakes about 20cm apart. The two outer stakes are width guides for a planting trench. Tie string close to the ground between these outer stakes and dig 2–3cm deeper than the depth of the hedging plants' pots, more if using large plants. Mix a handful of fertiliser through each square metre of removed soil.

4 When the trench is ready, tie a string line to the centre stakes as a planting guide. Before planting, soak potted plants in a bucket of water. Plant them with the stem at the same level as it was in the pot.

5 Fill in the trench and lightly firm soil around the roots with your hands to remove any air. Water and apply a mulch over the root area away from the stems.

6 As plants grow, lightly prune new growth with shears, using a string line to ensure that an even height is maintained. The base of the hedge must be wider than the top or leaves on the lower branches will die from lack of light.

SELECTING A SUITABLE HEDGE

Choose hedging plants with modest root systems that do not 'steal' nutrients from nearby flowers or fruit trees. Plants should be low growing and capable of regular trimming. Fast-growing cypress hedging is unsuitable for creating a 'garden room', and if allowed to grow rampant as a border hedge, will almost certainly upset your neighbours. The most versatile plants for hedging are the members of the box family. Box can be bought or raised from cuttings, and although somewhat slow growing, is easily maintained and survives drought, frost and snow once established.

A framing hedge

A bordering hedge is a natural way to transform any outdoor area into a 'garden room'.

MATERIALS
- tape measure
- hedge shears
- spade
- compost or well-rotted manure
- short stakes
- string
- spirit level
- hammer or mallet
- hedging plants

1 Seek advice from your garden centre on what hedging to plant. Position (sunny or shady) and drainage, for example, will be

relevant to the hedge's success. (Simply raising the bed may overcome drainage problems.)

2 Calculate the number of plants needed by measuring the total distance around the perimeter of your 'room' or garden and dividing this by the distance apart plants will be placed (ask your local garden centre or nursery about this). Small to medium-sized plants need to be at least 30cm apart.

3 Mark out the hedge's position with a string line. At each corner end, hammer in three

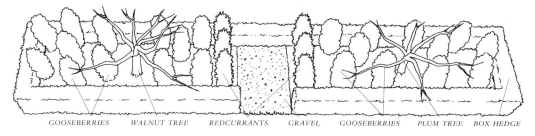

GOOSEBERRIES   WALNUT TREE   REDCURRANTS   GRAVEL   GOOSEBERRIES   PLUM TREE   BOX HEDGE

Topiary: Living Sculpture

*Encouraging hedging plants to assume the ornamental shapes of topiary adds a
distinctive look to your garden and is surprisingly easy to do. This ancient garden art form
is as fascinating a diversion for modern gardeners as it was in Roman times*

A hedged globe

*You can share in the revival of the ancient craft of
topiary by growing and training young plants. It's
easy, especially if you start with simple shapes such
as a pyramid, a globe or a standard, 'lollipop'
shape. For a formal subject, try this English box
hedge with a globe topiary set within it.*

MATERIALS
- 40-60 well-established, bushy
  English box plants for hedge
- 1 large English box plant, or
  contrasting plant, for globe
  (already clipped and trained)
- small wooden stakes, dowels
  or thin metal rods
- secateurs
- hedge shears
- string and stakes for string line
- spade

1 Begin by marking out a 4 × 6m rectangle.
Place wooden stakes at the corners and run
diagonal string lines from the stakes to find
the centre. To ensure that the corners form
90° angles, check that the measurements
from the centre to each corner are equal.
2 Dig the trench for the hedge plants and
a hole in the centre for the globe plant (in
partial shade, *Lonicera nitida* would make
a good choice for the globe).
3 Plant out the hedge, setting the English
box plants about 30cm apart. For more
information on planting hedging, see page 175.
To achieve an even, flat top to the hedge, use
a string line made from two stakes and a taut
length of string tied at the desired height. Use
the taut string as a guide to clip the tops off all
the plants with hedge shears.
4 Plant the globe. Begin shaping it by
trimming the top and snipping off any
protruding stems. Maintain a regular pruning
schedule throughout the year, cutting any
loose shoots back to the basic round shape.
5 Apply a suitable fertiliser according to
maker's instructions in spring and summer.

STARTING A POT TOPIARY

1 *A potted topiary plant looks particularly attractive if trained to a simple, classical shape. Use your eye to
judge the shape for the first trimming.*

2 *After twelve months, use a
pruning guide, such as the one above,
made from canes and wire rings.
Cut any growth outside the guide.*

3 *Once the plant has developed the
desired shape, trim it at least once
a year with secateurs to maintain a
clean, well-defined outline.*

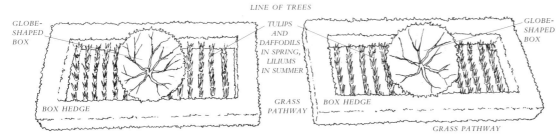

LINE OF TREES

GLOBE-SHAPED BOX

TULIPS AND DAFFODILS IN SPRING, LILIUMS IN SUMMER

GLOBE-SHAPED BOX

BOX HEDGE

GRASS PATHWAY

BOX HEDGE

GRASS PATHWAY

The beds bounded by twin box hedges (below left, plan at left) have cool root runs in which bulbs flourish in all seasons. The hedges are tied together by a grass path and a line of trees. The japonica pictured below is topiary in the making. It forms a plinth with a top portion that will be developed into a more complex shape as the plant matures.

PLANTS – THE RAW MATERIAL

FOR SUCCESSFUL topiary, choose evergreen plants with small leaves and a thick, dense growth habit. If possible, the plants should be fast growing and able to produce new growth fairly quickly after clipping.

Conifers such as cypress or juniper are a good choice for topiary; the evergreen box is a traditionally popular plant because it lends itself readily to shaping.

Other useful topiary subjects include box-leaved honeysuckle (*Lonicera nitida*), yew, the hollies (*Ilex* × *altaclerensis* and *I. aquifolium*), *Gardenia augusta* 'Florida', small-leafed privet (trim after flowering to prevent seeding), duranta, diosma, *metrosideros* (in frost-free gardens only), westringia, figs (*Ficus carica* and *F. benjamina*) and pittosporum. Climbers such as ivy, wisteria and potato vine are particularly attractive as topiary when trained in pots.

Bring a sense of humour to the garden by training your topiary plants into whimsical shapes such as these birds, or perhaps create a design that resembles a dinosaur (to the left in the background).

PRACTICAL IDEAS

TENDING TOPIARY

When pruning, work from the top of the plant down. Cutting guides can be made from canes and wire and placed over the plant.

Pinch off shoots every fortnight while the plant is growing strongly. Trimmings of topiary made with culinary herbs such as rosemary or bay can be dried or used fresh in the kitchen.

Some woody plants from dry climates, such as rosemary, may not reshoot if they are cut below a leaf bud, so when pruning make sure you always leave several leaves on the stem.

If topiary is grown in a container, remove the plant from the pot once a year and prune the roots.

Fertilise your topiary in spring and summer only – the main growing seasons. Apply liquid fertiliser monthly and slow-release fertiliser pellets in early spring and again just before the onset of autumn.

Bird topiary

Plants that are to be transformed into shapes more complicated than basic geometrical outlines can be grown on wire frames or templates.

MATERIALS
- 'bird' plants as required
- chicken wire
- wire cutters
- secateurs
- hedge shears
- stakes
- blocks of softwood
- file or plane
- paint and brush

1 Select a plant with a bushy habit and two main branches (the best plants to use are small-leafed varieties with strong but pliable stems such as rosemary, small-leafed privet, lonicera or ivy). The height of the plant can vary from 30cm to a metre or so.

2 Dig a hole of appropriate size, hammer a supporting stake into the ground and then plant the topiary, tying it lightly to the stake.

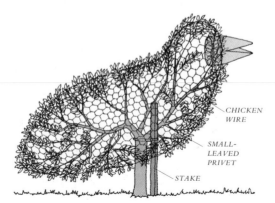

CHICKEN WIRE

SMALL-LEAVED PRIVET

STAKE

3 Remove lower leaves to an appropriate level so that the stem suggests the bird's legs.

4 Cut the chicken wire to the desired size, position it over the plant and form it into a rounded, body shape as a pruning guide (see left). Tie the wire to the stake in several places to keep it steady.

5 As the plant grows, loosen its ties to the stake. Pinch out stems that grow through the wire: this encourages new stems and shoots to form increasingly denser foliage.

6 Once the plant has reached the desired size, add the beak. Cut this from a small block of softwood, rounding the edges with a file or plane until the desired shape is achieved. Paint with all-weather gloss paint. Drill small holes on either side of the beak and thread fine-gauge wire through these before tying the beak to the head part of the wire frame.

◆ Water in the Garden ◆

*Whether still or moving, water brings a unique quality of tranquillity to a
garden. And you can enjoy the charm of restful water features in even the smallest of gardens with
our miniature barrel pond – complete with lilies – and gurgling wall fountain*

Barrel pond

If you crave the refreshing presence of water in the garden but do not have enough room for a conventional pond, try a barrel mini-pond.

MATERIALS
- a half wine or beer barrel (or an old laundry copper)
- sealant or liner (optional)
- selection of water plants
- aquatic compost
- small fish
- coarse gravel
- pump (optional)

1 Place the barrel in its permanent position – once filled with water it will be difficult to move. Unless the barrel has an oxygenating pump the water will need to be siphoned off on a regular basis; this can be a messy procedure so make sure there is a flowerbed or a drain nearby to receive the stale water.

2 If necessary, test the barrel for leaks. Use a spirit level to ensure the top of the barrel is level. Fill with water and leave for several days. If the water level drops or the outside becomes damp, empty the barrel, allow it to dry and seal the inside with a bituminous sealant.

3 Pot the water plants in water-plant baskets or, for an economical alternative, use black plastic pots with slits cut into the sides. Hold the plants around the crown allowing the roots to hang down into the container and fill with aquatic compost. Ensure the crown is not covered or the plant will rot. Cover the surface with coarse gravel to stop it floating out of the pot. Most water plants are heavy feeders so using aquatic compost is the ideal healthy start for plants.

4 Slowly submerge the pots in the water, letting air bubbles escape gradually so the soil is not disturbed. If the leaves of deep-water aquatics are totally submerged when the pots are placed on the base of the barrel, raise them on bricks until the leaves lie on the surface.

5 Allow time for the pond environment to stabilise before introducing fish. Two to three weeks should be sufficient but if the water looks cloudy or dark, wait until it clears.

6 Stock your barrel with floating and oxygenating plants to help maintain a healthy environment. Oxygenating plants grow completely submerged on the bottom of the pond. They are useful for keeping algae in check by adding oxygen. Floating aquatics provide shade which also helps reduce algae.

Aquatic plants such as waterlilies will thrive in a cut-off wine barrel filled with water. Cover the compost with coarse gravel to keep the water clear.

Wall fountain

For this fountain you need two wall pots (these have one flat side) of different sizes and one large pot (round or also with one flat side) to sit on the ground as a base. The base pot needs to be large enough to accommodate a pump.

MATERIALS
- 2 terracotta wall pots, 1 large 'base' pot, 1 small round pot
- sheet of glass-reinforced cement
- tiles and waterproof tile adhesive (optional)
- 4 bolts with nuts and washers
- 4 long screws (about 100mm)
- low-voltage submersible pump with suitable transformer
- up to 2m of 12mm diameter black irrigation tubing with 3 elbow joints
- scraps of plastic, waterproof adhesive and sealant (see step 1)
- paint and paintbrush
- electric drill, round file, adjustable spanners, screwdriver

After deciding on a location, hire an electrician to install an outdoor power point, if necessary. Ask the electrician's advice about connecting the pump cable to the transformer, which needs to be under cover.

1 Use a paintbrush to thoroughly coat the interior of the three pots with waterproof sealant. Cover any drainage holes with pieces of rigid plastic and waterproof glue. Seal edges.

2 If the top and middle pots have hanging holes, enlarge these to take fixing bolts; otherwise drill new holes: prevent cracking by starting with a small masonry bit and gradually increasing the gauge.

3 Drill pipe-inlet holes near the top edges of the top and base pots (see diagram).

4 With the round file, make a small notch in the front centre of the top and middle pots to let the water spill over.

5 Cut the cement backing board to a height that hides the top of your wall or fence.

6 Mark four drill holes for the bolts (top and middle pots), and two drill holes for pipe inlets (top and base pots). If using tiles, mark their positions, leaving a space for the pipe inlets.

7 Drill the six holes in the board. Make the pipe holes slightly narrower than the pipes themselves for a snug fit. On the bottom edge of the lower pipe hole, make a shallow notch to carry the pump cord. Attach the tiles with tile adhesive and allow to dry.

CONSTRUCTION

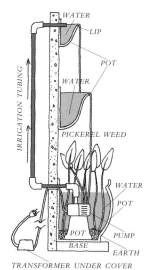

1 Stand board in position and bolt the pots to it; seal around bolt heads to avoid leakage.

2 Pass the pump cord through the bottom pipe hole and connect it via a lead to the transformer (see below).

3 Cut the pipes to the required length using the diagram as a guide (one long piece at the back and two short ones for the inlets to the pots). Place elbow joints on the pipes as shown in the diagram. Pass the pipes through the inlet holes.

4 Stand the base pot on a firm surface; a stone block or bricks are sufficient.

5 Put the small pot upside down inside the base pot and place the pump on it; connect the pump to the elbow joint of the pipe.

6 Attach the backing board to the wall or fence. If attaching to cross-members on the inside of a wooden fence, drill pilot holes and fix in place with screws. If attaching to a flat wall, use hardwood buffers to ensure that there is enough space to allow the plumbing to clear the wall. Attach the board to the wall with long screws and wall plugs in the wall.

7 Paint the backing board with two coats of masonry paint.

8 Fill the base pot with water and add plants, and small fish, if desired. Turn on the pump.

Constructing the fountain on a backing board allows access to back and front for plumbing. When it is complete, simply fix the board to a wall or fence.

♦ Paths and Edgings ♦

*Paths and edgings can act as frames for the various elements of the garden. If you spend
a little time considering your needs, and then provide the labour yourself, you can put a variety of paving
materials to work in distinctive designs especially created to complement your plantings*

Sandstone path

*Capitalise on the sculptural qualities of irregular
shaped sandstone slabs by combining them with fine
gravel to make an informal, meandering path.*

MATERIALS
- string and stakes
- shovel
- sandstone or similar stone slabs
- coarse sand
- cement
- fine gravel (optional)
- rake, tamper, levelling board,
  spirit level, mallet

For basic information on laying paving see
step-by-step instructions on page 160.
1 Decide on the best position and stone
pattern by laying the stone out on the ground
before making the path. To start, hammer in
a stake on either side of the chosen site, with
corresponding stakes at the other end of the
path. String a line between the stakes at either
end to form the outer edges of the path.
2 Dig out the path area to a depth equal to
the depth of the stone slabs plus 5-10cm. Mix
6 parts damp sand to 1 part dry cement and
spread a 5-10cm layer of the mix as a bed for
the stones. If the path is on soft ground, dig
the path area 5cm deeper, spread fine gravel
to a depth of 5cm and compact it with a
tamper before spreading sand over the top.
3 Level the sand-cement mix with a rake,
compact it down and then smooth it with a
levelling board. It may help to frame the path
site with narrow boards (formwork) flush with
the level of the sand as a guide for levelling.

*The character of a sandstone path is enhanced by
oxides in the stone that combine over time with tiny
lichens to form intricate patterns on the path surface.*

4 String a third line down the path site about halfway between the other string lines.

5 Place the stones onto the sand, using a spirit level to ensure that they lie flat. If you line one edge along the central string line, you will give the path a pleasing rough symmetry; however, you can break the symmetry if desired by laying stones to either side of the string line.

6 As you place each stone in position, gently tap it down with a rubber mallet.

7 When all the stones are laid, brush a dry mixture of 10 parts sand to 1 part cement between them and gently mist spray the path with a garden hose so the cement can set.

In an informal garden, you can create the simplest path of all using organic materials such as bark chippings, wood chip or sawdust. These materials keep the path relatively dry underfoot and, as long as they are laid to a depth of at least 2cm, will discourage the growth of weeds. Allow informal paths to meander (left) rather than follow a straight line and let the edges be similarly casual so that they become blurred as low-growing plants creep over them.

Bark chippings could also be used as an inexpensive alternative to gravel for the landing sections of a stepped path like the one shown (below).

Bring variety to a path that crosses a gentle slope or to a series of steps by mixing natural materials (above and right). Weathered sleepers laid flat make for an interesting punctuation mark in a mainly gravel path (above). Allow plants to overflow onto the path to soften the edging. Most types of stone or paver combine well with gravel – landings filled with gravel perfectly complement the stone and brick steps (right).

Block-edged path

Block gutters and edgings neatly confine loose material, such as gravel, and prevent soil spilling from a planting bed onto the path.

MATERIALS

- string and stakes
- spirit level, tape measure
- shovel
- dry pre-mixed sand and cement (optional)
- square paving blocks
- gravel
- plywood or timber strips about 12cm wide (optional)
- roller or mechanical tamper (optional)

1 Lay a string line (see step 1, page 182) on each side of your chosen gravel path area. Outside these lines on each side, lay another string line for the edging – the width of these outer guide lines needs to equal that of the thickness plus the length of your chosen block.
2 Between the lines on each side, dig a trench that is as deep as the thickness of your block. If desired, lay concrete (see Variation, below).
3 Along each outside string line, stand blocks in the trench, leaving small gaps between each. Along each inside line (next to the path) lay blocks flat to form a gutter, as pictured.
4 For the path, excavate the area between the two inside string lines to about 2cm below the level of the block gutter. Tread the ground, or use a wooden tamper, to form a solid base for gravel. For drainage, form a slight camber or slope from the centre to either side of the path.
5 Lay gravel over the earth. For a firmer surface, water the gravel then press with a roller or mechanical tamper, if desired.

VARIATION For a very firm base for paving blocks, dig the trench a further 5cm deep, mix up concrete, lay it in the trench then bed the blocks in this while it is still wet. If desired, build formwork for the concrete along the string lines using old floorboards or similar waste timber (for step-by-step information on laying a brick or paver path, see page 160).

Large paving blocks are ideal for giving garden borders a formal appearance. The kerb-and-gutter shown above provides a neat, clear-cut division between garden bed and pathway as well as helping channel water away from the path during heavy rain. An English box hedge planted along the path's other edge heightens its formality. The benefits of asphalt (left) as a way of making 'instant' paving are often overlooked. If laid carefully, in the right setting, it can strike a complementary note. An asphalt path looks neat and attractive when edged with blocks. Try using bricks laid end to end, and allowed to protrude by about half their thickness above the path surface.

• Lattice Style •

Whether used as a framework or a trellis to display a climber, lattice is one of the most
decorative and inexpensive garden materials as well as one of the easiest to fashion to your requirements.
With some basic skills you can make a range of patterns unique to your garden

Perspective illusion

An awareness of the intriguing way in which the manipulation of perspective can fool the eye of the beholder is the inspiration behind this project. To obtain the lattice strips (laths), try timberyards or specialist lattice suppliers. Laths come in standard sizes (such as 38 × 10mm); any size in treated pine or hardwood will suffice.

MATERIALS

♦ 80m of laths
♦ 2 litres exterior paint
♦ three 2400 × 900mm sheets of white (undercoated) hardboard
♦ 1 packet 25mm flat-head nails (about 1.8mm thick)
♦ eleven screws (about 65mm)
♦ 3m of string
♦ compasses and pencil, tape measure, saw, electric drill, hammer, steel block (or second hammer), try square, sandpaper

GETTING READY

1 Apply two coats of paint to all timber.
2 Lay the hardboard sheets on the floor as shown in diagram 1, as a 'layout' board.
  This lattice is made of two side panels and a top panel. Make the side panels first.

DRAWING A PLAN FOR THE SIDE PANELS

1 Near the top of the layout board, draw a rectangle 2000 × 750mm. Draw a basic plan of a side panel within this rectangle (see diagram 1); this takes a little time but ensures the other panels will be in proportion. Take a long piece of lath and use it to draw six evenly spaced laths across the rectangle as shown; also draw a lath at each short end of the rectangle.
2 Mark a point 1250mm along the bottom edge of the rectangle, then (using a try square for the angle) draw a perpendicular line (the 'centre line'), 1500mm long, from the point; hammer a nail at the end (see diagram 1).
3 Attach the string to the nail then tie the pencil to it 1m from the nail and draw an arc (see diagram 1). Fix the compasses at 75mm. Put the compass point at A and draw a mark on the arc; draw eight points on the arc towards B and five towards C (see diagram 2).

MAKING THE SIDE PANELS

1 For the first side panel cut six laths of 2m and three laths of 750mm. Lay two 2m laths and two 750mm laths in the shape of a rectangle (on the plan) with the long laths on top. Drill 1.5mm diameter holes for nails at the four corners. Hammer the nails in place (the points will pierce the board beneath).

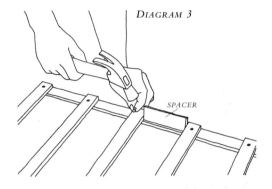

DIAGRAM 3

SPACER

2 Drill and nail the remaining four 2m laths, using the plan as a guide. To make nailing accurate, cut a small piece of lath as a 'spacer' between the laths (see diagram 3). The length of the spacer depends on your lath width.
3 Now the 'radiating laths' can be added (see diagrams 4 and 5, page 187). Pull the string taut along the centre line and lay your third 750mm lath on the frame (under, and centred on, the string). Nail the ends of the lath to the top and bottom laths of the frame.
4 Pull the string taut in line with the next mark along the arc. Measure the lath length needed to fit on the frame at this point – the length of string between top and bottom laths of frame – and cut a lath slightly longer than this. Lay the lath centred under the string

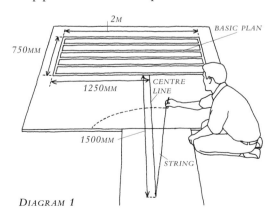

DIAGRAM 1

2M
750MM
1250MM
BASIC PLAN
CENTRE LINE
1500MM
STRING

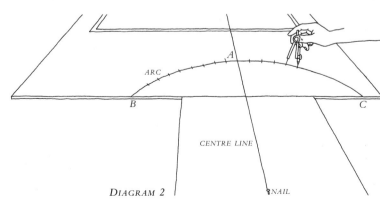

DIAGRAM 2

ARC
A
B
C
CENTRE LINE
NAIL

You can dress up the exterior of a window with this lattice, which has pieces attached at angles to give a perspective illusion. The 'gable' at the top of the lattice can be replaced with a lower, flat top (see pages 187-8) if there is insufficient space above your window.

DIAGRAM 4

RADIATING LATHS

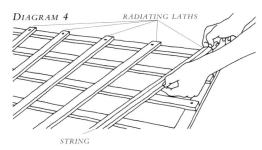

STRING

(see diagram 4), overlapping at ends, then nail in place. Trim off excess at the ends. Repeat for the other radiating laths (see diagram 5).

DIAGRAM 5

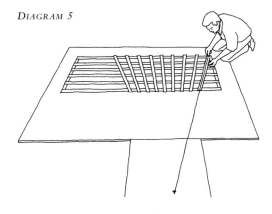

5 Drill holes and nail all the radiating laths to the other four 2m laths of the frame.
6 To save time later, mark on the layout board where the edges of the radiating laths meet the bottom and top laths of the frame.
7 Turn the panel over – it will come away easily from the layout board. Place the panel on the steel block (or on the head of a hammer) so that the block is under the flat head of one nail. Hammer the nail point flat; this is 'clenching' (see diagram at bottom of page 189). Clench all the nails.
8 The second side panel is the reverse of the first. To make it, first drill, nail and clench the basic rectangle (steps 1–3) and lay it – with the 2m lengths *underneath* – on the plan of the first side (lengths are marked underneath because the panel is a mirror-image of the first panel). Transfer the marks drawn for the radiating laths of the first panel onto the top and bottom of the frame. Turn it over; drill, nail and clench radiating laths at these positions.
9 Sand all the rough surfaces, then paint all the sanded surfaces and the cut lath ends.

MAKING THE GABLED TOP PANEL

1 To make a frame for the top panel, which has a pointed or 'gabled' top, cut one lath 2500mm long and two 1500mm long.
2 Lay them in the form of a triangle on the plan that you used for the side panels (see diagram 6). The long lath is on the bottom of the rectangle

DRAWN PLAN ON HARDBOARD

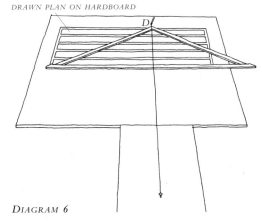

D

DIAGRAM 6

with its midpoint on the centre line. At the two lower corners, the long lath should sit on top of short laths. The shorter laths will meet at the top (point D, on the centre line) where they will overlap each other slightly.
3 Stretch the string taut and secure it at the top, above D. Use the string line as a guide for cutting the ends of the 1500mm laths (see

DIAGRAM 7

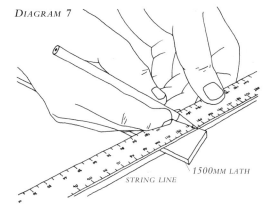

1500MM LATH

STRING LINE

diagram 7). When you have cut each one they will fit neatly together with no overlap. Drill and nail the two lower corners of the triangle.
4 Lay a short lath across the top corner, at 90° to the string line (see diagram 8). Drill and

DIAGRAM 8

SPACER

SPACER

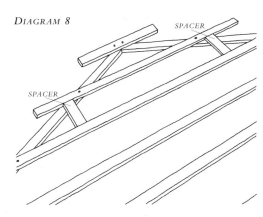

nail the joint as shown. Add four evenly spaced horizontal laths between the top and bottom of the frame; use the plan on the layout board as a guide for placing these laths, and cut them so that they overlap slightly at the sides. Cut spacers if desired and use when nailing. Drill and nail each lath then trim the ends (the top lath is trimmed to a small triangle, the shape of the top of the frame).
5 The radiating laths for the top panel are added in much the same way as for the side panels. The difference is that the top panel has six radiating laths on either side of the centre line (the side panel had eight on the left and five on the right). Make marks for the radiating laths using the string line method as before (for most of the radiating laths, you can save time by using the lath marks that you drew on the rectangular plan).
6 Drill and nail each radiating lath to the outer laths of the triangular frame. When all have been nailed, drill and nail all the remaining joints. Clench the nails (see diagram at the bottom of page 189). Saw off excess ends flush with the outer laths of the frame.
7 Paint all cut ends and touch up the nails on both sides. All three frames are now complete and ready to be attached to your wall. Attach with a screw at each corner of each panel. On a masonry wall, use wall plugs for the screws.

VARIATION: FLAT-TOP TRELLIS

The gabled top may make the lattice too tall to fit around some windows. The lattice can be lowered by making a rectangular, flat top instead (see diagram 10), reducing the height to about 2350mm.

1 Make the two side panels exactly as before.
2 Cut three laths 2500mm long and three laths 350mm long. On the layout board, lay two 2500mm laths and two 350mm laths in a rectangle, with the long laths on top at the corners. The bottom long lath should lie on the bottom of the drawn rectangle, midpoint on the centre line (as for the gabled top panel, see diagram 6). Drill and nail the laths together at the four corners.
3 Mark the midpoint of each short lath; drill and nail the third long lath on top of these, centred on the midpoints. Mark the midpoint of each long lath. Drill and nail the third short lath on top of these. Put a piece of scrap lath underneath to support the nailing point.
4 With string, place the radiating laths as for the side panels; there are seven points on the arc on each side of the centre (see diagram 9).

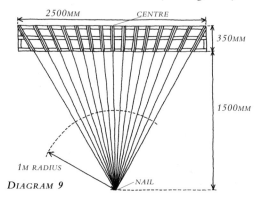

DIAGRAM 9

5 Drill and nail the radiating laths. Lift the panel off the layout board and clench all nails.
6 Sandpaper all rough surfaces then paint all sanded surfaces, lath ends and nails.

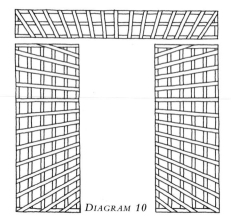

DIAGRAM 10

Wall trellis

Climbing plants will quickly cover a wall if they have a support. An easy-to-make trellis like the one shown here will show your plants off to good advantage. For information on the laths that are used to make the trellis, see the introduction to Perspective illusion, page 185.

MATERIALS

♦ 30m of laths
♦ tenon saw
♦ 1 litre exterior acrylic paint (a light shade emphasises foliage)
♦ 50mm-wide paintbrush
♦ 2400 × 900mm sheet of white (undercoated) hardboard
♦ 1 packet of 25mm flat-head nails (about 1.8mm thick)
♦ pencil
♦ tape measure
♦ try square
♦ electric drill
♦ hammer
♦ steel block, or second hammer
♦ sandpaper

Using the diagram at right as a rough guide, construct the trellis on the hardboard as it makes nailing much easier.
1 Apply two coats of paint to all the laths and leave them to dry.
2 Cut seven laths 1800mm long. Lay them vertically on the hardboard using diagram 1 as a guide (or lay them on a drawn plan).
3 Cut one lath 600mm long and one lath 700mm long. Lay the top edge of the shorter one 50mm from the top of the verticals as shown, and the longer one at the bottom of the verticals. Align the vertical laths to the measurements on the top and bottom laths as shown above.
4 Cut laths that will fit horizontally at the points shown on diagram 1. Cut the laths slightly longer than needed so they overhang at the sides – they will be trimmed later. Lay the laths on top of the vertical laths at the heights shown on the diagram (the measurements show the distance from the base). Use a try square to make sure the horizontal laths are perpendicular to the central vertical lath.

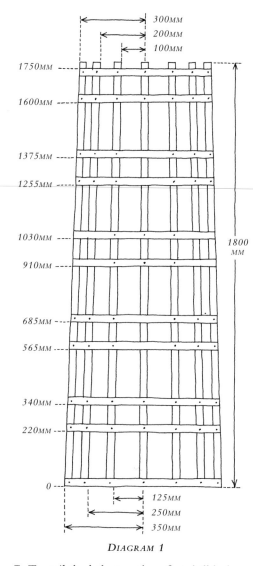

DIAGRAM 1

5 To nail the laths together, first drill holes for nails at the points where the laths cross. Hammer in a nail at each hole; the pointed end of each nail will dig into the hardboard behind. Note: most points where laths cross need to be nailed but some do not, as parts of the laths will be cut off at a later stage – for example the horizontal laths at 910mm and 1030mm are not nailed to the two vertical laths on each side. Use diagram 1 as a guide to non-nail points and diagram 2 on page 189 as a guide to parts that are to be cut away.
6 When all nails are in place, turn the trellis over and remove the hardboard (it should come away quite easily). Place the steel block

(or the head of your second hammer) under the trellis so that the flat head of one of the nails is on the block. Bend down the point of the nail and hammer it flat (the block supports the nail as you do this). This is known as 'clenching' and is illustrated in the diagram below. Repeat for all the nails. The basic structure of the trellis is now complete.

7 Saw off the shaded parts in the diagram at 25mm from each inter-section. The horizontal laths at 910mm and 1030mm are cut at the sides and the two offcuts are nailed to the outside two vertical laths between the horizontal laths just cut (see right).

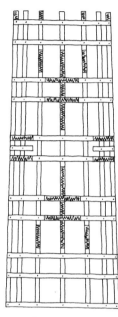

DIAGRAM 2

8 Trim the outside ends of the horizontal laths to the sides of the trellis so that the only ends that protrude are at the top of the framework. Also trim all the cut ends of the laths that are on the inside of the trellis so that they overhang by only 25mm.

9 Sand all the rough surfaces, then paint all the sanded surfaces and the raw lath ends.

CLENCHING

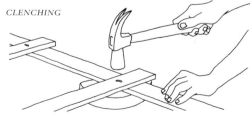

A seemingly intricate pattern in this trellis is easily achieved with some ingenious cutting. Allow it to stand proud of a wall so climbers can twine around the laths.

Gardeners' Friends

*Spending just ten minutes a day on small tasks such as weeding and dead-heading
makes caring for a garden much easier – and if small tools are kept to hand, you'll be more likely to
keep up with the chores. Our rack and holdall are attractive enough to hang in the porch*

A hanging rack

*Fix a rack near the back door on which to hang all
your gardening paraphernalia. For information on
the laths used to make the rack, see page 185.*

MATERIALS

- 8m laths
- 500ml paint in colour
  of choice, paintbrush
- hardboard sheet, 60 × 60cm
- 1 packet 25mm flat-head nails
- 4 coat hooks
- tape measure, try square,
  pencil
- tenon saw, sandpaper
- electric drill
- hammer and steel block

1 Apply two coats of paint to all timber.
2 Cut the timber to the following lengths:
Horizontal pieces: 560mm, 575mm, 590mm,
595mm (lengths differ to create tapering shape;
alternatively, cut 4 lengths of 560mm). Vertical
pieces: 4 × 490mm, 3 × 600mm. Diagonal
pieces: 4 × 470mm.
3 Place the horizontal pieces on the
hardboard, the shortest at the top and longest
at the bottom, then arrange the vertical pieces
over them, using the photograph as a guide.
Most pieces will not meet at 90° because of the
taper, but the central vertical does cross at right
angles so use a try square here (and for all
angles if you don't taper the rack).
4 Drill pilot holes for nails where laths cross
and hammer a nail in at each hole, so that
the points slightly pierce the hardboard.
5 When the pieces are nailed together, turn
the rack over and remove the hardboard. Put
the steel block under the rack so that the flat
head of one nail is on the block. Bend down
the point of the nail and hammer it flat with
the block supporting the nail (this is called

'clenching'). Repeat for all nails.
6 Turn the rack over to face you, lay down
the diagonals and drill pilot holes where they
cross. Then hammer in and clench the nails.
7 Trim overhanging laths, sand rough edges
and paint nails and sanded and trimmed ends.
8 Drill holes where the diagonals cross each
other and insert coat hooks.
9 Drill two holes in the second horizontal
from the top and screw or nail the rack to the
wall. Dab the screw or nail heads with paint.

Garden holdall

*This strong green canvas bag has lots of pockets on
one side and a divider compartment in the middle.*

MATERIALS

- 60cm of 180cm-wide canvas
  and thread to match
- sewing machine
- heavy-duty sewing
  machine needle
- masking tape
- 1 large press stud

1 Cut the following pieces from the canvas
(below): 20 × 50cm (pocket); 56 × 50cm
(front); 71 × 50cm (back); two straps 90 × 10cm.

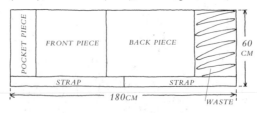

2 Machine a row of stitching 1cm from
the edge of one long side of the pocket piece.
Fold over along the line of stitching and stitch
close to the fabric edge. Repeat with the short
edges of the front piece, turning the hems in
opposite directions to each other.

3 Tape the pocket piece, hem under, to the
front piece, with top edges 8cm apart (below).
Stitch through both layers close to the bottom
edge of the pocket piece. Fold the front piece
up 18cm to form the bottom pockets (shown).
Stitch close to each side edge, top to bottom,
to hold both rows of pockets in place. Make
the pocket dividers by stitching two lines, top
to bottom edge, 15.5cm from each side edge.

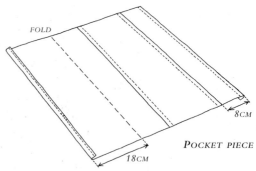

FOLD

8CM

POCKET PIECE

18CM

4 Stitch two hems as before on the short sides
of the back, turning them in the same
direction. Fold the back up 36cm from the
bottom hem to form a divider. Place the front
and back together with the divider between
them and stitch 1.5cm from one edge. Trim
the edge of the front piece close to the seam
and fold the edge of the back over once and
then again at the row of stitching and machine
through both. Join the edges of the other side.
5 Stitch along the bottom of the bag.
6 Turn all raw edges of the straps in and stitch
in half lengthwise. Double stitch each strap
3cm below top edge of bag, and 5mm either
side of the stitching of the pocket dividers.
7 Hand stitch the press stud in the centre of
the bag close to the top hem edge.

*This bag and rack will take all manner of small tools
and other oddments. Either can be customised to suit
your needs – by making larger or smaller, perhaps.*

◆ Scarecrow ◆

*Scarecrows have been used for centuries to frighten birds away from crops. Making
one is easy – just use your imagination and whatever old clothing you have to hand. Even if
your mock-farmer doesn't frighten the birds, he'll make the neighbours smile*

*Decorate your scarecrow's clothes and hat before
putting them on. Spoons, cloth patches, decorative
stitching – these all make amusing embellishments.*

MATERIALS

- 2 garden stakes, one 180cm long,
  one 120–140cm long (or old
  spade with a rake head on end)
- screw (to go through 2 stakes)
- hessian bag
- straw
- thin garden wire
- assorted clothes and accessories
- PVA adhesive
- needle and thread
- electric drill, screwdriver,
  scissors, pliers, hammer

1 Lay the longer stake on the ground and
centre the shorter one (or spade) across it,
30cm from the top. Where the stakes cross,
drill a hole for the screw that will hold them
together. Fasten the screw through the stakes.
2 Cut the hessian bag to a suitable size for
a head and put it over the top of the long
stake. Stuff it with straw and fasten it at the
throat with a piece if wire.
3 Create a face: we glued on a felt mouth and
sewed on buttons for teeth. We used wire to
fix on bits of plastic for the eyes and glued on
straw hair before wiring the hat to the head.
4 Put a shirt on the frame and fill with straw.
If using a stake for arms, use straw for hands.
Knot the bottom of the shirt to hold straw in.
5 Make a hole between the legs of the overalls
for the stake to pass through, put them on the
scarecrow and fill them with straw.
6 Hammer the stake into the ground.

*Add a whimsical touch to your garden – and keep the
birds out of the vegetable patch and the home orchard
– with an old-fashioned, straw-filled scarecrow.*

◆ Nesting Boxes ◆

Making your own nesting box is a good way to invite favourites into your garden.
Remember that location is everything — to persuade birds to use the box, be sure to mount it near
a source of water and a good supply of food, and not too close to the house

Robin's nest

Some birds, such as robins, swallows and blackbirds,
won't nest in an enclosed box. They prefer an open-
fronted design, known as a nesting shelf.

MATERIALS

- 405 × 255 × 18mm plywood for back
- 405 × 215 × 18mm plywood for roof
- 175 × 175 × 18mm plywood for base
- 2 pieces 265 × 190 × 18mm plywood for sides
- 173 × 25 × 18mm plywood for nest retainer
- 12 × 38mm No 8 countersunk brass woodscrews
- exterior woodworking adhesive
- clear silicone mastic
- 2 × 50mm brass woodscrews or garden wire, for hanging

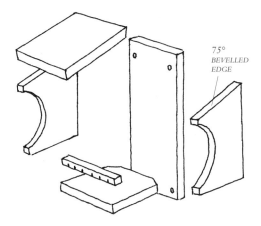

75°
BEVELLED
EDGE

A good way to encourage birds into your garden is
to build a nesting box. Tempt tits or nuthatches with
the box at the top; robins and blackbirds prefer a
nesting shelf (centre); while wrens may be attracted
to the house with the wood-shingled roof.

CUTTING THE BODY

1 This nesting box is made of 18mm thick exterior-grade plywood. Cut the back, roof, base and sides to the dimensions in the materials list. When you cut the top, bevel one edge at 75° (right). When you cut the sides, angle one end of each at 75° (see diagram, page 193). Nip the back corners off the bottom piece for drainage.

75° ANGLE

2 The curved cuts on the side walls are optional. Use a saucer or the base of a large coffee tin to draw the curve and cut with a jigsaw or coping saw.

3 A router was used to round some of the edges. You can achieve the same finish with sandpaper or simply leave them square.

4 To make the retaining ledge, cut the plywood to the dimensions given and then notch one 25mm face with a handsaw for drainage (right).

SHOWN BOTTOM SIDE UP

5 Make mounting holes in each corner of the back with a 6mm drill bit.

ASSEMBLING THE BODY

1 Hold the back and sides together, then drill pilot holes for the brass screws through the back and into the edge of each side. Countersink each hole in the back, then screw the back to the sides. Screw the floor into place, countersinking the screws slightly.

2 Run a bead of mastic along the back edge of the roof, then secure it with four screws.

3 Attach the nest retainer with adhesive.

INSTALLING THE NESTING BOX

Attach the nesting box to a trellis, a tall post or a creeper-covered wall using 50mm woodscrews through the mounting holes. If you are fixing the box to a tree, run wire through the mounting holes and around the trunk and secure it with pliers. To stop the wire cutting into the tree, pad it with strips of old tights or other bits of material.

Bluetit box

Some experts suggest that a lining of wood chips in the box makes small birds feel cosy. This design will also appeal to nuthatches. Locate it in partial shade.

MATERIALS

- 235 × 187 × 18mm plywood for front and back (cut 2)
- 102 × 102 × 18mm plywood for sides and base (cut 3)
- 190 × 178 × 18mm plywood for short side of roof
- 210 × 178 × 18mm plywood for long side of roof
- 190mm length of 28 × 28mm angle moulding for ridge cap
- 30mm sherardised panel pins
- 38mm no. 10 countersunk brass woodscrews (4 screws)
- 19mm diameter wardrobe rail end-socket and screws
- 19mm hardwood dowel or metal wardrobe rail for post

1 Use 18mm exterior-grade plywood, stained with wood preservative to the desired colour. Cut the floor piece 102 × 102mm. To provide drainage, make three notches each in two opposing

NOTCHES

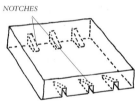

sides of the floor, as shown above. A few strokes with a handsaw will make each notch.

2 Cut the sides to 102 × 102mm with a 120° bevel on the bottom and a 105° bevel on top (below).

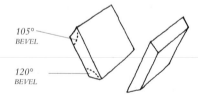

105° BEVEL

120° BEVEL

3 For the front and back, cut two pieces of plywood a little oversize and use the plan above to mark up their shape Cut them out with a fine-toothed saw. Drill a 28mm hole in

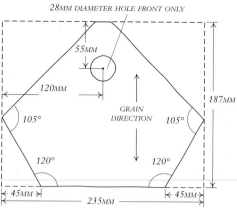

28MM DIAMETER HOLE FRONT ONLY

55MM

120MM

GRAIN DIRECTION

105° 105°

187MM

120° 120°

45MM 45MM

235MM

FRONT AND BACK PATTERN

the front panel as an entrance hole. Centre the hole 120mm from one side and 55mm from the top, as shown. Nail the front and back to the floor and sides with the panel pins.

4 Cut one roof piece to 190 × 178mm and the other to 210 × 178mm. Butt the short piece into the long piece and nail them together. The nesting box shown has a 6mm bevel routed around the top and bottom of the roof and the outside bottom edges of the front and back. If you want to add this detail, do the routing now. Cut the corner moulding 190mm long and glue it to the ridge with a 6mm overhang on each end.

5 Put the roof in place, centred front to back. Pre-drill and countersink four holes through the roof and fix with brass wood screws. This will allow you to remove the roof for cleaning.

6 Paint the outside of the box with primer, undercoat and two coats of all-weather gloss.

7 Pre-drill for the socket screws, being careful not to drill all the way through the floor. Attach the socket with its screws. Set the post

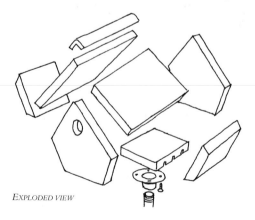

EXPLODED VIEW

in concrete and fit the house to the top of it. Depending on the length of dowelling you use, you can vary the height of the nest (see panel, right, for preferred heights). If you expect to attract a variety of birds, build two or three boxes and set them at different heights.

Wren box

Wrens are happy in nesting boxes both in cities and in suburban or country locations. Fix this box in a position that is sunny for part of the day.

MATERIALS

- 102 × 102 × 18mm plywood for base
- 240 × 102 × 18mm plywood for back
- 160 × 102 × 18mm plywood for front
- 249 × 138 × 18mm plywood for sides (cut 2)
- 190 × 165 × 6mm plywood for roof
- scraps of roofing felt for 'shingles'
- 165mm length of 22 × 22mm angle moulding for ridge
- 30mm sherardised panel pins
- waterproof wood adhesive
- clear silicone mastic

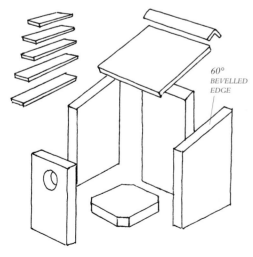

60°
BEVELLED
EDGE

EXPLODED VIEW

THE RIGHT HEIGHT

THE HEIGHT YOU HANG a nesting box can determine the species of bird that settles in. Set a box for tits about 2 to 3 metres above the ground on a post or tree. Nuthatches prefer to be higher – between 4 and 6 metres above ground, suspended from a tree branch or wired to the trunk of the tree. Wrens, on the other hand, are happier nearer to the ground. Fix their nesting box at a height of 1.5 to 3 metres.

CUTTING AND ASSEMBLING THE BODY

1 This box is made of 18mm exterior-grade plywood with a 6mm roof covered in felt 'shingles'. Cut the bottom, back, front, and sides to the dimensions in the materials list. Trim the corners of the bottom for drainage. When you cut the back, bevel the top edge as shown in the diagram (below, left). When you cut the sides, make a 60° bevelled edge on one side of each, as shown.

2 Use a 28mm flat wood bit to drill an opening in the front. Centre the hole 50mm from the top. Drill mounting holes in the back.

3 Use the panel pins to nail the sides to the back, and then nail the floor in place.

4 Hold the front piece in position on the house and pin it in place.

CUTTING AND ASSEMBLING THE ROOF

1 Cut a piece 6mm wide exterior plywood to 190 × 165mm to make the roof deck. Fix to the sides with three panel pins in each side.

2 Now make miniature shingles from scraps of roofing felt. Cut five pieces of felt, each 165mm wide and one each to the following lengths: 190, 165, 135, 95 and 55mm. Now use a utility knife to slice the pieces into random widths from about 15mm to 30mm.

3 Hold the box steady in a clamp or the jaws of a workbench so that the roof is level. This will stop the felt shingles from slipping off as you fit them and will keep adhesive from dripping off the roof.

4 Dry-fit your first course of shingles and trim the widths as needed so that they fit with only

---

tiny gaps between. Once you're satisfied with the fit, remove the shingles and spread the adhesive evenly over all but the bottom 25mm of the roof. Press the shingles into place.

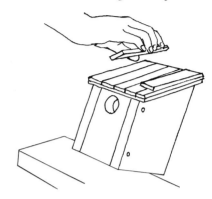

5 Repeat the process with the other courses of shingles, being sure to line up the top edges of each shingle with the top edge of the roof. To keep the roof as waterproof as possible, try to arrange the shingles so that joints in one course don't coincide with those in the previous course.

6 Place a weight on top of the shingles to keep them in place while the adhesive sets – a plastic bag half-filled with rice, baking beans or sand is ideal.

7 Cut the angle moulding to fit over the top edge of the roof and secure it with silicone mastic. Leave the box for a couple of days, keeping the roof level before mounting it outdoors.

8 Use the mounting holes to wire the box low on a tree. Or mount it on a pole as shown in the instructions for the Bluetit Box (see opposite page). You may have to build more than one of these boxes, because the male wren usually builds several 'cock' nests before the female eventually selects one and lines it with feathers in readiness for her eggs.

MAINTENANCE

Clean the nest immediately after the first brood has hatched, to cater for a possible second fledging. The birds like to bring up each brood in a fresh nest. Don't get rid of unused 'cock' nests until the end of August when you can remove all but one of these boxes, for a fresh supply for the next season.

• Feeding the Birds •

Bring nature into your garden by keeping a year-round buffet table stocked for the
birds that are native to your area and those that pass through on their annual migrations.
Once birds have found your feeders, they will keep coming back

Classic seed feeder

You can hang this feeder in a porch as shown in the
photograph on the facing page, or from a branch.
Mixed birdseed and bird nuts are widely available.

MATERIALS

- 229 × 190 × 18mm plywood for sides (cut 2)
- 255 × 190 × 18mm plywood for base
- 330 × 127 × 18mm plywood for roof pieces (cut 2)
- 291 × 38 × 18mm softwood for feeding lips (cut 2)
- 318 × 38 × 18mm softwood for perch supports (cut 2)
- 660mm of 12mm diameter wooden dowel for perches
- 248 × 140 × 3mm clear plastic (Perspex) sheet
- 135 × 10mm quadrant moulding (cut 10)
- 30mm panel pins
- 18mm veneer pins
- 12mm galvanised tacks
- bicycle inner tube offcut
- one 50mm round nail
- sandpaper (medium and fine)

1 This bird feeder is made of 18mm thick exterior-grade plywood. Cut the sides, base, and roof to the dimensions given above. Then cut the sides to the shape shown far right.

2 Fix the sides to the base with panel pins. Use three pins on each side and punch their heads in with a nail punch.

3 To cut the plastic to the dimensions required, leave the protective film on and score deeply with a sharp trimming knife, guided by a metal straightedge. Then snap it.

4 The quadrant moulding is used to hold the

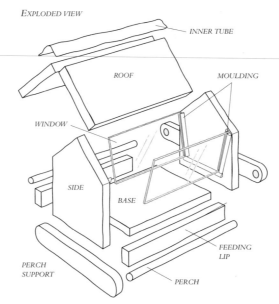

EXPLODED VIEW

INNER TUBE

ROOF

MOULDING

WINDOW

SIDE

BASE

FEEDING LIP

PERCH SUPPORT

PERCH

plastic. Attach the moulding to the sides with two panel pins per piece. Use a scrap of the moulding as a spacer to hold the bottoms of the inner pieces 10mm off the base. Centre the bottom piece and attach it. Align the outer pieces with the ends of the bottom piece and the upper corner of the sides, as shown in the Side pattern, right. Attach the moulding pieces. Use an offcut of plastic sheeting as a spacer to position the inner pieces. On one side, make the space big enough so that you can slide the window out easily for filling the feeder. The other side will be fixed permanently. Remove the protective film and fit the windows.

5 Put one roof piece over the side with the permanent window. Align the top of the roof piece with the peak and make sure the overhang is equal on both sides before attaching it with four panel pins.

6 Sand the top edges of the two feeding lips, then nail them to the front and back of the feeder, flush with the bottom, using two panel pins per connection.

7 Cut the two perch supports to the dimensions in the materials list. Use a 12 mm flat wood bit to make a 6mm deep hole at each end of each support. Centre the hole 19mm from each edge and the end. Cut the corners off each support at a 45° angle, then round the ends with sandpaper. Use panel pins to attach one of the perch supports.

8 Cut the dowel into two 330mm lengths. Test-fit and trim the dowels until the other perch support fits snugly against the side. Insert the dowels and nail the second perch support in place.

9 Cut a 330mm section from a bicycle inner tube for use as a hinge and tack it to the fixed side of the roof with galvanised tacks. Put the other roof piece in place and tack the inner tube to it. The single round wire nail is used as a locking pin for the flip-up roof. Drill a 3mm hole through the flip-up roof into the top edge of one side. Insert the nail. To fill the feeder, pull the nail out by hand. If squirrels are a problem, a little hook might be better and work more effectively.

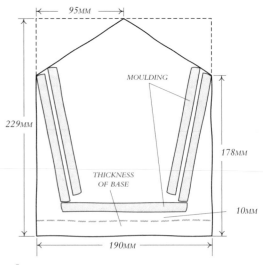

95MM

MOULDING

229MM

178MM

THICKNESS OF BASE

10MM

190MM

SIDE PATTERN

Hanging bird feeder

Here's a bird feeder made very easily with materials that you may already have and some very basic skills. It's a great project to make with children.

MATERIALS

- 460mm length, 110mm diameter uPVC drainpipe
- 110mm uPVC pipe end socket
- 12mm M3 machine screws and matching nuts
- round plastic food container, 125-150mm in diameter (or a child's plastic bucket)
- 235 × 10mm softwood dowels for perches (cut 3)
- solvent-weld cement
- 25mm panel pins × 6
- garden wire
- hanging chain

1 Use a hacksaw to cut the drainpipe to length and then sand off any burrs.
2 Mark the height and location of three perch holes, as shown in the photograph. Use a 10mm flat wood bit at slow speed to drill one hole at each height, spaced evenly around the diameter of the pipe. Put a scrap of dowel into the hole and mark the location for an opposing hole on the other side of the pipe. Drill those holes, too. Using a 5mm twist bit, drill a seed hole 38mm above each perch hole.
3 Cut a 38 × 60mm hole for the seed-viewing window. Start by drilling a hole with a flat wood bit. Complete the cuts with a pad saw or jigsaw. Make the window itself from a piece of clear plastic, 100 × 75mm, cut from a food container. Hold the window in the pipe with masking tape, and drill 2mm-diameter holes through the pipe into the window. Secure the window with machine screws and nuts, then remove the tape.
4 Make the feeder cap by cutting the plastic bucket or food container down to 60mm.
5 Rest the bucket upside down on top of the pipe, centre it, then drill two 5mm holes through its base, on opposite sides, just beyond the outside edge of the pipe. Drill another pair of holes 12mm below the top of the pipe.
6 Slip the three dowel perches into place,

lining up each one so that an equal amount of dowel protrudes on each side.
7 Fix the bottom cap in place with the solvent-weld cement.
8 To install the top cap, work some garden wire into the holes in the cap and then into the holes at the top of the tube; bend the wire ends over with pliers. To fill the feeder, slide the cap up the wire handle until the opening is clear.

Two bird feeders – one simply made from a length of plastic drainpipe and the other a classic in wood – hang from chains and hooks fixed in the beams of a patio. Make sure they are visible from indoors.

9 Hang the feeder by the wire handle from a length of chain suspended from a tree branch or a hook in the porch or patio frame.

• Birdbaths •

*To attract birds to your feeders or nesting boxes, you also need to provide
a ready source of water – for drinking and for bathing. Although after watching some birds
clowning around in a birdbath, you'd be convinced they come just for fun*

Stump birdbath

*This is an inexpensive project that calls for a
minimum of materials. It can be made using
any stump of wood you may have in the garden.
The stump serves as a shallow, rustic birdbath that
complements any garden. Fill it with fresh water
every day. If your log isn't cut square on both ends,
dig out a hole that will hold the top of it level.*

MATERIALS

- a log about 360mm in diameter
- 305mm diameter ceramic or
  plastic saucer – the type used
  under plant pots is ideal
- clear silicone mastic
- felt-tip pen to mark circle
- router with flat cutting bit (this
  tool can be hired)

1 Find a likely stump, then trace the diameter
of the saucer at the centre of its top surface. If
the diameter of the base is smaller than the
rim, draw the outline of the top lip, then mark
the outline of the base within.

2 Set up a router with a flat cutting bit.

3 Don't try to dig out all the wood at once –
you'll have to make at least three or four
passes, depending on the power of your router,
each slightly deeper than the previous one.
Start by making a 100mm diameter hole at the
centre of the log, and work your way down to
the depth of the saucer.

4 Reset the router for a shallow cut and begin
to enlarge the hole outwards. This technique
ensures that the base of the router always has
firm support while cutting.

5 Test-fit the saucer and adjust the hole as
needed. To stop water collecting beneath the
saucer, run a bead of clear silicone mastic
around the lip of the saucer and set it in place.

6 Paint the base of the log with wood
preservative before you position it.

Hanging birdbath

*Site this birdbath in a sheltered area – it will
attract more birds and it will be buffeted less
by breezes. A hanging birdbath should not be
left out in high winds. This is a reasonably
straightforward project, although working with
wire takes a little practice.*

MATERIALS

- 305mm diameter plant
  saucer (glazed ceramic
  or plastic to hold water)
- length of plastic-coated
  clothesline about 100mm
  longer than the
  circumference of
  the saucer
- 610mm 14-gauge
  galvanised wire
- 2.5m light gauge chain
- four 19mm S-hooks
- O-shaped metal key
  ring or large S-hook

1 Cut a length of plastic-coated clothesline
long enough to fit around the saucer just
beneath the lip, plus 100mm which you will
need for the overlap and for securing it. Form
it into a ring; then, to secure the ring at the
overlap, use pliers to twist a short length of
galvanised wire tightly around the clothesline
(below). Make 5 turns, then clip off the
excess. Trim away any excess clothesline, to
give a neat finish.

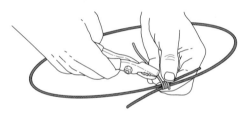

2 Cut three 125mm lengths of galvanised wire
to serve as guards for holding the saucer inside
the clothesline ring. Form a loop in one end of
each guard using long-nosed pliers. Hook the
loops over the clothesline ring at three
equidistant points and crimp the loops tight to

MAKING THE STUMP BIRDBATH

1 *Find a suitable log, and mark on
it the diameter of the saucer's rim and
base, roughly centred. For a snug fit,
the hole will need to be large enough
to accommodate the saucer's widest part.*

2 *Start by routing a 100mm hole in
the middle of the traced circle. Make at
least 3 or 4 passes, each slightly deeper
than the previous one, then enlarge the
hole outwards, staying within the outline.*

3 *Test-fit the saucer and enlarge the
hole if necessary. Run a bead of clear
silicone mastic around the lip of the
saucer and set it in place. The mastic
will protect the wood beneath.*

the ring with pliers. If you are using a ceramic saucer, bend the ends to fit over the sides. If you are using a plastic saucer, leave the ends straight for now.

3 Midway between the guard wires, slip three S-hooks over the clothesline at three equidistant places. The open top of the S should be facing outward. Crimp the S-hooks tight on the clothesline ring with pliers.

4 Place the ceramic saucer in the ring and slip the three wire guards over the lip. They will prevent the saucer from slipping out of the ring when birds land on it or a if a gust of wind should catch it. Clip the wire guards with wire cutters just short of the base of the saucer. If you are using a plastic saucer, drill holes in the saucer's rim directly above each guard piece. Put the straight ends of the guard pieces through the holes and bend them back over the rim of the saucer for security.

5 Cut three 610mm lengths of chain and slip the end of each over the open end of each S-hook. Crimp the hook to retain the chain.

6 Connect the opposite ends of the chains to the O-shaped key ring (or a large S-hook) for hanging the birdbath. Loop weatherproof cord around a suitable branch and hang the birdbath from it. Try to choose a position that will allow you to watch the antics of the birds using the bath, from indoors. Remember to fill the bath with fresh water daily and you will have endless pleasure watching visiting birds enjoying themselves.

Two birdbaths blend comfortably into a garden landscape. Both have shallow ceramic basins for water. In one case, the basin sits snugly in an old tree stump; in the other, it hangs from a wire and chain support.

• Party Lights •

Garden lighting can help to create a magical atmosphere for an outdoor party or dinner, and it doesn't have to involve fancy lights or complex installations. With a little imagination you can provide some gentle illumination with your own festive lights made from simple, everyday materials

Glass jar lights

Here are three ways to hang jars using wire. The measurements given are the ones we used, but you can vary them as desired. Read the section on wirework techniques, page 161, before proceeding.

MATERIALS
- selection of glass jars
- lengths of copper wire, brass picture wire, or similar
- thin and medium garden wire
- vice, pliers, thick screwdriver
- drill and cup hook
- tape measure
- candles, sand
- glass paints, paintbrush

Basic hanger

1 Measure the neck of the jar, add 80mm, and cut a piece of copper wire to this length. Bend the wire around the neck of the jar and use pliers to hook the two ends securely together. Loop the wire around a screwdriver and twist the screwdriver to form two 'eye' loops (see left).
2 Take another piece of wire, about 800mm long, for the hanger. Use pliers to twist a loop (for hanging from a hook) at its midpoint.
3 Thread 20-30mm of each end of the hanger wire through the loops (left) and twist the ends back on themselves as far as they will go.

Twisted-wire hanger

1 Loop a piece of medium garden wire, 2m long, into a circle and use pliers to hook the

two ends together. Shape the wire around the top of the jar, just below the lip (see below) so that there are two loops of about 900mm each on either side of the neck.

900MM LOOP OF WIRE
HOOKED ENDS OF WIRE
LOOP AT END

2 With pliers, twist the left-hand loop hard up against the neck of the jar. Fit a cup hook where you would normally insert a drill bit and slip one of the loops over the cup hook.

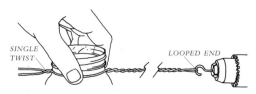

SINGLE TWIST
LOOPED END

3 Holding the wire firmly on either side of the jar's neck as shown (above), run the drill at its lowest speed so that it twists the wire tightly right up to the jar. Then repeat this procedure for the other loop.
4 Neatly cut off the two end loops from the twisted wire. Bend the two strands up above the jar and, about 100mm from their ends, bind them together with finer wire. Use pliers to form decorative coils of about 30mm diameter at the ends (see cage hanger illustration, next column, and photograph, opposite).

Cage hanger

1 Take two pieces of the medium wire, each 1m long. Cross them at their midpoints (see right) and bind them together at this point, using the finer wire.
2 Centre the base of the jar over the join and, holding it firmly in place, bend the wire up over the sides. Bind the four pieces together, 150mm from their ends, using finer wire. Form a decorative coil on each end by twisting it in on itself with pliers.
3 Cut a piece of the medium wire to measure the circumference near the top of the jar plus a few centimetres. Loop this around the four wire strands just below the lip of the jar. Fix to each of the four strands using the finer wire.

LOOP
CROSS

Finishing off

Paint some of your jars, following the paint manufacturer's instructions (see page 123 for more detail on glass painting). To completely coat a jar with one colour, squirt the paint on and then spread with a brush. Put 50-60mm sand in each jar to hold the candles steady.

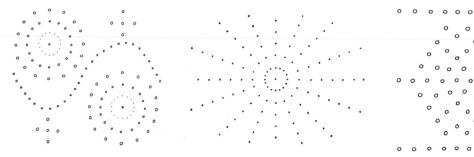

Tin can lights

Candlelight glints through the holes in these cans. The pattern is transferred onto paper and then you can drill or punch it into the can.

MATERIALS
- clean tin cans
- paper, pencil and compasses
- ruler and tape measure
- adhesive tape
- thick piece of dowelling
- vice, pliers, hammer, drill
- paint and paintbrush
- fine and medium garden wire

1 Make a hole pattern on paper to wrap around your can. Use a photocopier to enlarge one of the designs opposite, or cut a piece of paper to size and copy the designs onto it freehand, or make up your own patterns – you could theme the designs to a particular event – perhaps by punching numbers or initials for a child's birthday party.

2 To make circle designs, use compasses to draw concentric circles and mark equidistant points around the outer circumference. Draw lines from the centre to these points to divide the circle into even sectors. Then make a hole dot at each intersection.

3 For the diamond design, draw a small diamond shape made of two equilateral triangles and enclose this with two larger triangles. Add dots to the outlines at evenly spaced intervals to indicate holes.

4 Tape the paper pattern to the can.

5 Place one end of the dowelling lengthways in the vice; slip the can over the other end.

6 At each dot on the pattern, punch a small hole with a large nail and then enlarge the holes with a drill. Make holes for the handle in the top of the can in the same way.

7 Make a handle by bending a 500mm length of wire at its midpoint then bending small hooks at each end to attach to the can; twist the other end into a small loop for hanging.

Create a special atmosphere at an outdoor party or barbecue with soft candlelight from simple holders made using old jam jars and perforated tin cans.

• Pots with a Difference •

Here are some unconventional yet charming containers that you can recycle or make
to introduce some individual touches to your garden. With the right planting, items such as
broken pots, old buckets or wheelbarrows can be given a new lease of life

Recycled pots

When an attractive pot is cracked or broken its
useful life need not necessarily be over. An imperfect
object can be recycled to add its own special charm
and character to your garden.

MATERIALS
- a broken pot (with enough
  bowl remaining to hold some
  potting compost) and shard
  that has broken away
- small shards or pebbles
- potting compost

1 If you don't have a cracked or broken pot,
look out for a second at your local nursery or
pot shop. Damaged items are usually available
at a greatly reduced price. Use a bolster and
hammer to carefully chip away any sharp
points or irregular or jagged pieces off the
shard (the piece that has broken away).

2 Cover the drainage hole with smaller shards
or a few pebbles to prevent the potting
compost being washed out. Add potting
compost to the damaged pot to the level of
the lowest point of the break.

3 Press the shard into the potting compost,
placing it about one third in from the rear of
the pot. Firm the potting compost around
the shard to keep it in place.

4 Fill the pot with plants. Those that require
good drainage are best placed at the rear; those
that prefer moist conditions at the front. Plants
with large rootballs should also be positioned
at the rear where their roots have more room
to grow. For dry-climate plants or cacti, add
some coarse sand to the potting compost to
further improve drainage.

VARIATION To age a newly bought second,
smear it with dirt and moss or a handful of
peat moss and watery cement.

Use a large pottery shard to create a miniature
terrace and restore a broken pot to being a useful
container that can be planted up in two levels (above
and left). The shard also helps to hold potting mix
in place until plant roots are well enough established
to do the job. In this Australian planting, Scirpus
'Fairylights', Coprosma *and* Schleranthus biflorus
help to capitalise on the imperfections of the
unconventional container above. The pot at left
becomes a miniature folly with its use of a water-
worn aquarium stone as a makeshift replacement
for a missing shard. The impact of the display of
Pelargonium *'Pretty Lady',* Sedum *and* Erigeron
'Los Angeles Pink' is enhanced by placing the pot
on a weathered sandstone step.

Mock stone pots

*A stone trough is one of the most handsome –
but expensive – garden containers. Here is an
inexpensive and easy alternative – mock stone.
This material that you make yourself simulates
the texture of real stone at a fraction of the cost.*

MATERIALS

- containers with rigid sides
  (polystyrene vegetable cartons,
  cardboard boxes), small sheet
  of plywood
- 12cm length of 2cm diameter
  dowelling
- peat moss or shredded coconut
  husk
- sand-and-cement mix
- wire brush
- potting compost
- ground cover plants

1 Combine the dry peat moss or coconut
husk and the sand-and-cement mix using two
parts peat moss to one part sand-and-cement.
When thoroughly mixed, add small quantities
of water until the mixture is the consistency
of dough – sticky but not wet.

2 To make a simple mould, insert two 6cm
lengths of 2cm diameter dowelling into the
bottom of the box to form drainage holes. Line
the bottom of the box with 3cm of the mix.
For the inner walls of the mould, cut lengths
of plywood 6cm shorter than the outside
dimensions of the box and stand them corner
to corner inside to mimic the container's
shape. Support them on the inside with a
layer or two of bricks or half-bricks.

3 Fill the space between the two with the
peat-cement mix, pressing it down firmly as
you go with a blunt stick.

4 Allow to dry under cover for 24 hours.

5 Next day, slide out the inner sides and tear
away the polystyrene or cardboard outer walls.

6 Remove the dowelling drainage plugs.

*You may want to add coloured oxides to boost the
natural look given to the mock-stone mix by the peat
moss. Stir them in once or twice only and they will
introduce haphazard, sediment-like streaks to the pot.*

7 Rub the sides of the container with a small,
stiff floor-scrubbing brush or a wire brush to
slightly roughen the surface, giving it the
appearance of hewn stone.

8 Leave the container unplanted for 3-5 days
(depending on the weather) to ensure that the
mix firms properly, and then fill with plants.

VARIATION For a round pot, line the bottom
of a plastic container of the desired diameter
and height with 3cm of the mix. Centre a
garden pot with a diameter about 6cm less
than the plastic container on the mix so that
the gap between the two is even all round.
Fill in the gap with the mix and firm down.

Painted pots

These decorative pots are as practical as they are good looking. They can be used as highlights to bring colour to a garden corner and they make excellent gifts. Painted as subtly or as boldly as you like, they are a cheerful ingredient in giving the garden your own individual touch.

MATERIALS
- tin buckets or pails and terracotta pots of various sizes
- stiletto hole punch for tin
- cloth rag
- raw metal paint sealer
- household or artists' paints
- paintbrushes of various sizes to suit tin sizes

1 Make sure all containers are free of rust and in good condition.

2 Some of our metal containers were purchased with rims already scalloped. If yours are straight-edged and you would like them to be scalloped, draw a semi-circular pattern around the top rim with a sharp pencil, using a jam jar lid as a template. Cut the design out with sharp tinsnips.

3 If you wish to use the metal containers for planting (they can serve as rustic-looking vases if you wish), punch three or four drainage holes in the base of each one with a stiletto hole punch. Remember to cover the holes with pebbles or shards, before planting.

4 For best results, wipe down the work surfaces of the containers with a damp clean cloth before you start painting them.

5 Coat the metal containers inside and out with a raw metal paint sealer. Allow to dry.

6 Working in an airy, dust-free environment, paint each container with two or three coats of semi-gloss exterior, oil-based paint. Make sure each coat is dry before you start the next one. The number of coats required will depend on the colour of the paint you choose. Allow the containers to dry thoroughly before use.

Use a simple coat of paint to bring style to inexpensive tin containers or to help containers of all kinds to blend in with a particular colour scheme.

Where space is limited, plant bulbs and annuals in galvanised bowls, tubs and buckets for displays that can be moved readily from place to place. Ensure that containers have drainage holes before planting.

Novelty planters

Just about any type of container that will hold soil and can be drained will serve as a novel, eye-catching planter. Old galvanised buckets or watering cans make ideal plant containers; new ones can be aged to give them character.

Use found or discarded objects such as this old wheelbarrow as feature planters. Grouping small and large containers together in a corner or against a wall makes for an effective display.

MATERIALS
♦ potting mix
♦ slow-release fertiliser
♦ range of flowering plants
♦ containers such as old galvanised buckets and watering cans

1 To give an aged look to a new galvanised bucket or watering can, smear a handful of moist clay loam haphazardly over the surface. Let this dry and then use a gloved hand to scrape or wipe off any lumps that have stuck to the surface. Do not wash it off as moisture will remove the dirt that dulls the silver gloss finish of the galvanising process.

2 If an old container is still watertight, punch two or three 1cm diameter holes in the bottom. Cover the holes with a layer of pottery shards or pebbles so that they do not become clogged with potting mix or allow the mix to wash away. If the bottom has rusted you may need to line it with thick plastic to ensure that the drainage is not too free.

3 Fill the containers with a free-draining but moisture-retentive potting mix, add a handful of slow-release fertiliser pellets and plant as you would any other container. Check moisture daily by pressing your finger into the top few centimetres of the potting mix – if this top layer has dried out then it is time to water. In hot, dry or windy conditions, water at least once daily, and once a week dunk small containers in a bucket or tub of water to ensure that roots are thoroughly soaked.

QUIRKY INSPIRATIONS

O LD WORK BOOTS, wooden crates, metal teapots or kettles, even birdcages can be adapted to hold plants. Why not attach a length of chain or weatherproof cord to the top to make an unusual hanging basket?

Inexpensive plastic pots can be given character with a coat of matt enamel paint; age them with a coating of wet soil or a rough sponging of limewash. You can individualise them by tying a length of rope around the neck and hanging them with ornaments such as pine cones, seashells or small bells.

Fill containers with bulbs mixed with low-growing annuals such as violas and pansies.

Wire Pot Stands

The ancient craft of of wirework produces an intriguingly novel form of indoor and outdoor decoration. Choose either of two versions of this elegant but sturdy wire pot stand, or tailor the style and proportions to suit a particular pot you want to display

Read the section on wirework techniques, page 161, before proceeding with this project.

MATERIALS

- rolls of wire: thin, medium, thick and thickest
- saucepan, 26cm diameter or less
- ruler or tape measure, felt pen
- vice, pliers, screwdriver, gloves
- piece of 40mm-diameter plastic waste pipe
- jar, about 70mm diameter
- drill, with cup hook
- full-gloss spray paint, or small jar of paint and paintbrush

MAKING THE BASE

1 To make a cross-shaped base, take two pieces 600mm long, of the thickest wire, marking the midpoint of each and then marking a point 90mm either side of this.

2 To shape the four 'foot' rings to sit beneath the cross-piece, secure the pipe horizontally in a vice. Rest one cross-piece on the pipe at one of the 90mm marks, holding it in place with your thumb. With the other hand, bend the long end of the wire around the pipe so that it overlaps the other end and forms a 40-50mm diameter ring. When released, the long end should spring back to form a neat ring (try a few times until you get the right size).

3 Repeat the above at the other 90mm mark and then do the same with the other piece. Bend a kink into one piece at its midpoint, rest the second piece in this to form a neat cross and secure at the midpoint with the thin wire.

4 Make an outer hoop to sit on the cross-shaped base by protecting your hands with gloves and unwinding enough of the thickest wire to go around the saucepan. Make a hoop of approximately 880mm circumference (260mm diameter). Cut the wire 20mm longer (approximately 900mm). Use pliers to hook the ends together to secure the hoop.

5 Lay the hoop on top of the base, cutting back the four ends of the cross-piece so that only 10mm extends beyond the hoop. Secure the two together by tightly hooking the ends around the hoop with pliers.

6 Use pliers to bend 3m of the thick wire into a spiral of an outer diameter to fit within the outer hoop. Leave 10mm free at each end.

7 Lay the spiral on the base. Hook the 10mm at the spiral's centre around the centre of the cross-piece and the 10mm at the other end around the outer hoop wherever the two meet.

8 Secure the spiral to each cross-piece with an 800mm length of the thin wire. Wind the wire across so that it loops around each point where the two pieces intersect. Secure neatly at each end to the outer hoop.

DECORATING WITH PETALS

1 Use the drill with a cup hook to twist 1m double strands of the medium wire into 'plaits' (see illustration, page 200) and cut these into sixteen 320mm lengths with 10mm hooked ends.

2 Bend each length into a V-shaped 'petal'. Then lay a jar on its side and press each petal over it to give the petal a gentle curve.

MAKING THE POT STAND

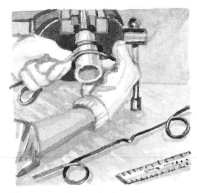

1 To start the stand's base take two lengths of wire and make two 'foot' rings in each by bending around a pipe. Make a small kink at the midpoint of one piece, rest the other in it and join the two here.

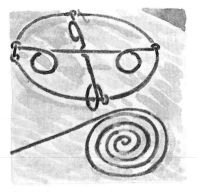

2 For the second part of the base, make an 880mm diameter hoop, place it on the cross-piece and secure with hooks at the end of each piece. Finish the base by winding the thickest wire into a spiral that fits inside the hoop.

3 Lay the spiral within the hoop and attach it to the cross-piece by winding on the thin wire so that it secures the two wherever they intersect. Ensure that the wire is also wound around each of the 'feet'.

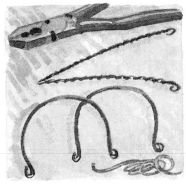

4 For a decorative trim round the perimeter, make 16 V-shaped 'petals' of plaited medium wire and press each over a jar to make a curve. Alternatively, use thick wire scallops bent on the pipe in the vice.

3 With curve and hooks facing outwards (use the picture above as a guide), connect a petal to the base hoop with hooks about 100mm apart. Close the hooks with pliers. Attach the next petal half overlapping the first. Continue in this way around the hoop back to the start. Where the petals cross each other, secure them with the thin wire.

4 Finish by painting the stand, if desired.

DECORATING WITH SCALLOPS

1 Cut 18 lengths of the thick wire, each 250mm long and with 10mm hooks at each end.

2 Bend each piece of wire around the waste pipe secured in the vice until it forms almost a complete hoop. Remove from the pipe and let it spring out to make a half-ring or scallop shape (see picture above) with ends about 90mm apart. Repeat for each length.

Use these sturdy stands to support pots on the verandah or patio, or vases indoors. Paint them with a metal primer before coating in your favourite colour.

3 Attach in the same way as the petals (step 3, column 1, at left), but with hooks facing inwards rather than outwards.

4 The stand can be painted, if you wish.

◆ Relaxing in the Garden ◆

Summer leisure is all about being able to live in your garden as you would in any other room of the house. A versatile awning that provides far more shade than an umbrella and some director's chair covers in cheerful fabrics are the perfect 'furniture' combination to tempt you outdoors

Canvas awning

This awning, made of strong material and fully adjustable, can be used in many ways in the garden – stand it on the lawn, suspend it from two trees, or attach it to a wall or the side of the house.

MATERIALS

- two 2400mm lengths of planed softwood, 50 × 25mm (its actual size will be about 45 × 22mm)
- two 2400mm lengths of 40mm-diameter PVC tubing
- 4 PVC caps to fit tubes
- 4 eye bolts with 15mm eyes, at least 50mm long (extra 2 bolts if attaching to wall)
- two 2350mm lengths of 16mm-diameter aluminium tubing
- two 1500mm lengths of 25mm diameter dowelling (plus an extra two lengths, at least 2m, if attaching to wall)
- two 100mm-long nails or thin steel rods
- lightweight (250g) canvas, 2500 × 1900mm
- 35 small plastic rings (as sold for Roman blinds)
- 2m of 7mm-wide cotton tape
- 5m light rope (sash cord)
- 4 tent pegs (we used plastic ones)
- 20m synthetic blind cord
- quick-drying epoxy adhesive
- full-gloss paint, paintbrush
- sewing machine, heavy-duty needle, scissors, plane, electric drill, chisel

MAKING THE TUBES AND RODS

1 Plane the edges of the softwood so that the lengths fit snugly inside the plastic tubes. Insert the pine into the tubes, to reinforce them.
2 Drill two holes for eye bolts 500mm from each end of one plastic tube, ensuring the bolts

Bringing the indoors outside is easy with the awning and chair-cover projects which make the garden as comfortable for lunch as the dining room.

DIAGRAM 1
100MM NAIL HOLE
CAP
500MM
385MM
45MM

NAIL HOLE
CROSS-SECTION
SOFTWOOD
EYE BOLT

pass through the 40mm width of the pine inside the pole (see cross-section, left). Insert bolts and fix them with nuts and washers.

3 Starting 45mm from one end, drill seven holes in the tubes at 385mm intervals (see diagram 1); drill in line with the two eye-bolt holes, making the new holes just large enough for the blind cord.
4 Quarter-turn the tube and drill two holes for the 100mm nails so that they will pass through the 22mm depth of the softwood (see cross-section). Drill midway between each eye-bolt hole and the nearest cord hole (see diagram 1). Glue a cap on each end of the tube.
5 Prepare the second PVC tube in the same way, then paint both tubes.
6 Drill three holes in each aluminium rod – at the midpoint, and 270mm from each end.
7 To make poles to support the awning on a lawn (see illustrations, page 210), taper one end of each dowel to a sharp point (see diagram 2) using a chisel, plane, or sanding disc on the drill. At the other end of each, drill a

NAIL
50 MM

DIAGRAM 2

PEG

hole 50mm from the end. Then drill a hole into the blunt end of the dowel and hammer in a long nail or steel rod, fixing with glue if necessary. Paint both poles. Make longer poles (2m) to use the awning on sand at the beach.
8 Cut two 2m lengths of rope (3m for long poles). Tie one end to the hole in a tent peg and the other through the hole in the pole (diagram 2).

MAKING THE CANVAS AWNING

1 On each 1900mm side of the canvas, turn over 50mm, then fold under 10mm of raw edge and hem with the sewing machine. Do the same for the 2500mm sides, leaving these hems open-ended to take rods later.
2 On the other side of the canvas – the side not showing hems – measure and mark the positions for the small plastic rings in seven equally spaced rows of five across the width of the canvas (see diagram 3). The seven rows of rings have to line up with the seven holes in

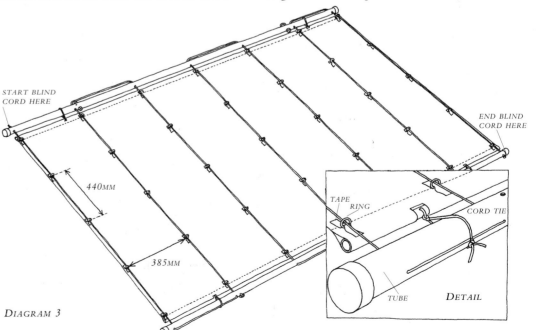

START BLIND CORD HERE

END BLIND CORD HERE

440MM

385MM

DIAGRAM 3

TAPE
RING

CORD TIE

TUBE   DETAIL

the tubes, so lay the long side of the canvas next to a pole and mark the canvas accordingly. In each row, the rings should be about 440mm apart, with those at either end about 20mm from the canvas edge. Place a 50mm piece of cotton tape through each ring and glue 20mm of each end of the piece to the canvas (see detail of diagram 3).

ASSEMBLING THE AWNING
1 Lay all the completed parts on the floor.
2 Thread a 500mm length of blind cord through each hole in the aluminium rods and knot to secure. Insert the rods into the open hems of the canvas. Cut three holes about 20mm square in the hem at the points where the lengths of cord are tied (see detail of diagram 3). Pull the cords through the holes and tie them around the PVC tubes.
3 Starting at one end of one tube (see diagram 4), thread blind cord continuously through the holes and plastic rings. When you get to the end (see diagram 3), tie a knot in the cord. It is best to thread the cord under the ties holding the aluminium rods to the tubes.
4 Dab adhesive on all knots to secure them.

USING THE AWNING
There are three main ways to erect the awning – on a lawn, between two trees or attached to a wall. The side with the adjustable cord should always be the outer or upward-facing side.
1 To place it on a lawn, use short pieces of rope to tie the bolts of one of the tubes to tent pegs secured in the ground, then support the other

Trees are not essential for the canvas awning; use poles and guy ropes to provide almost instant shade for a garden picnic.

tube with the dowels, placing the nails at the ends of the dowels into the holes in the tube. Push the pointed ends of the dowels into the .

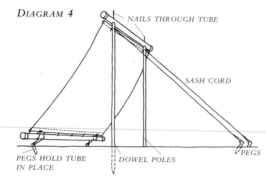

DIAGRAM 4

NAILS THROUGH TUBE

SASH CORD

PEGS HOLD TUBE IN PLACE

DOWEL POLES

PEGS

ground and keep them upright by pulling the sash cords taut and hammering their pegs into the ground.
2 To hang the awning between two trees, attach sufficient sash cord to each of the four eye bolts and adjust it as appropriate.
3 To attach to a garden fence or wall or the side of a house, insert two eye bolts into the fence or wall and join them with short pieces of rope to the eye bolts of one of the tubes. Use the the longer (2m) poles to prop up the other tube or tie it with rope to a tree, a sturdy post or a similar solid support.

The awning can be adjusted to give as much or as little shade as desired, as the sun moves.

Chair covers

These simple loose covers can protect new chairs or brighten up old director's chairs.

MATERIALS
♦ 2 metres of 115cm-wide fabric per chair
♦ matching machine thread
♦ sewing machine
♦ pins, scissors
♦ tape measure
♦ large sheets of clean scrap paper for patterns

MEASURING THE FABRIC
Each cover is composed of three pieces – a central piece and two arm pieces. As factory-made director's chairs can vary in size, make sure that you carefully measure your chairs before starting. The cover described here has a skirt that drops to about two-thirds of the way between the seat and the floor – but you can make it with a full skirt if desired.
1 To calculate the width of the central piece, measure from A to A on diagram 1 (across the back of the chair). To calculate the length of the piece, measure from B to B (from about two-thirds of the way between the front edge of the seat and the floor, across the seat from front to back, then up over the back rest and down to about two-thirds of the way between the seat's back edge and the floor). Add a 15mm seam allowance to all edges. Use large sheets of scrap paper taped together to make a paper pattern first, or cut straight from the fabric if you are confident.
2 The two arm pieces are identical. To calculate the length of the piece, measure from C to C on diagram 1 (from about two-thirds of the way between seat edge and floor, up over chair arm and down to side edge of seat). For the width of the piece, measure from D to D (from front to back of armrest). Add a 15mm seam allowance to all edges. Cut out two arm pieces, making a paper pattern first.

ASSEMBLING THE COVER
Seam edges may be pressed open and zigzagged on each side, or overlocked together, as desired.

Dress up your outdoor chairs with some stylish, brightly coloured, slip-on covers. If it rains, the chairs look equally good indoors.

1 Drape the central piece on the chair as shown in diagram 2, with the wrong side of the material facing you and the front and back edges at the same height. Using pins, mark positions (see diagram 3) on both sides of the piece for the top of the uprights (E), top of the arm rests (F), seat back (G) and seat front (H). Remove the piece from the chair. Pin, then stitch the edges together from E to F on each side (top of uprights to top of arm rests).

2 Place the central piece on the chair as before with the pins in the correct positions. Pin then stitch the short edge of each arm piece to the central piece between G and H as shown in diagram 3. At G and H cut 15mm of the fabric – from edge to seam allowance – so the central piece will turn easily at these corners.

3 Place the cover on the chair and drape each arm piece up over a chair arm and down the outside of the chair as shown in diagram 4 (the arm piece edges should be level with the front and back edges of the central piece). Pin each arm piece to the central piece from G to I on diagram 4 (do this on both sides of the chair's arm); from I to the bottom of the skirt is left free on each side for a slit, as shown.

4 Place the cover on the chair. Pin, then stitch from J to K on diagram 4 (front edges of arm pieces and down to bottom of skirt).

5 Zigzag all raw edges to prevent fraying. Press hems for the slits in place then stitch them close to the edge of the fabric. Press a hem around the bottom of the cover and stitch close to the fabric edge.

6 Put the cover back on the chair. Pin, then stitch a short seam across the width of the arm at the top of and at right angles to the front seam. Press seams open and zigzag edges.

7 Turn the cover right side out, check all corners carefully, and place it on the chair.

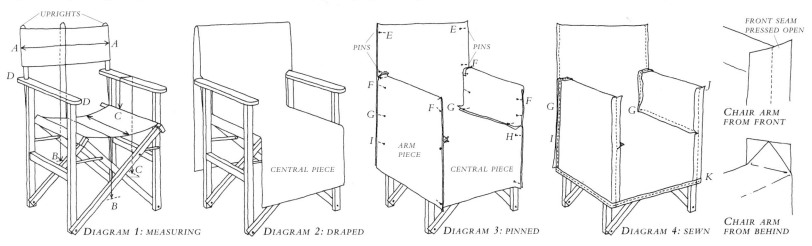

DIAGRAM 1: *MEASURING*   DIAGRAM 2: *DRAPED*   DIAGRAM 3: *PINNED*   DIAGRAM 4: *SEWN*

The Ultimate Hammock

*Shop-bought hammocks rarely live up to their claims of comfort but this garden indulgence has
been especially designed for the do-it-yourselfer to provide comfort without folding in on the user. Its strong
end pieces provide a sense of security for those wary of reclining while suspended above the ground*

*This hammock does not need a large garden with
conveniently placed trees — it can simply be attached
to a sturdy post at one end and a large ring bolt in a
wall at the other. It requires some woodworking
competency but only basic sewing skills.*

MATERIALS

- six lengths of planed softwood
  900 × 65 × 38mm
- approximately 500mm of
  10mm-diameter dowel
- PVA waterproof wood adhesive
- two eye bolts with 26mm eyes
  and 125mm shafts
- gloss paint
- two lengths of planed hardwood
  900 × 42 × 32mm
- clear polyurethane varnish
- four 150mm long, 6mm-
  diameter bolts
- 2.2 × 9.5m heavy natural canvas
- 17m heavy sash cord
- sewing machine with upholstery
  gauge needle
- poly-cotton sewing thread,
  upholstery weight
- sandpaper, scrap paper, pencil,
  saw, plane, drill, clamps,
  paintbrush, scissors

MAKING THE TIMBER END PIECES

This hammock has timber end pieces, made of
three 900mm pieces of softwood, at each end.
Before making the end pieces, draw a full-sized
plan on paper to work from; it makes measuring
easier and ensures the two will be identical.
The following instructions show how to
make one end piece; repeat for the second.

1 Use diagram 1 as a guide to drawing the
plan. Draw a rectangle 900 × 650mm, then
mark points A, B and C as shown; join A to B
and A to C with solid lines; draw a solid line
from B and C to the bottom corners then join

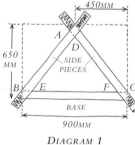

DIAGRAM 1

the bottom corners
with a solid line.
This sets the outer
edge of the end
piece. To draw the
inside edge (to join
points D, E and F)
lay a piece of soft-
wood down on its
65mm side with one edge abutting the inside of
the triangle just drawn; draw a line along the
other edge of the wood. Do this on all three sides.

2 Lay one side piece on the plan and trim its
ends (the shaded areas in diagram 1). Repeat
for the other side piece. Lay the base piece
down and give it a slight trim near points B
and C. (If preferred, you can leave some wood
untrimmed at the ends, then trim neatly after
the gluing is finished.)

3 Make joints at each of the three corners:
where overlaps occur, draw lines around the
overlapping pieces (see dotted line, diagram 2).
Saw halfway through the timber along the
lines so that when all the joints are cut, the

The recommended materials and the way they have been combined will make you a relatively weatherproof hammock that is stronger than most and should last a lifetime. After you have made the hammock, take time out to relax and enjoy its gentle swinging motion. All that's required is a summer's day, a cool drink and a good book.

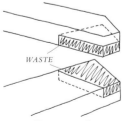

DIAGRAM 2

three pieces will slot together as shown in diagram 3. Glue the pieces together at each corner and clamp. Leave to dry.

4 Strengthen each join with two pieces of dowel: drill holes the diameter of the dowels, smear them with adhesive and push into place. They should be long enough to protrude at either side; when dry, saw off the ends.

5 Measure and cut a small triangular piece to fit inside the apex of the timber triangle (see diagram 3). Glue it in place. Also trim off the point of the timber triangle so that it is flat.

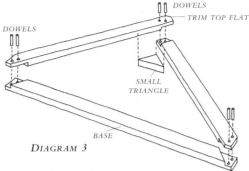

DIAGRAM 3

6 Drill three holes for bolts: two of 6mm diameter in the triangle's base, 155mm from each corner, and one of 10mm diameter through the triangle's apex (see diagram 6).

7 With a plane, bevel all outer edges of the triangle to approximately 45°. Sand the end piece (medium, then fine sandpaper) then paint with two or three coats of paint, allowing drying time between each coat.

MAKING THE SUPPORT RODS

These connect to the end pieces (diagram 6) and prevent the canvas from folding inwards.

1 Bevel the long edges of the two 900mm lengths of hardwood so each piece looks octagonal when viewed from the end.

2 In each rod, drill two 6mm diameter holes 155mm from the ends for bolts, and two holes big enough to accept the sash cord 20–30mm from the ends.

3 Sand the rods (medium, then fine) then apply one or two coats of clear varnish.

MAKING THE CANVAS SLING

Ensure that all seams turn to the same side (there is no wrong or right side to canvas).

DIAGRAM 4

1 To make the loops that hold the supporting rods, cut four slits at one short end of the

canvas (see the dotted lines in diagram 4). Fold over as indicated in the diagram and machine stitch. There is no need to turn the raw edge under. Repeat for the other end.

2 Reinforce the edges at the bottom of the slits with a piece of canvas roughly 90 × 50mm folded in half. 30mm slits on either side of the fold allow it to slide into place. Glue it around the bottom of the slot, as shown on diagram 5.

3 Fold over 10mm at the top edges of the loops and stitch; then fold the loops over in half so the top edge is in line with the bottom of the slots (see diagram 5). Machine two rows of stitching.

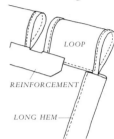

DIAGRAM 5

4 On the long sides of the canvas, turn over 50mm, fold under the raw edge and hem. (At the ends of the long sides, where the slits were cut, fold the raw edge over and hem it before you stitch the long hem.)

ASSEMBLING THE HAMMOCK

1 Insert the support rods in the hems.

2 Thread the sash cord through the support rods and side hems of the canvas and knot together at one end, between the timber end pieces and the rods.

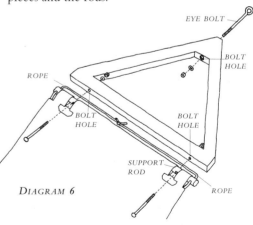

DIAGRAM 6

3 Attach the support rods to the end pieces with 150 × 6mm bolts and acorn-nuts. Screw an eye bolt into the top of each end piece. Attach 5m of heavy sash cord to each eye bolt and tie the hammock to its supports.

· Homemade Compost ·

The best additive for your garden beds is homemade compost and the best place to make it is in a no-nonsense compost bin you made yourself. These straightforward projects show you how quick and easy it is to turn garden and kitchen waste into valuable nutrients for your plants

Compost bin

Proper composting depends on good aeration. This stake and wire mesh bin allows a free flow of air while at the same time giving you access through one side to turn the contents with a fork.

MATERIALS
- nine 1200mm lengths of 25mm-diameter hardwood, or nine 1200mm pre-cut garden stakes
- 3m × 900mm-width light welded mesh
- 800mm-square piece of 6mm-thick exterior-grade hardboard, for lid
- five 450mm lengths of 25mm-square hardwood (buy a 2.4m length and have it cut to size)
- medium garden wire
- thin garden wire
- six 75mm-long galvanised bolts with nuts and washers
- fence paint
- paintbrush
- tape measure
- long ruler (optional)

MAKING THE BIN

If you choose to make the lid first, you can use one of the stakes as a long ruler to help with its measurements.

1 To make the stakes, shape the bottom end of each 1200mm length to a point using a plane; if you have bought pre-cut stakes this won't be necessary.

Make a bin with straight wire sides to allow the air to penetrate and your garden need never be short of compost, the essential ingredient for healthy plants.

2 Drill three holes in each stake, one about 100mm from the top, another 400mm below this and a third 300mm from the bottom. Ensure that the holes are slightly larger than 2mm in diameter.

3 Dig holes about 300mm deep for the stakes and insert them in the ground. Place them about 300mm apart to form a shape approximately 600mm square (see diagram 1).

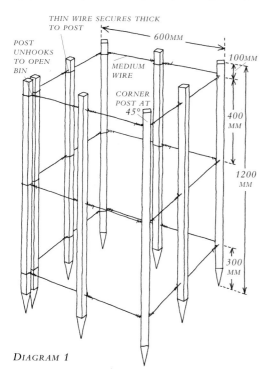

DIAGRAM 1

Put two stakes at the most accessible corner – one of these will form the opening edge of the bin's 'door'. Twist the corner stakes by about 45° (see diagram 1) so that a flat surface faces inwards – this allows for ease of wiring later. Fill in the holes and tamp down the soil.

4 Starting with one of the stakes at the double-stake corner and working round to the other, thread three rows of medium garden wire through the holes in the stakes. At each hole, secure the medium wire with thin wire anchored on either side of the pole. The row at the bottom of the stakes should be at ground level or a bit below; it may help to dig a small trench to make it easier to attach this row.

5 Wrap one end of the mesh around one of the 'double' stakes and secure it with thin wire

to the three rows of medium wire.

6 Roll the mesh around the square on the inside of the stakes (see diagram 2). As you work, connect the mesh to the top row of medium wire with the thin wire, making a tight weave every 100mm or so (see diagram 2). Do not take the mesh past the second 'double' stake as this is the edge of the 'door'.

7 Run thin garden wire along the other two rows of medium wire, weaving through the mesh and medium wire as before.

8 Anchor the mesh to the top of each stake with a loop of medium wire (see diagram 2).

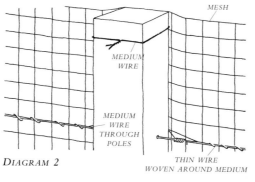

DIAGRAM 2

MAKING THE LID

1 Mark out six holes for bolts to attach the handle to the hardboard lid. To do this, mark a point 225mm up from each corner – you should have two marks on each edge 350mm apart. Rule straight lines across the lid to join each mark to its opposite and the result should

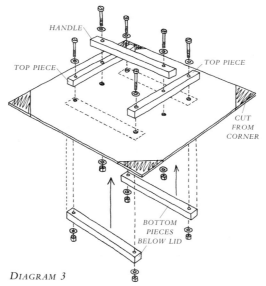

DIAGRAM 3

be a 350mm square in the middle of the lid. Mark drilling holes where the lines intersect then mark two more holes halfway between these holes (see diagram 3). At the six marked points, drill holes big enough for the bolts you have chosen.

2 For the handle, mark drilling holes 50mm from each end of each 450mm-long piece of hardwood – ensure that these correspond to the drill holes on the lid. Drill the holes. Also mark and drill a hole at the midpoints of the two top pieces (see diagram 3).

3 With the lid sandwiched between, position the two top pieces and the two bottom pieces at right angles to each other and bolt them together (see diagram 3). Lay the handle across the two top pieces and bolt it to them through the holes at their midpoints.

4 To make removing and replacing the lid easier, you can saw off small triangles from the corners of the hardboard – these are shown as shaded areas on diagram 3.

FINISHING OFF

If desired, stain all timber and the hardboard lid with fence varnish. This is not essential but will greatly increase the life of the bin.

MAKING THE BEST COMPOST

Position your bin or heap in a reasonably sunny position. The warmth of the sun will provide extra heat to encourage the decomposition process.

If you are unable to turn the compost regularly, drill holes in a wide, plastic drainage pipe that matches the height of the bin and place it in the centre of the heap to encourage aeration.

Do not start your heap under a tree – its shade will lower the heap's temperature and any roots under the compost will quickly pilfer its nutrients.

If you have the space in your garden, make an individual wire enclosure for recycling leaves. Although leaves may take up to two years to rot down completely, the wait is worth it because they make excellent homemade potting composts.

Compost heap

The rich humus formed by composting is not only a vital part of the makeup of soil but it is also the cheapest soil conditioner available and the easiest to obtain because you make it yourself. Without it, plants will not flourish no matter how much love and attention is lavished upon them.

HOW A COMPOST HEAP WORKS

The basic ingredients of a compost heap are nitrogen, carbon, oxygen and moisture. Nitrogen-rich materials include most fresh, green forms of vegetable matter: kitchen peelings, green leaves and grass clippings. Carbon-rich materials include those that have already started to decompose by drying out: straw, paper, dried leaves and bark. Green materials also contain some carbon but an effective heap requires at least twice the amount of 'dry', carbon-rich material as it does of green, nitrogen-rich matter.

Oxygen is absorbed from the air so the heap must be turned regularly or, if it is enclosed, air should be able to penetrate through the sides (see previous page). Too much water is as bad as too little – excess water will decrease the amount of oxygen in the heap – so to keep the heap damp but not wet it should be covered. This way if it starts to dry out you can spray it with a hose for a few minutes.

The interaction of all these elements, combined with the heat generated by microbe activity, breaks the organic matter down. Regular turning of the heap maintains a high temperature and adds fresh oxygen which reacts with the nitrogen to provide additional heat. In summer, a fresh heap takes about two weeks to reach its maximum temperature, and, if it is well maintained, will mature in two to three months. The end result should be a dark-coloured, sweet-scented, crumbly medium for mixing into garden soil.

HEAPS VERSUS BINS

A simple, open heap is the traditional and most common way to compost materials but being exposed to the elements means that heat build-up is slow. Bins such as the one described on page 215 are more efficient. A series of three containers will ensure a regular supply: one in the process of being filled, a full one with waste left to decompose and a third with fully decomposed waste being used as needed on the garden.

MAKING A HEAP

1 In a sunny position, measure out an area at least a metre square (this is the minimum size necessary to generate the required heat in the shortest possible time). The bigger the heap the more rapidly it generates heat.

2 Arrange coarse materials such as sticks, prunings and bark pieces to form the base. These allow air to filter into the centre of the heap but should not completely smother the soil surface otherwise worms will not be able to enter the heap.

3 Place about 5-10cm of other organic matter, such as kitchen waste or grass clippings mixed with dry leaves, animal manure or weed-free garden loam, over this.

4 Lightly water each layer with a fine spray and build further layers of material 10cm deep. Turn the heap about once a fortnight.

MAKING A COMPOST HEAP

1 *Start your heap on an open, sunny site a minimum of 1m square. Make a base by spreading a loose layer of coarse garden waste such as twigs and bark over the soil.*

2 *Build up the heap with layers of organic matter – vegetable peelings, leaves and grass. If it starts to dry out, spray with a hose until it is just damp but not wet.*

3 *For every 10cm layer of waste add a handful of blood and bone or a spadeful of manure. Use a fork to turn the heap regularly – about every two weeks.*

VARIATION *A plastic compost bin, whether a proprietary model or a bottomless garbage bin, is useful where space is limited. Build up layers of waste with soil in between.*

• Keeping Your Garden Healthy •

*Beautiful flowers and bountiful vegetables depend on good rich soil,
regular doses of fertiliser, and protection from harmful pests and diseases. Here's how
to do it all with a little ingenuity and without toxic chemicals*

Know your soil

*Unless you know what type of soil you have in
your garden, you could waste time and money
trying to grow unsuitable plants.*

Soil-testing

A complete soil test is the best investment you
can make in your garden. Buy a soil-testing kit
from your local nursery or garden centre, and
test the pH – the acidity or alkalinity – of your
soil. There is also a test available that indicates
the nutrient content of the soil. The results will
give you a good indication of the lime, trace
elements and fertiliser your soil needs. When
you know what your soil needs you can create
the right conditions for the plants you choose.

Homemade starter compost

All-natural: Mix one part sifted garden loam,
one part peat or leaf mould and one part
coarse sand. To eliminate soil-borne diseases,
place the mixture in a shallow baking pan with
a small potato. Bake at a very low temperature
until the potato is cooked.
Lightweight potting compost: Mix thoroughly
one part vermiculite, one part leaf mould and
one part perlite. Moisten before using.

Killing weeds

A chemical-free way of clearing weeds is by
smothering them. Cover the area you wish to
clear with some kind of mulch. This can be an
old carpet or a sheet of black polythene, with
the edges tucked securely into the soil, or a
layer of old newspapers or sheets of cardboard
held in place by bricks or stones. It takes a
couple of months to kill annual weeds in this
way, but up to two years for perennial weeds.

Natural fertilisers

*No matter where you live, good sources of free
fertiliser may be available. Is there a riding stable
nearby? Or does a neighbour have a pet rabbit or
chickens? Here are some other possibilities.*

Seaweed

Seaweed is actually richer in nitrogen and
potassium than most animal manures. To get
rid of the salt, stack the seaweed in an out-of-
the-way place (because it smells) where the
runoff won't end up in your lawn or garden.
Let several rains wash through it before adding
it to the compost heap or digging it into the
garden in late autumn.

Wood ash

Save your wood ash (but not the ash from a
coal fire). It is an excellent source of potassium
and a way to improve the hardiness of plants
and the flavour of fruits.

Coffee grounds and tea leaves

Apply coffee grounds or tea leaves as a light
mulch around acid-loving plants to provide a
mild, but complete food.

Organic plant food

For an organic food for plants, put two
bucketfuls of fresh horse manure into a hessian
sack. Tie the sack shut with one end of a long
rope and put it in an empty barrel. Fill the
barrel with water and leave the sack to steep
for a week, using the rope occasionally to jerk
it up and down and mix the liquid. Dilute
until it is the colour of weak tea and apply it
monthly to the soil around plant roots.

Keep pests at bay

*One of the best non-chemical ways to deter pests is
to inspect the garden daily and pick off caterpillars,
snails and slugs from foliage, rub off aphids with a
finger and thumb and spray plants with water to
deter red spider mites. To keep mice out of newly
sown seedbeds, scatter holly leaves or prickly twigs,
such as pyracantha or berberis, over the drills.*

Natural predators

To attract insects that eat other insects, such as
ladybirds and hover flies, dot your garden with
poached egg flower (*Limnanthus*), sweet
alyssum, asters, daisies, marigolds, sunflowers
and members of the parsley family, such as
yarrow, fennel, and dill. These flowers provide
the nectars and pollens that predatory insects
need to supplement their diet.

Rabbits

Plant French marigolds amongst lettuce and
carrots in the vegetable garden. The marigolds'
strong odour repels rabbits. Alternatively, try
sprinkling ground black pepper around plants
– but remember to renew it after a rainfall.

Slugs

Sink old saucers or tin cans into the ground
and fill them with beer. Slugs are drawn to the
beer bait, fall in and don't get out again.
Replenish after rain. Alternatively, cut an
orange in half, scoop out the flesh and put the
hollowed-out skins, cut side down, near
vulnerable plants. Check in the morning and
dispose of the slugs hiding underneath. Orange
peel also deters cats; they hate the smell of it.
Grit, gravel or crushed eggshells scattered
around plants will also deter slugs and snails.

CRAFTED
with care

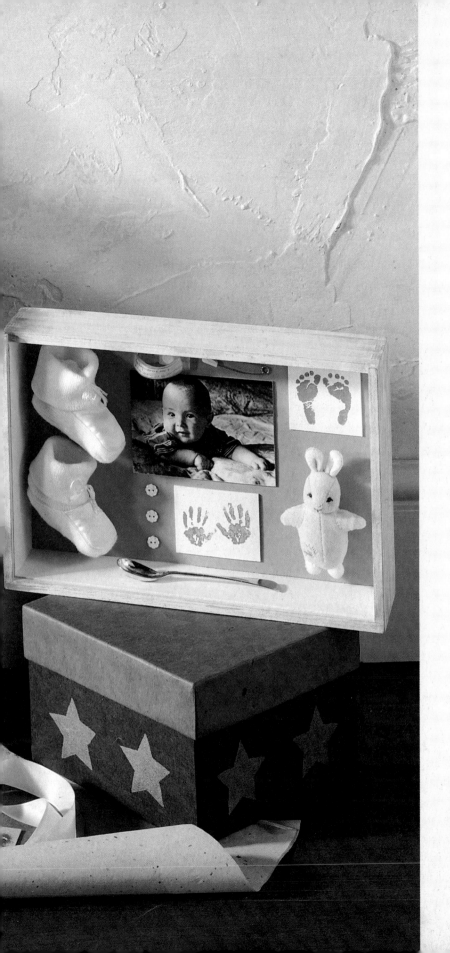

Here is a wide-ranging collection of inspiring ideas with easy-to-follow instructions for things you can make yourself, from cut-out projects for children to elegant, handmade greetings cards. Personal items, gifts for friends and family, ornaments, decorations for the home – you can give them all your own individual stamp, crafting them to suit you and your friends. Make a pressed-flower card or picture, using leaves and flowers that represent the recipient's birth-month.

Help the children make papier-mâché egg cups and then fill them with marbled eggs to display or give at Easter. Sew a patchwork baby's quilt that can just as easily double as a wall hanging. Make sundresses and sunsuits for toddlers, or go high, wide and handsome with multicoloured kites for older children.

Make a display with shells that you have collected, and frame it. And for the cat in your family, there's a window perch and a comfortable sling bed.

For Christmas, there are homemade wrapping papers, gift tags and cards – you can even make and decorate your own gift boxes. You'll be really proud of Christmas trimmings you make yourself – especially the crackers that can be filled with personalised gifts. With these and many other ideas, there are endless possibilities for creativity and fun, making items which are both beautiful and practical.

BEFORE YOU BEGIN...

*Nothing compares to the thrill of satisfaction you experience when a friend admires your
handiwork and you can say, 'I made it myself'. All of the projects in this chapter are within the scope of
even a beginner and your skills and confidence will increase with each new task you undertake*

To complete the projects in this chapter you will usually need only basic materials and tools. Each project gives a full list of what you need, and you should read this carefully before you start. To buy the materials, look in art supply shops, craft shops, hardware stores, newsagents and supermarkets. Occasionally, you may need to go to a specialist shop to find the right materials.

For many of the projects you will need to protect your work surface with cloth, paper, cardboard or timber. When using paints, varnishes and glues, always work in a well-ventilated area as the fumes may be toxic.

The instructions accompanying each project explain the special techniques you will need to use. Some useful basic craft techniques and skills are described below and in the following pages.

Applying colour and making patterns

Colouring techniques have developed and become refined over time. Many techniques in this chapter, such as marbling, are hundreds of years old, but the time-honoured effects can be achieved better than ever with today's paints. Some projects employ more recent methods such as applying paint with rubber stamps.

To achieve the various effects you will need a range of brushes. A stiff brush is good for stencilling, for example, while a soft round one is better for delicate designs. If a particular brush is specified, it is advisable to match this as closely as possible, asking your art supplier

for help if needed. For other projects the type of brush is not important, and you can use whatever you have to hand. You may choose to experiment with different brushes or everyday objects, such as kitchen sponges, to vary the methods given.

Paper...more versatile than it looks

A sheet of paper is the beginning point for any design or image used in crafts, but this versatile material has many applications and lends itself to more than its traditional combination with pen, pencil or brush. For centuries, paper has been cut, folded, painted and moulded by everyone from artisans in Venetian courts to small children amusing themselves with strings of cut-out figures.

Specialist paper shops or art suppliers provide the best selection of paper types. If you are prepared to buy in bulk, paper merchants are also a good source (ten sheets is usually the minimum order). The charm of the craft is that the raw material is inexpensive and readily available; sometimes the most rewarding projects are those made from found or recycled paper. A number of outlets sell clean industrial wastepaper. Contact the nearest recycling depot through your local council.

The large variety of papers available means that this is a craft that lends itself well to creative innovation. While different textures and strengths mean that certain papers will be preferred for particular crafts, experimentation is the key to your own style.

ENLARGING WITHOUT A PHOTOCOPIER

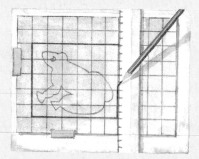 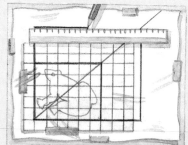 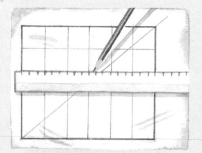 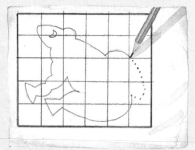

1 *Decide how large you want the design to be; make a note of the desired width. Trace the design onto tracing paper, tape it to a flat surface, then draw a grid over it using a ruler. Mark a rectangle around the perimeter of the design in thick pencil.*

2 *Tape a second piece of tracing paper over the design. Rule a diagonal line (bottom left corner to top right) and extend it as shown. Extend the rectangle's base to the desired width. Rule a line from this point up to the diagonal. Complete the large rectangle.*

3 *Remove the underlying tracing paper. On the enlarged rectangle, measure and rule the same number of rows and columns as you ruled over the original design, so that you have an identical grid but with larger squares than the original.*

4 *Working square by square, copy the design lines from the original grid onto the corresponding squares on the larger grid. It is easier if you mark a dotted line first, particularly making dots where the design lines intersect the squares of the grid.*

With just a few basic materials – and a little creativity – you can make a whole range of beautiful craft pieces.

Placing your image where you want it

There are a number of ways of placing a picture, outline or design on the material you are to work with. Stencilling is a relatively easy way of achieving an accurate reproduction, particularly for an image that is to be used repeatedly. For simple stencils try plain cardboard, although this can allow paint to seep through. A better choice is acetate, a semi-transparent plastic available from art suppliers; place your design underneath and trace the design directly onto the acetate. You can also use waxed cardboard, which is quite firm and therefore better for large stencils. Place the design on top and transfer it using the techniques given in the next section.

Many of the stencilling projects in this chapter give you specific designs to copy, but you may like to choose your own – designs from other projects may also provide inspiration. Any design can be enlarged or reduced by using a photocopier (or without one, as shown at left).

You will need a sharp scalpel or craft knife to cut stencils. A backing board or mat should be placed underneath. Cut towards you, turning the stencil and backing around as you work. To make the cutting out easier you can use masking tape to secure the stencil.

To stencil, use an almost dry brush and do not thin the paint. Apply paint to the tip of the brush only, hold the brush upright and apply to the stencil cut-out with a light dabbing motion.

To trace or to transfer?

A simple way of moving an image from a sheet of paper to another material is by tracing or transferring. The method you choose depends on what material you are using.

To trace a design onto plastic, such as stencil acetate, place the plastic over the design and trace the design using a whiteboard or overhead transparency marker pen. To trace onto transparent or semi-transparent fabric, place the fabric over the design and trace the lines with a water-soluble pen, or a fade-out pen for fabric that cannot be washed (marks last up to 48 hours). Backlighting can help you to outline a design: place on a light box or tape the fabric and design to a window.

To trace onto opaque surfaces such as cardboard, first trace the design onto tracing paper. Using small pieces of masking tape at each corner, attach the tracing paper to the surface to be decorated. Then slip transfer (graphite or carbon) paper underneath the tracing paper and, using light pressure, trace over the design lines with the end of a stylus or an empty ballpoint pen. Remove the lines with a pencil rubber. To transfer design lines onto opaque fabric, the method is similar. Trace the design onto tracing paper then place in position on the right side of the fabric and pin at the corners. Slip dressmaker's carbon paper, carbon side down, between the fabric and the design. Draw over the design lines using a tracing wheel or a stylus.

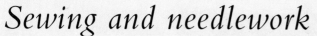

Sewing and needlework

There are many types of stitches, each with its own special uses. For the selection of projects in this chapter, which features quilting, feltcraft, embroidery and various sewing projects, the stitching techniques you will need are shown on this page.

SLIPSTITCH

This type of slipstitch, known as uneven slipstitch, is used to join a folded edge to a flat surface. Work the stitching from right to left, as shown below.

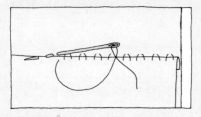

Fasten the thread and bring the needle and thread out through the folded edge. Take a small stitch into the garment fabric, catching one or two threads of the fabric. Insert the needle back into the fold of the hem. Slide the needle along the inside of the fold for about 6mm, then bring the needle out and draw the thread through. Continue alternating stitches from the garment to the fold, keeping them even and ensuring that the thread is not pulled too tight, so that the stitches on the right side are as invisible as possible.

BLANKET STITCH

This stitch is used to neaten raw edges of thick fabrics. Work from left to right, with the point of the needle and the edge of the fabric towards you.

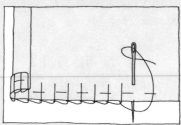

Tack the edge of the fabric. Bring the thread out below the edge of the fold. Insert the needle from the right, bringing it down below the hem edge. With thread from the previous stitch under the needle point, draw the needle through to form a stitch over the edge.

RUNNING STITCH

Running stitch is a very short, even stitch used for fine seaming, tucking, mending, gathering and other such delicate sewing. Work from right to left.

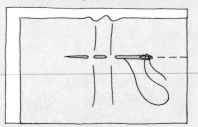

Weave the point of the needle in and out of the fabric several times before pulling the needle through. Keep the stitches and the spaces between them small and even. This stitch is like even tacking except that the stitches are smaller and usually permanent.

STEM STITCH

Primarily an outlining stitch, this stitch is often used for embroidery, to work plant stems in floral designs, and other solid lines.

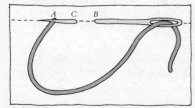

1 *Working from left to right, bring the needle out at A. Insert it at B and bring it out at C, half a stitch-length back.*

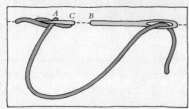

2 *Repeat this sequence, keeping the thread below the needle and to the left. Keep stitches even in length.*

STRAIGHT STITCH

This is a single stitch that can be of any length and worked in any direction. It can be used to cover straight design lines, or scattered to make an open filling. In ribbon embroidery, it can be used for sewing such things as flower buds. For the best results as you work, make sure that the thread or embroidery ribbon is not carried too far on the wrong side between the stitches.

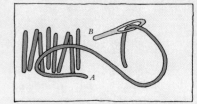

Bring the needle up at A and take it to the back at B, then on to another point A for the next stitch. Work as many straight stitches as needed for the desired design. Embroidered flower buds are 2 to 3 straight stitches on top of one another.

Mitring

The key to mitring is accurate pressing of folds at the corner.

1 *Press the fabric to the wrong side on the seamlines of the crosswise and lengthwise edges, to form a corner. Mark both raw edges at the point where they cross.*

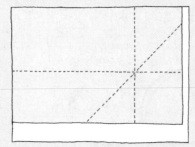

2 *Unfold the fabric and lightly mark or crease a diagonal line from the junction points through the corner of the pressed seamline to form the mitre stitching line.*

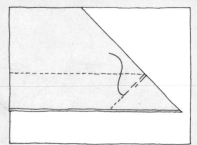

3 *Fold the fabric diagonally (on the bias), right sides together, aligning the edges. Stitch the mitre along the diagonal line, back-tacking at the beginning and the end.*

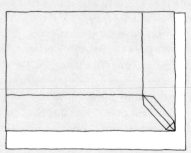

4 *Trim the mitre, making sure to leave a 6mm seam allowance. Press the seam open, then finish by turning the corner right side out and pressing.*

◆ Baby's Patchwork Quilt ◆

*This traditional patchwork design is a simple, restful pattern, especially
suitable for a baby's cot quilt. The quilt can also double as a wall hanging in a child's
room — a treasured memento, once it is no longer needed for the cot*

*We have chosen blue and white for this quilt, which
measures 92 × 114cm when finished.*

MATERIALS
- 75 × 115cm-wide blue
  patterned cotton fabric
- 1.2m × 115cm-wide white
  cotton fabric
- 1.2m × 115cm-wide backing
  cotton fabric (subdued print or
  plain pale colour)
- matching thread
- 1.5m × 96cm-wide thin wadding
- quilting hoop
- quilting needles
- white quilting thread
- rotary cutter
- self-healing cutting mat
- ruler
- small scissors
- thimble
- tracing paper
- pencil
- cardboard
- blue washout pen

CUTTING
All cuts are across the width of fabric. Use
a rotary cutter, mat and ruler. A 7.5mm seam
allowance is included in all measurements.
1 *Blue fabric* Cut seven strips 6.5cm wide; cut
two of these in half. Cut four strips 6cm wide;
put aside for binding (see page 225).
2 *White fabric* Cut ten strips 6.5cm wide; put
four of these strips aside for borders (see page
225); cut two of the remaining strips in half.
Cut two strips 16.5cm wide; cut each into six

*This patchwork quilt for a baby's cot is well within
the scope of the first-time quilter. Make it for your
child or grandchild and it may well become a precious
heirloom, a reminder of fond family ties.*

16.5cm squares (total of 12 squares). Cut one extra strip 25cm wide; cut into four 25cm squares. Cut these squares diagonally twice to make 16 triangles (14 are needed). From remaining fabric, cut two 12.5cm squares; cut each square diagonally once to make the four corner triangles.

SEWING

1 To make triple strip A, machine stitch one blue strip on either side of a white strip. Make two. Make another triple strip A using the short blue and white strips. Press *all* seams towards the darker colour after stitching.

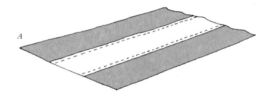

2 To make triple strip B, stitch one white strip on either side of a blue strip. Make one. Make another triple strip B with the short white and blue strips.

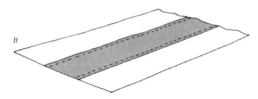

3 Cut all triple strips at 6.5cm intervals. In all, you will need 40 cut sections of triple strip A and 20 sections of triple strip B.

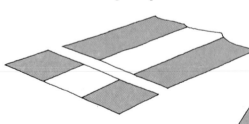

4 Sew one section of triple strip A to either side of a triple strip B section to make a patchwork square. Make up 20 squares in this way.

The design above shows the layout of the quilt. The quilting pattern is shown as dotted lines. The binding is attached after all the hand quilting has been completed.

QUILTING DESIGN

TO MAKE UP

1 Position the patchwork squares, white squares and white triangles on a flat surface. Machine stitch the squares and triangles together, one row at a time, to make eight diagonal rows as indicated below. Press seams. Join the diagonal rows to form the quilt top.

2 Place the quilt top flat and measure down each long side (both measurements should be the same). Cut the side borders to this length from two of the reserved white strips, matching the centre of each strip to the centre of each side. Pin and sew the side borders to the quilt top. Repeat with the top and bottom borders, which should extend to each edge of the side borders (see diagram, left).

3 Press the quilt top on the wrong side, pressing the border seams towards the border. Turn right side up and mark the quilting lines (see 'Quilting Design', right).

4 Leaving the backing and wadding slightly larger than the quilt top, sandwich the three pieces together with several rows of large tacking stitches – work out from the centre.

5 Fold the excess backing to the front and tack around all four sides; this will protect the edges during quilting.

QUILTING

Quilting is an even running stitch that is worked through all layers of fabric and wadding. Use a single strand of quilting thread about 50cm long with a small knot tied at the end. To protect your finger from the needle – and give extra control – use a thimble on the middle finger of your sewing hand.

1 Position the hoop in the middle of the quilt and work out towards the edges. Make sure the tension of the fabric is even on the top and the backing, with no puckers.

2 Insert the needle into the top only, about 2cm away from where you want to make your first stitch. Gently pull on the thread until the knot pops through into the wadding. Take a small backstitch, then make a small running stitch. Continue to take one or two small, even running stitches at a time, making sure the thread is going through all layers. Aim to have the stitches the same length on both sides of the quilt. Quilt whatever is within the hoop – when doing the long straight vertical and horizontal lines, you can leave the thread dangling when you reach the edge of the frame, if you wish, and rethread your needle as you move the hoop to the adjoining area.

3 To finish off each piece of stitching, make a knot in the thread near the quilt, do a single backstitch, and pull the knot into the wadding; pass the needle through the wadding and away from the stitch. When you cut the thread, this end will disappear into the wadding.

BINDING

1 Join the four 6cm wide blue strips together to make a continuous length; fold in half lengthways with wrong sides together and press.

2 Trim the excess backing and wadding so that all three layers are the same size.

3 Leaving a 1cm seam allowance, pin and machine stitch the binding to the front of the quilt. Begin 15cm from one corner, and sew through all layers; stop sewing 7.5mm from the first corner, backstitch, lift the machine foot and remove the quilt. Turn the quilt. Fold the binding back to form a 45° angle, then continue folding back along the raw edge – a mitred corner should form automatically. Lower the foot and continue sewing.

4 When you reach the starting point, overlap the ends of the binding by 3cm, making sure you tuck the raw edge under before finishing.

5 Turn the binding to the back and hand stitch along the machine line, mitring each corner to match the front. Remove tacking.

QUILTING DESIGN

TRACE the quilting design (page 224) and transfer it to cardboard; cut out. With a washout pen, draw around the shape onto the quilt as indicated in the diagram on page 224 (test the pen on a scrap of fabric before using). Trace the border design (below) in the same way. Use a design of your choice, if desired.

BORDER QUILTING DESIGN

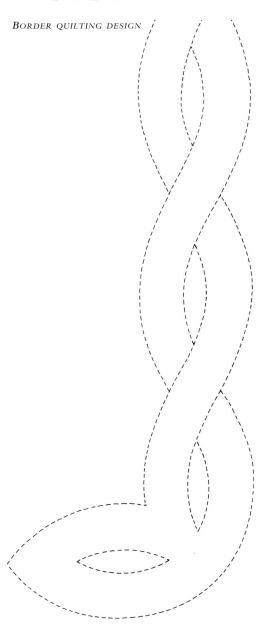

• A Cosy Crib •

*This thick, soft cot bumper protects the baby from the crib slats and also enlivens the
nursery with bright colour and lively pattern. Team the bumper with the patchwork quilt
on page 223 and you'll have a charming homemade crib set*

page 223

*A thin layer of wadding allows machine-quilting in
this easy patchwork project. The extra thick wadding
is used only as stuffing. Made in four parts for easier
washing, the finished bumper has two end panels
(about 23 × 73cm) and two side panels (about
23 × 145cm). All seam allowances are 5mm.*

MATERIALS

- 3.25m × 115cm-wide calico print
  fabric
- 2.10m × 110cm-wide white fabric
- 1.5m × 96cm-wide lightweight
  wadding (cotton or polyester)
- 2.25m × 96cm-wide extra
  thick polyester wadding
- 41.75m × 4cm-wide
  pregathered white eyelet
- rotary cutter or scissors
- self-healing cutting mat
- transparent ruler
- threads to match fabrics
- dressmaker's pins
- scissors

CUTTING

1 From the print fabric, cut two pieces
17.5 × 75cm and four pieces 17.5 × 150cm
for the diamond pattern which covers the
front of the bumpers.

2 From the remaining print, cut two pieces
25 × 75cm and two pieces 25 × 150cm for
the backs of the bumper guards, six pieces
2.5 × 150cm for the ties, and two 20cm
squares to piece the corners of the panels
(step 5, Sewing, opposite). Cut the squares
diagonally in each direction to make eight
triangles. Set all these pieces aside.

*Pretty and practical, these cot bumpers come in four
sections, so you can wash individual ones if there are
unexpected spills. The four parts also balance better in
a washing machine than does one continuous strip.*

QUILTING SECRETS

Rotary dressmaker's cutters can be bought at any good fabric store or haberdashers. They are a particular boon to quilters because they make quick work of cutting out a stack of pieces of the same size. They are also efficient in cutting out other patterns. Some come with a pinking blade. When you use a rotary cutter, you should work on a self-sealing mat because the cutters are very sharp and could mar any other type of work surface.

Always wash and iron the fabric used in patchwork and quilting before cutting the pieces out. You don't want to discover after you have the quilt made that some of the fabric shrinks in the wash and some of it doesn't. When cutting out quilting pieces, place the longer measurement along the lengthways selvage edge of the fabric.

3 From the white fabric cut one piece 17.5 × 75cm and two pieces 17.5 × 150cm to make the diamond pattern for the bumpers.
4 From the remaining white fabric cut two pieces 25 × 75cm and two pieces 25 × 150cm. These will be used as the backing layers, under the wadding, for the quilted front panels of the bumper guards.

SEWING

1 Match the strips in groups of equal length, with two print strips for each white strip.
2 With right sides together, sew one print strip to each side of a white strip (below) and press the seam allowances toward the print.

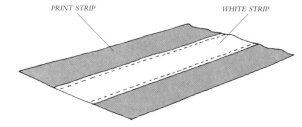

PRINT STRIP   WHITE STRIP

3 Cut at right angles across the seams on each of the patchwork units at 18cm intervals adding a 7.5mm seam allowance to each piece to yield a total of 3 strips for each end panel and 6 strips for each side panel – a total of 18. There will be two superfluous strips.

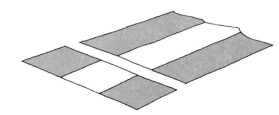

4 For each panel, sew together its allocated number of strips so that the corners of the white squares meet the seamlines 'on point,' beginning to make the diamond pattern of the finished bumper guards. The ends of the strips will be staggered, forming points, as seen in the drawing below.

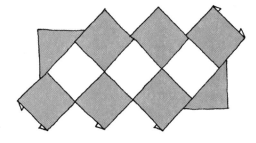

5 With right sides together, centre, pin, and stitch the long edge of one triangle over the unstitched edge of the white squares on the ends of the panels. Press these outer seams inward and all other seams in one direction.
6 Trim the pointed edges of each panel into a straight line by placing the edge of the transparent ruler 5mm outside each white point; align the ruler carefully over the full length of the edge before cutting. The end panels should now measure 24.5 × 72.5cm, and the side ones 24.5 × 140cm.
7 Using the backing rectangles cut from the white fabric as a pattern, cut out a matching lightweight piece of wadding.
8 Layer the wadding on top of the white backing fabric. Centre a patchwork piece, right side up, on top of each wadding piece of similar size.

Pin the layers together. Then use long stitches to hand-tack them together, following the grain line, through the centre of each square in each direction. Also tack around the edges together 5mm inside the edges of the patchwork layer.
9 With the patchwork side up, machine-quilt 5mm inside each white square. Pull the thread ends to the wrong side and knot them together. Remove the centre basting.
10 From the eyelet, cut two pieces 75cm long and two 150cm long. With right sides together, pin the centre of one strip to the centre of the tacked top seam of a panel of comparable size and match the eyelet binding edge to the cut edge of the patchwork. Continue pinning along the top. When nearing the corners, turn the cut ends of the eyelet outward so that the embroidered top edge of the eyelet is at the corner tacking line; ease the fullness of the cut edge into gathers and trim off any excess. Machine-tack the eyelet to the panel.
11 To sew the ties, press 5mm to the wrong side on each long edge and then fold and press again so the long edges meet; edgestitch each tie piece. Cut each length into 50cm pieces to yield 16 ties. Finish each cut end with a tight slip knot.
12 Fold the length of each tie in half and pin the fold 1cm inside each top and bottom corner. Secure the knotted ends with pins to keep them away from the seamlines.
13 With right sides together, pin a print back rectangle to each quilted front panel of the same size; place the pins on the side with the white backing fabric. Following the perimeter tacking lines, stitch the layers together, starting and stopping about 25cm inside the bottom corners. Trim away the excess wadding and print fabric to about 5mm from the seam and diagonally trim the corners. Turn the panels right side out and remove the pins holding the ends of the ties.
14 From the thick wadding, cut two pieces 43 × 70cm and two 43 × 135cm. Fold each piece so that the 43cm become 21.5cm. Insert the wadding, stuffing it through the bottom seam opening into its comparable cover size. Slipstitch the openings closed.
15 To dress the crib with the bumper guards, place one guard inside the slats on each end and side with the eyelet edging at the top. Secure the ties to the corner posts of the crib.

❖ Sundresses and Sunsuits for Toddlers ❖

Our cool and comfortable outfits include a reversible dress and a classic sunsuit.
To decorate them, we've included designs for four colourful appliqués, each of them suitable
for use on either outfit. The one-size pattern is for toddlers' sizes 3 to 4

Easy appliqués

The directions for our sundress and sunsuit indicate when to add the appliqués, which can be made with scraps of fabric. Enlarge the appliqué patterns on 2.5cm graph paper (page 220).

MATERIALS

- 1 pack (1m × 45cm) paper-backed, iron-on interfacing
- small embroidery scissors
- dressmaker's tracing paper
- needle

FOR THE TURTLE

- green, floral print, pink, and yellow cotton remnants; 15cm piece of 1cm-wide lace edging; green and pink thread

FOR THE WHALE

- white-background print and pink cotton remnants; turquoise thread; 1 pack white jumbo rickrack

FOR THE SAILBOAT

- blue, red, and yellow fabric; black thread; 1 pack blue jumbo rickrack; blue thread

FOR THE BEACH BALL

- yellow, hot pink, and green-dot cotton fabric; white thread

1 Enlarge the appliqué design of your choice.
2 Cut pieces of fusible webbing slightly larger than each part of the appliqué. Using a steam iron, fuse the webbing to the wrong side of each piece of fabric. Use some dressmaker's tracing paper to transfer the pattern pieces onto the fabric (right). Cut out the pieces.

FUSIBLE WEBBING

FABRIC WITH PATTERN TRACED ON

3 The dotted lines on our patterns indicate where one piece will be covered by another when all the pieces are in place. Starting with the pieces that have dotted lines, fuse the pieces onto the dress or sunsuit.
4 Appliqué the motifs in place. Use a dense, medium-width zigzag stitch to cover the edges and to stitch the sailboat's mast. With a needle and doubled thread, embroider the eyes and mouth of the turtle and whale and the centre of the flower and the starfish.

Reversible sundress

Use coordinating fabrics to make this charmer. Be sure to choose colours that will not run.

- 2.5cm graph paper, ruler, pencil
- scissors
- 70 × 110cm-wide solid or print fabric
- 70 × 110cm-wide coordinating print fabric
- thread to match fabrics
- needle
- 135 × 1cm-wide lace edging or 1 package piping
- 2 buttons, 30cm in diameter (optional)
- 4 large snap-fasteners (for lapped-shoulder dress only)

1 Using 2.5cm graph paper, enlarge the dress pattern as directed on page 220.
2 Choose between long, tied shoulder straps or shorter straps with snaps. Cut out two pieces from each of the fabrics, adding a 1cm seam

Ready for a summer outing are a toddler girl's two choices of appliquéd sundresses and a toddler boy's two choices of appliquéd sunsuits.

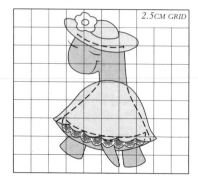

FLIRTATIOUS TURTLE APPLIQUÉ

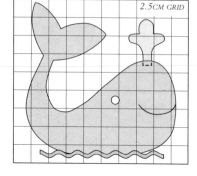

SPOUTING WHALE APPLIQUÉ

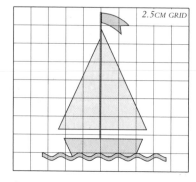

SPORTY SAILBOAT APPLIQUÉ

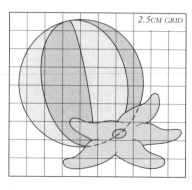

BEACH BALL AND STARFISH APPLIQUÉ

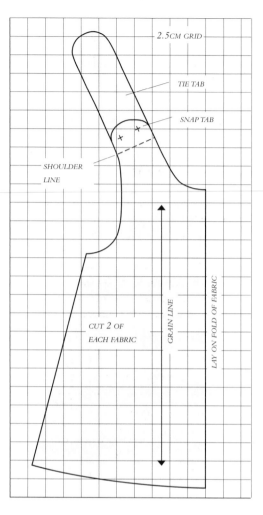

The pattern — for both front and back — outlines the dress; add a 1cm seam allowance all around.

allowance to all cut edges.

3 Follow step 4 of Easy Appliqués to apply a motif to one front piece, 7.5cm above the hemline. For the boat or whale, sew one side seam of the dress before adding the rickrack. A single row of rickrack goes across the front and around the back of the dress (below).

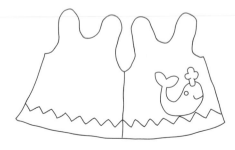

4 For each set of dress pieces, sew and press open the side seams.

5 Select one dress layer. With the right side facing you, pin the lace edging or piping along the hemline, matching the flat edge of the trim with the raw edge of the hem. Sew in place, lapping the ends of the trim. Fold under the edges to the wrong side of the fabric.

6 With right sides together, pin and sew the two dress layers together all the way around the top; clip curves and trim the seam allowances (below). Turn the dress right side out and press. Topstitch along the top seam.

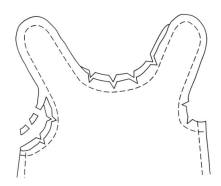

7 Matching the side seams, pin the hems of the dress layers together, turning under 1cm on the layer without the trim. The trim should be visible from both sides. Edgestitch the newly turned hem (below).

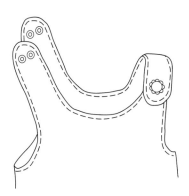

8 For the lapped shoulders, sew on snaps to close the dress. Add buttons on one side, if you like. For the other sundress, tie the straps.

Reverse sides of girls' dresses, refreshingly different, literally give two dresses for the price of one.

Sunsuit

This carefree summer suit has snap shoulders and crotch, making it easy to put on and take off.

- 112 × 110cm-wide fabric
- thread to match fabric
- 4 buttons, 1cm diameter
- 4 large snap fasteners
- 25 × 1.5cm-wide snap-fastener tape

1 Using 2.5cm graph paper, enlarge pattern as directed on page 220. For sunsuit, add 4cm hem allowances to the legs and 1cm seam allowances to the other edges. For the facings, retrace front and back from the facing line up and add 1cm seam allowances.

2 Cut two pieces each of the front and back. Cut one piece each of the facings, placing the centres on a fold of fabric.

3 Apply motif, following step 4 of Easy Appliqués. Sew centre seam first to centre motif.

4 With right sides together, sew the front centre seam. Repeat on the back. With right sides facing, sew the front and back together along the sides. Sew the facings together on the side seams. Turn under the bottom edge of the facing 5mm and stitch. Press all seams open.

5 Follow Step 6 of the sundress instructions to sew the top seams, using the facings for the second dress layer. Sew two snap-fasteners at each shoulder and buttons for decoration.

6 Fold and press the leg hems under 1cm and then 2.5cm; stitch the hem edges.

7 Press front crotch edge under 1cm. Press back crotch edge 1cm toward right side of fabric. Pin half of the snap tape to cover the raw edge on either side, centring snaps and turning the ends under; sew the tape along each edge.

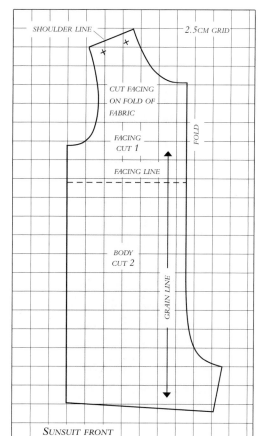

SUNSUIT FRONT

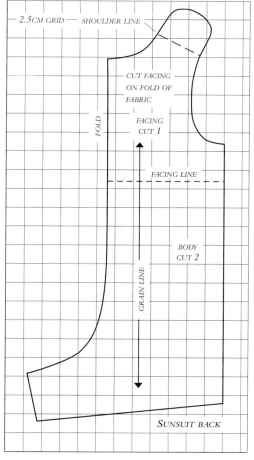

SUNSUIT BACK

◆ High Flier ◆

The joy of flying a kite can be surpassed only by flying a kite that you've made yourself.
Our kites are made with ripstop or spinnaker nylon, which is extremely light, flexible and strong. A 'hot knife'
is used to cut the nylon, giving it clean, sealed edges and eliminating any fraying

Kite-making basics

The tools and basic techniques listed below are essential to making all kites, including ours.

MATERIALS

- 2.5cm graph paper
- pencil, chalk
- metal ruler, French curve
- dressmaker's carbon paper, tracing wheel (to transfer design onto poster board)
- 4 to 6 pieces of poster board (for making pattern templates)
- masking tape
- craft knife
- 'hot knife', pencil-type (flat or sharp-tip soldering iron, to cut ripstop nylon fabric)
- scissors
- water-soluble glue stick
- newspaper
- sewing machine with zigzag capabilities
- white nylon or polyester sewing thread
- 30cm square spinnaker or flag fabric for frame sleeves
- spindle of kite string, 10-20kg breaking strain, for bridle and for flying

TEMPLATE PREPARATION

1 Enlarge the design to its full size, using 2.5cm graph paper and the instructions on page 220. Add the perimeter hem measurements required by the design.

2 Make a separate template for each section of the design; such pieces as tail bows or teeth, which are repeated, need only one template. Make the large templates first, taping poster boards together to achieve the needed size.

3 To make a template, place the carbon side of the dressmaker's paper against the poster board and centre a section of the enlarged design on top. Trace the section, including dotted line

These kites are in two favourite styles – diamond and delta. One brings a blazing comet to an afternoon sky, the other might cause a sensation on the beach.

edges and perimeter hem allowances. Remove the pattern and carbon paper and cut out the poster board template using the craft knife with the ruler for straight edges and the French curve along curves. On asymmetrical pieces, mark 'up' on the template to indicate the right side.

Comet kite

This traditional diamond-shape kite is about 1m high when finished, with another 3m or so of tail.

MATERIALS

- basic tools, at left
- 150cm wide ripstop nylon: 120cm royal blue; 70cm orange; 60cm each fuchsia, red, and yellow; 25cm gold
- 5mm wooden dowels; one 100cm long and one 92cm long

1 Arrange the templates right side up on the right side of the fabric. For the main portion of the kite, cut one piece of fabric from each template, including the large star, using the colour fabric indicated in diagram 1. In addition, cut out two small gold stars; eight tail-bow halves from mixed colours; and three tail strips 2 × 112cm (not shown in diagram).

2 To make the multicoloured comet: spread newspaper on a work surface. Place the top section of orange fabric face down and apply the glue stick in a thin line along the top and bottom edges. Turn right side up and glue in position on the blue background fabric.

3 Apply the remaining comet sections in the same manner, lapping each new piece over the former by 5mm until the bottom orange section is in place.

4 Set the sewing machine with a long, wide zigzag stitch. Zigzag each edge of the comet sections from the outer to the inner edge.

5 Turn the kite wrong side up. Using scissors, trim away the blue layer of fabric from behind

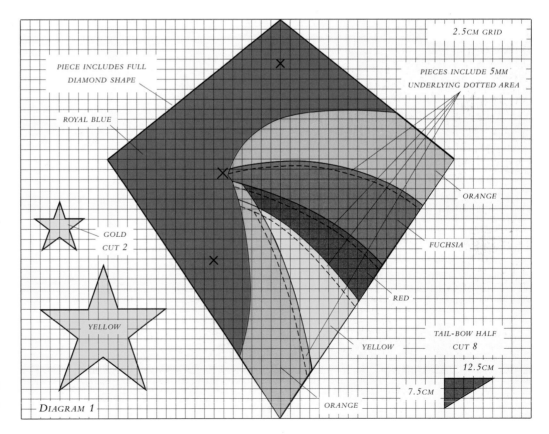

DIAGRAM 1

2.5CM GRID

PIECE INCLUDES FULL DIAMOND SHAPE

ROYAL BLUE

PIECES INCLUDE 5MM UNDERLYING DOTTED AREA

ORANGE

GOLD CUT 2

FUCHSIA

RED

YELLOW

YELLOW

TAIL-BOW HALF CUT 8

12.5CM

7.5CM

ORANGE

each comet tail section, leaving about 4mm of fabric beyond the stitches.

6 Turn the kite right side up. Using the same gluing technique, glue the large star over the large *X* mark and the small stars over the small *x* marks. Zigzag the stars to the kite, switching to a straight stitch at the top of each point.

7 Turn the kite face down and trim away the background fabric from behind the stars.

8 Working on one outside edge of the kite at a time, double-fold a 5mm-wide hem and stitch with straight stitch.

9 From the flag fabric (see materials list, Kite-making Basics) cut out four 1 x 7.5m 'frame sleeves', to hold the dowels in place at the kite corners (diagram 2). Fold each frame sleeve so that the bottom of the fold extends 5mm beyond the top. Position a sleeve at each corner with the fold overlapping the hemmed edges. Edgestitch the sides.

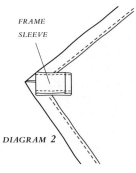

FRAME SLEEVE

DIAGRAM 2

10 To make the tail of the kite: seam the three tail strips together, end to end, using a 5mm seam allowance. On one end, fold 4cm to the wrong side twice and edgestitch. Use the hot knife to burn an 8mm hole at the centre of the hemmed end.

11 To make the bows for the tail: select two triangular bow halves and overlap the long points about 5cm. Position one bow over a seam in the kite tail and stitch in place (diagram 3); repeat, covering the other seam. Position and sew the remaining bows equally spaced between the first two.

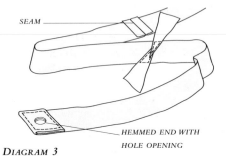

SEAM

HEMMED END WITH HOLE OPENING

DIAGRAM 3

12 Place the kite on a protected work surface. Chalk a dot 22cm down from the top corner of the kite and one 20cm up from the bottom corner. Use the hot knife to burn a 3mm hole at each mark for the kite bridle string.

13 To assemble the kite: select the longer dowel. Insert one end through the hole in the tail piece and then into the bottom frame sleeve. Insert the opposite end in the top sleeve, bowing the dowel slightly. Insert the ends of the shorter dowel in the side sleeves. If necessary, reduce the dowel lengths so there is no distorted tension. Knot string around the dowels where they cross.

14 Using the hot knife, cut a length of string for the bridle, 150cm long. Insert one end through each of the prepared holes and tie the ends to the vertical dowel. Turn the kite right side up

PRACTICAL IDEAS

CUTTING TIPS

Cut one layer of ripstop fabric at a time. The dull side of ripstop is considered the right side.

For symmetrical pieces, make a half-template, dividing pattern in half, vertically. Before cutting the fabric, chalk a fold-line on the fabric. Align the template edge that represents the piece's centre along one side of the line and cut that half; flip the template to the other side of the line and cut the other half.

Use a hot knife to cut ripstop fabric on a glass-top table or another safe, hard, work surface. Move the knife swiftly and smoothly along the edge of the template. Gently pull the excess fabric away; if the cut is not clean, retrace the area with the hot knife.

If the template and fabric edges become joined during the cutting process, insert a ruler between the two layers and gently pull it around the edges to separate them, as you would with a book with uncut pages.

Position templates on the ripstop fabric along the grain of the fabric, following the selvage. The symmetry of the grain will give the kite optimum strength, which is critical for good construction and long life. It also makes it easier to sew, as the pieces will not be so likely to pull out of shape.

and pull the centre portion of bridle string to the front of the kite. Measure about 50cm along the string from the top hole and make a looped slipknot for attaching the kite's flying string. The loop can be repositioned higher or lower on the bridle string for different wind conditions. Lower the knot for stronger winds.

15 Tie the spindle of string to the bridle loop.

Jaws kite

When finished, this delta-wing kite is about 92cm high. Read Kite-making Basics and the Comet Kite instructions to familiarise yourself with kite-making materials and techniques before you begin.

MATERIALS

- ◆ basic tools (p.233)
- ◆ 150cm-wide ripstop nylon in the following lengths and colours: 60cm green; 25cm each blue, white, orange, purple and black
- ◆ four 5mm wooden dowels, each 60cm long

1 After enlarging the pattern (diagram 1), add 15mm to each perimeter line on kite body and keel pieces before making the cutting templates.

2 Place the templates right side up on the right side of the fabric. Cut out one piece from each template in the colour indicated except for the following: 16 orange teeth; two black eyes; two each of the two blue triangles; two each purple bottom fins and side fins.

3 Using the methods described in steps 2 to 4 of the Comet Kite, glue and stitch the following pieces in the order described: orange teeth on top of white mouth; mouth and teeth on top of green head; black eyes on head.

4 Turn the kite face down and trim away the green fabric within the edge of the mouth.

5 Lap the sides of the purple top fin over the sides of two blue top fin triangles and zigzag. Centre this piece at the top of the kite, lapping it under the edge so that it forms a continuous line with the sides of the kite. Zigzag the edge.

6 Lap one edge of each purple side fin over the edge of a blue side fin triangle and zigzag. Position these pieces at the lower sides of the

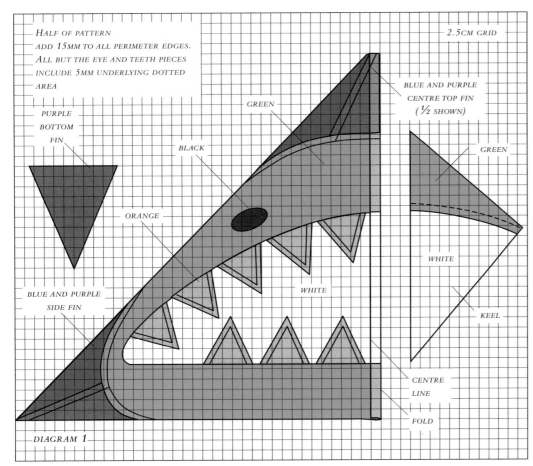

HALF OF PATTERN
ADD 15MM TO ALL PERIMETER EDGES.
ALL BUT THE EYE AND TEETH PIECES
INCLUDE 5MM UNDERLYING DOTTED
AREA

2.5CM GRID

PURPLE
BOTTOM
FIN

GREEN

BLUE AND PURPLE
CENTRE TOP FIN
(½ SHOWN)

BLACK

GREEN

ORANGE

WHITE

BLUE AND PURPLE
SIDE FIN

WHITE

KEEL

CENTRE
LINE

FOLD

DIAGRAM 1

kite, lapping them under the edge. They should form a continuous line with the sides and bottom of the kite. Zigzag the edges.

7 For the two bottom fins: turn under 5mm on one side edge and hem; repeat on other side edge. With right sides together, align the top edge of the fin with the bottom edge of the kite so that, when the edge is turned under 1cm, the side and bottom fins meet at the corner. Stitch the fins 5mm in from the edge.

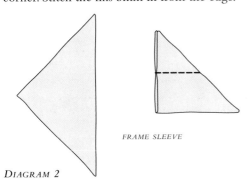

FRAME SLEEVE

DIAGRAM 2

8 From the flag fabric (see materials under Kite-making basics) use a hot knife to cut one triangle with 5cm sides for the keel reinforcement and one 7.5cm square. Cut the square in half diagonally; fold the long edge of each portion in half and stitch 2.5cm from the fold to create two frame sleeves (diagram 2).

9 The side hems of the kite double as dowel casings. Fold the side edges 1.5cm to the wrong side. Tuck a frame sleeve into each fold, 40cm from the bottom of the kite: the opening of the frame sleeve should face upward, as shown in diagram 3.

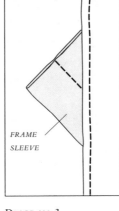

FRAME
SLEEVE

DIAGRAM 3

Stitch each hem casing as follows: starting at the bottom, stitch for 5cm; skip 2.5cm (for a dowel opening). Backstitch at both ends of the dowel opening. Continue stitching to the top of the kite. Make sure the frame sleeve is caught in the stitching. About 26 inches up from the bottom, stitch across the casing to prevent the dowel from riding up.

10 On the bottom edge of the kite, fold under and stitch a 5mm double hem (the bottom fins will hang downward). Trim any excess hem at the corners. Seal the corners by running the hot knife over the edges.

11 Lap the curved edge of the green keel piece over the white keel piece and zigzag. Tape the keel reinforcement triangle just inside the corner where the pieces meet. Stitch 5mm double hems on the two sides, as shown in diagram 4. Catch the reinforcement corner inside as you sew.

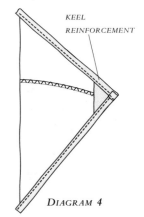

KEEL
REINFORCEMENT

DIAGRAM 4

12 Use the hot knife to burn three 3mm holes in the keel reinforcement triangle; one at the point, the others 15mm away along the sides. Hot-cut a 20cm piece of kite string. Fold the string in half and knot the ends together. Thread the looped end of the string through the hole at the point of the keel and pull the knotted end through the loop; tighten.

13 To make the centre dowel casing: turn the kite wrong side up. Using a ruler, chalk a line vertically down the centre of the kite. Then chalk a parallel line, 15mm away, to one side of the centre. With the right side of the kite facing, align the long edge of the keel along the centre: match the coloured sections, as shown in diagram 1. Tape the keel in place.

14 On the wrong side, fold the kite along the centre line. Stitch across the bottom end between chalk lines, pivot and stitch along the second chalk line for 1cm. Leave a 2.5cm opening and continue stitching to the top and across the casing area.

15 Insert the dowels into the casings and tie the flying string onto the keel string.

• Novelty Stamps •

Children will have fun creating and using easy-to-make stamps, which can be applied
to a wide variety of surfaces – even fabric – but they will need help with cutting the blocks
and the foam shapes. Get them to choose a bold design from a picture book

Frogs and lily pads

Use a clean paintbrush or foam applicator for
each new colour you apply to the stamps.

MATERIALS

- ◆ wood offcuts (pine or MDF for example)
- ◆ saw (optional)
- ◆ high-density foam rubber sheet (from foam rubber specialists and craft stores)
- ◆ double-sided adhesive tape
- ◆ tracing paper, masking tape
- ◆ pencil
- ◆ trimming knife
- ◆ artist's acrylic paints
- ◆ small foam applicators, brushes or ink pads

1 Cut four blocks of wood big enough to accommodate your chosen designs. We used jolly frogs and lily pads, but other simple designs are just as effective – flowers, steam trains, dinosaurs, butterflies – let your imagination run riot. Timber suppliers will often be happy to cut the wood for you and may even give you small offcuts, free.

2 Using the trimming knife, cut pieces of high-density foam to fit the wooden blocks.

3 Apply double-sided tape to the whole surface of each block, laying the strips of tape edge to edge. Stick each piece of foam onto its corresponding block, making sure that the smooth side of the foam is facing out.

4 Trace the outlines of your stamp designs onto sheets of tracing paper using a soft pencil.

5 Cut each piece of tracing paper to fit its block and use strips of masking tape to attach the pieces of tracing paper to the blocks.

6 Use the trimming knife to cut around the designs, slicing through both the paper and foam. Peel away the unwanted paper and foam and neaten the edges so they are smooth and even. Your stamps are now ready for use.

APPLICATION Use a foam roller, a brush or an ink stamp pad to apply paint to the stamps. A foam roller will give even coverage without a build-up of colour at the edges. Paint is easy to apply with a brush, particularly when applying more than one colour to the same stamp, but you may need to blot away any surplus.

A stamp pad will allow you to work quickly. This method gives the best results when applied to paper or cardboard, producing an even-coloured design with well-defined edges. The stamped designs will appear more translucent when they are worked with ink.

Fabric paints are usually stickier than acrylic paints, but since fabric is quite porous it will take up a lot of paint. You may need to experiment with fabric paints and different applications, including using a foam roller or a brush to achieve the best result. Make sure the stamp is not overloaded with paint or the paint will bleed and make the edges uneven.

We applied our frog and lily pad designs to boxes
and sketchbook covers in bold colours, creating a
cheerful coordinated range for the playroom.

MAKING THE FROG STAMPS

1 *Cut a piece of foam to fit the wood block. Lay double-sided tape edge to edge on the block, to cover the whole surface. Lay the foam on the block, shiny side out.*

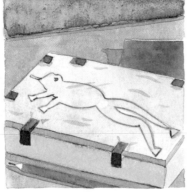

2 *Trace your chosen design onto tracing paper with a soft pencil. Cut to the size of the block, place over the foam and fix it in place using small pieces of masking tape.*

3 *Use a scalpel or trimming knife to cut around the design outline, cutting through both the tracing paper and the foam. Work slowly with a steady hand for best results.*

4 *After cutting, remove the tracing paper and excess foam, and tidy up the edges of the foam outline. The neater the outline, the clearer the final stamped image will be.*

Dinosaur Magnets

Cheerful monsters like these will brighten any spot from the fridge door or a magnetised bulletin board to the side of a filing cabinet. Children will love them and, with a little help from an adult, they'll be able to make a set of these lovable lizards for themselves

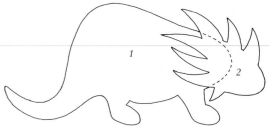

Assemble the dinosaurs on the oven tray they are to be baked on, to avoid moving the soft clay too much.

MATERIALS

- tracing paper
- lightweight cardboard (shiny surface is best)
- transfer (graphite) paper
- stylus
- small scissors
- rolling pin
- white modelling compound ('Sculpey' or 'Fimo')
- scalpel or craft knife
- 600 grade sandpaper
- acrylic paints
- small paintbrush
- small magnets
- craft glue

1 Using tracing paper and a pencil, make a tracing of the dinosaurs from the patterns given (above and on opposite page). Trace the basic body shapes and the extra body parts (legs, frills, etc) separately. On the patterns, the numbers show how many separate parts there are for each dinosaur, and the dotted lines show where pieces overlap.

Give your imagination free rein when you are decorating your collection of Dinosaur Magnets – the brighter the colours and patterns you choose, the more fun they will be for the lucky recipients.

2 Place a piece of lightweight cardboard on a flat surface. Place a piece of transfer paper on this and place the tracing paper with the dinosaur patterns on top. Use a stylus to trace the shapes onto the card, leaving enough space to allow you to cut each part out separately. Cut out all the shapes with scissors.

3 With the rolling pin, roll out the modelling compound to approximately 3mm thickness.

4 Place the cardboard stencil of the body shape on the compound and carefully cut out the shape. Do the same for body parts. Smooth any raw edges with your fingertips.

5 Place the separate body parts on the base body shape (frills are attached beneath the body; head and legs are attached on top of the surface). It is best to do this on the baking tray, so that the soft compound will not need to be moved before being placed in the oven. Gently press the pieces together. For a more rounded shape, place extra compound under the body. Using the scalpel, clean up the raw edges and then smooth with your fingertips.

6 Use the round shaft of the stylus and pressing very lightly, roll the stylus over the whole figure in order to make the extra pieces adhere to the base body shape.

7 Roll a small piece of compound between your fingertips to make an eyeball. Gently position on the figure.

8 Bake, following the compound manufacturer's instructions. Allow to cool and use sandpaper to smooth the rough surfaces.

9 Refer to the picture of the dinosaurs as a guide for drawing decorations on your creations, or use your imagination to design your own decorations.

10 Paint with artist's acrylic paints. When dry, attach a magnet to the back of each dinosaur with craft glue.

MAKING THE DINOSAURS

1 *Trace each dinosaur shape onto tracing paper. Place light cardboard (preferably with a shiny surface to prevent sticking) on a flat surface, cover with transfer paper and place the tracing paper on top. With a stylus, trace the shape onto the cardboard.*

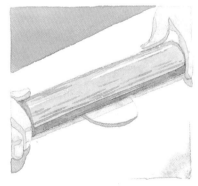

2 *Remove the tracing paper and transfer paper and cut out the cardboard shape with scissors. With a rolling pin, roll out a piece of modelling compound to about 3mm thick. Roll carefully so that the compound is perfectly even in thickness.*

3 *Place the cardboard shape on the flat compound and press very slightly so it holds firm. Cut around the shape with a scalpel, slowly and accurately cutting around all curves and corners. When finished, remove the surrounding compound.*

4 *Assemble all the parts of the dinosaur on a baking tray. Using the round shaft of the stylus and pressing very lightly, roll over the whole body to make the parts adhere. Bake in the oven for the time specified by the manufacturer of the compound.*

❖ Bracelets and Buttons ❖

Turn ordinary wood or plastic items into things of beauty with these faux finishes.
It may take a little practice to get your hand in, so use some spare craft wood or stiffened cardboard
to hone your skills. The finished items make exciting wearables and welcome gifts

Tortoiseshell finish

Tortoiseshell has an infinite number of variations in pattern and colour. Choose one that you like and use it as the model for your bracelet or buttons.

MATERIALS
- small round brush (no. 2 or 4)
- wooden or plastic bangle
- acrylic gold paint
- gloss polyurethane lacquer
- artist's oil paints: burnt umber, burnt sienna, black
- saucer
- soft-bristled brush (badger softener, hake, or even a blusher brush)

1 Using the round brush, paint the bangle inside and out with the gold paint. Allow to dry thoroughly.
2 Paint the bangle with a generous layer of lacquer. Do not let it dry; but proceed quickly and carefully.
3 Place a blob of each oil paint around the edge of the saucer and put a tablespoon of lacquer in the centre. Using the brush, draw off a bit of lacquer, about the size of a match head, towards the burnt sienna then mix to a creamy consistency. Do not allow this to mix with the lacquer in the centre.
4 Apply a small number of oval dots with the burnt sienna around the bracelet (this colour should be the least obvious one when the bracelet is finished). Do not allow any drying time at this stage, but move straight on.
5 Repeat the process using burnt umber, but apply two or three times the amount, overlapping the sienna with the umber to create larger shadowy areas.
6 Repeat the process using black, but apply only as much as the first colour, again slightly overlapping the existing ovals.
7 Using the soft-bristled brush, soften the edges of the dark colours. You need to use a gentle touch, blurring the hard edges rather than moving any paint. It is very important to work quickly – you need to do the softening before the lacquer and the colours get tacky. Allow to dry thoroughly – this will take several days or even longer in damp weather.
8 Apply two or three coats of lacquer to give depth and sheen.

Oxidised finish

This technique allows a lot of copper to show through, and on a tiny object, such as a button, this gives it a sense of being precious.

MATERIALS
- small round brush (no. 2 or 4)
- artist's acrylic paints: copper, peacock green, antique or grey-green
- short-bristled coarse brush
- foam brush
- paper
- scumble
- saucer to mix on
- coarse sea sponge
- matt lacquer or acrylic sealer

1 Using the round brush, base coat the button in copper. Allow it to dry.
2 Using the coarse brush, pick up a tiny amount of peacock green. Tap out the excess on some scrap paper and then proceed to stipple (dab lightly with the top of the bristles only) onto the copper. Make it very irregular and try to colour only a third of the copper

---

TORTOISESHELL

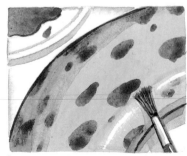

1 *To mimic the appearance of tortoiseshell, paint all over a lacquer finish with gold and let dry, then apply oval dots using a round brush dabbed in burnt sienna oil paint.*

2 *Complete the colouring with a more generous application of burnt umber followed by black daubs at about the same intervals as the burnt sienna paint.*

OXIDISED COPPER

1 *Apply a coat of copper paint to the object and let dry. Stipple in an irregular fashion with a small amount of green paint, covering about one-third of the surface.*

2 *Apply a glaze then, before it dries, use a sea sponge to take off just enough to allow patches of the copper base to show through. Finish by sealing with a coat of lacquer.*

area in total. Allow it to dry.

3 Using a foam brush, mix up a glaze of 1 part scumble, 1 part water and 1 part antique green or grey-green and paint the whole button. Before the glaze dries, touch the surface lightly with the coarse sea sponge to remove some of the glaze and open up areas of the copper. Allow to dry thoroughly.

4 Seal with one coat of lacquer or sealer.

Any of these finishes can be applied to either buttons or bracelets. Tortoiseshell buttons, for example, would look fabulous on a black coat or sweater. The process is the same for achieving either a black or white marble finish, depending on your fashion desires.

Marble finish

A precious-looking marble finish will add impact to buttons or other items receiving this treatment.

MATERIALS

- small round brush (no. 2 or 4)
- acrylic paints: black, white
- saucer to mix on
- feather (collect one or buy from craft shops)
- sea sponge
- gloss acrylic lacquer

1 Base coat the button in white. Allow to dry.
2 Dab some black and white onto the saucer and mix a deep charcoal colour and a medium-to-light grey. The mixture needs to be the consistency of pouring cream. Add water in drops to achieve this consistency, if necessary.

3 Using only the tip of the feather dipped in the charcoal, draw a jagged, erratic line on the button. Using the brush loaded with a dot of white paint and lots of water, run along the line, letting the charcoal bleed into the watery white. Blot up excess with the sponge and allow to dry.

4 Repeat this process with the grey. Allow to dry thoroughly.

5 Apply two or three coats of lacquer.

VARIATION To make a black marble finish, base coat in black then repeat as above using white and soft grey-white. Use a dot of black on the brush instead of the white.

◆ Painted Malachite Box ◆

In nature, malachite is a stone with rich green colour and striations that give it a distinctive appearance. Re-create this unique finish with paints and a few simple tools and apply it to any number of surfaces, such as timber or cardboard, for a striking ornamental effect

The distinctive green bands of this beautiful copper-based mineral present a challenge to the decorative painter, but the technique used in this project results in a really effective finish.

MATERIALS

- ◆ medium sized, soft-bristled brush
- ◆ artist's acrylics: peacock green, deep marble green
- ◆ acrylic scumble
- ◆ stiff but flexible cardboard to make wipe-out tools
- ◆ 12mm-wide masking tape
- ◆ medium-sized, flat-bristled brush
- ◆ old toothbrush (optional)
- ◆ acrylic or polyurethane lacquer
- ◆ lacquer brush

1 If you are applying this finish to a box (as pictured), remove the decorative corners and hinges before you start to apply the paint.

2 Using the soft-bristled brush, apply a strong, even base coat of peacock green. Allow to dry thoroughly.

3 Mix up a glaze in the ratio of 1 part acrylic scumble, 2 parts deep marble green paint and ½–1 part water.

4 To make wipe-out tools, tear the cardboard in straight lines into several pieces. Different shapes and sizes will create varying patterns, to more closely resemble natural malachite. It's also a good idea to experiment with different kinds of cardboard; each gives a different result, but you'll soon find those that best suit your requirements.

5 Before applying the glaze, mark off two or three separate inlay panels with masking tape, making sure that they, too, are of varying shapes and sizes.

6 Still using the soft-bristled brush, apply an even coat of marble-green glaze to one panel; the coating should be neither too thin nor too generous. To break up the brush strokes, lightly stipple it with the tip of the brush.

PERFECTING TECHNIQUE

When wiping-out with cardboard, don't press too hard – you'll squash the ragged points on the cardboard and end up wiping off the glaze.

Keep one end of each piece of cardboard in a fixed position and move the work around so that you can execute a smooth curve comfortably and without stopping. It is important to make even strokes, because every time you stop and start there will be an obvious ridge.

If you don't like the shape you've made, recoat with the glaze and try again. This is one of the few painted finishes that allows the opportunity to get each small part exactly right.

To finish off boxes or other containers, paint the inside of the box with artist's acrylic paint in a rich gold and allow to dry.

CREATING A MALACHITE EFFECT

1 *Apply a base coat of peacock green to the whole surface using a soft-bristled brush. Mark off two or three separate inlay panels with masking tape. Vary the shapes and sizes of the panels and make sure the tape is applied in neat, straight lines.*

2 *Mix up a glaze of deep marble green paint, scumble and water. Apply an even coat of the glaze to one masked-off panel with the soft-bristled brush. Lightly stipple the glaze with a flat-bristled brush to break up the brush strokes.*

3 *Using a piece of cardboard that has been ripped to produce an uneven edge, remove semi-circles of the wet glaze by swivelling one end of the cardboard in an arc while keeping the other end still. Vary the sizes of the patterns for a more natural effect.*

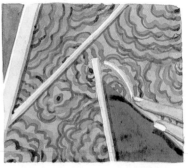

4 *Remove the tape and let dry completely before painting an adjoining panel. When dry, lay new tape along the edge of the painted panel, butting up exactly to the edge of the adjoining panel. Apply the glaze. Continue in this way for the whole surface.*

7 Using a wipe-out tool, remove semi-circular shapes of glaze by swivelling one end of a piece of cardboard in an arc while keeping the other end still.

8 After you have completed each inlay panel, assess your work for line quality and finish. When you are satisfied with the results, remove the tape and allow the paint to dry completely before masking off an adjoining panel. Each section must butt up to the one next to it.

9 When the final panel has been completed, remove the last of the masking tape. Allow the glaze to dry thoroughly.

10 As a final touch, you may like to spatter each surface very finely with the glaze. To do this, dip the tip of an old toothbrush into the glaze, hold the brush down almost perpendicular to the surface, and lightly run the index finger of your other hand along the edge of the bristles to produce a fine spray; the spatters should be almost imperceptible. Allow to dry.

Inspired by nature, this beautiful faux malachite box is likely to become a treasured keepsake. Any piece treated in this way will necessarily be unique.

11 Using the lacquer brush, apply three or four coats of lacquer. Sand lightly and evenly. Clean the surface thoroughly before applying a final coat of lacquer. If you have applied a malachite finish to a box, replace the decorative corners and hinges after the lacquer has dried.

◆ Great Ideas for the Table ◆

Personalise your entertaining with table linen and serving bowls you make
yourself. Match fabrics or create stunning contrasts using a simple photocopying technique and
apply it to papier-mâché bowls, paper plates – anything that takes your fancy

Table linen

Make this beautiful set of table linen for six as a gift or as an addition to your own table. Finished size: placemats, 50 × 35cm; table napkins, 45cm square. A seam allowance of 1cm is used here.

MATERIALS
- 2.3m × 120cm-wide main fabric
- 2m × 120cm-wide trim fabric
- 50 × 122cm-wide fusible woven medium-weight interfacing
- thread to match both fabrics

MAKING THE TABLE NAPKINS

1 Cut six 49cm squares of washed and ironed main fabric.

2 Stitch a row of matching thread 1cm inside all edges. Using the stitching line as a guide, fold and press a 1cm wide double hem, mitring the corners neatly (see page 222). Machine-stitch close to the hem edge.

MAKING THE PLACEMATS

1 For the front, cut six rectangles of washed and ironed main fabric, 42 × 27cm, with the long sides across the grain. Cut six rectangles of interfacing, 40 × 25cm.

2 Follow the manufacturer's directions, fuse the interfacing to the wrong side of the fabric; leave the seam allowance clear of interfacing.

3 From the trim fabric, cut 10 strips 7cm wide and the width of the fabric. From these, cut 12 strips 52cm long and 12 strips 37cm long. With right sides facing and centring each strip, pin, then stitch, the 52cm strips to the long sides of the placemats, leaving 1cm unstitched at each end of each placemat. To prepare the corners for mitring, fold each end of the border back towards the centre at a 45° angle (along broken line in following diagram).

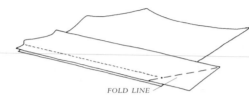

FOLD LINE

4 Repeat for the 37cm strips on short sides, stitching just to the edge of the long strips.

5 Press each of the borders away from the centre of the placemat (see below).

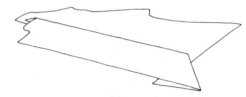

6 At each corner, pin and stitch a seam along the pressed diagonal folds from each stitched corner to the outside edge (see below). Press seams open and trim away excess fabric.

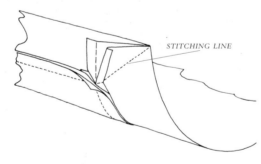

STITCHING LINE

7 For the backs of the placemats, cut six rectangles of trim fabric, 52 × 37cm. With right sides facing, stitch fronts to backs, leaving a 10cm-wide opening on one side of each placemat. Trim the corners diagonally and turn right side out. Press the raw edges to the inside of the opening and slipstitch closed.

8 Press. With right side up, machine stitch all around inside the border through all layers.

Decorative bowls

The versatility and low cost of papier-mâché are not the only advantages of turning unwanted paper into useful objects. Match them to your table linen by photocopying the fabric. Varnishing will protect them a little, but the bowls are best used for dry objects.

MATERIALS
- 2 items with circular shapes of different diameter, such as a mug and a large plate
- 1 large sheet cardboard
- marking pen
- scissors
- masking tape
- newspaper
- PVA woodworking adhesive (diluted 3 parts glue to 1 part water)
- white paper
- photocopies of chosen images
- artist's acrylic paints
- spray varnish

TO MAKE THE FORM

1 Trace the outline of the plate onto cardboard. Measure the diameter to find the centre point, then draw a straight line from the centre to the edge of the circle (right).

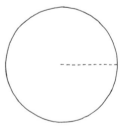

This fully coordinated table is set with our attractive handmade table linen – napkins and placemats – and decorative bowls of papier-mâché patterned with photocopied motifs. Use this idea simply as a change from the everyday look of your table setting or extend it to introduce a special theme for festive occasions.

2 Cut out the circle, then draw a line from the outer rim to the centre point. Cut down the line.

3 Overlap the cut edge to form a cone (right). When you are happy with the shape, cut away the overlap and roughly tape the two edges together.

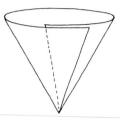

4 Place the point of the cone inside the mug, adjusting the position until the top of the cone is level (right). Trace a line around the cone, using the top of the mug as a guide.

5 Untape the join, cut around the small circle to remove the centre (right), then retape the join firmly.

6 To make the base, place the mug, top-side-down, on the cardboard, then trace around the top of the mug and cut out.

7 Upend the cone onto the mug and tape loosely. Then tape the cardboard base into position (right). Carefully remove the mug, cutting the tape as necessary.

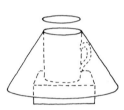

TO MAKE THE BOWL

1 Tear the newspaper into strips. Place the diluted glue in a bowl and, dipping each piece of paper in as you go, apply five to eight layers to the inside of the form. Allow to dry. (Depending on the weather, this could take from one to four days; a hair dryer can speed up the process.)

2 When the inside is dry, repeat the process on the outside of the form. Allow to dry.

3 Tear the white paper into narrow strips, dip them into diluted glue, and apply two layers over the newspaper.

4 Cut out the photocopied images. Position around the outside of the bowl, taping to the bowl with masking tape, if necessary. Once you are happy with the appearance, glue each to the bowl. Allow to dry.

TO FINISH

1 To achieve the colour-wash look as photographed, paint the bowl with acrylic paints mixed with a little glue. Apply two or three coats for an even finish.

2 When the paint is dry, apply four coats of varnish. This will help seal the bowl so that when you need to clean it, it can be wiped over with a damp cloth.

Octagon mat

This octagonal placemat is quilted for good looks and durability. It is made with two cotton fabrics: one side with a soft floral print and the other with a toning solid colour. Flip the mat over for a new look and an instant colour change. The materials listed below are sufficient to make two mats.

MATERIALS
- 1cm graph paper
- 40cm print fabric, 144cm wide
- 40cm solid colour fabric, 144cm wide
- 40cm fusible fleece interfacing, 112cm wide
- thread to match fabrics
- buttonhole twist for quilting
- transparent ruler
- pencil
- water-soluble marking pen
- scissors, needles, pins

1 With the graph paper, ruler and pencil, enlarge the pattern from the octagon placemat diagram (below). See page 220 for information on enlarging without a copier.

2 For each placemat, cut one piece of print fabric, one piece of solid colour fabric and the fusible fleece interfacing. Add a 1.5cm seam allowance around the edges of the print and solid colour fabrics, but not for the fusible fleece interfacing.

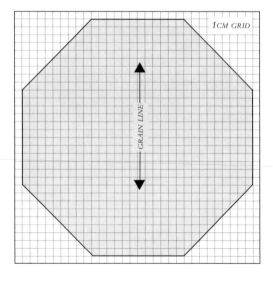

1CM GRID

GRAIN LINE

This quilted placemat will look equally attractive for afternoon tea or for a sophisticated dinner party. As an addition to individual place settings, why not make a large central mat for serving dishes?

PRACTICAL IDEAS

CHOOSING FABRIC

Placemats that are used on a regular basis need to be made with practicality in mind. Choose a fabric that is easy to wash and iron such as cotton or polycotton. Furnishing or dress-weight fabrics are both suitable, although furnishing fabric will give a more substantial result and dress-weight fabric will have a crisper finish. For special occasions, linen, damask or organdie will create a more formal look.

With so many attractive print fabrics available, there is no lack of choice when selecting a design. Avoid over-large patterns that will not be shown off to their best advantage on a mat. Medium to small-scale prints are ideal, as are ginghams and other checks. If you have patterned china, a plain fabric might be more appropriate.

It is a good idea to sandwich medium-weight wadded interfacing between the front and back of placemats to give some degree of protection from warmed plates to the table. However, remember that these placemats will not be fully heatproof and a table surface must be more adequately protected against very hot dishes. Place a cork mat underneath each placemat, or you could use a heat-resistant rubberised fabric such as Bulgomme in place of the wadding.

Plasticised fabric is often the choice for placemats to be used out-of-doors. This fabric is also ideal for children's placemats when spills are more likely. However, plasticised fabric is more difficult to seam if used with a normal turned-through method, as the bulk of the fabric will create a nasty lumpy edge. The most successful method to use is to place the front and back wrong sides together and bind the edges with bias binding (see page 225). Remember that not all plasticised fabric is heat-proof, so be careful about putting hot items on it (test a small piece of extra fabric).

3 Following the manufacturer's directions and using a hot iron, fuse the fleece interfacing to the wrong side of the solid colour fabric. Make sure that the special bonding agent on the fleece is face down onto the fabric so that it does not adhere to the surface of the iron and cause a mess.
4 With right sides together, pin and tack the bonded layers to the print fabric. Using a complementary-coloured thread, machine-stitch the mat leaving a 10cm opening along one edge. Trim the corners diagonally with sharp scissors and turn the mat right side out. Press and slipstitch (see page 222) the opening.

5 Change the top and bobbin threads on the sewing machine to the buttonhole twist ready for quilting the octagonal stitching lines.
6 Test the water-soluble marking pen on the underside of the print fabric before drawing the final quilting lines. Spray a reasonable quantity of water onto the placemat, so that it is quite damp, to make sure the marked lines can be removed successfully.
7 Use the ruler and water-soluble pen to lightly draw quilting lines on the print fabric (see the diagram on page 248). Begin 2.5cm away from the edge of the mat and draw two concentric octagons, 2.5cm apart.

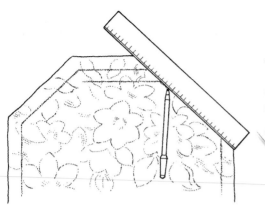

Pear placemat

Use a vibrant, modern print for this mat which has an appliquéd pear pocket to hold a napkin or cutlery. The mat is lightly padded for insulation and trimmed with colourful piping. The materials given below are sufficient to make two placemats.

MATERIALS

- 1cm graph paper (mark a 3cm grid)
- pencil and transparent ruler
- 50cm solid colour lightweight fabric, 144cm wide
- 1m print lightweight fabric, 144cm wide
- 20 × 40cm medium-weight interfacing
- 50cm fusible fleece interfacing, 112cm wide
- thread to match fabrics
- transfer paper (optional)
- stranded embroidery cotton
- 4.5m of 6mm-wide piping cord
- water-soluble marking pen
- scissors, needle, pins

1 With the graph paper, pencil and ruler, enlarge the pear placemat diagram on page 249 following the instructions on page 220. Enlarge the pear pocket diagram (right) by the same method. Add a 1.5cm seam allowance around each piece.

2 Cut four pear motifs from the solid colour fabric and two from the medium-weight interfacing for the pocket. Working on the bias of the remaining solid colour fabric, cut a series of 4.2cm-wide strips. These will need to equal the length of the piping cord when seamed end to end (see Making Piping, below).

3 For each placemat, cut two identical pieces of print fabric and one matching piece of fleece interfacing to the required size.

4 Pin the medium-weight interfacing to the wrong side of one pear piece. With right sides together, place a second pear piece with the first. Pin and stitch around the shape, leaving an opening as shown on the diagram (see below).

5 Trim the interfacing with sharp scissors close to the stitching. Clip the curves around the pear and trim the seam allowance to 1cm.

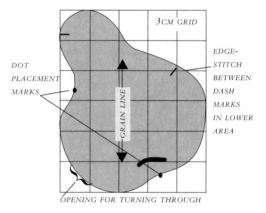

Press onto the fabric with a firm hand to obtain a solid line and work reasonably quickly to avoid ink spots.

8 Beginning at one corner of the outer octagon, correctly position the machine foot and needle and stitch along the marked quilting line until the shape is complete. Leave long threads at each end of the stitching. Repeat this process for the other octagon.

9 Finish off the thread ends by working them through to one side of the placemat and hand sewing several invisible backstitches into the seam line. Spray sufficient water around the edge of the placemat to remove the marked lines now that the stitching is complete. Gently iron the mat if the fabric is creased.

MAKING PIPING

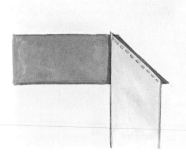

1 To join bias strips, place two lengths at 90°, with right sides together and the two diagonals matching. Make sure that there is an equal triangle of fabric at each end of the seam line. Stitch with a 5mm seam.

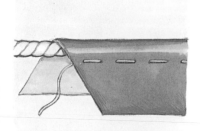

2 Cut the piping cord to fit round the mat, then add an extra 5cm. Wrap the bias strip around the cord and tack it close to the cord. Machine-stitch along the tacking line, using a zipper foot. Remove the tacking.

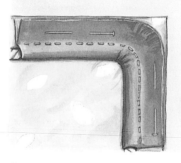

3 With the cut edges of the piping facing outwards, pin the piping to the right side of the mat front. Make sure that the stitching line on the piping matches the seam allowance line on the mat. Tack in place.

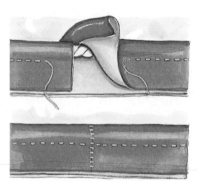

4 To join the piping, unpick 1cm of the bias strip at each end and turn it back. Trim the cord so that the ends abut. Fold the bias strip back over the cord, turn under the overlapping end, and sew in place.

6 Turn the pear right side out and press with a hot iron. Trace on the design at the bottom of the pear, and sew it, using three strands of embroidery cotton and straight stitch (see page 222), keeping your stitches close together and within the outline.

7 Working on one piece of previously cut print fabric for the front of the mat, and using the water-soluble pen, make placement marks to indicate the position of the pocket. Draw corresponding marks on the pear. Pin the pear in place, then machine-stitch around the edge, sewing between the indicated dash marks. Leave the pocket top open.

8 Trim 1.5cm from the edge of the fleece interfacing and fuse it to the wrong side of the other piece of print fabric for the back.

9 To make the piping, follow the instructions in steps 1 and 2 of Making Piping (below left). Tack, then stitch the piping to the right side of the placemat front, as shown in step 3. Clip the seam allowance around the curves with scissors. To join the piping ends neatly follow the instructions in step 4 and complete the piping seam to create a complete circle.

10 With right sides together, pin and tack the back of the placemat to the front. Machine-stitch around the outside, leaving a 10cm opening for turning through. Trim and clip the curved corners with scissors.

11 Turn the mat right side out through the opening, then push out the rounded corners and press with a hot iron. Neatly slipstitch the opening to close (see page 222).

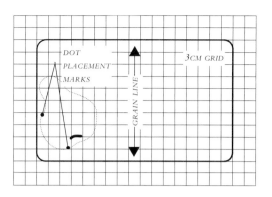

This Pear Placemat is perfect for a casual table setting outdoors, and will be fun to use for al fresco meals or a barbecue where the napkin pocket will really come into its own.

◆ Flower and Shell Decorations ◆

Here are two interesting ways of using flowers and shells – two types of decorative material that always lend themselves to new forms of display. You can pick the flowers from your own garden, while the shells are 'found' objects from the seashore

Tiered flowers

A spectacularly tall arrangement of beautiful flowers cleverly disguises the tiered tin buckets that provide its support. This novel display can be put together in a formal or informal manner depending on the time and equipment available. The cool colours that dominate, both in the flowers and the containers, make it ideal for a dresser with a mirror at its back, or for a cheerful spring or summertime celebration. The flowers used in the arrangement shown here are listed on the right, but you can use seasonal flowers in whatever combination you prefer.

MATERIALS
- 3 large floral foam bricks ('oasis')
- 3 metal buckets or similar containers of diminishing sizes, approximately 30cm, 20cm and 14cm
- scissors

Simple materials and natural objects are combined here to make memorable decorations. The final appearance of such arrangements is limited only by the maker's imagination.

FLOWERS
- ½ bunch magnolia leaves
- ½ bunch pieris
- ½ bunch photinia
- 1 bunch poppy seed heads
- 1 bunch (10 stems) mauve rose
- 1 bunch (10 stems) purple anemone
- 1 bunch sweet pea
- 7 cream tulips
- 1 bunch forget-me-nots

1 Soak the foam for about an hour in water. Make sure it is waterlogged.

2 Start with the largest container. Cut up one brick of foam and fill the container to about halfway with the pieces. Place the second largest container inside the first and pack foam around the edges. Repeat the process of filling and packing the second and third containers.

3 Fill the three containers with water.

4 Add the cut stems to the three containers, holding the foam firmly as you go. Place the shorter stems (those about 10cm) closer to the edges of the containers and gradually build up an even density of flowers so that there are no gaps in the arrangement.

PRACTICAL IDEAS

VARIATIONS ON THE THEME

Include sea shells or starfish in your arrangement for a summery feel. Attach them to the container, or tuck them in among the flowers.

If you wish to include ornamental fruit or vegetables such as pomegranates or globe artichokes, they can be held in place with wooden skewers. Try a variety of leaves, as well. They fill out an arrangement without detracting from the flowers.

In wintertime, when flowers may be in short supply, try making a dried arrangement, mixing textures and shapes as you would with fresh flowers.

As a final touch you could add ivy, tucking the stems into the floral foam and allowing it to hang in drifts over the side of the middle container.

5 Arrange the pieris and the photinia over the rim of the largest bucket and trail the pieris towards the front, so the display does not look too formal.

THREE-BUCKET TIERS

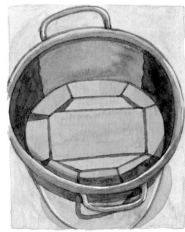

1 *Using a sharp, long-bladed knife, cut the foam carefully so that it fits the shape of the bucket and provides an even base for the first insert. Pack the foam in so that it makes an even fit to about halfway up the container's sides.*

2 *Stand the second container inside the first and, holding it steady, pack in more foam around the sides to keep it in position. Repeat this procedure with the smallest container. Fill the containers with water until the foam is soaked; pour off any excess.*

3 *Fill the top container and the outer edges of the other two containers with flowers, making sure that the stems are graduated – shortest at the front, longest at the back. The final result should resemble the photograph at left.*

ALTERNATIVE METHOD *In order to save time and money, you can support the second and third containers on half-bricks or similar solid supports. Pick fresh flowers from the garden and arrange them in the buckets in an informal way.*

251

AN ALTERNATIVE METHOD

A quick, easy and less formal way of arranging the tiered flowers with simple, inexpensive materials is described here.

1 Pick fresh flowers and leaves in the early morning. Cut the stems at an angle to create a maximum surface area to absorb water. Place the flowers in clean water while arranging.

2 Choose three containers of graduated size so that they will fit one within the other, creating a pyramid effect. Stack them together using half-bricks or similar flat-sided supports; half fill each with water.

3 Arrange the flowers and leaves informally around the buckets. Or, starting with one type of flower, place one stem in the top container and then one in the middle container to the right and one in the bottom container to the left, to create a zigzag effect. Repeat with other flowers and add leaves as you choose.

4 Continue until the containers are full and the arrangement looks complete. Top up with clean water every few days.

Using half-bricks as internal supports, the result here is just as attractive, in an informal way, as the first method. The 'insert' pots should be barely visible.

Shell picture

Many decorative objects – here seashells – lend themselves to framing, either formally or informally.

MATERIALS

- 1 sheet Foamcore board, 5mm thick (from art supply shops)
- 4 sheets mount board, in four harmonious colours (from art supply shops)
- steel ruler
- soft pencil (2B) and rubber
- craft knife, with spare blades
- glue gun
- cutting mat, or thick solid cardboard
- shells and starfish
- hole puncher

MAKING THE BASE

1 Cut the Foamcore to 60.5 × 53cm; your first colour mount board to 60.5 × 53cm; and the second colour mount board to 60.5 × 53cm.

2 Take the second colour mount board and, using pencil and ruler, mark a 'window' in the middle. To do this measure 8.5cm from each outer edge and draw a line, then cut. The window will be 43.5 × 36cm. Avoid making unnecessary pencil marks on mount board as erasing can cause damage.

3 Using the glue gun, join the three layers together, as shown below.

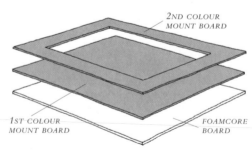

2ND COLOUR MOUNT BOARD

1ST COLOUR MOUNT BOARD

FOAMCORE BOARD

MAKING THE DISPLAY

1 Make sure all the shells and starfish are clean and dry. Within the base frame, arrange shells

of the same kind in rows, aiming for harmony of shape, size and colour. Make subtle breaks in the pattern, such as a turned shell or starfish, to avoid an overly rigid design.

2 When you are pleased with the arrangement, use a small amount of glue to attach the shells to the surface. Allow to dry.

MAKING THE FRAME

1 Cut eight strips of Foamcore: two pieces 53 × 3cm (see 'A' on diagram at bottom left of opposite page); four pieces 59.5 × 3cm ('B'); and two pieces 45 × 3cm ('C').

2 Glue the two 'A' pieces on the bottom and top edges of the base so that the edges are flush.

3 Glue two of the 'B' pieces to the side edges of the base piece, between the already glued 'A' pieces, ensuring that the edges are flush. Glue the other two 'B' pieces so that they are 3cm in from, and parallel to, the previously glued 'B' pieces.

4 Glue the two 'C' pieces so that they are 3cm in from, and parallel with, the previously glued 'A' pieces.

5 Reinforce the frame by gluing short strips of Foamcore 3cm wide (length not important, whatever will fit best) in an even zigzag pattern in the cavities of all four sides.

COVERING THE FRAME

1 Cut four strips of mount board (using your 2nd colour): two pieces 45 × 3cm ('D' on diagram at bottom right); and two pieces 52.5 × 3cm ('E').

2 Glue the two 'D' pieces to the inside of the Foamcore frame as shown bottom left. Glue the two 'E' pieces to the inside of the frame as shown.

3 Cut four strips of mount board (using your 3rd colour); two pieces 60.5 × 3.7cm ('F'); two pieces 53.2 × 3.7cm ('G').

4 Glue the two 'F' pieces to the outside of the Foamcore frame as shown. Glue the two 'G' pieces to the outside of the frame as shown.

5 Cut a piece of mount board (using your 4th colour) 60.7 × 53.2cm. Measure and cut a 47.7 × 40.2cm window in this board, 6.5cm from each outer edge.

6 Glue this sheet of mount board over the top of the frame, ensuring that all edges on the outside are flush.

ATTACHING THE HANGER

1 Cut a 4.5 × 5.5cm piece from any of the mount boards.

2 Rule a line 1.5cm from one short end and bend the board along the line. On the opposite end punch a hole 5mm from the top edge and centred.

3 Mark a centre line down the back of the Foamcore frame and position the hanger 4cm from the top and centred. Hang the project away from direct or strong sunlight.

A simple, symmetrical arrangement of objects looks just as impressive in an informal, glassless frame as when formally placed behind a pane as on page 250.

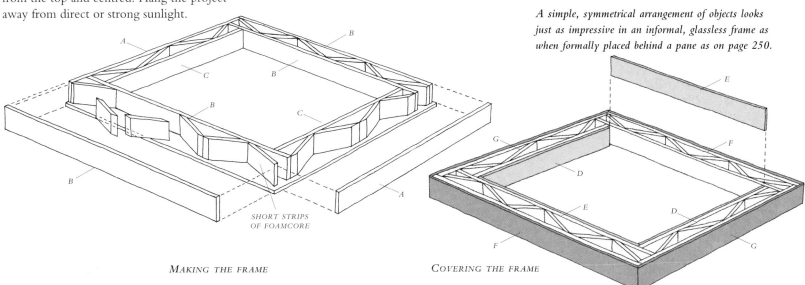

SHORT STRIPS
OF FOAMCORE

MAKING THE FRAME

COVERING THE FRAME

◆ Keep your Cat Happy ◆

Cat owners, who may also want to save their upholstery, can make a cosy bed
to keep their cat out of draughts and off the sofa. If your house doesn't have window seats for
viewing the world, your cat will consider our window perch the next best thing

Cat sling

A cosy spot for a favoured feline, this perch calls
for modest woodworking and sewing skills.

THE FRAME
- 4 stair balusters
- 3 wooden dowels, 12mm diameter and 1.2m long
- sandpaper (120 grit)
- PVA wood glue
- clear varnish
- 4 floor protectors

THE SLING TOP
- 1m fleece fabric
- 50cm of 25mm elastic
- 2 yards matching double-fold bias binding

CONSTRUCTING THE FRAME

1 For the legs: cut each baluster to a length of 410mm. The squared section of each baluster – which will be the bottom of the leg – should be at least 180mm long.

2 Put a 12mm flat wood bit in your drill. On one flat face of each leg, centre and drill two 16mm-deep holes, one 50mm, the other 150mm, from the bottom. On an adjacent face,

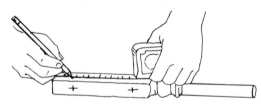

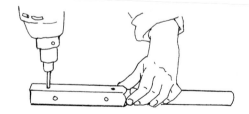

centre and drill two 16mm-deep holes, one 38mm, the other 165mm, from the bottom.

3 Cut eight dowels 400mm long. Sand the ends to fit easily into the leg holes.

4 With sandpaper, smooth any sharp edges on the legs, and round the tops of the legs.

5 To assemble the frame: put a light dab of glue into each hole before inserting a dowel. Use a hammer and a block of wood to seat the dowels firmly. When the glue is dry, apply a coat of the varnish, let it dry, and apply a second coat. When the surface is dry, fit a floor protector to the bottom of each leg.

CONSTRUCTING THE SLING

1 For the sling, cut out a 430mm square of fleece. For the pockets (for hanging the sling from the frame), cut out four 210mm squares and fold each in half diagonally.

2 Cut four pieces of elastic 12mm longer than the top of a leg. Wrap each piece of elastic into a ring that will fit tightly over the leg. Stitch one elastic ring onto the long side of each pocket triangle (right).

3 Arrange the triangles, ring side down and ring inside, at each corner of the sling. Pin and machine-stitch in place, rounding the corners slightly. Trim the corners.

4 To finish the edges of the sling with the bias binding, pin the binding to the edge, right side to right side. Stitch along the foldline of the binding, then fold the binding over to the wrong side of the sling and pin it to fit. Then stitch it neatly by hand. (The edging reinforces the soft edges of the fabric and gives the sling a finished look.)

5 To assemble the cat sling, slip an elastic ring over the top of each leg for security. Then let the sling hang from the legs by the pockets.

Window perch

This cat perch is designed to fit a window that is
at least 620mm wide.

MATERIALS
- 560 × 255 12mm plywood base
- two 598 × 50 × 25mm lengths of softwood for front and back edges
- two 100mm steel repair brackets
- two 255 × 50 × 25mm lengths of softwood for side edges
- 635mm strip of decorative beading for the front (optional)
- two 305mm strips of decorative beading for the sides (optional)
- PVA wood glue
- 38mm oval wire nails
- sandpaper (120 grit)
- 25mm panel pins (optional)
- 305 × 100 × 25mm softwood for the brace
- two 38mm woodscrews
- 150mm foam weatherstripping

1 Cut the base of the perch from plywood. Measure the depth of the window sill (below). To bend one end of each repair bracket so that it hooks over the outside of the sill, secure it in a vice and hammer it against a block of wood until it forms a 90° angle.

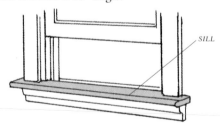

SILL

2 The perch has a rim made of 50 × 25mm softwood (actual dimensions, 44 × 22mm). The rim pieces are mitred at the corners. Place the rim pieces against the base and mark the inside of the mitre cuts. Make the cuts in a mitre box.

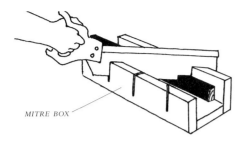

MITRE BOX

Using glue and 38mm wire nails, attach the pieces so that they are flush with the bottom of the plywood.

3 To attach the perch to the window, position the brackets on the bottom of the perch 115mm from the ends and outline them with a pencil. Clamp the perch to the work surface and use a chisel to chop out two 3mm-deep recesses so that the brackets will sit flush with the base.

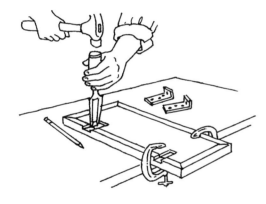

4 Screw the brackets to the bottom of the perch, and test-fit it to the window. To prevent the plates from interfering with the window, mark where they overlap the back of the sill and chisel shallow recesses in the sill.

5 The perch shown here has decorative beading around the front and sides. Place a piece of beading against the front of the perch and mark the inside of the mitres. Cut the mitres and attach the beading flush with the bottom of the perch with glue and panel pins. Mitre one end of two oversize pieces of beading for the sides. Attach them with glue and pins, then cut them flush with the back of the perch.

6 Make the brace by cutting a 305mm length of 100 × 25mm wood, with a 45° angle on each end. Draw a centre line on the bottom of the perch, from front to back. Put the perch in

position on the window, place the brace on the centre line, and mark where the front of the brace should start on the perch, as shown below. If the brace extends beyond the front of the perch, shorten the brace.

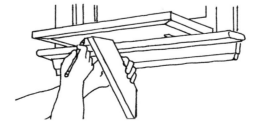

House-cat comforts include a sling bed and a perch for watching the world go by from the window.

7 Drill two countersunk pilot holes for 38mm screws through the top of the perch and into the brace. Screw the perch to the brace. Attach self-adhesive weatherstripping foam to the free end of the brace to protect the wall.

8 Screw through the mending plate and into the back edge of the sill.

9 Line the perch with a piece of foam covered with a fabric or an offcut of carpet.

Easter Breakfast Gifts

*Make these delightful egg cups from instant papier-mâché mix or using your
own paper pulp. And for lasting Easter mementos, why not make and give marble-finish eggs?
They make charming ornaments for home or office and look like real marble eggs*

Egg cups

*You can use these egg cups as candle holders or,
filled with sweets, as gifts at an Easter brunch.*

MATERIALS

- petroleum jelly (or vegetable oil)
- egg cup moulds (use existing egg cups or small cups)
- plastic wrap
- instant papier-mâché mix (or paper pulp, see box)
- kitchen knife
- PVA glue
- fine sandpaper
- flat spatula brush (no. 6)
- white gesso
- round brush (no. 1)
- selection of coloured acrylic paints
- gold and black water-based markers (optional)
- satin water-based varnish

1 Rub petroleum jelly on the outside of the mould and then cover with a sheet of plastic wrap (this will make it easy to remove your papier-mâché egg cup).

2 Make up the instant papier-mâché mix as instructed on the packet (or see box on this page for paper pulp recipe). Roll the papier-mâché into balls about the size of marbles. Starting from the centre top, press the balls onto the plastic wrap on the mould, smoothing as you go to achieve an even thickness. When you get to the edge, trim off any excess with a kitchen knife. Leave to dry for about 5 days.

3 To make the stem, slightly flatten out and shape three papier-mâché balls (one slightly larger than the other two). Place them on top of each other with a dab of PVA glue between each one, the largest going on the bottom as the foot. Leave to dry for about 5 days.

4 Remove the papier-mâché egg cup by gently lifting it off the mould. Test the size of your egg cup with an egg. If the cup is too big, simply add a small coil of papier-mâché to the inside lip of the cup, smoothing and blending it into the edge. Allow this addition to dry for about 2 days.

5 Sand down any rough spots and attach the stem to the cup with PVA glue. Leave until the glue is set.

6 Using the flat brush, base coat the egg cup with gesso and leave until touch dry (this will take 10 minutes or less).

7 Using the round brush, paint on your decorations with the acrylic paints. Use the patterns given above as a guide. Leave each colour until touch dry before starting another.

8 Outline your decoration with the gold and black markers for added detail. Allow the egg cup to dry thoroughly.

9 With the flat brush, apply two coats varnish.

MAKING PAPER PULP

INSTANT papier-mâché mix is available from craft stores, but it's easy to make at home. Tear newspaper into thin strips and process to a pulp in a blender with water added. Strain the pulp in a fine sieve, squeezing it in your hands to remove excess water. Put about 1 cup pulp in a mixing bowl, add 2 tablespoons PVA glue and 1 teaspoon plaster of paris and stir thoroughly. Add more water or PVA glue if the pulp is a little tough and dry. The mixture is now ready and should be used within 1 hour.

ACHIEVING A MARBLED EFFECT

1 *Paint the egg with white gesso and leave until touch dry. With a damp sea sponge, dab on several layers of a coloured acrylic mixed with gesso.*

2 *Apply a watery mixture of the acrylic to a feather with your fingers. Separate out the filaments so that the paint is not in large clumps.*

3 *Lightly dab and drag over the egg in a random pattern. Wash the feather and repeat with gesso, then wash and repeat with gold acrylic.*

Marbled eggs

With their deep marbled finish, these beautiful and unique keepsake eggs may look complicated, but they are, in fact, quick and easy to make. You will need only basic materials for these eggs, which will last in a way traditional painted eggs do not.

MATERIALS

- flat spatula brush (no. 6)
- wooden eggs (available from gift and craft shops)
- white gesso (or white acrylic paint)
- selection of coloured acrylic paints
- artist's palette or clean ice-cream container lid
- sea sponge
- feather (collect one or purchase from craft shops)
- gloss water-based varnish

1 With the flat brush, base coat the egg (or eggs) with gesso and leave until touch dry.

2 Place a small amount of your chosen coloured acrylic paint and white gesso onto the palette or lid. With a damp sea sponge pick up a little of each paint and dab the sponge all over the egg, letting the two paints blend and tone. Repeat until you have reached your desired depth of sponged colour. Leave the eggs until touch dry (about 10 minutes).

3 Apply a watery mixture of the coloured paint to the feather with your fingers, making sure you separate the filaments of the feather.

4 Lightly dab and drag the feather over the egg. Wash the feather and repeat with gesso (no need to water down but you may choose to). For added effect, go over the egg a third time with the feather dipped in a watery solution of acrylic gold or contrasting colour. Allow to dry thoroughly.

5 Apply four to six coats gloss varnish.

Marbled Eggs, with the subtle colours and distinctive patterns of real marble, will grace any shelf or kitchen table centrepiece. Or you can place them in hand-painted papier-mâché egg cups – together they make an Easter morning celebration of colour.

Botanical Cards

Every sign of the zodiac has its own flowers, shrubs and trees. For a homemade birthday card that will be treasured long after the celebrations are over, use the flower and leaf symbolising the recipient's star sign or special date as a decoration. And the pressing and drying of the flowers and leaves is a joy in itself

Pressing flowers by hand

Specially designed flower presses are available from craft shops, but if you aren't doing a lot of pressing, there's no need to buy one, as this simple method will work just as well.

MATERIALS
- A4 blotting paper
- newspaper
- flowers and leaves of choice
- 2 telephone directories or heavy books

1 Lay 3-4 sheets of newspaper on a flat surface (for very succulent flowers use a few more sheets). Top with a sheet of blotting paper.
2 Carefully place the flowers on the blotting paper, making sure they do not overlap.
3 Cover with another sheet of blotting paper then 3-4 more sheets of newspaper (extra for succulent flowers).
4 Place the telephone books on top.
5 Leave for three weeks in a cool, dry place such as a cupboard. Check the plants daily for the first week, straightening out any flowers or leaves as necessary. When checking, peel off the blotting paper carefully: place your finger-nail (or the curved side of a teaspoon) on the blotting paper and run it along as you pull up the paper, to prevent flowers or leaves from sticking. Replace the newspaper daily during the first week as it absorbs the moisture. For the next two weeks, check the flowers and replace the newspaper 2 or 3 times a week.
6 After three weeks, test whether the flowers are sufficiently dry. There are three ways to determine this: they should feel dry, they should be rigid and not limp, and the newspaper should be dry. Almost all types of flowers will dry within three weeks, but leave larger, more solid flowers, such as peonies, for one week extra, if necessary. It is worth allowing extra time to achieve a perfect result.

Pressing flowers by microwave

Be sure to use a medium to low microwave setting. Flowers dry too quickly if set on high, which leaves them brittle. Microwave ovens get hotter the more they are used. If you are drying several batches of flowers, later batches will take less time to dry. Watch carefully and adjust your timing.

MATERIALS
- kitchen paper towel
- blotting paper
- flowers and leaves for pressing
- heavy, flat microwave dish

1 Lay 3-4 sheets of kitchen paper towel on a work surface or on the removable turntable from a microwave (if drying particularly succulent flowers use a few more sheets). Top with a sheet of blotting paper.
2 Carefully place the flowers on the blotting paper, making sure they don't overlap.
3 Cover with another sheet of blotting paper and place 3-4 more sheets of kitchen paper towel on top (extra for succulent flowers).
4 Place the flowers and paper in a microwave, placing a dish or casserole lid on top of the whole arrangement to keep it flat.
5 Heat on medium (or low-medium for dark flowers) for 3-4 minutes. Check at 1-minute intervals, to straighten any flowers or leaves if necessary and to check for dryness. There are two ways to determine dryness: the flowers should feel dry and they should be rigid, not limp. Note that the newspaper may still be slightly damp. Usually 3-4 minutes is required, although times may vary according to the flowers being used – an extra minute or so may be needed for some flowers. Be careful not to overcook the flowers – when they feel dry or very nearly dry, leave them in the microwave for a few minutes with the power off. This will finish off the drying process. Experiment with less-than-perfect specimens.

HOROSCOPE FLOWERS

CAPRICORN : DECEMBER 22 – JANUARY 19
Ivy and Pansy, Pine, Elm, Yew,
Aspen and Poplar
AQUARIUS : JANUARY 20 – FEBRUARY 18
Orchid and Golden Rain
All fruit trees
PISCES : FEBRUARY 19 – MARCH 20
Water lily and water-loving plants
Willow, Fig and trees near water
ARIES : MARCH 21 – APRIL 19
Honeysuckle, Thistle and Bryony
Hops and Hawthorn
TAURUS : APRIL 20 – MAY 20
Rose, Poppy, Foxglove, Daisy and Primula
Apple, Fig and Cyprus
GEMINI : MAY 21 – JUNE 20
Lily of the valley and Lavender
Maidenhair fern and Hazel
CANCER : JUNE 21 – JULY 22
Lily and White rose
Cow parsley and Maple
LEO : JULY 23 – AUGUST 22
Sunflower and Marigold
Laurel, Bay and Walnut
VIRGO : AUGUST 23 – SEPTEMBER 22
Forget-me-not and Buttercup
Oak and other nut-bearing trees
LIBRA : SEPTEMBER 23 – OCTOBER 22
Rose, Bluebell and Hydrangea
Ash, Poplar and Maple
SCORPIO : OCTOBER 23 – NOVEMBER 21
Geranium, Honeysuckle and Rhododendron,
Hawthorn, Blackthorn and Box
SAGITTARIUS : NOVEMBER 22 – DECEMBER 21
Dianthus (Pink) and Carnation
Birch, Oak and Ash

Making the card

Some flowers may be too large for a card. You can press these flowers and use the petals to create free-form designs or stylised representations on cards.

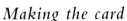

MATERIALS

♦ a purchased plain card (available from stationery or craft shops), or heavy sheets of A4 paper, folded in half
♦ pressed flowers and leaves
♦ tweezers
♦ clear-drying craft glue
♦ small paintbrush, for glue
♦ calligraphy pen

1 Using tweezers, place the flowers on the card, trying different arrangements if using several specimens. Smaller flowers and leaves can be used to fill any gaps, if desired.

2 Leave space for any writing at the top or bottom of the card.

3 Remove flowers from the card using the tweezers. For delicate fronds or flowers it may be easier to leave them on the card when applying glue, using tweezers to gently lift each segment.

4 Starting with the plant material that is the feature plant, or that will lie closest to the surface of the card, dab a little glue on to the back of the petals, stem and leaves.

5 Stick in place, applying a little more glue if necessary after the final positioning.

6 Repeat until all the flowers and leaves are in place, cutting away the stems if too bulky.

7 Remove excess glue from around the flowers. Leave for five minutes to allow the glue to set. If there is no excess glue, place a piece of paper over the top and a heavy book. This will stop petals and leaves curling from the moist glue.

8 Leave for several hours or overnight in a cool, dry place.

9 Using a calligraphy pen, write the flower name and month, if you wish. Practise the wording two or three times before starting.

These pretty Botanical Cards can serve as reminders of a bouquet received on a happy occasion or of a friend's garden in which the flowers were picked.

◆ Decorations for Christmas ◆

*The festive season gives you lots of opportunity to create a distinctive look for the home.
Try a novel Advent Calendar, make a wreath you can use year after year – or even personalise
the Christmas Crackers that will adorn your table on Christmas Day*

Advent calendar

This beautiful wall hanging can be used year after year. Children will enjoy putting the charming decorations in place each day and, at the end of the season, the calendar can be rolled up for storage.

MATERIALS
- 130cm of 90cm-wide cream felt
- cream machine thread
- stranded embroidery thread to match cream, green, brown and red felt, and to match small felt squares
- crewel needle
- tracing paper
- 30cm of 90cm-wide green felt
- 10cm square brown felt
- 12cm square red felt
- felt squares, 6–8cm each, in a variety of colours for decorations
- variety of glass beads, sequins, gold cord and ribbons to trim decorations
- clear-drying craft glue
- 24 small gold safety pins
- two 58cm lengths 15mm-diameter wooden dowelling
- length of silk cord

1 Cut two 76 × 62cm pieces cream felt to form the background. From the remaining cream felt, cut two 58 × 7cm pieces for the rod pockets.

2 Centre the pocket pieces across the top and bottom edges of one background piece 3cm in from the edges. Using cream thread, machine stitch the pockets to the background, leaving the ends open. Put this piece aside.

3 Trace the tree pattern on page 262 and enlarge it on a photocopier until it measures 53cm from the base of the pot to the top of

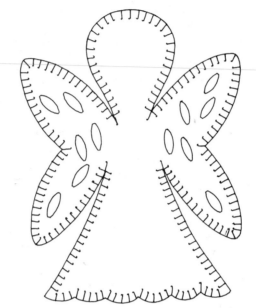

the tree. To enlarge without a photocopier, see page 220. Pin patterns to the green felt and cut out the shape. Do the same for the tree trunk outline in brown felt and the tree bucket in red felt. Position the felt shapes on the remaining background piece, with the top of the tree 14cm down from the top edge, and the bottom of the bucket 9cm up from the bottom edge. Pin in place, overlapping the pieces slightly. Using two strands of matching thread, sew each shape onto the background with blanket stitch (see page 222 for all stitches used in this project).

4 Trace the decoration patterns (above and on page 262). For each decoration, cut out two identical pieces from the desired coloured felt, 48 pieces in all. Decorate the front of each shape as desired, using craft glue to attach the trimmings. Join the front and back of each pair by blanket stitching around with two strands of matching embroidery thread. Take a small gold safety pin and sew the side with the catch head to the back of the decoration.

5 Trace the outlines of all the decorations onto tracing paper. Pin to the tree, then, using two strands of yellow embroidery thread, work the outlines in running stitch (see diagram, page 262). These indicate the positions for each decoration.

6 Pin the two cream background pieces together, with the tree to the front and the rod pockets to the back. Join the pieces by blanket stitching around them with two strands of matching embroidery thread.

7 Insert the dowelling in the rod pockets and attach the silk cord to hang up the calendar.

8 Place the decorations along the sides of the background. Beginning December 1, place one decoration on the tree each night until, on Christmas Eve, the tree is complete.

CALENDAR TRIM

Decorate the tree with gold cord for extra sparkle.

Dowel rods can be stained in a colour to blend with your wall and extended beyond the width of the hanging with fancy ends, if preferred. Attach a decorative cord to the ends of the top rod for hanging.

The patterns for the ornaments are simply guides to the types of decoration you can use for your tree. You may wish to design your own, such as mini wreaths or candy canes. Or make them all in one design, if you wish – a tree full of stars, for example.

Store the decorations in a box to avoid crushing.

The personal touch. An Advent Calendar for the children, a Christmas Wreath to say 'welcome' to family and friends, and a box of Christmas Crackers to make sure the occasion goes off with a bang.

PRACTICAL IDEAS

PERSONALISED CRACKERS

Insert glitter and stars in the crackers for an extra surprise when pulling them.

Choose trinkets that are safe for young children.

Start saving toilet paper tubes and tiny gifts to put inside the crackers weeks before you make them.

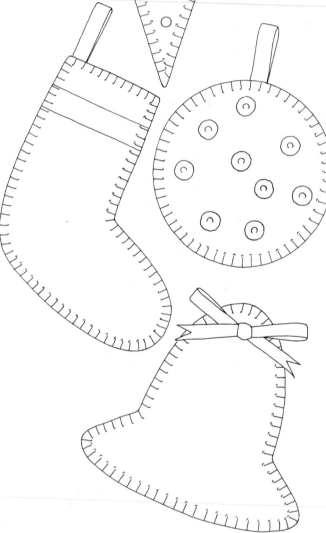

The patterns above are the actual size for the Advent Calendar; the tree pattern, right, must be enlarged (see directions). You can also trace the shapes to use on cards, tags and other items you create for Christmas.

Christmas crackers

Make these individual Christmas crackers to adorn your own or your host's table and fill them with small, carefully chosen gifts. If you can't buy cracker snaps, cannibalise a set of cheap crackers.

MATERIALS

- crepe paper, for hats
- ruler
- sharp scissors, pinking shears
- double-sided sticky tape and plain sticky tape
- sticker stars
- 8 toilet paper tubes or other cardboard tubes cut to size
- 6 cracker snaps
- 3-4 sheets different decorative papers
- ribbon or cord, about 3m
- gifts for inside crackers
- seals, tassels, coloured pens
- 2 colours of tissue paper
- box to fit crackers

1 Cut six pieces of crepe paper 58 × 15cm. Make six party hats, using the pattern and instructions on page 264. Decorate the hats with sticker stars.

2 With sticky tape, secure a cracker snap in the centre of each of six cardboard tubes.

3 Insert a gift, surprises and rolled-up hat.

4 Cut six pieces of decorative paper 37 × 17cm. Use pinking shears to trim the short edges. Place one tube in the centre along the long edge of a piece of the decorative paper.

Continued overleaf

A box of Christmas Crackers makes an excellent gift for your host or hostess. For your own table make enough for all your guests. Choose colours to match your linen and china, or use the most colourful paper you can find. You could also write out riddles or humorous messages to include with the gifts.

MAKING THE CRACKERS AND BOX

1 *Take a toilet paper tube and secure a cracker snap in the centre with sticky tape. The snap will stick out at each end. Insert a party hat, a small gift and any other surprises you wish to include, pushing them in so that they do not protrude.*

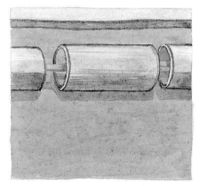

2 *Place the tube on your chosen paper, not far from one edge, and secure with sticky tape. Place an extra tube on either side of the central tube, with a short gap between each. Roll the paper tightly around the tubes and secure with double-sided sticky tape.*

3 *Carefully tie a piece of ribbon or cord on either side of the central tube, drawing in the paper evenly (the extra tubes help the cracker to keep its shape). Make a neat bow or fancy knot. Remove the two end tubes. Decorate the cracker as desired.*

4 *Fit two sheets of coloured tissue paper inside the box, cutting out a square of excess paper at the corners to neaten. Let the paper fall over the rim, if you wish, and cut the edges in a zigzag pattern. Arrange the crackers in the box with the ties up.*

Secure the paper to the tube with sticky tape. Place one of the extra tubes on each side to keep the cracker in shape. Roll the paper tightly around and secure with double-sided sticky tape.

5 Carefully tie a 50cm piece of ribbon or cord around the cracker on either side of the centre tube, drawing in the paper evenly. Make a neat bow or fancy knot. Remove the two extra end tubes.

6 Repeat to make the other crackers then decorate as you wish with tassels, seals, sticker stars, ribbon or coloured pens.

7 To line the box, place two sheets of tissue paper on top of one another and trace the bottom of the box in the centre. Measure out the height of the box and add 5cm to that measurement to all four sides of the tracing of box bottom. Cut a square out of each corner so the tissue paper will fit the corners neatly. Cut the top edge of the paper in a zigzag pattern. Place the tissue in the box and fold the zigzag edge down over the rim.

Fresh pine foliage – with its wonderfully evocative aroma – is employed to great effect in this version of the Christmas wreath described below.

CONSTRUCTING A CHRISTMAS CRACKER HAT

Fold the crepe paper in half lengthways, twice. Cut to the shape above. Unfold, then join the ends with tape on the inside; overlap the ends slightly. Decorate with sticker stars. Fold up the bottom of the hat 5cm, to fit inside the tube. Roll the hat up and insert in the tube.

Christmas wreath

Celebrate Christmas elegantly with this colourful wreath. Hung on the front door or an inside wall, it will be a cheery sight all through the festive season. If you choose to use artificial greenery (as on page 261), your wreath will last a lifetime.

MATERIALS
- four 50cm lengths ribbon, width and colour of choice
- wreath base made from twisted vines
- artificial holly, real box, or other real or artificial greenery
- artificial fruit
- hot-glue gun

1 Tie the lengths of ribbon into four bows.

2 Arrange the holly, fruit and ribbons on top of the wreath, trying various placements.

3 When you are happy with the appearance, cut the holly to the desired length. Using the hot-glue gun, glue the cut ends of the holly to the wreath base.

4 Repeat with fruit, and finish off with bows.

5 There is no need to add a loop for hanging as the wreath is easily hung on a nail or hook. Hang the wreath on a door or wall, making sure the nail or hook is not visible.

VARIATIONS FOR PINE WREATH

For a traditional Christmas wreath, substitute fresh pine needles for the holly or box. Cut a few small, healthy fir branches. Submerge the ends in water until you are ready to assemble the wreath. Strip small clumps of needles from the branches, trimming the ends – leave a few centimetres of twig to poke into the wreath base. Attach the pine needles in the same manner as the holly wreath. Small clumps are easier to work with than big unruly bundles. Decorate as above, or in any way you wish.

Tags, Cards and Boxes

*Use many techniques to create homemade cards and gift tags: stencilling, stamping or
simply cutting and pasting. Two unusual ideas are suggested below. You could mix or match them
with wrapping paper you make yourself and even devise a clever box for your gift*

Greetings cards

*Cards can be made from any number of common
objects – magazine pictures, cut-outs of fabric or
coloured paper, and stencils are all possibilities.*

Magazine-weave card

*The impact of this type of card comes from the blend
of shades and tones – it's like a woven carpet.*

MATERIALS

- card
- coloured paper
- glue stick
- colourful images at least
  11cm wide, from magazines
- craft knife
- scissors
- ruler
- masking tape

1 Cut a piece of card 26 × 15cm, so that,
when folded, it will be 13cm wide and 15cm
high. Score the fold line with a craft knife; fold.

2 Roughly cut a piece of the coloured paper a
little smaller than the front of the card. Apply
the glue stick to the back of this and press
firmly to the card front.

3 Cut the magazine images into strips about
1cm wide. You will need about 20 strips.

4 Lay nine of the strips edge to edge, taping
the top ends so that all strips are held down
– this is called the warp.

5 Weave the other strips (called the weft)
through the warp until you have a woven mat
of images. Carefully tape the bottom ends of
the warp. Peel the two pieces of tape off your
work surface along with the woven square.
Trim any ragged ends, turn the square over
and carefully apply the glue stick to the whole
area. Press the mat onto the front of the card,
leaving even margins all round.

Fabric-covered card

Use motifs from the fabric to create a floral montage.

MATERIALS

- thick cardboard
- fabric and coloured paper
- length of ribbon
- craft knife, ruler, scissors, PVA
  glue, hole punch

1 Cut out two separate pieces of card 14cm
wide and 19cm high.

2 On one of these, draw a window 7cm
square. This should sit 3.5cm from the top and
sides and 8.5cm from the bottom. Cut this out
using a craft knife and ruler.

3 Cut a piece of fabric 17 × 22cm. Apply PVA
glue to one side of the piece of cardboard with
the window and place the glued side on the
wrong side of the fabric so that there is a
1.5cm border of fabric all round.

4 Trim the corners diagonally, fold the fabric
flaps around the edge of the cardboard and stick
them with PVA glue to the
back of the card.

5 Cut a 5cm square in the
fabric in the centre of
the window. Cut diagonally
from the corners of the
square to the corners of the
window. Fold flaps over
the edge of the window and
glue them to the back of
the card.

6 Cut another piece of
fabric 13.5 × 18.5cm. Draw
a 6.5cm square window
about 3.5cm from the top
and sides and 8.5cm from
the bottom. Cut out
this square.

7 Apply PVA to the back
of the half-covered card,
ensuring that it is coated
with glue to the edges.

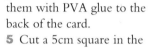

*The elaborate Fabric-covered
Card (blue flowers) will take
a little time to make, but the
Magazine-weave Card (orange
background), or more basic ones
made with stencils or paper
cut-outs, are quicker.*

Lay the piece of fabric with the window cut out over the back, positioning it 2.5mm in from all outside edges. Press down firmly and allow to dry.

8 Cover the second piece of cardboard with the coloured paper.

9 Determine the centre point on the left edges of both pieces. Using a hole punch make a hole on either side of the centre point on each piece, about 1cm in from the edge.

10 Thread the ribbon through the holes and secure with a bow. Do not make the bow too tight as the card needs to open easily – experiment until you have the right amount of give.

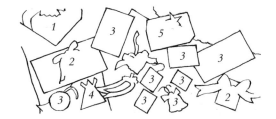

A variety of wrappings, cards and tags can be made using the projects on these pages. You can make them as simple or as ornate as you like, from a quick thankyou card to a stunning giftwrap for a special friend: Potato-print Wrap (1), Stencilled Tag and Card (2), Variety Tags and Cards (3), Ribbon Christmas Tree (4), Corrugated Wrap (5).

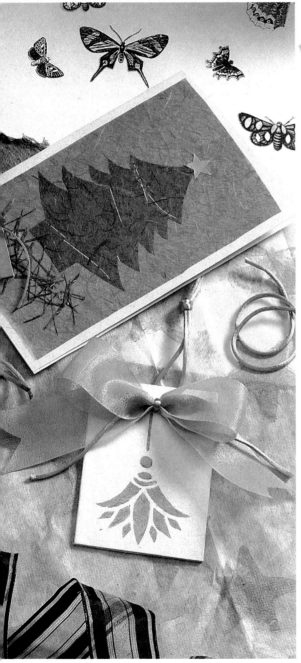

Giftwraps

Take any attractive paper and dress it up to make imaginative wrapping for Christmas gifts.

Potato-print wrap

Get the children to help make wrapping paper using this simple but effective technique.

MATERIALS
♦ sheets of appropriate paper for wrap
♦ sheet of tracing paper
♦ acrylic paints
♦ potato
♦ craft knife
♦ paintbrush

1 Trace the outline of the star motif from page 262. Choose a potato that, when cut in half, will have a surface area large enough to accommodate the motif. Place the tracing on top of the cut side of the potato. With the craft knife, cut along each line of the star to a depth of about 1cm. Turn the potato on its side and carefully cut out the negative area of the motif – that is, the area that will not print – by cutting a line 1cm down from the top of the potato between each star point.

2 Lay the paper you intend printing on a flat surface. Using the paintbrush, dab paint on the potato star to cover the motif completely. Firmly stamp the motif on the paper, then, holding the paper with one hand, carefully lift the potato off. Repeat until the sheet is covered. Allow the paper to dry.

Scribble wrap

Making scribble paper is similar to dyeing eggs at Easter. Vary wax applications for different effects.

MATERIALS
♦ coloured sheets of paper for wrap
♦ white candle
♦ acrylic paint
♦ sponge

1 As this technique can be quite messy, spread plenty of newspaper on a flat surface before

you start. Lay the paper to be coloured on top.

2 Take the candle and scribble all over the paper with it until the paper is well covered.

3 Dilute the chosen colour of paint with water to a thin, watery consistency. You will need enough to cover all the sheets you intend to colour. Dip the sponge in the diluted paint and drag it over the paper to cover the sheet completely. Allow each sheet to dry.

4 For a deeper colour, you will need to do about three layers of paint. Alternatively, for a more subtle effect, you can do more wax scribbles over the first layer of paint and each subsequent layer. Allow each layer to dry.

Corrugated wrap

The texture of corrugated paper gives dimension to a gift wrap. Even the smallest gift can look special. It is best if the present is a squarish shape, such as a box, but with a little imagination, most objects can be wrapped in this way.

MATERIALS
♦ sheet of coloured paper
♦ 1 sheet of thin, coloured corrugated cardboard (or colour it with acrylic paint)
♦ sheet of tracing paper
♦ craft knife
♦ ribbon and 12cm of cord

1 Wrap the present with the coloured paper.

2 Lay the present on the corrugated cardboard and cut a piece large enough to wrap around it. Trace the outline of the star motif from page 262 and lay the tracing on the cardboard in the position you want the cut-outs to appear. Using the craft knife, carefully cut out a star. Repeat, so that you have a cut-out on two sides and two stars to decorate the top.

3 Tie the ribbon so that the two edges of the corrugated cardboard are held together. Finish with a knot.

4 Pierce a hole through the centre of both stars. Thread the cord through one star and tie a knot in the end. Thread the other end of the cord through the other star and tie a knot in the other end of the cord. Push both stars so that they are against the knots. Attach the centre of the cord to the knot of the ribbon.

Make an assortment of gift tags in your spare time throughout the year, so that when Christmas comes, you have a good supply to choose from.

Spatter wrap

Use richly coloured paper and gold or silver paint to impart a seasonal richness with this technique.

MATERIALS
- coloured sheets of paper for wrap
- acrylic paint
- large brush

1 As this technique can be quite messy, spread plenty of newspaper on a flat surface before you start. Lay the paper to be spattered on top.
2 Wet the brush with plenty of paint and, with a flicking action, spatter the wrapping sheet. The size of spatters and coverage of the paper will depend on the size of brush, the viscosity of the paint and flicking technique. It is a good idea to experiment with scrap paper until you have a result you are happy with.
3 Allow the paper to dry.

PRACTICAL IDEAS

MAKING THE JOB EASIER

Wrapping paper made from black and white photocopies can be given colour by copying on coloured papers, or by adding colour highlights with acrylic paints. It is also possible to make colour photocopies in many print shops – create your original and then get as many colour copies as you need.

A hole punch is useful for punching holes in cardboard and paper, especially if you are making a large number of tags.

To pierce holes in thick cardboard, use a nail and hammer. Place the nail tip at the hole position and hit the head until the nail protrudes through the card. Do this on some scrap wood or a few sheets of scrap card so that you don't make marks on your table or floor.

Ribbon is often cheaper from craft shops than from haberdashers, and is usually available in larger rolls.

Gift tags

Use the wrapping paper for your gift as material for the tag, or adapt our Christmas card ideas to this use. Below are more suggestions.

Variety tag

Tags can be made from any number of found objects, photocopies, cut-outs of fabric or coloured paper, magazine pictures, tassels, ribbons – the key is your imagination.

MATERIALS
- card
- glue stick
- PVA glue
- ribbon or cord
- craft knife
- scissors
- ruler

1 Cut the card to a suitable shape. If the tag is to be shaped (a Christmas bell for example, as shown on page 266), glue all the elements onto the card first, then cut out the shape.

2 Arrange coloured paper, photocopies, magazine pictures or found objects on the card until you are happy with the result.
3 Glue the elements to the card. Use the glue stick for paper and PVA glue for any heavy or bulky items.
4 Punch a hole in the top or corner of the tag and attach the ribbon or cord for the tie (see the box on decorative ties, page 269).

Stencilled tag

Stencilling is one of the quickest ways to make gift tags – perfect for mass production at Christmas time. A large selection of stencils can be purchased from craft stores or you can design and cut your own.

MATERIALS
- card
- acrylic paint
- ribbon or cord
- craft knife
- ruler

1 Cut the tag to the size and shape required and position the stencil on the card.

2 Wet the brush with a small amount of paint – it is best if the brush is not saturated to avoid bleeding around the edges of the motif. Being careful not to wipe the paint under the stencil edges, dab the paint over the cut-out until the area is covered. Holding the paper with one hand, carefully lift off the stencil and allow the tag to dry.

3 Punch a hole in the top or corner and attach the ribbon or cord for the tie.

Ribbon Christmas tree

Here's a gift tag that definitely says Christmas. Vary the colours, perhaps blue and silver or green and gold, to get away from the standard green and red. Or coordinate the colours with your giftwrap.

MATERIALS
- thick cardboard (if you can't buy the colour you want, colour it with acrylic paint)
- craft knife
- ruler
- scissors
- 120cm × 2mm-wide ribbon for each tree
- 30 × 1cm-wide ribbon for each tree
- darning needle

1 Cut out triangles about 9.5cm wide at the base and 11cm high. Paint the triangles at this point if the board is not the right colour.

2 On a scrap of card, mark 11 intervals 8mm apart along the edge. This will be the template for cutting the notches for the ribbon. Lay the template along one side of the triangle and, with the scissors, cut a 2-3mm notch at each mark on the template, starting 1.5cm from the base. Repeat on the other side. Between the two notches at the top of the triangle, pierce a hole about 2mm across (see 'Making the job easier', opposite page).

3 Fold a 120cm length of 2mm ribbon in half to determine the centre point. Place the centre point midway between the first two notches at the base of the triangle and start criss-crossing the ribbon around the tree, pulling it into the notches and crossing each end over as if you were threading shoe laces. Pull the ribbon

tightly into each notch as you go. When you have reached the last two notches at the point of the triangle, thread both ends of ribbon through the eye of the darning needle and push this through the hole.

4 Fold the 30cm length of 1cm ribbon in half to determine the centre point. Cross the two ends at the centre point to form loops and tails. Pass the double strand of 2mm ribbon around the centre of the bow and back through the hole. Pull the needle through until the bow is held tightly – this forms the 'knot' of the bow as well as securing the bow to the card. Remove the darning needle and tie the two ends in a knot behind the hole. Trim the ends of the 2mm ribbons about 15cm above the triangle and knot them together neatly.

Paper tassels

You can use these tassels to wrap around napkins for the Christmas table, to coordinate with your giftwraps, or as an attractive trim for the tree.

MATERIALS
- thick cardboard
- craft knife
- sheet of white paper of the size you want your 'cord'
- PVA glue
- acrylic paints
- brush

1 Cut out two cardboard tassel shapes and punch a hole in the top of each.

2 Roll and twist the white paper to look like a cord. (If you want cords that are longer than your paper, tape strips together and roll them with the tape on the inside.)

3 Thread one end of the cord through one of the cardboard tassels, repeat with the other tassel and the other end of cord. Glue the ends of the cord to the back of each tassel with PVA glue.

4 Cross the cord over until the tassels are sitting well together. Glue the point of crossing with PVA glue. When the glue is dry, paint the cord and cardboard with acrylic paint. Add black lines as shown in the photograph on page 268 to give the tassels definition; the finer and more subtle the lines, the better.

page 268

DECORATIVE TIES

TIES MADE FROM ribbon or cord can finish off a card or tag with flair. Ribbon comes in many colours, textures and widths. When making a card with a specific theme and in specific colours, it is a good idea to take samples to the haberdasher so that you can choose a ribbon that suits. A few strands of raffia also make an effective tie for a parcel wrapped in even something as simple as white butcher's paper or plain brown paper.

ATTACHING A BOW TO A GIFT TAG
Method 1 – one wide and one narrow ribbon
Fold the wide ribbon in half to determine the centre point. Cross the two ends at this point to form loops and tails. Thread one end of the narrow ribbon through the hole in the tag from the back and pass it around the centre of the two loops and tails. Thread the narrow ribbon back through the hole and pull it tight – this forms the 'knot' of the bow as well as securing the bow to the card.
Method 2 – two equal ribbons
This tie uses two different-coloured ribbons. Bring one end of the first ribbon through the hole from the back, take it around the side and thread it back through the hole from the back. Take it around the other side and in through the hole from the back again. Pull the two ends tight and trim the ends. Tie the second ribbon in a plain bow around the first ribbon.

ATTACHING CORD AND RIBBON TIES
Place the two ends of the ribbon together and tie in a firm knot. Pass the loop through the hole in the card or tag, pull through a short way and thread the knotted end through the loop. Let go of the loop and pull the knotted end firmly. Alternatively, simply loop a length of ribbon or cord through the hole and tie the ends together in a knot.

Don't forget to finish off your ribbon ends with either a diagonal cut or a fishtail. This is not only a decorative element but a practical one, as it will prevent the ribbon from fraying.

Gift boxes

Bright and imaginative presentation gives a thrill of pleasure even before the gift itself is revealed.

Wrapped and painted

Plain boxes of all sizes and shapes can be bought from many gift stores and craft shops at a reasonable price. Once you have added a decorative touch, they can even become a gift in their own right.

MATERIALS: PAINTED BOX
♦ acrylic paints
♦ paintbrush

FABRIC-COVERED BOX
♦ fabric to cover
♦ PVA glue
♦ ribbon

PAPER-COVERED BOX
♦ paper to cover
♦ glue stick
♦ acrylic paint
♦ stencil
♦ paintbrush

Painted box

1 Paint the box in colours the recipient will find pleasing. You may need up to three coats of paint for even coverage.
2 When the paint is dry, PVA glue a home-made or bought figurine to the top of the lid. The figurine we have used was made from a blend of papier-mâché and glue.

Covered boxes

1 Cover each box with fabric or paper. To achieve the neatest finish, experiment with the folds before you glue them down.
2 Apply the stencils to the paper-covered box and allow to dry. Glue ribbon to the lid of the fabric-covered box with PVA glue. Bulldog clips are useful for holding the ribbon in place while the glue dries. Tie the ribbon bow and glue it to the top. For contrast, we painted parts of the fabric on the lid with acrylic paint mixed with a little PVA glue. Instead, when covering the lid, you could reverse the fabric, if the underside provides a pleasing contrast.

Doric column box

This intriguing container may have the recipient puzzled for a few moments about how to open it – the bottom pulls out. Fill it with tempting sweets, coloured pencils, rolled-up fabric or paper items.

MATERIALS
♦ thick cardboard
♦ corrugated cardboard
♦ craft knife
♦ ruler
♦ pencil
♦ PVA glue
♦ gold acrylic paint
♦ brush
♦ 2 small bulldog clips
♦ hair dryer or a small fan heater

1 Cut out the corrugated cardboard as shown below (note the direction of the corrugations in pieces A, B and C): one piece 19 × 32cm (A); one piece 18 × 4.5cm (B); and two pieces 5.5 × 14cm (C). Cut out two pieces of the thick cardboard 7 × 7cm (D). Paint one side of pieces A, B and D and both sides of pieces C with gold paint and allow to dry.
2 On pieces A and B, mark a line 1cm from one end. Score this line with the blunt side of the craft knife on the corrugated side. Clip out triangle shapes in the 1cm border, leaving the last 2cm clear for the overlap made when the pieces are glued into cylinders.

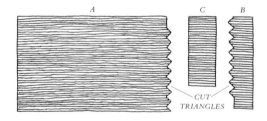

A   C   B

CUT
TRIANGLES

3 Apply PVA glue down the long edge of piece A and fit the two edges together (with a 2cm overlap) to form a tube. Hold in place with bulldog clips while glue dries – use a hair dryer to speed up the process. Repeat with piece B, with an overlap of a little more than 2cm, so that the tube fits inside the tube formed by A.
4 On each cylinder, bend triangles inwards, apply glue to them and press each cylinder onto the centre of a piece D. Allow to dry.

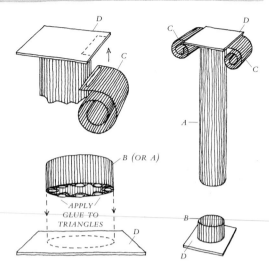

D   D   C

C

A

C

B (OR A)

APPLY
GLUE TO
TRIANGLES

D

B

D

5 Take two pieces C and curl into a spiral by rolling them tightly and then easing the spiral out. When you are satisfied with the spiral, apply glue to the top of the edge and attach to the column as shown above. Hold firmly while drying with a hair dryer.

Simple box

You can make this perfect cube any size you wish.

MATERIALS
♦ cardboard
♦ craft knife
♦ ruler and pencil
♦ PVA glue

1 Decorate one side of a piece of cardboard with potato prints, stencils, or by covering with some attractive paper. The side you have decorated will be called the 'right side'.
2 Using the template (page 271), mark the dimensions you require on the right side of the cardboard with a pencil and ruler.
3 Cut around the outside edges with the knife.
4 Score the fold-lines on the right side with the blunt side of the craft knife for thin cardboard, and lightly with the sharp side for thicker cardboard.
5 Fold into a box along the scorelines with all the tabs inside. Glue the two top tabs down over the side tabs with PVA glue. It is not necessary to glue the side tabs in place. Bulldog clips are excellent for holding the top tabs in place while they dry.

This selection of boxes of all sizes and shapes is quite within the scope of even a beginner at making things. Covered with fabric or paper, decorated with stencils and tied with ribbon, they are dressed-up enough to go to any party.

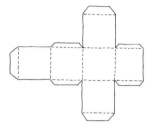

DIAGRAM OF WHOLE PIECE

PRACTICAL IDEAS

A PROFESSIONAL FINISH

When gluing awkward objects, use bulldog clips to hold the elements together while the glue is drying.

To achieve a clean fold on card, score the fold-line first. With the blunt edge of a craft knife, score a line on the right side of the card. The idea is that you are not cutting the card, just indenting it.

On thick cardboard, score the fold-line first to achieve a clean fold. With the sharp edge of a craft knife, lightly score a line on the right side of the cardboard. This will cut it just deep enough to allow the cardboard to fold easily.

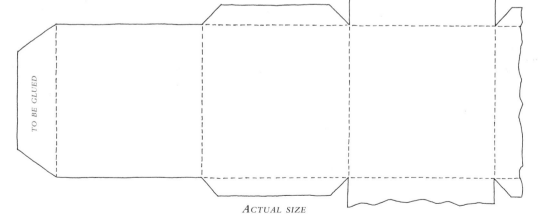

ACTUAL SIZE

To make a simple box, use this template, extending it to its complete shape using the small diagram as a guide. Note that there are seven tabs, three slightly larger (to be glued) and four smaller (no need to glue).

Innovative Giftwraps

*With some of these novel ideas, the wrapping can become part of the gift. Give a little
thought to coordinating the wrap and gift – you might choose a rose-patterned fabric to make a cover
for a book on roses, for example, or a wine-coloured napkin to wrap a bottle of red wine*

Kitchen giftwrap

*Choose a colourful tea towel for this cute present-
ation idea for a kitchen tea or similar occasion.*

MATERIALS
- new tea towel
- needle and thread, to match
  tea towel
- rope, enough to go around
  package twice and leave 6cm
  at each end
- 2 biscuit cutters
- 2 wooden cooking spoons

1 Wrap the gift in the tea towel, as you would
with a sheet of paper. Fold over the ends
neatly and tack down with the matching
thread – don't stitch too securely.
2 Make a neat knot at each end of the rope.
Tie the package with the rope, looping the
biscuit cutters and wooden spoons into the
final tie. For a homespun touch, make a
knot instead of a bow.

Japanese giftwrap

*Choose filmy fabric or scarves for this project.
Different fabrics of various textures and thicknesses
will add interest to your wrap.*

MATERIALS
- 2 squares of fabric or 2 scarves
- needle and thread, or sewing
  machine

1 Hem all edges of the fabric by hand or
machine (not necessary if using scarves).
2 Lay one piece of fabric on top of the
other and place the item to be wrapped on
a diagonal in the centre of the fabric. Bring
two opposite corners of the fabric together and
fold neatly over each other. Bring the other
opposite corners together and tie. Tuck all
the edges in to make a neat parcel.

Book giftwrap

*For a special book, create a wrapping that will later
act as a decorative and protective envelope. A book
for a man could be wrapped in corduroy, a country-
style cookbook in gingham.*

MATERIALS
- rectangular piece fabric,
  for pocket (see step 1)
- contrasting fabric, for flap (see
  step 2)
- fabric scissors
- needle and thread, or sewing
  machine
- 2 buttons, about 25mm each
- silk cord, about 30cm

1 Measure the height, width and thickness
of the book. Cut a rectangle of fabric – the size
will vary according to the size of the book.
The length will be double the book's height,
plus the thickness, plus 1cm seam allowance.
The width will be the book's width, plus the
thickness, plus 2cm. One of the rectangle's
short sides should be on the selvage.
2 Cut a square of contrasting fabric the size
of the width of the rectangle. With right sides
facing, stitch one side of the square to the
non-selvage end of the rectangle. Press. Turn
down a 1cm hem on the opposite side of the
square. Press.
3 Fold each end of the combined strip in to
meet at the join, right sides facing (see below).

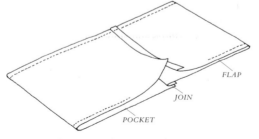

FLAP

JOIN

POCKET

Pin, then stitch along each side, 1cm in from
each edge. Turn the pocket and flap right side
out. Slipstitch along the pressed hem to close
the open end of the flap.
4 Slip the book into the bag and mark the
position of the two buttons, one on the flap
and one on the pocket, centred. Sew on the
buttons. Tie one end of the cord around the
thread attaching the flap button, and tie a knot
in the other end of the cord.
5 With the book inside the bag, wind the
cord around the buttons in a figure 8 pattern
to secure the parcel.

Potplant giftwrap

This is a quick way to dress up a plain potplant.

MATERIALS
- 2 large new handkerchiefs or
  colourful square napkins
- sticky tape

1 Fold one handkerchief diagonally in half,
and tie around the rim of the pot with a simple
knot (the folded edge runs around the rim and
the loose points of the handkerchief hang
down). Tuck the pointed end of the triangle
under the pot and tape it in place.
2 Repeat with the other handkerchief, tying
the knot on the opposite side of the rim.

Nappy giftwrap

The nappy and pins will be as useful as the present.

MATERIALS
- nappy
- 3 nappy pins
- small teddy bear
- ribbon, for bow

1 Lay the nappy flat on a table with a corner
towards you. Place the gift item (a square or

rectangular shape is best) in the centre of the nappy, at 45° to the sides. (For a gift that is too large to be accommodated in a nappy, you could use a baby's towelling bath square, bound around the edges with bias binding.)

2 Fold the top corner of the nappy down over the gift, then fold in the two side corners. Finally fold up the bottom corner to overlap the other corners. Pin the four corners together with two nappy pins, making sure you don't damage the item inside.

3 Tie a ribbon bow around the teddy's neck. Thread the ribbon through the hole at the end of the nappy pin, and attach teddy to the gift.

Bottle giftwrap

Turn a bottle of wine, or whatever you choose, into an elegant gift with this easy giftwrap.

MATERIALS
♦ colourful cloth napkin
♦ sticky tape
♦ contrasting ribbon, for bow

1 Lay the napkin on a table. Place the bottle on one edge of the napkin with the bottom of the bottle about 4cm from the bottom of the napkin. Secure the napkin to the bottle with sticky tape, about halfway down the bottle,

The extra thought that has been given to the wrapping of these gifts has added greatly to their charm. Clockwise from back left: Nappy Giftwrap; Bottle Giftwrap; Japanese Giftwrap; Kitchen Giftwrap; Book Giftwrap; and Potplant Giftwrap.

and fold down the top edge of the napkin a little higher than the top of the bottle.

2 Roll the bottle up tightly and secure the end of the napkin with sticky tape.

3 Tuck the bottom of the napkin under the bottle and secure with sticky tape. Tie a bow around the neck of the bottle.

· Mounting Photographs ·

Precious photographs and keepsakes deserve special presentation. It is surprisingly easy to give images a professional finish with decorated mounts, or create a special display box frame. Take time to match colours, textures and the style of your photograph for long-lasting heirlooms

Vintage frame

This old photograph has a border of a double mount of card and paper. The corners are decorated with an embossed design, and the photograph is edged with a gold ruled line. The simple embossed shapes complement the delicate lace of the bride's dress.

MATERIALS

- gold picture frame
- photograph
- cream-coloured card
- cream 150g paper
- scrap paper
- fine gold pen
- set square
- metal ruler
- clear, bevel-edged ruler
- trimming knife
- burnisher or round-ended spoon
- gummed paper

RULING THE CARD MOUNT

1 Remove the backing board from the frame. Draw around the recess of the frame onto the cream card, paper and scrap paper. Use a set square for right-angled corners. Cut them out.
2 Measure the photograph and use the scrap paper rectangle to make a practice mount. Transfer the measurements of the photograph centrally to the paper as a dotted pencil line. Draw a solid line at least 2mm inside the rectangle; this will enable the mount to overlap the photograph. Cut along the solid inner edge using the trimming knife.
3 Transfer the measurements to the card mount and cut out the aperture (above right).

The moulded gold frame blends subtly with the sepia tones of the photograph. A double mount of cream with a gold line continues the toning colour scheme.

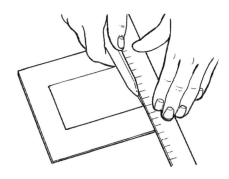

4 Turn the bevel-edged ruler upside down on the card mount; this will prevent the ink from smudging. Draw a line 7mm in from the aperture with the gold pen.

EMBOSSING THE PAPER MOUNT

1 Cut an aperture in the paper rectangle, 1cm larger all round than the card aperture. Transfer the motifs and marker lines (above) to a scrap of card and cut out. To alter the size, use the directions on page 220.

2 Match the corner with a corner on the paper. Place the paper and card, card side down, on a flat surface. Rub through the motif with the burnisher or back of spoon to emboss the design. Repeat for all the corners.

3 Secure the card mount over the photograph with gummed paper. Repeat for the embossed mount and reassemble the frame.

FRAMING MATERIALS

To ensure that you do not tear the paper or card mount as you cut, change the blade of the trimming knife regularly and work on a self-sealing cutting mat. When cutting thick card, do not attempt to cut right through the board during the first stroke. Gradually cut deeper and deeper, and always start at a corner when cutting an aperture.

Gummed paper is best for gluing lightweight paper and card because it does not cause wrinkling or staining. Ideally use acid-free paper, card and tissue paper. Although it is more expensive than non-acid-free materials, it will last longer and will not adversely affect other materials.

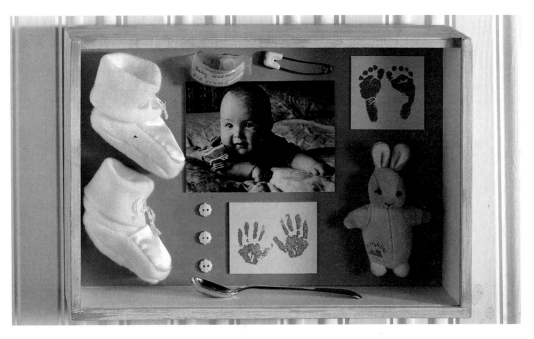

Baby frame

This ensemble makes a lovely gift for doting grandparents. The foot and hand prints, and the other personal mementos make it really special.

MATERIALS

- box frame
- thick card
- white and blue emulsion paint
- personal mementos such as a nappy pin, booties, stamps
- PVA glue
- needle and strong sewing thread
- tissue paper
- small decorator's paintbrush
- sandpaper
- kitchen paper towel
- set square
- ruler

1 Remove the glass from the frame and paint the box white. When dry, lightly sand it before applying a second coat. Cut a piece of thick card to fit the back of the box and paint it blue. Dip a dry brush into the blue paint, dab the excess onto the kitchen paper towel, and lightly brush the paint over the frame. Allow areas of white paint to show through.

Box frames are ideal for creating a commemorative collage. Choose items that are of sentimental value and paint the box to match.

2 Spread a thin layer of glue over the back of the photograph and secure it to a piece of thick card. Stamp the foot and hand prints onto additional pieces of card. Shape the booties by stuffing with acid-free tissue paper.

3 Place the memorabilia onto the painted card and move them about to form a pleasing arrangement. Try not to group all three-dimensional pieces or similarly coloured items together as they will balance more harmoniously if placed around the frame.

4 When satisfied with the arrangement, secure the photograph, stamped prints and buttons in position with PVA glue. Use a set square and ruler to ensure they are square to the frame and evenly spaced.

5 Sew the fabric booties and the toy to the painted card. Use a sharp needle to make small stitches, and fasten the thread tightly on the back of the card. Secure the nappy pin and birth tag in a similar way, adding a dab of glue. Stick the painted card to the back of the frame with PVA glue, place the spoon in position and replace the glass.

LOOKING GOOD
feeling good

Beauty and body-care products based on plant
extracts instead of synthetic ingredients are
growing in popularity every day. Because
such 'natural' products contain no harsh
ingredients they clean and condition your
hair and skin gently. The good news is that
you can make your own beauty products at
home – products which are every bit as
effective as the commercial version – using
ingredients that are readily available and
relatively inexpensive.

Preparations for women, men and children;
bath oils and lotions for the skin and hair –
even fragrances that you can make yourself –
they are all included in this compendium of
time-honoured formulas. Because they are
made of herbal extracts and infusions, these
products are kinder to the skin than many
factory-prepared products. Best of all, you
know exactly what each contains because
you made it yourself.

This chapter also contains eight pages of
home remedies to treat common complaints
such as stuffy noses, calluses or minor burns.
So choose from these traditional recipes to
help yourself and your family to not only
look good but feel good too.

BEFORE YOU BEGIN...

Making your own cosmetics and remedies offers you many satisfactions. You select the ingredients yourself – and you save money. Because you control the content of your health and beauty regimen, you can be sure the products you use are pure, natural and entirely suitable for you

Most of the ingredients used in these recipes can be obtained easily. Look in pharmacies, health-food shops, plant nurseries or the appropriate sections of major retail stores. It is best to buy essential oils that carry a brand name – those which carry no brand can vary greatly in quality. It's even possible for you to grow some ingredients yourself (see Chapter 3 for growing scented herbs).

Read and follow recipes carefully. Take note of what each calls for and do not exceed amounts given. In particular, do not confuse 'oils' with 'essential oils'. Oils, such as almond oil and vegetable oils, are non-volatile; they are called fixed oils. Essential oils are volatile substances. This means that they evaporate at low temperatures and are potentially toxic if used incorrectly. With the exception of lavender and tea tree, essential oils must be diluted in a fixed oil, which acts as a 'carrier', before they are applied to the skin.

Equipment

You will need only basic kitchen equipment. To avoid any chance of contaminating food, it is better not to use your normal cookware. It is preferable to buy secondhand equipment and to store it separately from cookware. If this is not practical, clean equipment thoroughly before using it again for cooking. Implements of absorbent material, such as wooden spoons, must be new to avoid contamination from foodstuffs. Keep these only for making natural products.

For heating and boiling, use only non-reactive pans, that is, pans made of material that will not react chemically with the materials you'll be using. Non-reactive materials include stainless steel, glass, enamel and pans with a non-stick coating. Take care that enamel pans have no holes or chips in the enamel. Non-stick pans must be of good quality and not scratched. You must not use pans made from aluminium, brass, copper or tin – all of which are reactive.

Any spoons which you use should also be of a non-reactive material. Use a stainless-steel spoon for measuring and a wooden or stainless-steel spoon for stirring the mixtures. You will need a 5ml teaspoon and a 15ml tablespoon, or the equivalent measuring spoons.

Bottles and jars used for storing need not be expensive, but make sure they are cleaned and sterilised properly. Lids should be non-porous to prevent evaporation – glass stoppers and metal or solid plastic lids are suitable. Although bottles with cork stoppers are often sold, cork on its own is too porous for storing products satisfactorily. A cork stopper can be used, however, if a piece of strong cling film is folded several times and placed under it to create an airtight seal. This will prevent air coming into contact with products.

A stainless-steel funnel is ideal for straining and pouring liquids into bottles, but a plastic one can be used as long as pouring is done rapidly. Be sure that you clean the funnel well immediately after use.

Sterilising and labelling

Sterilise all containers and lids before you use them. For sterilising jars and bottles, follow the step-by-step method below. If you are using containers and lids that will not withstand very high heat, wash them well in hot soapy water, then dry thoroughly. Keep them covered with a cloth until needed.

STERILISING JARS

1 *Wash the jars and lids thoroughly in warm, soapy water, using a bottle brush. Rinse well in cold water, making sure to remove all traces of soap residue.*

2 *Place the jars on a baking tray and put the tray in the oven. Heat the oven to 110°C (225°F, gas mark ¼). Leave on for 45 minutes, then turn off.*

3 *Remove the jars when cool. If you need to remove the jars while still hot, use tongs and an oven mitt. Place the jars upside down on a cloth and leave until needed.*

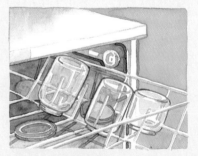

ALTERNATIVE METHOD *Instead of steps 1 and 2, wash jars and lids in the dishwasher on the hottest cycle. Remove when cool, then place on a cloth until needed.*

You need little specialised equipment to make beauty and health products at home. All that's required is basic kitchen equipment, some common herbs and flowers from the garden or nursery and a few simple ingredients from your health-food shop.

It is essential that you keep equipment scrupulously clean. Wash and dry bowls, saucepans and utensils before using them.

Label everything you make with its name and the date on which it was prepared and bottled. This is important as preparations can look very similar, and some must be used within a certain period.

Storing natural products

Heat, light and contact with air will all cause natural products to deteriorate. Keep the products in a cool, dark place such as the refrigerator, or a closed cupboard if you are storing in quantity.

Because the recipes do not use preservatives, you must check products regularly to make sure that they have not deteriorated.

Pronounced discoloration or an unusual smell indicate that the product's constituents may have broken down. If this should occur, discard the product immediately without using any of it. In general, unless you intend the product for family use, it is best to make only enough for use in a short space of time.

A word of caution

While side effects are not common in normal use, some can occur because of individual skin sensitivity. Effects can include rashes, nausea, sneezing, skin irritation and breathing difficulties. If you experience any of these, stop using the product.

When using essential oils:
◆ Do not exceed the amount recommended.
◆ Do not ever swallow the essential oils. Keep bottles sealed and out of reach of children.
◆ If an essential oil is accidentally swallowed, do not induce vomiting. Give the affected person a glass of water and seek medical advice and/or take the person to a hospital immediately.

Do not use essential oils without professional advice if you have any pre-existing chronic or acute disorder such as heart disease, epilepsy, asthma, diabetes or kidney disease. Do not use essential oils on young children or while you are pregnant.

Certain herbs may cause allergic reactions in sensitive people, in particular those who suffer from hay fever or plant allergies. Should this be a cause of concern, patch test each herb or remedy before using it by applying a small amount of the remedy to the tender skin under the arm and waiting for several hours. If redness, swelling or any other form of irritation occurs, do not use the herb or remedy.

Total Body Treatment

Soothe your skin and indulge your senses with
these creams and lotions which you can make yourself.
You'll feel silken and scented all over – naturally

Soothing footbath

At the end of a busy day, give tired feet a real treat
– soak them in a reviving footbath. Relaxing the
feet often has a calming effect on the whole body.

INGREDIENTS
- 1 tablespoon sea salt
- 2 drops lavender essential oil
- 1 drop rosemary essential oil
- 1 drop bay essential oil
- 1 drop geranium essential oil
- rose petals, optional

As well as the above ingredients, you will also
need a large basin or bowl and a clean towel.
1 Fill the basin with enough warm water to
cover the feet. Stir the sea salt into the warm
water until it dissolves (use your toes to stir if
you like). Add the essential oils, mixing them
in well. For an attractive look and pleasant
aroma float some richly scented rose petals on
the surface of the water.
2 Soak your feet in the basin for 10 minutes,
or until the water is cool. Remove feet and pat
dry with the towel. You can finish off by
massaging your feet with Eucalyptus Foot
Lotion (see right), massaging the toes well.

Leg massage cream

This soothing cream will help to firm and moisturise
the skin, keeping it soft and supple. Massage it over
feet, legs and knees, using firm upward strokes.

INGREDIENTS
makes about 125g (4½oz)
- 50g (1¾oz) anhydrous lanolin
- 50ml (2fl oz) olive oil
- 30ml (1fl oz) sweet
  almond oil

You will need a non-reactive double boiler,
a wooden spoon and a sterilised 125g (4½oz)
glass jar with a tight-fitting lid.

1 Warm all the ingredients together in the
double boiler over a low heat until the lanolin
has liquefied (about 5-10 minutes).
2 Stir for several minutes, then pour the
mixture into the jar and allow to cool. Keep
in a cool, dark place.

Eucalyptus foot lotion

The feet are very often neglected when it comes
to moisturising, and the skin can easily become
cracked. Rubbed regularly into the heels and feet,
this lotion will soften the skin and prevent cracking.

INGREDIENTS
makes about 30ml (1fl oz)
- 1 tablespoon sweet almond oil
- 1 teaspoon avocado oil
- 1 teaspoon wheat germ oil
- 10 drops eucalyptus
  essential oil

Put all of the ingredients in a sterilised
glass bottle with a tight-fitting lid and shake
the liquid vigorously until it is completely
combined. Keep the bottle in a cool, dark
place. Shake well before using.

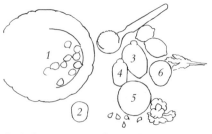

Give the body protection and nourishment with
these natural products: (1) Soothing Foot Bath,
(2) Lemon Hand Cream, (3) Quick-and-easy Hand
Lotion, (4) Eucalyptus Foot Lotion, (5) Leg Massage
Cream and (6) Gardener's Hand Cream.

Lemon hand cream

A fresh-smelling, soothing and smoothing cream to protect and help repair damaged skin.

INGREDIENTS

makes about 450ml (16fl oz)

- 1-2 tablespoons fresh or 1-2 teaspoons dried lemongrass
- 300ml (10fl oz) boiling water
- 40ml (1½fl oz) sweet almond oil
- 4 teaspoons avocado oil
- 1 teaspoon wheat germ oil
- 1 tablespoon beeswax
- 2 teaspoons lemon juice

You will need a heatproof ceramic or glass bowl, a fine sieve, two non-reactive saucepans, a non-reactive double boiler, a wooden spoon and two sterilised 250ml (9fl oz) glass jars with tight-fitting lids.

1 Put the lemongrass in the bowl and add the boiling water to make an infusion. Cover and allow to steep for 15 minutes.

2 Strain the water into one of the saucepans and heat to lukewarm. In the other saucepan, heat the oils to lukewarm.

3 In the double boiler, melt the beeswax completely over simmering water. Add the warmed oils, then, drop by drop, stir in 4 teaspoons of the warmed infusion.

4 Remove from the heat, add the lemon juice, and beat until thick and smooth.

5 Pour into the jars. Keep one handy for use and the other in the refrigerator until needed.

Moisturising body lotion

Soothe and repair dry, scaly skin with this easily prepared lotion. Shake well before use.

INGREDIENTS

makes about 125ml (4fl oz)

- 50ml (2fl oz) glycerin
- 50ml (2fl oz) rosewater
- 1 tablespoon sweet almond oil
- 1 teaspoon wheat germ oil
- 1 teaspoon jojoba oil

Put all the ingredients in a sterilised glass jar with a tight-fitting lid and shake vigorously until thoroughly mixed. Keep in a cool, dark place.

FOOT CARE

FOR ALL-DAY COMFORT it is important to take special care of your feet. Perspiration and hardened skin around the heels are both common problems. You can minimise the effects of these with a few easy steps:

TO DEODORISE SHOES, sprinkle a small amount of powdered chamomile inside them each day, brushing the powder out before wearing. Another trick is to fill a spare pair of socks with a mixture of coarsely crushed dried herbs and spices – any combination of rosemary, bay leaves, cinnamon sticks, whole cloves, orange peel, lemon peel, thyme, lavender and pine needles. Tie the socks at the top and leave them in the shoes between wearings. For a gift idea, fill a new pair of socks with the mixture and tie them with ribbons.

TO SOFTEN HARD SKIN around the soles of the feet or the backs of the heels, massage in equal quantities of olive oil and cider vinegar.

TREAT A FUNGAL INFECTION between the toes with applications of cider vinegar diluted with an equal amount of water over the affected area, or a fungicide made by diluting 2 drops tea tree essential oil with ½ teaspoon water.

For a quick foot treatment, if you haven't time for a separate foot bath, rub the feet with a mixture of cider vinegar and water in equal amounts, or 1-2 drops of rosemary essential oil in a teaspoon of vegetable oil, and massage into the feet for 5 minutes before taking your bath.

Gardener's hand cream

Apply this special cream after a day in the garden, before bedtime, and your hands will be cared for while you sleep. For added protection, rub some into your hands before working in the garden.

INGREDIENTS

makes about 350ml (12fl oz)

- 2 tablespoons avocado oil
- 1 tablespoon clear honey
- 2 teaspoons glycerin
- about 225g (8oz) finely ground almond or oatmeal

You will need a ceramic bowl, a spoon and a pair of cotton gloves.

1 Thoroughly mix the avocado oil, honey and glycerin in the bowl. Stir in sufficient almond or oatmeal to form a thin paste.

2 Rub the paste over the hands, then put on the gloves and leave them on overnight. The gloves can be washed and re-used.

Rose and honey body lotion

Apply this gentle lotion regularly to protect your skin and replace natural oils lost through bathing, swimming and exposure to the sun.

INGREDIENTS

makes about 250ml (9fl oz)

- 60-125g (2¼-4½oz) fresh or 1-2 teaspoons dried rose petals
- 300ml (10fl oz) boiling water
- 250ml (9fl oz) distilled or boiled water
- 1 teaspoon quince seeds
- 100ml (3½fl oz) sweet almond oil
- 2 teaspoons avocado oil
- 2 teaspoons wheat germ oil
- 1 teaspoon clear honey
- 5 drops geranium essential oil

As well as the above ingredients, you will also need a medium-sized heatproof ceramic or glass bowl, a fine sieve, a cup, a non-reactive saucepan, a stainless-steel spoon, a dessert bowl and a sterilised glass jar with a tight-fitting lid.

1 Place the rose petals in the medium-sized bowl and add the boiling water to make an infusion. Cover and leave for 15-20 minutes.

2 Strain the infusion into the cup.

3 Put the distilled or boiled water and the quince seeds into the saucepan. Bring slowly to the boil, then simmer over a moderate heat for about 15 minutes, stirring to prevent sticking. The mixture will thicken into a gel. Using the back of the spoon, push the gel through the sieve into the dessert bowl. The seeds can be dried and kept for future use.

4 In the saucepan, combine the infusion and the sweet almond, avocado and wheat germ oils. Warm over a low heat, then stir in the honey until combined. Remove from the heat and allow the mixture to cool.

5 Add 85ml (3fl oz) of the quince gel, then the geranium essential oil, 1 drop at a time. Finish by stirring the mixture until smooth.

6 Pour the body lotion into the jar and seal. Store in a cool, dark place.

Cellulite massage oil

Good diet and regular exercise are the first defence against cellulite, but an effective massage oil can also be beneficial. Regular massage with this oil may help increase circulation and break down fatty deposits.

INGREDIENTS
makes about 35ml (1¼fl oz)
- 30ml (1fl oz) sweet almond oil
- ¾ teaspoon jojoba oil
- ¾ teaspoon carrot oil
- 14 drops geranium essential oil
- 6 drops lemongrass essential oil
- 4 drops cypress essential oil

As well as the above ingredients, you will need a small sterilised glass jar with a tight-fitting lid.

1 Put all the ingredients in the jar, screw on the lid and shake vigorously to combine.

2 After a bath or shower, pat the skin dry and massage a small amount of the oil on cellulite-affected areas, using circular movements. Use ¼-½ teaspoon, depending on the size of the area you are treating. Apply once a day only and do not exceed the recommended amount. If using the oil regularly, you may choose to double the quantities in the recipe.

Herbal deodorant

This pleasant deodorant will control odour and inhibit the growth of some micro-organisms that thrive on perspiration. Choose from rosemary, thyme, lavender, sage, spearmint, eucalyptus leaves, marjoram and deeply scented rose petals.

INGREDIENTS
makes about 300ml (10fl oz)
- 100ml (3½fl oz) cider vinegar
- 100ml (3½fl oz) distilled or boiled water
- 3 tablespoons dried herbs or flower petals of choice
- 85ml (3fl oz) rosewater

You will need a heatproof ceramic or glass bowl, a non-reactive saucepan and a sterilised glass bottle with a tight-fitting lid.

1 Heat the cider vinegar and water in the saucepan to just below boiling.

2 Place the herbs or flower petals in the bowl and pour the heated liquid over them. Cover and leave to stand for 15-20 minutes.

3 Strain the liquid into the bottle, then add the rosewater. Shake to combine, then store in a cool, dark place. Use within a few days and make more as needed. When making more, vary the herbs to prevent bacteria developing a resistance to the deodorant.

Summer body splash

An invigorating body splash for those hot, humid days and nights of summer.

INGREDIENTS
makes about 600ml (1 pint)
- 100ml (3½fl oz) vodka
- 10 drops lavender essential oil
- 10 drops lime essential oil
- 5 drops lemon essential oil
- 5 drops lemongrass essential oil
- 500ml (18fl oz) distilled or boiled water

You will need a sterilised glass bottle with a tight-fitting lid (or a few smaller bottles), a ceramic or glass bowl and a paper coffee filter.

1 Put the vodka and essential oils into the bottle, seal and shake for several minutes.

2 Add the distilled or boiled water and shake for several minutes. Leave to stand for at least 48 hours (3 weeks for a better fragrance).

3 Drip through the paper filter into the bowl, then pour back into the bottle or into a few smaller sterilised bottles. Keep one bottle in the refrigerator and store the others in a cool, dark place until needed.

Quick-and-easy hand lotion

An old favourite valued by generations of women long before the advent of commercial cosmetics. Massage regularly into your hands.

INGREDIENTS
makes 250ml (9fl oz)
- 150ml (5fl oz) rosewater
- 100ml (3½fl oz) glycerin
- 1 drop yellow food colouring, optional

Pour all ingredients into a sterilised glass bottle with a tight-fitting lid and shake vigorously to combine. Keep the lotion in a cool, dark place.

PRACTICAL IDEAS
HAND-CARE HINTS

Wipe the hands with the cut flesh of a lemon to lighten skin discolorations. You can also remove dead skin cells by adding caster sugar to the lemon juice and rubbing this into the backs of the hands.

Massage a little avocado flesh into the hands and cuticles as a moisturiser to soften dryness.

When using rubber gloves for household chores, wear a pair of cotton gloves inside to keep hands dry.

To shine nails without using nail polish, dust with cornflour and polish vigorously with a chamois cloth.

Rub untidy cuticles with Lemon Hand Cream (page 282) then gently push back with a clean fingernail.

Eat lots of seafood, nuts, lean meat and raw fruit and vegetables to promote nail health.

Always file towards the centre of the nail, in one direction only. Use an emery board, not a metal file.

Bathtime Indulgences

*Sink into bliss as you spoil yourself with these delightfully scented bath salts,
bubble baths, soaps and scrubs. You know they're pure because you've made them yourself.
Presented in a pretty bottle, any of them would make a wonderful gift*

Almond-oatmeal body scrub

*This natural body scrub will remove dead skin
cells, improving skin colour and texture.*

INGREDIENTS
makes enough for 2 applications
- aloe vera leaves
- 2 tablespoons clear honey
- 2 drops geranium essential oil
- 2 drops palmarosa essential oil
- 150g (5½oz) ground almonds
- 150g (5½oz) ground oatmeal

You will need two ceramic or glass bowls, a
small stainless-steel spoon, and a sterilised glass
bottle with a tight-fitting lid.
1 Cut the aloe vera leaves in half lengthways
and scoop out 1-2 tablespoons of the clear gel
(the pigmented gel can be irritating) into one
bowl. Mix in the honey and essential oils.
2 Put the ground almonds and oatmeal in the
second bowl. Stir in the liquid, adding a little
water as required to make a thick paste.
3 Rub the scrub all over your body, paying
special attention to dry, scaling areas of skin.
Rinse off in the bath or shower, then apply
an aromatic body oil (see box, opposite page).
4 Put cling film over the leftover mixture
in the bowl and keep in the refrigerator.

Fragrant bath powder

*A delightfully aromatic powder to use after a
bath. Choose your favourite essential oil.*

INGREDIENTS
makes about 150g (5½oz)
- 75g (2¾oz) rice flour
- 75g (2¾oz) cornflour
- 5-10 drops essential oil

You will need a food processor or electric
blender (or a clean jar with a lid), a spoon
and a clean, dry container for storage.

1 Blend all the ingredients in the processor
or blender for 1 minute (or shake in a clean
covered jar for several minutes).
2 Leave the powder to settle. Spoon into a
clean, dry container and set the mixture aside
for 2 weeks before use.

Rose-scented bubble bath

*An aromatic bubble bath that is both nourishing
and softening to the skin. Shake well and add a
teaspoon to the water while the taps are running;
then lie back and relax.*

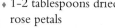

INGREDIENTS
makes about 700ml (1¼ pints)
- 1-2 tablespoons dried
  rose petals
- 1 litre (1¾ pints) boiling water
- 100g (3½oz) pure soap flakes
- 50ml (2fl oz) glycerin
- 2 teaspoons sweet almond oil
- 1 teaspoon wheat germ oil
- 1 teaspoon geranium
  essential oil
- 30ml (1fl oz) witch hazel
  lotion

You will need a heatproof ceramic or glass
bowl, a fine sieve, a non-reactive saucepan,
a stainless-steel spoon and one or more clean,
airtight plastic bottles.
1 Put the petals in the bowl and pour the
boiling water over them. Cover and leave for
15-20 minutes. Then strain into the saucepan.
2 Heat the water over a medium heat; add the
soap flakes and stir until they dissolve.
3 Put the glycerin, oils, essential oil and witch
hazel lotion into the bowl and mix well. Add
the soap mixture and stir well.
4 Pour into small bottles. Keep one in the
bathroom for immediate use and the others
in a cool, dark place until needed.

Bubble bath for kids

*Wash away grime and make bathtime fun
with this fresh bubble bath. Shake, then add
3 tablespoons as the taps are running.*

INGREDIENTS
makes about 600ml (1 pint)
- 2 tablespoons dried
  rose petals
- 2 tablespoons dried
  lavender flowerheads
- 300ml (10fl oz) boiling water
- 300ml (10fl oz) natural
  baby shampoo
- 12 drops lavender
  essential oil

You will need two bowls, a fine sieve, and
one or more clean, airtight plastic bottles.
1 Put the rose petals and lavender into one
bowl and add the boiling water. Cover and
leave for 15-20 minutes.
2 Strain into the other bowl, squeezing out
all liquid. Add the shampoo and essential oil.
3 Pour into bottles and shake for several
minutes. Keep in the bathroom, and put
any extra bottles in a cool, dark place.

Rosemary shower gel

*For a gentle cleansing and softening effect, rub
this gel all over your body while showering.*

INGREDIENTS
makes about 150ml (5fl oz)
- 4-6 teaspoons dried
  lavender flowerheads
- 4-6 teaspoons dried rosemary
- 4-6 teaspoons dried
  chamomile
- 1 litre (1¾ pints) boiling water
- 125g (4½oz) pure soap flakes
- 10-20 drops lavender
  essential oil

You will need a non-reactive saucepan, two heatproof ceramic or glass bowls, a fine sieve, a wooden spoon, a potato masher (optional) and two or three clean wide-mouthed plastic bottles with tight-fitting lids.

1 Put the lavender, rosemary and chamomile into one bowl and add 500ml (18fl oz) of the boiling water to make an infusion. Cover and leave for 15-20 minutes. Strain into the second bowl, squeezing all liquid from the herbs.

2 Put the soap flakes and the rest of the water into the saucepan. Stir constantly over a low heat to dissolve the soap flakes (use a potato masher if necessary); keep below simmering point. Add the infusion and stir until well blended. Remove from the heat.

3 When the mixture has started to cool, stir in the lavender essential oil, a drop at a time, until sufficiently scented. Pour into the bottles and leave until a soft gel has formed. Keep one bottle handy to the shower and the others in a cool, dark place until needed.

Almond-rose soap

Use this fragrant soap to clean the skin gently and remove dead cells from its surface.

INGREDIENTS

makes 6 soap cakes
- 6 teaspoons dried red rose petals
- 250g (9oz) pure soap flakes
- 165ml (5½fl oz) boiling water
- 8 tablespoons rosewater
- 6 teaspoons ground almonds
- 9 drops geranium essential oil

You will need a pestle and mortar, a large basin, a wooden spoon and waxed paper.

1 Pound the petals with a pestle and mortar.

2 Place the petals and soap flakes in the basin and make a well in the centre. Add the boiling water and stir until the mixture is smooth (if the soap starts to solidify, place the basin over near-boiling water). Stir in the rosewater and ground almonds, then leave to cool.

3 Mix in the essential oil. Shape into six balls and flatten them slightly; leave them to set hard between sheets of waxed paper. Keep unused soap in a cool, dark place until needed.

Relaxing bath salts

Add two handfuls of these salts to the bath.

INGREDIENTS

makes enough for about 5 baths
- 500g (1lb 2oz) bicarbonate of soda
- 15g (½oz) dried lavender or rose petals
- 8 drops lavender essential oil
- 8 drops geranium essential oil

Collect a ceramic bowl, a wooden spoon and a sterilised glass jar with a tight-fitting lid.

1 Put the bicarbonate of soda and dried petals into the bowl, add the essential oils and mix thoroughly with the spoon to combine.

2 Pour the salts into the jar and keep in a cool, dark place, handy to the bath.

Invigorating bath salts

Use these salts to refresh your body and lift your spirits after a long, hard day.

INGREDIENTS

- 500g (1lb 2oz) bicarbonate of soda
- 8 drops rosemary essential oil
- 4 drops rosewood essential oil
- 4 drops tangerine essential oil

Follow the directions for preparing and storing Relaxing Bath Salts (left).

AROMATIC BODY OILS

USED REGULARLY after a bath or shower, body oils moisturise the skin and keep it feeling and looking great. Choose the oil blend suited to your skin from the list on the right.

Put the ingredients in a small sterilised glass jar and shake the mixture well. Pour a little oil into your palm, rub the hands together and apply. Use firm circular movements on the chest, stomach and buttocks, and firm upward strokes on the arms and legs.

Each blend is sufficient for four complete body applications. Store in a cool, dark place.

To 4 teaspoons of almond oil, add your choice of essential oils from the following list.

NORMAL SKIN
8 DROPS LAVENDER
6 DROPS GERANIUM
4 DROPS NEROLI
2 DROPS CHAMOMILE

DRY SKIN
8 DROPS PATCHOULI
6 DROPS PALMAROSA
4 DROPS GERANIUM
2 DROPS CARROT

OILY SKIN
10 DROPS LEMON
6 DROPS GERANIUM
4 DROPS SANDALWOOD

SENSITIVE SKIN
15 DROPS PALMAROSA
3 DROPS GERANIUM
2 DROPS PATCHOULI

A Pampered Face

The range of natural possibilities seems endless when it comes to facial care.
There's a recipe here to suit every skin type and meet every skin-care need — all free of
the chemicals and preservatives that can lead to allergies

Rose moisturising cream

Here is an everyday moisturiser that is especially good for dry or sensitive skin.

INGREDIENTS
makes about 175g (6oz)
- 2 tablespoons rosewater
- 125ml (4fl oz) sweet almond oil
- 10g (¼oz) beeswax, finely chopped
- 25g (1oz) lanolin
- a 400 IU vitamin E capsule
- 4 drops geranium essential oil
- 2 drops red food colouring

You will need a non-reactive saucepan, a double boiler, a wooden spoon and a sterilised, wide-mouthed glass jar with a tight-fitting lid.
1 Warm the rosewater in the saucepan.
2 In the double boiler, gently warm the almond oil, then add the beeswax and lanolin, stirring continuously until melted. Remove from the heat and stir until combined.
3 Add the warmed rosewater, drop by drop, and beat until the mixture is cool and smooth.
4 Add the contents of the vitamin E capsule; then add the geranium essential oil and food colouring, and stir well to combine.
5 Spoon into jar. Store in a cool, dark place.

MOISTURISING YOUR SKIN

Use light, gentle strokes of the hand when applying moisturising preparations — don't drag on the skin. Smooth on, then after about 15 minutes blot off any lotion or cream that hasn't been absorbed.

Excess creams and lotions should be removed with a soft piece of sterile cloth or a pad of cotton wool. Dab it off; do not pull and stretch the skin.

Cleansing milk

Suitable for regular use, this gentle cleanser will remove all traces of oil and make-up.

INGREDIENTS
makes about 50ml (2fl oz)
- 150ml (5fl oz) buttermilk
- 1 tablespoon each dried elder flowers and lime flowers
- 1 teaspoon dried chamomile
- 1 tablespoon honey

You will need a non-reactive saucepan, a spoon, a fine sieve and a sterilised glass bottle with a tight-fitting lid.
1 Bring the milk and dried ingredients to a simmer. Leave on a low heat for 30 minutes.
2 Remove from the heat, stir in the honey and allow the mixture to cool.
3 Strain into a bottle and keep in a cool, dark place. Use within 7 days. Shake before use.

Everyday facial moisturiser

This moisturiser will replace natural oils lost through cleansing and toning. Choose essential oils to suit your skin type (see box, page 289): normal – 20 drops geranium, 6 drops lavender, 2 drops lemon, 2 drops neroli; dry – 14 drops palmarosa, 6 drops neroli, 6 drops sandalwood, 4 drops geranium; oily – 16 drops geranium, 10 drops lemon, 4 drops juniper; sensitive – 6 drops lavender, 4 drops neroli.

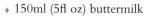

INGREDIENTS
makes about 50ml (2fl oz)
- 40ml (1½fl oz) sweet almond oil
- 1 teaspoon jojoba oil
- 1 teaspoon wheat germ oil
- essential oils

Place all the ingredients in a sterilised glass jar with a tight-fitting lid and shake well. Store in a cool, dark place and use within 2 months.

Galen's cold cream

The original cold cream recipe is believed to have been invented by the Greek doctor and philosopher Galen in the 2nd century AD.

INGREDIENTS
makes about 150g (5½oz)
- 35g (1¼oz) beeswax
- 100ml (3½fl oz) light olive oil
- 2 tablespoons distilled water or rosewater
- 3 drops geranium essential oil

You will need a non-reactive double boiler, a non-reactive saucepan, a wooden spoon and a wide-mouthed jar with a tight-fitting lid.
1 Melt the beeswax in the double boiler. In the saucepan, heat the oil slightly, then pour it into the melted wax and beat until combined.
2 In the saucepan, heat the water or rosewater, then stir it, drop by drop, into the oil and wax mixture. Remove from the heat and stir until the mixture is cool and thick. Stir in the geranium essential oil.
3 Spoon the cold cream into the jar and keep in a cool, dark place.

Ideal face cleanser

This cleanser is beautifully scented and is beneficial for all skin types.

INGREDIENTS
makes about 100ml (3½fl oz)
- 65ml (2¼fl oz) sweet almond oil
- 2 tablespoons sesame oil
- 2 teaspoons wheat germ oil
- 4 drops lavender essential oil
- 1 drop geranium essential oil

Place all the ingredients in a sterilised glass bottle with a tight-fitting lid and shake for several minutes. Store in a cool, dark place.

NATURAL FACIAL CARE

If skin tends to be oily, add a few drops of lemon juice to cleansing creams and lotions.

Keep an aloe vera plant on hand. Smooth the gel from the leaves onto the face to refresh the skin.

To make a gentle liquid face cleanser, cover 20g (¾oz) crushed soapwort root with 1 litre boiling water and leave for an hour before straining and bottling.

Crush petals of calendula until they are juicy and rub gently onto irritated areas of skin to relieve irritation and promote healing.

If using soap on the face, choose a gentle one containing natural oils. Follow with a herbal toner to remove all traces of the soap.

Brush the skin regularly with a soft cosmetic brush designed especially for the face, to stimulate the circulation and remove dead skin.

If your eyes are sensitive to mascara, a small amount of petroleum jelly applied to the lashes with a fingertip gives them the appearance of thickness.

To reduce puffiness under the eyes, soak a couple of tea bags in boiling water for a moment, let cool, and then place over the eyes for 10-15 minutes.

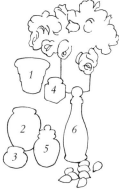

Use these preparations to give your face a fresh and healthy glow: (1) Galen's Cold Cream, (2) Rose Moisturising Cream, (3) Anti-wrinkle Eye Cream, (4) Peppermint Moisturising Lotion, (5) Basic Skin Toner and (6) Cleansing Milk.

Anti-wrinkle eye cream

Avoiding the eye itself, gently apply this cream around the eye area with small, circular strokes.

INGREDIENTS
makes about 175ml (6fl oz)
- 2 tablespoons elderflower water
- 4 tablespoons avocado oil
- 2 tablespoons sweet almond oil
- 4 teaspoons wheat germ oil
- 2 tablspoons lanolin
- 2 teaspoons glycerin
- 2 drops geranium essential oil
- a 400 IU vitamin E capsule

You will need a non-reactive saucepan, a non-reactive double boiler, a wooden spoon and a sterilised, wide-mouthed 175ml (6fl oz) glass jar with a tight-fitting lid.

1 Warm the elderflower water in the pan.

2 Gently warm the three oils in the double boiler. Stir in the lanolin until melted, then remove from the heat. Gradually beat in the warmed elderflower water.

3 Stir in the glycerin, essential oil and the contents of the vitamin E capsule. Spoon into the jar and store in a cool, dark place.

Treatment for large pores

Try this simple but effective herbal treatment to tighten large pores. After cleansing the face, gently dab the ointment onto the skin with cotton wool. Use morning and night as needed.

INGREDIENTS
makes about 300ml (10fl oz)
- 1 teaspoon dried sage leaves
- 1 teaspoon dried yarrow leaves
- 1 teaspoon dried witch hazel
- 300ml (10fl oz) boiling water

You will need a small bowl, a fine sieve and a sterilised glass bottle with a tight-fitting lid.

1 Place all the dry ingredients in the bowl and add the boiling water. Cover and allow to steep for 15 minutes.

2 Strain into the bottle and store in a cool, dark place. Use within 7 days, checking daily to ensure that it hasn't deteriorated.

Peppermint moisturising lotion

Moisturising lotions are more easily absorbed than creams because they contain more water. The peppermint gives this lotion a refreshing aroma.

INGREDIENTS
makes about 175ml (6fl oz)
- 1 teaspoon dried peppermint
- 200ml (7fl oz) boiling water
- 90ml (3¼fl oz) sweet almond or vegetable oil
- 25g (1oz) beeswax, chopped
- 2 drops peppermint essential oil
- 1 drop green food colouring

You will need two cups, a fine sieve, a non-reactive double boiler, a wooden spoon and a sterilised, wide-mouthed 175ml (6fl oz) glass jar with a tight-fitting lid.

1 Place the dried peppermint in one cup and add the boiling water. Cover and leave for 15 minutes. Strain into the other cup.

2 Slowly warm the almond or vegetable oil in the double boiler. Add the beeswax and stir until completely melted.

3 Remove from the heat and gradually add about 60ml (2¼fl oz) of the infusion, beating continuously until well combined. Stir in the essential oil and food colouring.

4 Pour the mixture into the jar and store in a cool, dark place. Apply sparingly, massaging in gently with small, circular strokes.

Rich neck moisturiser

The neck is often neglected in everyday skin care yet it can show the first signs of ageing. This recipe has oils that will keep the skin supple. Massage in a small amount, from the collarbone up to the chin, at least once a day.

INGREDIENTS
makes about 175ml (6fl oz)
- 1 teaspoon dried chamomile
- 200ml (7fl oz) boiling water
- 50ml (2fl oz) avocado oil
- 50ml (2fl oz) sweet almond oil
- 2 teaspoons jojoba oil
- 25g (1oz) beeswax
- 2 teaspoons glycerin
- 20 drops lemon essential oil

You will need two cups, a fine sieve, a non-reactive saucepan, a non-reactive double boiler, a wooden spoon and a sterilised, wide-mouthed glass jar with a tight-fitting lid.

1 Place the chamomile in the cup and add the boiling water to make an infusion. Cover and leave for 15 minutes. Strain into the other cup.

2 In the double boiler, gently warm the three oils. Add the beeswax and stir until melted.

3 Remove from the heat and beat in 2 tablespoons of the infusion, drop by drop, until the mixture thickens and cools. Mix in the glycerin and the essential oil thoroughly.

4 Spoon into a jar. Keep in a cool, dark place.

APPLYING FACE CREAM

1 *Press the fingers of both hands into the centre of the forehead and work the cream slowly outwards. Pat a little cream gently around the eyes.*

2 *Work the cream in evenly around the jawline, chin and mouth with the middle fingers of both hands, using small, firm circular movements.*

3 *Massage the cream over the throat with alternating hands. Use upward strokes, starting from the collarbone and moving up to the chin.*

Basic skin toner

This toner will stimulate circulation, reduce oiliness and refine the pores. Choose from these essential oils to suit your skin type (see box, right): normal – neroli, geranium, lavender or palmarosa; dry – neroli, patchouli, sandalwood or geranium; oily – rosemary, lavender, lemon or geranium; sensitive – neroli or lavender.

INGREDIENTS
makes about 100ml (3½fl oz)
- 1 teaspoon dried chamomile
- 100ml (3½fl oz) boiling water
- 2 drops essential oil

You will need a cup, a fine sieve, a sterilised 100ml (3½fl oz) glass bottle with a tight-fitting lid, and a paper coffee filter.

1 Place the chamomile and boiling water in the cup. Cover and leave for 15 minutes.
2 Strain through the sieve into the bottle. When cool, add the essential oil and shake well to mix. Allow to stand for 48 hours, shaking periodically.
3 Drip through the paper filter into the cup. Re-sterilise the bottle and fill. Seal and keep in a cool, dark place until needed.

Scented vinegar toner

Diluted vinegar is an effective toner that also helps protect the skin from infections. As it evaporates it cools and refreshes the skin. Choose herbs or flower petals to suit your skin type (see box, right): normal – chamomile, lemon balm, spearmint or rose; dry – violet, rose, jasmine or borage; oily – lavender, peppermint, rosemary or marigold; sensitive – borage, violet or parsley.

INGREDIENTS
makes about 100ml (3½fl oz)
- 1 teaspoon dried or 3 teaspoons fresh herbs or flower petals
- 100ml (3½fl oz) cider vinegar

You will need two sterilised bottles with tight-fitting lids, a fine sieve and a bowl.

1 Place the herbs or flower petals best suited to your skin type in one of the bottles and cover with the vinegar. Seal and leave for 10 days until the vinegar is perfumed.

2 Strain the vinegar into the bowl, then pour it into the second bottle. (If you want a stronger fragrance, add fresh herbs or petals and leave for a further 10 days, then strain.) Keep in a cool, dark place.
3 To use, dilute 1 tablespoon of the scented vinegar in 125ml (4fl oz) distilled or boiled water and splash gently on the face as required.

Lip gloss in a tube

Lip gloss protects the lips from cracking and drying. It can be used on its own or over lipstick, in which case it helps extend the life of the lipstick. This recipe shows you a good way to recycle those used lipstick holders that are usually thrown away.

INGREDIENTS
- 2 teaspoons finely chopped or grated beeswax
- 1 teaspoon jojoba oil
- 1 teaspoon liquid paraffin
- a 200 IU vitamin E capsule
- 3 drops geranium essential oil

You will need a used lipstick holder, non-stick baking paper, kitchen paper, a small white cup, a saucepan and a thin skewer for stirring.

1 Remove any lipstick residue from the holder – put the residue aside for possible use (see 'Variations', below). Using a piece of kitchen paper, wipe the tube until clean.
2 Screw down the end of the holder until the small plastic insert that holds the lipstick is at the bottom. Form a 6cm (2½in) square piece of baking paper into a tube and insert into the holder until it touches the bottom. Insert a finger to ensure that it maintains its shape.
3 Place the cup in the saucepan. Pour water into the saucepan so that it comes partially up the side of the cup. Place the beeswax, jojoba oil and liquid paraffin in the cup. Gently heat until the beeswax has melted. Remove the cup from the water and allow the mixture to cool a little, stirring constantly.
4 Add the essential oil and the contents of the vitamin E capsule and stir until combined.
5 Carefully pour into the holder. Leave in a cool place until the gloss has set.
6 Screw the gloss stick up and carefully take off the baking paper (if the stick lifts off, pour

a little melted gloss onto the insert then quickly replace the stick). Test the texture of the gloss. If too soft, remelt and add a little more beeswax. If too hard, remelt and add a little more jojoba oil. You will then need to repeat the baking paper process.

VARIATIONS To colour the gloss, use some of the residue lipstick, an amount about the size of two peas. Add after the beeswax has melted in step 3. Stir until the lipstick has melted and the mixture is evenly coloured.

To give your lip gloss flavour, replace the geranium essential oil with a drop of clove or cinnamon essential oil. Alternatively, add 5-10 drops of one of the flavoured culinary oils available from health-food shops and gourmet suppliers. Some of the flavour choices include lemon, lime and orange, and even black and white truffle. Add at step 4.

Green herb steam facial

Choose herbs to suit your skin (see box, page 289): normal – lemon balm, spearmint, chamomile; dry – parsley, violets, rose petals; oily – peppermint, sage, lavender. Do not use on sensitive or inflamed skin.

INGREDIENTS
- 2 handfuls herbs or flowers
- 1.5 litres (2¾ pints) boiling water

You will need a large bowl and a thick towel.

1 Coarsely chop the herbs or flowers and place them in the bowl. Add the boiling water.

2 Lean over the bowl and cover your head and the bowl with the towel. With your eyes closed, remain under the towel for 10 minutes.

3 To finish, splash with lukewarm then cool water. Keep out of the sun for an hour or so.

Honey-almond face scrub

Good also for areas such as elbows, legs and hands.

INGREDIENTS
makes enough for one or two applications
- 1 tablespoon honey
- 2 tablespoons ground almonds
- 1 drop geranium essential oil

You will need a cup, a bowl and a small stainless-steel spoon.

1 Place the cup in a saucepan of hot water. Warm the honey in the cup. (Alternatively, warm the honey in a cup in the microwave.)

2 Place the almonds in the bowl, then stir in sufficient warmed honey to make a spreadable paste. Stir in the essential oil.

3 To apply, first rinse your face with tepid water, then carefully massage in the scrub, paying attention to any flaky skin. Keep any leftover mixture in the refrigerator, covered with cling film, until you wish to use it again.

Lip balm

Lips often react quickly to extreme forms of weather. This balm will soothe and soften lips affected by too much sun or cold winds.

INGREDIENTS
makes about 60ml (2¼fl oz)
- aloe vera leaves
- 2 teaspoons distilled water
- 2 tablespoons hazelnut oil
- 1 teaspoon jojoba oil
- 1 teaspoon wheat germ oil
- 1 teaspoon beeswax, finely chopped
- ¾ teaspoon anhydrous lanolin
- 2 drops lavender essential oil
- 2 drops sandalwood essential oil

You will need a non-reactive saucepan, a heatproof ceramic or glass bowl, a small stainless-steel spoon and a sterilised glass jar with a tight-fitting lid.

1 Cut the aloe vera leaves in half lengthways and scoop out 2 teaspoons of gel into the saucepan. Add the distilled water and the hazelnut, jojoba and wheat germ oils, then warm over a low heat.

2 In a bowl sitting in hot water, melt the beeswax and anhydrous lanolin until they are completely liquefied. Stir in the oil/aloe mixture and mix well until combined.

3 Remove the bowl from the water and allow the mixture to cool slightly. Stir in the essential oils and beat until cool.

4 Spoon the balm into the sterilised jar and store in a cool place.

REFRIGERATOR FACIALS

SOME OF THE BEST cosmetics can be found in the refrigerator. For example, roll an avocado stone around in your hands, then massage the residue into the face and hands to leave them supple. A teaspoon of mayonnaise gently massaged into the face will do the same.

Blend a few cabbage leaves in a food processor and strain to collect the juice. Use on oily skin to cleanse and tighten the pores. Or mash very soft pears and apply to the face to clear oily skin.

Watermelon juice is another effective cleanser and pore tightener. Strain, to remove pulp and seeds, then pat the juice all over the face.

Fresh corn kernels, blended with the corn silks to produce a milky slush, are a skin soother. Strawberries will also soothe the skin – mash two and apply to the face.

Wipe some cut pieces of cucumber or halved grapes over your face for a pleasant, refreshing feel. Or process some cucumber in a blender and use the juice as a skin cleanser.

To soften the skin, apply a small amount of mashed papaya to the face and leave for a few minutes only, then wash off. This is not suitable for sensitive or problem skin.

Face Masks

Whether you wish to tighten pores or simply to refine the skin, there is a natural product that will work wonders for you. Follow our directions and these masks will, over time, give you a glowing complexion. Each recipe makes one mask

Strawberry yoghurt mask

Strawberry and yoghurt have long been used for bleaching and refining the skin.

INGREDIENTS
- 1 handful ripe strawberries
- 1 tablespoon ground almonds
- 2 tablespoons natural yoghurt

In a bowl, mash the strawberries and almond meal until completely blended together. Stir in the yoghurt to make a spreadable paste, then apply as directed in the box on this page.

Fresh herb mask

Refreshing and invigorating, this face mask is especially beneficial for oily skin.

INGREDIENTS
- 1 tablespoon fresh chopped peppermint
- 1 tablespoon fresh chopped cabbage leaves
- 1 tablespoon apple juice
- 1 tablespoon ground almonds
- 1 egg white

You will need a pestle and mortar, a fine sieve, a cup and a spoon.

1 Place the peppermint, cabbage and apple juice in the mortar and use the pestle to pound to a paste. Strain off excess juice into the cup and put aside for later.

2 Add the ground almonds and egg white to the paste and beat to combine, then apply according to directions in the box on this page.

3 After removing the mask, tone the skin with the excess juice diluted with a little boiled water, or refrigerate and use within two days.

VARIATION Similar masks will suit other skin types. For normal skin, substitute lemon balm and cucumber for the peppermint and cabbage.

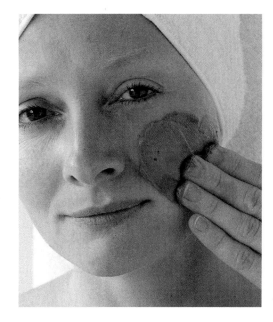

For dry skin, substitute calendula flowers and finely grated carrot for the peppermint and cabbage, and egg yolk for the egg white.

Aloe and honey mask

This combination of aloe and honey is just right for soothing and nourishing dry skin.

INGREDIENTS
- aloe vera leaves
- 1 egg yolk
- 1 teaspoon warmed honey
- about 3 teaspoons powdered milk

Cut the aloe vera leaves in half lengthways and scoop out 1 teaspoon of the gel into a cup. Add the egg yolk and honey and beat with a spoon. Add sufficient powdered milk to make a thinly spreadable paste, then apply as directed in the box on the right.

Green clay mask

Clay masks leave skin feeling pleasantly firm and smooth. While green clay suits all skin types, if you have oily skin substitute the honey for brown clay and 1 teaspoon egg white for an even better result. Do not apply a clay mask more than once a week.

INGREDIENTS
- 1 teaspoon honey
- 2 tablespoons green clay powder
- 1-2 tablespoons warm water

In a bowl, mix the honey into the clay with a spoon and add sufficient water to make a spreadable paste, then apply as directed below.

APPLYING A MASK

FACE MASKS have been used for centuries to cleanse and tone the skin. Used regularly, they leave the skin glowing with vitality.

Cover the shoulders with a clean towel. Place a towel on the area where you will lie down once the mask is on. Make sure you have a damp towel or face flannel available to wipe any areas the mask may drip onto.

Use cotton wool or your fingers to spread the mask, covering the skin up to the hairline and down to the chin, avoiding the area immediately around the eyes. Leave it on for 15 minutes (you can gradually increase the duration of future applications to up to 30 minutes, depending on sensitivity of the skin and effectiveness of the mask).

Next, use your fingers to remove as much of the mask as possible. If it has dried, splash the face with warm water, then remove with your fingers. Use a wet face flannel, if needed, to clean away the remainder. To finish, splash the face with running water and apply a toner.

❖ A Winning Smile ❖

Ensure a fresh-tasting mouth and white,
healthy-looking teeth with these preparations, all of which are
made from purely natural ingredients

Cinnamon mint tooth powder

Peppermint and cinnamon essential oils both help
in relieving the discomfort of sensitive or aching
teeth. Dip a toothbrush into the powder, wet the
brush slightly, and clean the teeth, paying particular
attention to chewing surfaces and the gum line.

INGREDIENTS

makes about 300g (10½oz)
- 200g (7oz) calcium carbonate
  (from chemists)
- 70g (2½oz) bicarbonate of soda
- 1 teaspoon salt
- 25 drops peppermint
  essential oil
- 12 drops cinnamon essential oil

You will need a food processor or blender, a
spoon and a sterilised, wide-mouthed 300g
(10½oz) glass jar with a tight-fitting lid.
1 Place all the ingredients in the processor or
blender and blend for 1 minute to combine
well. Leave the powder to settle.
2 Spoon the powder into the jar and keep in
the bathroom cupboard. It lasts well if the lid is
always replaced after use.

Citrus antiseptic mouthwash

Use this refreshing mouthwash to help fight bacteria.
Dilute it and rinse the mouth, or gargle after you
brush your teeth. Do not swallow the liquid.

INGREDIENTS

makes about 500ml (18fl oz)
- 200ml (7fl oz) vodka
- 30 drops lemon
  essential oil
- 25 drops bergamot
  essential oil
- 300ml (10oz) distilled water

You will need a sterilised 500ml (18fl oz) glass
bottle with a tight-fitting lid.

1 Place the vodka and essential oils in the
bottle and shake vigorously to combine.
2 Add the distilled water and shake until well
mixed. Leave for a week to mature, shaking
from time to time.
3 To use, shake the bottle and mix 1 part of
the mixture to 3 parts lukewarm distilled water
in a small tumbler to rinse around your mouth.

Minty-fresh toothpaste

This natural toothpaste is easy to make and a pleasure
to use for adults and children alike. If you want the
toothpaste to look as 'minty' as it tastes, you can use
a drop or two of green food colouring.

INGREDIENTS

makes about 150g (5½oz)
- 100g (3½oz) calcium
  carbonate (from chemists)
- 50g (1¾oz) bicarbonate
  of soda
- 1 teaspoon salt
- about 7 tablespoons
  glycerin
- 3 or 4 drops peppermint
  essential oil
- 2 drops green food
  colouring, optional

You will need a small ceramic or glass bowl,
a spoon and a sterilised, wide-mouthed glass
jar with a tight-fitting lid.
1 Place the calcium carbonate, bicarbonate of
soda and salt in the bowl and stir in sufficient
glycerin to make a thick paste.
2 Stir well, then add the peppermint essential
oil, drop by drop, until the paste is pleasantly
flavoured. Add the green food colouring at
this stage, if desired.
3 Spoon the paste into the jar and keep in
the bathroom cupboard. Make sure that the
lid is always replaced after use.

Herbal mouthwash

The herbs in this mouthwash will keep your breath sweet and your mouth feeling fresh and clean. It can also be used as a soothing gargle.

INGREDIENTS

makes about 300ml (10fl oz)

- 1 teaspoon dried sage
- 1 teaspoon dried rosemary
- 1 teaspoon dried peppermint
- 250ml (9fl oz) boiling water
- 60ml (2¼fl oz) cider vinegar

You will also need two bowls, a fine sieve, a paper coffee filter and a sterilised glass bottle with a tight-fitting lid.

1 Place the herbs in one bowl and add boiling water. Cover and leave for 15-20 minutes.

2 Strain through the sieve into the second bowl, discarding the herbs.

3 Drip through the paper filter into the bottle. Add the vinegar and shake. Store in a cool, dark place and use within a few days, shaking the bottle well before use.

PRACTICAL IDEAS

REFRESH YOUR MOUTH

Rub two or three fresh sage leaves over the teeth regularly to whiten and clean them.

The oil from cashew nuts has been shown to fight tooth decay. Chew some cashews after a meal to help prevent the production of plaque acids.

Clean teeth and fresh breath can easily be achieved with homemade products: (1) Cinnamon Mint Tooth Powder, (2) Citrus Antiseptic Mouthwash, (3) Lip Balm, see page 290, (4) Minty-fresh Toothpaste and (5) Herbal Mouthwash.

◆ Especially for Men ◆

Homemade products can be strikingly successful in meeting men's special skin-care requirements. The soothing properties of these herbal components are perfect for their specialised needs, such as preparing skin for the razor and calming aftershave irritation

Tangy body cologne

Pat on this invigorating body lotion to refresh the skin and revive the spirits.

INGREDIENTS
makes about 500ml (18fl oz)
- 250ml (9fl oz) vodka
- 10 drops lime essential oil
- 10 drops lavender essential oil
- 5 drops lemon essential oil
- 3 drops lemongrass essential oil
- 250ml (9fl oz) distilled water

You will need a sterilised 500ml (18fl oz) glass bottle with a tight-fitting lid.

1 Pour the vodka and essential oils into the bottle and shake well to disperse the oils. Leave to mature for 4 weeks.

2 Add the distilled water to the bottle and shake for several minutes. Leave to mature for a further 2 weeks, shaking periodically.

3 Store in a cool, dark place. Shake the cologne well before use.

Fragrant shaving soap

Rinse the face, then lather with this gentle soap.

INGREDIENTS
makes about 200g (7oz)
- 160ml (5½fl oz) rosewater
- 125g (4½oz) pure soap flakes
- 4 drops rosemary essential oil
- 3 drops lemon essential oil
- 2 drops bay essential oil
- 1 drop sage essential oil

You will need a non-reactive saucepan, a non-reactive double boiler, a wooden spoon, a potato masher (optional) and a sterilised, shallow glass jar with a tight-fitting lid.

1 Warm the rosewater in the saucepan.

2 Place the soap flakes in the double boiler, add the warmed rosewater and stir to moisten.

To keep the skin in good condition, and make shaving easy, use these simple preparations: Oatmeal Body Scrub (left), Fragrant Shaving Soap (centre), Aftershave Splash (right).

At a gentle simmer, stir the soap until it has melted to a smooth gel (if necessary, use a potato masher to help dissolve the soap). Remove from the heat and cool to lukewarm.

3 Stir in the essential oils and spoon the soap into the jar. Leave to harden for 3-5 days. Keep handy in a cool, dark place.

Aftershave splash

Delightfully aromatic, this mildly antiseptic lotion can be used as a refreshing aftershave or to protect the skin before using an electric shaver. Simply dab it on with a piece of cotton wool before using the shaver.

INGREDIENTS
makes about 200ml (7fl oz)
- 75ml (2½fl oz) orange flower water
- 75ml (2½fl oz) cider vinegar
- 50ml (2fl oz) witch hazel lotion
- 18 drops bergamot essential oil
- 18 drops lemon essential oil
- 6 drops neroli essential oil

Put all ingredients into a sterilised glass bottle with a tight-fitting lid and shake well. Leave to mature for several days, shaking each day. Store in a cool, dark place. Shake before using.

Oatmeal body scrub

Removes dead skin cells to give the skin a smooth texture and natural colour.

INGREDIENTS
makes enough for 1 application
- 1 handful brown lentils
- 1 handful coarse rolled oats
- ½ teaspoon carrot oil
- ½ teaspoon jojoba oil

You will need an electric blender, a spoon and a small bowl.

1 Reduce the lentils to a coarse powder in the blender. Add the rolled oats and blend to a powder, then add the oils and blend again. Blend with water, a little at a time, until the mixture becomes a thick paste.

2 Spoon the mixture into the bowl. Massage the scrub all over the body before a shower or bath, paying particular attention to dry areas.

Shaving cut lotion

A little razor nick need not cause discomfort. Dab a drop of this lotion on the cut to help stop the bleeding and prevent infection.

INGREDIENTS
makes about 4 teaspoons
- 4 teaspoons witch hazel lotion
- 13 drops lavender essential oil
- 7 drops geranium essential oil

Put all the ingredients into a small sterilised glass bottle with a tight-fitting lid and shake well to combine. Keep in a cool, dark place. Shake well before using.

Pre-shave moisturiser

Shaving can be made so much easier and more effective with a little preparation. To soften bristles and avoid razor cuts, massage in this moisturiser.

INGREDIENTS
makes about 120g (4¼oz)
- 40ml (1½fl oz) orange flower water
- 2 teaspoons beeswax
- 1 teaspoon anhydrous lanolin
- 60ml (2¼fl oz) sweet almond oil
- 1 teaspoon wheat germ oil
- 12 drops lemon juice
- 6 drops bergamot essential oil

You will need a cup, a ceramic or glass bowl, a non-reactive double boiler, a wooden spoon and a sterilised glass jar with a tight-fitting lid.

1 Warm the orange flower water in a cup sitting in hot water.

2 Melt the beeswax, lanolin, almond oil and wheat germ oil in the double boiler. Stir in the warmed orange flower water. Remove from the heat and stir well.

3 When the mixture has cooled, stir in the lemon juice and the bergamot essential oil. Beat until it becomes creamy.

4 Pour the moisturiser into the jar and keep handy in the bathroom in a cool, dark place.

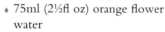

✦ Hair-care Secrets ✦

*For glossy, healthy hair, free from dandruff and split ends, you can't beat natural
substances such as honey, chamomile, lavender and rosemary. These shampoos and treatments
can be used on any type of hair every day, if you wish, with complete safety*

Chamomile shampoo

*Chamomile makes a mild shampoo that is gentle
to the hair. About one large spoonful is sufficient for
one wash. Use leftover pieces of pure soap instead
of soap flakes if you prefer.*

INGREDIENTS

makes about 400ml (14fl oz)
- 1 handful fresh or dried
  chamomile flowers
- 300ml (10fl oz) boiling water
- 50g (1¾oz) pure soap flakes
- 1 tablespoon glycerin
- 5 drops yellow
  food colouring

You will need two heatproof bowls, a wooden
spoon, a sieve and a clean airtight bottle.
1 Place the flowers and boiling water in
one bowl. Let it stand for 15 minutes to make
an infusion, then strain into the second bowl.
2 Clean the first bowl and add the soap flakes
and hot infusion. Leave for a few minutes until
the soap softens. Stir in the glycerin and food
colouring and beat until well combined.
3 Pour the mixture into the bottle. Keep in
a cool, dark place.

Instant dry shampoo

*Perfect for when you don't have time to wash and
dry your hair, or when full washing facilities are
not available, such as on camping trips.*

INGREDIENTS

enough for 1 application
- 1 tablespoon cornflour
  or finely ground oatmeal

1 Sprinkle small amounts of the cornflour or
oatmeal onto the hair, lifting up the hair in
sections so that the powder reaches the scalp
and does not merely settle on the top. Rub it
through the hair to absorb excess oil.

2 Comb the hair to remove tangles, and
then spend 5-10 minutes brushing (depending
on the length and thickness of the hair) to
remove all traces of the powder and prevent
the suggestion of dandruff. Shake and blow on
the brush to clean it while brushing the hair.

Dandruff treatment

*This strong infusion of rosemary and thyme can
help to eliminate dandruff. Shampoo and rinse the
hair thoroughly, then massage a small amount into
the scalp. Between shampoos, massage in a small
amount before going to bed.*

INGREDIENTS

makes about 300ml (10fl oz)
- 2 teaspoons rosemary
- 2 teaspoons thyme
- 150ml (5fl oz) boiling water
- 150ml (5fl oz) cider vinegar

You will need a heatproof ceramic bowl, a
fine sieve and a clean, airtight plastic bottle.
1 Place the herbs and boiling water in the
bowl. Cover and leave for 15-20 minutes.
2 Strain into the bottle, add the vinegar and
shake. Keep in a cool, dark place.

Soapwort shampoo

*Soapwort root can help relieve itching and dermatitis.
It makes an excellent shampoo, even though it does
not lather. To shampoo, apply 3 or 4 tablespoons,
working into the hair with your fingertips. Choose
herbs from the box on the opposite page.*

INGREDIENTS

makes enough for 6-8 shampoos
- 1½ tablespoons dried
  soapwort root, chopped
- 500ml (18fl oz) water
- 2 teaspoons dried herbs

You will need a non-reactive saucepan with
lid, a fine sieve and an airtight 500ml (18fl oz)
sterilised glass or plastic bottle.
1 Place the soapwort root and water in the
saucepan and bring to the boil. Cover and
simmer for 20 minutes.
2 Remove the saucepan from the heat and
add the dried herbs to the mixture. Cover and
leave to stand until cold.
3 Strain the mixture into the bottle and keep
in a cool, dark place handy to the shower.
It must be used within 7-10 days, so be
generous and share it with the family. Check
the soapwort shampoo regularly to make sure
it has not deteriorated.

Herbal rinse

*After shampooing, give your hair a lingering
fragrance with this rinse. For an itchy scalp, double
the quantity of herbs and use daily. Choose herbs
from the box on the opposite page.*

INGREDIENTS

makes enough for 1 application
- 1 tablespoon dried herbs
- 1 litre (1¾ pints) boiling
  water
- 40ml (1½fl oz) cider vinegar
- 1 drop green food
  colouring, optional

You will need two large heatproof ceramic
or glass bowls, a fine sieve and a cup.
1 Place the herbs in one bowl and pour the
boiling water over them. Cover and leave to
stand for 15-20 minutes.
2 Strain the infusion into the second bowl and
add the vinegar, and food colouring if desired.
3 After shampooing and rinsing your hair in
the normal way, hold your head over the bowl
and pour cupfuls of the herbal rinse over your
hair and comb through.

Constant shampooing can cause hair to lose its natural shine. For a gentle alternative to the strong chemicals that are found in many commercially available products, try these simple homemade preparations: Chamomile Shampoo (left), Pre-wash Honey Treatment (centre) and Herbal Rinse (right).

Pre-wash honey treatment

Your hair can often become damaged by exposure to the sun or harsh chemicals. Before washing your hair with shampoo, use this special treatment made with natural ingredients to condition the scalp and repair damaged hair. Use the treatment regularly if your hair is dry or splitting.

INGREDIENTS
makes enough for 1 application
- 2 tablespoons olive oil
- 2 teaspoons clear honey
- 5 drops rosemary, lavender or geranium essential oil

You will need a small cup, a ceramic or glass bowl, a small stainless-steel spoon, a plastic shower cap and a comfortably hot towel.

1 Warm the olive oil and the honey in a cup that is sitting in hot water (or you can use the microwave for heating). Stir in the essential oil of your choice and mix well.

2 While the mixture is still warm, apply it all over your hair, massaging well into the scalp. Cover the hair with the plastic shower cap, wrap the towel around the head, and leave these on for 10–15 minutes.

3 Remove the towel and shower cap and wash the hair with a mild shampoo, such as the Chamomile Shampoo (on the oppposite page).

HERBS FOR HAIR

CATMINT	Traditionally believed to promote hair growth.
CHAMOMILE	Can help to keep the scalp and hair follicles healthy, so that new hair grows well, and to heal scalp irritations.
COMFREY	Can soothe and heal scalp irritations.
ELDERBERRY	A berry traditionally used to add colour tones to greying hair.
LEMON BALM	Leaves a fresh citrus fragrance on the hair.
LEMON-GRASS	Has astringent properties, and can be effective in toning the scalp.
LEMON VERBENA	Leaves a fresh citrus fragrance on the hair.
NETTLE	An astringent herb that is beneficial in the treatment of skin irritations and itching.
PARSLEY	This common plant can be helpful in relieving skin irritations.
ROSEMARY	Is said to enhance the colour of dark hair, and to help control dandruff.
SAGE	An astringent for oily hair, and can be beneficial for damaged or fragile hair.
THYME	Has antiseptic, tonic and astringent properties.
YARROW	Acts as a tonic for the hair.

A Splash of Fragrance

In these days of costly and often quite similar commercial essences, what luxury
to wear a scent that says 'you'! Making your own splashes and colognes lets you vary ingredients
to create subtle fragrances that suit every mood and your personal taste

Essential eau de cologne

Eau de cologne was favoured by Napoleon. He is said to have used more than 50 bottles a month!

INGREDIENTS
makes about 200ml (7fl oz)
- 150ml (5fl oz) vodka
- 60 drops orange essential oil
- 30 drops each bergamot and lemon essential oil
- 6 drops neroli essential oil
- 6 drops rosemary essential oil
- 50ml (2fl oz) distilled or boiled water

You will need a sterilised glass bottle with a tight-fitting lid, a bowl and a paper coffee filter.
1 Pour the vodka and essential oils into the bottle, then leave for 1 week, shaking daily.
2 Add the water, shake and leave for 4-6 weeks.
3 Strain through filter into the bowl, then pour into bottle. Keep in a cool, dark place.

Lavender toilet water

The old-fashioned scent of lavender is one of the most popular – perfect for a present.

INGREDIENTS
makes about 250ml (9fl oz)
- 200ml (7fl oz) vodka
- 25 drops lavender essential oil
- 5 drops bergamot essential oil
- 50ml (2fl oz) distilled water
- 1 drop blue and 1 drop red food colouring, optional

Pour the vodka and both essential oils into a sterilised glass bottle with a tight-fitting lid. Shake well. Add the water and food colouring and leave for 2 weeks, shaking frequently.

Fruity body splash

If you like a citrus scent, this one is for you.

INGREDIENTS
makes about 600ml (1 pint)
- 1 tablespoon lemon peel
- 1 tablespoon orange peel
- 50ml (2fl oz) vodka
- 10 drops mandarin essential oil
- 10 drops orange essential oil
- 5 drops lemon essential oil
- 5 drops grapefruit essential oil
- 50ml (2fl oz) white wine vinegar
- 500ml (18fl oz) distilled or boiled water

You will need a fine sieve and a sterilised glass bottle with a tight-fitting lid.
1 Finely chop all the peel and place with the vodka in the bottle. Leave for 1 week.
2 Press the mixture through the fine sieve to extract all the liquid.
3 Pour the liquid back into the re-sterilised bottle. Add the essential oils, vinegar and water. Leave for 2 weeks, shaking often. Keep in a cool, dark place.

Rosewater perfume

Sprinkle a few drops of this onto your handkerchiefs for a delightfully scented dressing table drawer.

INGREDIENTS
makes about 50ml (2fl oz)
- 2 tablespoons vodka
- 2 tablespoons rosewater
- 8 drops bergamot essential oil
- 4 drops geranium essential oil
- 2 drops patchouli essential oil

You will need a sterilised glass bottle with a tight-fitting lid, a bowl and a paper coffee filter.

1 Place all the ingredients in the bottle, shake vigorously, and leave to stand for 2 weeks.
2 Strain the liquid through the paper filter into the bowl, then pour back into the bottle. Keep the perfume in a cool, dark place.

Carmelite water

Carmelite nuns in 14th-century France invented one of the earliest scents. Use sparingly as a perfume, or dilute for more liberal use.

INGREDIENTS
makes 300ml (10fl oz), or 800ml (1 pint 9fl oz) with water added
- 25g (1oz) lemon balm leaves
- 20g (¾oz) fresh lemon peel
- sprig sweet marjoram
- ½ cinnamon stick
- 5 whole cloves
- 1 teaspoon grated nutmeg
- 2cm (¾in) piece angelica stem
- 300ml (10fl oz) vodka
- 500ml (18fl oz) distilled water, optional

You will need a pestle and mortar, two or more sterilised glass bottles with tight-fitting lids, a fine sieve and a paper coffee filter.
1 Using the pestle and mortar, crush the dry ingredients. Place them in a small bottle, add the vodka and leave for 10 days, shaking daily.
2 Strain through the sieve into the bowl, pressing to extract all liquid. Drip through the paper filter into a freshly sterilised bottle.
3 To dilute, pour it into a larger bottle, then add the distilled water and shake. Leave for at least 2 weeks. Keep in a cool, dark place.

Clockwise from back, Carmelite Water, Rosewater Perfume and Lavender Toilet Water, three delightful fragrances you can make using your own ingredients.

◆ Natural Home Remedies ◆

The earliest cures were based on herbs. All ancient monasteries featured the herbarium
where the plants needed for healing work were grown. Many modern complaints respond well to
herbal treatments, which may have fewer side effects than commercial remedies

Acne and pimples

HERBAL STEAM FACIAL Place one handful
each of fresh thyme and calendula flowers in a
heatproof bowl. Add 1.5 litres (2¾ pints) of
boiling water. Lean over the bowl, cover the
head and bowl with a towel. With eyes closed,
remain for 10 minutes, then gently splash the
face with lukewarm water and pat dry.
MEDICATED STEAM FACIAL Put 2 drops of
essential oil (lemon, lavender, rosemary, tea tree,
geranium or cedarwood) in a bowl. Pour on
1 litre (1¾ pints) of boiling water, and proceed as
directed in the Herbal Steam Facial (above).
ESSENTIAL OIL TREATMENT Rub 1 or 2 drops
of tea tree or lavender essential oil on the
affected area. For a wide area, dilute in 20-40
drops light olive oil. Use once or twice a day.
ALOE VERA GEL Cut a fresh aloe vera leaf and
scoop out the gel. Rub in twice daily.
WITCH HAZEL INFUSION Dab the affected
area three times a day with an infusion (see
box, opposite page) of witch hazel leaves.

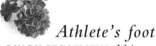

Athlete's foot

QUICK TREATMENT Using a cotton bud,
apply 2 drops tea tree essential oil directly to
the skin. For an extensive area, apply an oil
blend made by mixing 3 drops tea tree essential
oil in 1 teaspoon light olive oil.
HEALING OINTMENT Warm 50ml (2fl oz)
vegetable oil in a cup sitting in hot water.
Finely chop 10g (¼oz) beeswax and stir it into
the warmed oil until the wax melts. Remove
the mixture from the heat and stir until it
cools. Beat in 50 drops geranium, lavender, tea

An enormous range of herbs, flowers and natural
oils can be used to make safe and effective remedies
to relieve any number of common ailments.

tree, pine or peppermint essential oil (or make a combination of tea tree with any of these, not exceeding 50 drops in total). Spoon the ointment into a small, sterilised wide-mouthed jar with a tight-fitting lid. Keep in a cool, dark place. Massage a small amount into the affected area twice a day.

Bad breath

HERBAL BREATH SWEETENER Chew 1 or 2 fresh leaves of spearmint, peppermint, fennel or parsley for a minute or two, or several fresh or dried seeds of caraway, cardamom, fennel or dill. Alternatively, make an infusion (see box, right) with any of these herbs or seeds. For seeds, you will need to infuse 1 teaspoon for 30 minutes. Allow to cool before use. Gargle with this several times a day.

Bee stings and insect bites

First remove the sting by grasping near the base with tweezers and pulling carefully, or by pushing it out with a fingernail. Then you can use any of the following recipes to relieve the pain. Anyone prone to severe allergic reaction should follow the treatment they have been recommended by their doctor.
INSTANT RELIEF As an immediate step, you can apply some crushed leaves or flowers of chamomile to relieve the pain and prevent swelling. Simply applying ice to the spot will also provide quick relief.
BICARBONATE OF SODA PASTE To relieve itching, apply a paste that is made by combining ¼ teaspoon bicarbonate of soda with a little water.
ESSENTIAL OIL SOOTHER Essential oils have both soothing and healing properties. Fill a bowl with enough cold water to wet a small cloth or cotton wool pad. Swirl 1 drop of lavender, eucalyptus or tea tree essential oil through the water, then soak the cloth or pad. Squeeze gently to remove any excess water and apply the cloth to the skin. Hold it in place with your hand for as long as possible, or cover with cling film and leave on for 1 hour.

CAUTION

THE REMEDIES GIVEN here are not suitable for acute or chronic conditions. If an ailment fails to respond to a home remedy, consult your doctor immediately.

MAKING AN INFUSION

MAKING A HERBAL infusion is similar to making a cup of tea. In a cup place 3 rounded teaspoons of fresh herb leaves or 1 rounded teaspoon of dried herb leaves. Pour 100ml (3½fl oz) boiling water over the leaves, cover with a saucer and leave to stand for 5-10 minutes. Strain the infusion through a fine sieve or a piece of muslin, then discard the herbs. Drink the infusion while it is hot, or leave it to cool if you are going to use it as a lotion or gargle. Infusions can be kept in the refrigerator for up to 24 hours and heated whenever you want to use them.

Blisters

ESSENTIAL OIL APPLICATION Place 1 drop of tea tree or lavender essential oil onto the blister, gently massaging it in and taking care not to break the skin. Do not use this treatment on open blisters.
CALENDULA TREATMENT For open blisters, make an infusion (see box, above) of calendula flowers. Dab on and let dry. For foot blisters, apply a small amount of the Simple Calendula Ointment (see box, page 303) to a clean piece of gauze and cover the blister. Remove the gauze when not wearing shoes.

Body odour

FRESH HERB BATH Put a large handful of herbs in a piece of gauze. Choose from rosemary, lovage, lavender, lemongrass, sage, parsley or peppermint, individually or in combination. Tie the gauze and throw it in the bath. Rub the herbal pouch all over the skin, paying particular attention to areas where odour is a problem.
ALMOND MASSAGE OIL In a bowl, mix 2 tablespoons sweet almond oil with 10 drops lavender essential oil, 10 drops eucalyptus essential oil, 5 drops peppermint essential oil and 5 drops pine essential oil. Massage the body with the oil once or twice a week.

Boils

COMPRESS Put 30ml (1fl oz) hot water in a bowl. Swirl 2 drops lavender, lemon, tea tree or nutmeg essential oil through the water, then soak a pad of cotton wool or gauze. Gently squeeze out excess fluid and apply the cloth directly to the area of the boil. Cover the boil with cling film and secure in place with a bandage or tape. Leave on for at least an hour. Repeat the treatment twice a day.

Bruises

CIRCULATION STIMULANT Use two face flannels, or pads of cotton wool or gauze large enough to cover the bruise. Put 3 or 4 drops tea tree, lavender, geranium or rosemary essential oil into a bowl of cold water and swirl it around to disperse evenly. Swirl 3 or 4 drops of one of these essential oils in a bowl of hot water. Soak a flannel or pad in each bowl, and gently squeeze out excess fluid. Apply the hot and cold compresses alternately, directly to the area of the bruise, leaving each on for 2-3 minutes. Repeat several times.

FRAGRANT MASSAGE OIL Mix 5 drops essential oil with 1 teaspoon vegetable oil and massage into the bruise. For the essential oil, choose from lavender, geranium, rosemary or tea tree, using one or a combination.

Burns and sunburn

These suggestions are for the treatment of mild burns. For severe burns, seek medical attention immediately. Before applying a treatment, immerse the burnt area in cold, but not ice-cold, water or soak a clean cloth in water and apply to the burn to reduce the sensation of heat; then pat dry with a towel.

CALENDULA JUICE Apply the juice of crushed calendula petals several times a day. Crush the petals in your fingers or use a pestle and mortar if you need a larger amount.

ALOE VERA GEL Cut an aloe vera plant leaf, scoop out the gel and apply directly to the burn.

SOOTHING PASTE Mix a little bicarbonate of soda with water to make a thick paste and apply to the burn. Do not use on broken skin.

QUICK OIL RUB Apply 1 drop of tea tree or lavender essential oil to the skin and gently massage it in. For a more extensive area, dilute 1 drop essential oil in ¼ teaspoon olive oil and apply when the skin is cool. Use several times a day, but do not apply more than 10 drops of essential oil in 24 hours.

INFUSION FOR BROKEN SKIN If the skin is broken, dab on a cooled infusion (see box, page 301) of calendula flowers, raspberry leaves or ordinary tea leaves.

Chilli burns

NATURAL TREATMENT For burns caused by chillies, first wash the area with milk or cream. Then apply mashed avocado or banana flesh to the skin and leave on until the pain subsides. After eating chillies, alleviate the burning sensation in the mouth by drinking a glass of milk or eating a piece of avocado or banana. Do not drink water, as this can make the sensation worse.

Chilblains

FOOTBATH For unbroken chilblains, have a footbath once a day to stimulate circulation. Place 1 tablespoon ground ginger or hot chilli powder in a basin, stir in 500ml (18fl oz) hot water, then fill with hot water. Fill another basin with cold water. Soak the feet in the hot and cold baths alternately for 3-5 minutes each. Repeat this process six times, adding hot water as needed.

CHILLI OIL Chop 15g (½oz) fresh hot chillies with a sharp knife, holding the chillies with a fork to avoid contact with the skin. Spoon them into a clean jar and cover with 250ml (9fl oz) of vegetable oil. Seal tightly, shake well and leave for 10 days, shaking periodically. Strain the oil through a paper coffee filter into a sterilised 250ml (9fl oz) glass bottle with a tight-fitting lid and store in the refrigerator. Rub a few drops into the chilblains as needed. Do not use this preparation on broken skin.

TREATMENT FOR BROKEN CHILBLAINS For broken chilblains, dab on an infusion (see box, page 301) of calendula leaves, or rub in a small

amount of Simple Calendula Ointment (see box, opposite page).

Colds

FRAGRANT OIL BATH Fill a bath with comfortably hot water. Swirl in 6-8 drops lavender or peppermint essential oil and relax in the bath for 10 minutes. Pat gently dry, to retain essential oils on the skin.

CINNAMON SOOTHER Stir 1 teaspoon each of powdered cinnamon and lemon juice into a cup of hot water and sip slowly.

TRADITIONAL HERBAL REMEDY Mix 2 parts dried peppermint leaves, 2 parts dried lemon balm leaves and 1 part dried yarrow leaves, and store in an airtight container. Make an infusion (see box, page 301) with these as needed and drink three times daily.

Constipation

FRUIT AND FIBRE Soak about 5 prunes in orange juice or water overnight. Eat the prunes and drink the liquid before breakfast.

LINSEED DRINK Stir 1 teaspoon whole linseeds into a glass of water and drink. Follow with a second glass of water. Always drink at least 500ml (18fl oz) of fluid when ingesting linseeds. Use three times a day as a laxative.

Corns

NATURAL REMOVAL Crush a small dandelion leaf or a clove of garlic, scrape the inside of a banana or fig skin (about a teaspoon) or use the flesh of a squeezed lemon. Apply the pulp to the corn, binding it in place with a small adhesive bandage. When the skin is soft, gently rub the top layer of the corn away with an emery board. Repeat daily until the corn disappears. For several days after, massage the area with a small amount of Simple Calendula Ointment (see box, opposite page).

Coughs

VIOLET COUGH SYRUP Place 75g (2¾oz) fresh violet flowers in a heatproof bowl, pour on 500ml (18fl oz) boiling water, then cover and leave until cold. Strain the water through a fine sieve into a saucepan. Stir in 350g (12oz) granulated sugar and cook, still stirring, on a low heat, until dissolved. Simmer, without stirring, for 10-15 minutes until syrupy. Pour the syrup into a sterilised 500ml (18fl oz) glass bottle with a tight-fitting lid. The cough syrup will keep for about a year in the refrigerator. Take 1 teaspoon as needed.

HERBAL HONEY Place 1 tablespoon dried rosemary, thyme, aniseed or horehound in a sterilised 400ml (14fl oz) glass jar with a tight-fitting lid. Warm 400ml (14fl oz) honey in a bowl sitting in hot water, then pour this over the herbs. Leave in a warm place for about a week. Strain through a sieve and then pour into a freshly sterilised jar. Sip a teaspoon of the syrup as required.

Cuts and abrasions

ANTISEPTIC WASH Make an infusion (see box, page 301) using calendula flowers, garlic cloves or leaves of thyme, winter savory, sage or blackberry. Cool and keep in a cup or bottle. Bathe the cut or abrasion with the antiseptic wash several times a day.

TRADITIONAL CALENDULA OINTMENT To heal the skin, apply a small amount of Simple Calendula Ointment (see box, right) twice a day to the affected area.

GENTLE TEA TREE OINTMENT Warm 100ml (3½fl oz) olive oil in a double boiler. Add 20g (¾oz) beeswax to the oil and stir until it has melted. Remove the mixture from the heat and continue stirring until it cools and thickens. Add 1 teaspoon of tea tree essential oil and beat until cold. Spoon into a small sterilised jar or bottle. Gently spread the ointment onto the skin as required.

Diarrhoea

BERRY LEAF TEA Make an infusion (see box, page 301) of dried raspberry or blackberry leaves. Drink a small cup 3 times a day, and make sure you drink plenty of other fluids to prevent dehydration. If diarrhoea persists for more than 24 hours, see your doctor.

Eczema and dermatitis

CALENDULA FLOWER LOTION For quick relief, crush several calendula flower petals between your fingers (for larger amounts use a pestle and mortar) until they are juicy, then rub both petals and juice onto the skin.

SOOTHING BATH OIL Choose from pine, geranium or lavender essential oils and add 6-8 drops to a hot bath. Swirl the water around to disperse the oil, then relax in the bath for 10 minutes. After the bath, you can massage in any of the essential oil that is still left on the skin. Do not take this bath more than once in 24 hours.

ANTI-ITCH OINTMENT To ease symptoms of itching and dryness, apply a small amount of Simple Calendula Ointment (see box, below) to the affected area twice a day or as needed.

FLORAL INFUSION Dab a cooled infusion (see box, page 301) of fresh or dried calendula flowers onto the irritated area of skin several times a day or as needed.

SIMPLE CALENDULA OINTMENT

CALENDULA IS HIGHLY regarded as a soothing and healing herb and is used in a number of commercially available preparations for the treatment of skin problems. For this ointment, use only the old-fashioned variety (*Calendula officinalis*), which has several rows of bright orange or yellow ray flowers around a circular centre. Do not use the modern named cultivars or African, French or Mexican marigolds (*Tagetes* spp.).

Place 40g (1½oz) of fresh calendula petals in a double boiler and crush slightly with the back of a spoon. Add 110ml (3¾fl oz) light olive oil and then heat gently for 2 hours over a low heat. (Alternatively, place the crushed petals and the oil in a sterilised glass jar, seal and keep in a warm place for 2 weeks.)

Strain the liquid into a bowl, squeezing to extract all the oil, and then return it to the double boiler. Over a medium heat, add 20g (¾oz) chopped beeswax and stir until it melts. Remove bowl from the heat and beat the mixture until it cools and is thick and creamy. Add the contents of a 400 IU vitamin E capsule and mix in well.

Spoon the mixture into the jar, seal and keep in a cool, dark place, or divide the ointment between two smaller jars, keeping one handy and storing the other in the refrigerator. This recipe makes 125ml (4fl oz) of ointment.

CHICKWEED VARIATION Chickweed is renowned for treating inflamed skin. To make chickweed ointment, replace the calendula petals in this recipe with 60g (2¼oz) chickweed leaves.

Headaches and tension

LAVENDER WATER To ease tension after a hard day, soak a face flannel in Lavender Toilet Water (see page 298). Lie down on your back, place the flannel on your forehead and relax for 15 minutes or longer.

HERBAL TEA Make an infusion (see box, page 301) using chamomile or lemon balm leaves. Take a few minutes to slowly sip a cup of the hot tea while sitting in a quiet spot. You can sweeten the drink with a teaspoon of honey, if desired.

FEVERFEW Chewing a leaf of the feverfew plant can bring relief if you have a headache.

ESSENTIAL OIL FRESHENER Place 2 drops lavender, peppermint or geranium essential oil in a small bowl of lukewarm water. Swirl the water around to disperse the essential oil, and then leave a face flannel in the liquid until it is fully soaked. Gently squeeze out any excess water, lie back, place the flannel on the forehead and relax for as long as possible.

Hunger pangs

STOMACH SETTLER To alleviate hunger pangs at inappropriate times and to control stomach rumbling, you can chew on a few seeds, or a small piece of the stem, of fennel. Fennel is easy to grow from seed as long as it is protected from frost.

Indigestion and flatulence

SEED REMEDY Chew 1 teaspoon aniseed, dill or caraway seeds for a minute three times a day. Do not swallow the seeds.

DIGESTIVE BREW Place 1 teaspoon dill, aniseed or caraway seeds in a cup, crush with the back of a spoon, and add 100ml (3½fl oz) boiling water. Cover and leave for 30 minutes, then strain. Drink three times a day.

PEPPERMINT TEA A cup of peppermint tea is a traditional remedy for gas pains and is also a pleasant way to end a meal. Make an infusion (see box, page 301) of peppermint leaves and drink as needed. For persistent flatulence, drink three times daily for 2-3 days.

BACK MASSAGE

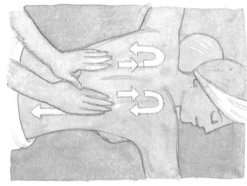

1 *Pour a little massage oil onto one palm and warm it by rubbing the hands together. With a gliding movement, slide the hands up and down the back to spread the oil, repeating this process once to spread it evenly.*

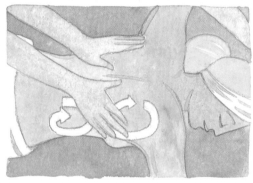

2 *Using small, circular movements, move your hands slowly from the buttocks up to the neck, pressing firmly but not too deeply. Repeat for 5-10 minutes as needed, increasing pressure gradually as the muscles relax.*

3 *Place one hand on each side of the back. Using small, circular movements, move each hand across to the other side then back again. Repeat twice. Continue like this down to the buttocks, then repeat the whole process several times.*

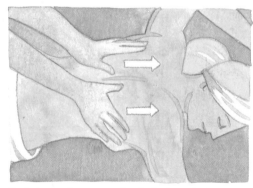

4 *As in step 2, move your hands slowly up the back to the neck, using small, circular movements. Repeat several times, decreasing pressure to wind down the massage. Finish with some light gliding strokes up and down the back.*

Insomnia

HERBAL NIGHTCAP Before going to bed, sip an infusion (see box, page 301) of chamomile or lemon balm. When sleep comes more easily, halve the concentration of the herb (continued use of the stronger concentration can cause sleeplessness to return). Stop taking the tea for a week after each 3 weeks of continuous use.

QUICK LAVENDER RUB Massage a single drop of lavender essential oil into the temples (that is, 1 drop for the two temples, not 1 drop each) before going to bed.

FRAGRANT LAVENDER PILLOW Dry a bunch of fresh lavender in a pillowcase kept in a warm linen cupboard. When needed, remove the lavender and insert a pillow into the case (put the lavender in another pillowcase for future use – it can be used like this for up to a year). The herb's sedative properties will help to induce a good night's sleep, and will last until the pillowcase is washed. Alternatively, you can place a single drop of lavender essential oil on the corner of your pillowcase each night.

Itching

ANTI-ITCH INFUSION Bathe the affected area with a cooled infusion (see box, page 301) of calendula flowers. This remedy is particularly effective in relieving the itchiness associated with childhood diseases such as chickenpox. Bathing with cooled chamomile or chickweed infusion also provides relief.

TOTAL BODY SOAK For extensive itching, mix 275g (9½oz) cornflour to a paste with a little water, and then add this mixture and 140g (5oz) bicarbonate of soda to a lukewarm bath. Swirl the water around to disperse the mixture, and immerse your body in the bath.

Low spirits

BATH OIL Fill the bath with comfortably warm water. Add no more than 6 drops of essential oil – any combination of lavender, geranium, pine, sandalwood or bergamot – and swirl the water around. Relax in the bath for about 10 minutes. The combination of warm bath water and the inhaled essential oils will help to calm the mind and lift the spirits.

Mouth ulcers

HERBAL MOUTHWASH Make an infusion (see box, page 301) of thyme or sage leaves, or marigold flowers. Alternatively, make an infusion using equal quantities of thyme leaves and marigold flowers, then add 50ml (2fl oz) cider vinegar. Use either of these liquids as a mouthwash three times a day.

Muscular aches

HERBAL MASSAGE OIL Place a large handful of fresh rosemary or lavender in a wide-mouthed jar. Add 500ml (18fl oz) vegetable oil, cover and leave for 10 days. Strain and store in a sterilised glass bottle in a cool place. It should keep for up to 6 months.

QUICK MASSAGE OIL In a glass or ceramic bowl, dilute 5 drops rosemary, tea tree or eucalyptus essential oil in a teaspoon of vegetable oil. Massage into aching muscles.

MASSAGE CREAM FOR SORE MUSCLES Pour 50ml (2fl oz) vegetable oil into a cup and stand it in hot water to warm. Finely chop 10g (¼oz) beeswax and stir it into the oil until melted. Remove the cup from the hot water and stir the mixture until cool. Beat in 50 drops tea tree, rosemary or eucalyptus essential oil, or a combination of these, not exceeding 50 drops in total. Spoon the cream into a small wide-mouthed jar. Massage a little into the painful area twice a day.

NECK-MASSAGE OIL Pour 2 tablespoons of vegetable oil into a small jar and add 30 drops of rosemary, lemon, ginger or peppermint essential oil, or a combination of these, not exceeding 30 drops in total. Shake well for several minutes and store in a cool place. Massage into the neck as required. For an effective neck-massage technique, use the step-by-step method given below.

BACK-MASSAGE OIL Pour 2 tablespoons of vegetable oil into a small jar and add 30 drops of peppermint, eucalyptus, lemon or rosemary essential oil, or a combination of these, not exceeding 30 drops in total. Shake the mixture vigorously for several minutes. Store the bottle in a cool, dark place until needed. For an effective back-massage technique, you can use the step-by-step method given on the opposite page.

MASSAGE FOR TIRED FEET Put 2 tablespoons of vegetable oil into a jar and add 30 drops rosemary, juniper, peppermint or lavender essential oil, or a combination of these, not exceeding 30 drops. Shake well for several minutes. Massage gently into the feet.

TREATMENT FOR CRAMP To soften the immediate effects of cramp, mix 2 teaspoons of vegetable oil with 10 drops lavender or rosemary essential oil, or a combination of these essential oils, not exceeding 10 drops. Massage a little into the muscles. To relieve the pain that follows a cramp, make a poultice: mix 2 teaspoons chilli or mustard powder with 1 tablespoon cornflour or rice flour, add a little hot water and stir to form a thick paste. Or you can mix the chilli or mustard powder with any mashed vegetable leftovers. Place the mixture in a cloth and fold to form a pad. Apply while comfortably hot to the site of the cramp and leave in place for up to an hour.

NECK AND SHOULDER MASSAGE

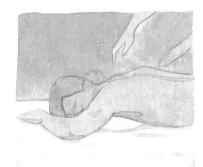

1 *Lay the person face down with a pillow under the chest. Pour a little massage oil onto one of your palms and warm it by rubbing your hands together. Spread the oil over the shoulders and neck, repeating once to ensure that it is spread evenly.*

2 *Place your hands on the shoulders as shown. Squeeze and knead the shoulders, moving from the outside to the centre. Repeat this movement for 5-10 minutes, as needed, gradually increasing the pressure as the muscles relax.*

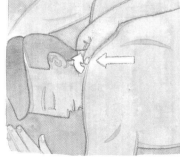

3 *Moving up from the base of the neck, massage the left side of the neck with your right hand, using small, circular thumb movements. Continue for 3-4 minutes, gradually increasing pressure. Repeat for the right side, with your left hand.*

4 *Place your hands on the edge of the shoulders and massage across to the base of the neck. Continue up each side of the neck using circular thumb movements. Repeat this several times, decreasing pressure to wind down the massage at the end.*

A steaming inhalant made from chopped fresh thyme is excellent for clearing nasal congestion. Acne and pimples also respond well to herbal steams.

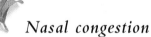

Nasal congestion

FRESH STEAM INHALANT Place 3 teaspoons finely chopped fresh thyme, sage, peppermint or pine needles in a small heatproof bowl and add enough boiling water to half-fill the bowl. Lean over the bowl, cover your head and bowl with a thick towel and inhale for 10 minutes. Repeat 2-3 times a day as needed.

INHALANT FOR SINUSITIS Put 2 drops of tea tree, eucalyptus or pine essential oil in a heatproof bowl with 1 litre (1¾ pints) boiling water. Lean over the bowl, cover your head and the bowl with a thick towel and inhale for

10 minutes. Stop before this time if you begin to feel uncomfortable. Sinusitis sufferers may find that difficulty in breathing is eased if they smear 2 drops tea tree essential oil over the palms, cup the hands over the nose and inhale deeply through the nose.

INSTANT DECONGESTANT Place 1 drop of tea tree, peppermint or rosemary essential oil on a handkerchief and inhale as needed.

Nosebleeds

HEALING AID With your head tilted forward, pinch the lower part of the nostrils with your thumb and forefinger. Hold for 5 minutes or longer until the bleeding stops. Then soak a ball of cotton wool in an infusion (see box, page 301) of witch hazel or calendula and gently insert into the nostril for a few minutes.

Rashes

HEALING OIL Put 1 drop lavender or tea tree essential oil directly onto the rash, gently smoothing it over the surface. To treat a large area, apply a blend made by mixing 3 drops essential oil in 1 teaspoon light olive oil.

GENTLE NAPPY RASH TREATMENT For nappy rash, wash the baby's bottom with an infusion (see box, page 301) of calendula or chamomile flowers. Pat the skin dry, then massage in a small amount of Simple Calendula Ointment (see box, page 303). Alternatively, combine 2 teaspoons sweet almond oil, 15 drops wheat germ oil, 5 drops borage oil and 1 drop lavender essential oil (note that, of these, only the lavender is an essential oil) and massage into the affected area. Leave the baby without a nappy for as long as possible.

Rheumatism and arthritis

RELIEVING COMPRESS For temporary relief of aching joints, fill a small bowl with warm water. Swirl in 2 drops rosemary, lavender, lemon or eucalyptus essential oil and soak a pad of cotton wool or gauze. Gently squeeze out any excess fluid and apply directly to the affected area. Cover with cling film or a bandage and leave for at least an hour.

SOOTHING BATH To relieve pain, soak in a comfortably hot bath in which 4 drops of rosemary, lavender or eucalyptus essential oil have been swirled. Gently massage in any oil still left on the skin after the bath.

CABBAGE LEAF WRAP Bruise a cabbage leaf with a rolling pin until soft. Wrap it around the painful joint and bind with a bandage.

BRACING MASSAGE OIL With a pestle and mortar, pound together 1 tablespoon chopped rosemary leaves, 3 teaspoons celery seed and 1 fresh chilli. Spoon into a jar with a tight-fitting lid and add 250ml (9fl oz) vegetable oil. Shake vigorously, then leave for 10 days, shaking periodically. Strain through a paper coffee filter into a sterilised glass bottle and keep in a cool, dark place. Rub 1 or 2 drops onto the skin to test for any adverse reaction. If there is no reaction, gently massage a little of the oil onto the aching joint twice a day.

Sore eyes

CUCUMBER TREATMENT Place a slice of fresh cucumber on each eye for several minutes.
EYEWASH INFUSION Make an infusion (see box, page 301) of calendula or chamomile flowers or borage leaves, strain twice through paper coffee filters and cool to lukewarm. Use in a glass eye bath, or soak a pad of cotton wool in the infusion and wash it into the eyes. Alternatively, soak two cotton wool balls and place them on the eyes for 10 minutes.

Sore throat

SOOTHING GARGLE Make an infusion (see box, page 301) using sage or thyme leaves. Gargle warm for a minute at a time, as needed. Gargling with a simple solution of ½ teaspoon salt in 250ml (9fl oz) warm water can also help to remove the pain of a sore throat.

Sprains

First soak the sprained limb in a bucket or sinkful of icy water or cover the sprain with an ice pack for 15-20 minutes. Repeat several times in the first 4 hours, then use any of the following remedies.
COLD COMPRESS Fill a small bowl with water and add 3 or 4 drops lavender, rosemary, eucalyptus, nutmeg or pine essential oil. Swirl the water to blend the oil, then thoroughly wet a face flannel or gauze pad. Squeeze gently to remove any excess water, then apply to the sprain. Cover the pad with cling film, then with a bandage. Leave on for at least an hour and repeat twice a day.
OLIVE OIL MASSAGE Pour 2 tablespoons light olive oil into a small jar and add 15 drops rosemary, 10 drops nutmeg and 5 drops eucalyptus essential oils. Shake well for several minutes, then massage into the sprained area.
FRESH LEAF POULTICE Bruise several fresh leaves of comfrey, cabbage and plantain with a rolling pin, then place in a clean cloth and fold to form a pad. Dip in comfortably hot water, squeeze, then apply to the skin and secure with a bandage. When cool, remove the pad, dip in hot water and reapply. Alternatively you can use a hot-water bottle to keep it hot.

Tiredness

BATH OIL If you are tired and you want to relax, put 6-8 drops essential oil into a comfortably hot bath, swirl the water to disperse the oils, then relax in the bath. For the essential oil you can choose lavender, geranium or cinnamon leaf. If you are tired and you want a lift, use peppermint or rosemary essential oil instead.
ROSEMARY AND GINSENG Slowly drink a cup of an infusion (see box, page 301) made from ½ teaspoon dried rosemary leaves and ½ teaspoon dried ginseng root, sweetened with a little honey, if desired.

Toothache

CLOVE BUD RINSE For relief from the pain until you can see a dentist, rinse the mouth with an infusion (see box, page 301) using a teaspoon of clove buds.
SIMPLE OIL RUB As a temporary measure, put 1 drop clove essential oil on a cotton bud, dip in water, then rub on the aching tooth and gum area. See a dentist as soon as possible.

Travel sickness

SIMPLE GINGER REMEDY An effective remedy is to chew on a lump of crystallised ginger as required. This is particularly effective for children. Always keep a packet in the car so it is there when you need it.
LEMON SETTLER Make a warm drink using the juice of 1 lemon in a cup of hot water sweetened with 1 teaspoon of honey. Sip as required. Keep the drink warm in a vacuum flask when travelling.

Warts

MILKY SAP TREATMENT Use the milky sap that exudes from freshly cut dandelion stalks. Apply the sap once or twice a day for several days or until the wart pulls away from the skin. Keep the sap away from the skin around the wart and from sensitive areas such as the eyes. If you are using this treatment on a child, cover the wart area with an adhesive bandage.

ALWAYS MAKE SURE you use the correct species of plant. You can't tell from a plant's common name which species it is, as several species may have the same name and even look similar to one another. If in doubt about identification, consult your local herbalist or nursery. The following is a list of plants that are referred to in this section, alongside their Latin names to ensure that you have exactly the right plant for your needs.

ALOE VERA *Aloe vera*
ANISEED *Pimpinella anisum*
BLACKBERRY *Rubus* spp.
BORAGE *Borago officinalis*
CALENDULA *Calendula officinalis*
CHAMOMILE *Chamaemelum nobile* or *Matricaria recutita*
CARAWAY *Carum carvi*
CARDAMOM *Elettaria cardamomum*
CHICKWEED *Stellaria media*
CINNAMON *Cinnamomum zeylanicum*
COMFREY *Symphytum officinale*
DANDELION *Taraxacum officinale*
DILL *Anethum graveolens*
FENNEL *Foeniculum vulgare*
FEVERFEW *Tanacetum parthenium*
HOREHOUND *Marrubium vulgare*
LAVENDER *Lavandula angustifolia*
LEMON BALM *Melissa officinalis*
PARSLEY *Petroselinum crispum*
PEPPERMINT *Mentha* x *piperita*
PINE *Pinus sylvestris, P. palustris, P. pinaster, P. radiata*
PLANTAIN *Plantago major, P. lanceolata*
RASPBERRY *Rubus idaeus*
ROSE *Rosa* spp.
ROSEMARY *Rosmarinus officinalis*
SAGE *Salvia officinalis*
SPEARMINT *Mentha spicata*
THYME *Thymus vulgaris*
VIOLET *Viola odorata*
WINTER SAVORY *Satureja montana*
WITCH HAZEL *Hamamelis virginiana*
YARROW *Achillea millefolium*

Index

herbal honey 303
honey-almond face scrub 290
honeycomb 89
lavender ice cream 86, *87*
pre-wash honey treatment 297
rose and honey body lotion
    282-3
horoscope cards 258, *259*
hummous 40, *41*

I

ice bowls 97
ice cream 15, 86-89
indigestion, treatments for 304
infusions, making 301
inhalant, fresh steam 306
insomnia, treatments for 304
interior decoration *see* decor
itching, treatments for 303, 304-5

J

jams 24-27
    acid 26
    bottling 14-15
    making 27
    pectin 26
    recipes 24-27
    sugar 26
jars, sterilising 278-9
jellies (preserves) 30-31

K

kirsch, peaches preserved in *82*, 83
kitchen
    cooking *see main entry*
    garden 162-7
    giftwrap 272, *273*
    shelves 143
    tiles 154, 155
    utensils 14, *15*, 278
    white goods cleaner 157
kites 232–5

kiwi fruit sorbet 90
Kourambiedes 78, *79*
Kugelhopf 63
kumquat marmalade 29

L

lampshades, stencilling 122
lattice, garden 185-8
lavender
    dried 146
    fragrant lavender pillow 304
    growing *164*
    ice cream 86, *87*
    insomnia, treatments for 304
    linen, in 157
    oil 278, 304
    quick lavender rub 304
    sachets 157
    tension, treatment for 304
    toilet water 298, *299*, 304
laxatives 302
Lebkuchen 80
leeks
    freezing 95
    leek and ham flamiche 45
leg massage cream 280, *281*
lemons
    fig and lemon jam 24
    lemon and almond cake 62
    lemon and lime chutney *21*, 22
    lemon hand cream *280*, 282
    lemon madeleines *60*, 61
    lemon-mint sorbet *87*, 92
    lemon settler for travel sickness
        307
    lemon spray-on furniture polish
        156
    lemon syrup 74, 77
    preserving 38
    see also citrus fruits
lettuce *see* salads: growing
lights, garden 200-1
limes
    Key lime pie 68
    lemon and lime chutney *21*, 22
    lime curd 27
    lime shred marmalade 28-29

spicy lime pickle 18
    see also citrus fruits
linseed drink for constipation 302
lips
    balm 290
    gloss 289
liver
    chicken liver pasta sauce 43
    chicken liver pâté 48, *49*
lotions
    body 282-3
    foot 280, *281*
    hand *281*, 283
    peppermint moisturising
        lotion *287*, 288
low spirits, treatment for 305

M

macadamia biscotti 64, *65*
macaroni, baked 43
magnets, dinosaur 238-9
malachite effect 242-3
mangoes
    mango chutney 20, *21*
    mango ice cream 86, *87*
    mango passion fruit sauce 88
marbling 144-5, 221, 241, *256*, 257
marmalades 28-29
    acid 26
    bottling 14-15
    making 27
    pectin 26
    recipes 28-29
    red onion *32*, 34
    sugar 26
marshmallows *71*, 72
massage
    almond massage oil 301
    back *304*
    back-massage oil 305
    bracing massage oil 306
    bruises, for 302
    cramp, for 305
    cream for sore muscles 305
    foot 305
    fragrant massage oil 302
    herbal massage oil 305

leg massage cream 278, *281*
neck *305*
neck-massage oil 305
oils 283, 301, 302, 305, 306, 307
olive oil massage 307
quick massage oil 305
shoulder *305*
mayonnaise
    Aïoli 36
    facial 290
meat
    barbecuing 38
    Caribbean spicy meat mixture 39
    freezing 97
    stock 50
    see also beef; ham; lamb; pork; veal
melons
    melon and peach sorbet 92
    watermelon facial 290
meringues *82*, 84, 85
mildew remover 157
mincemeat 78, *79*
mint *see* herbs
mirrors
    découpage 140-1
    disinfectant cleaner 156
    mosaic effects 114-15
moisturisers
    everyday facial moisturiser 286
    peppermint moisturising lotion
        287, 288
    pre-shave moisturiser 295
    rich neck moisturiser 288
    rose moisturising cream 286, *287*
mosaic effects 114-15
mounting *see* framing/
        mounting
mouth care
    citrus antiseptic mouthwash
        292, *293*
    herbal mouthwashes 293, 305
    teeth *see main entry*
    ulcers, treatments for 305
muffins
    apple and sultana 67
    blueberry 66
    herb and bacon 66
    orange and date 66
muscles, aching, treatments for 305

curry 37–38
dessert 85, 88
pasta 42–43
sausages 48–49
scarecrows 192
scents
  Carmelite water 298, *299*
  essential eau de cologne 298
  fruity body splash 298
  lavender toilet water 298, *299*
  rosewater perfume 298, *299*
  summer body splash 283
  tangy body cologne 295
scones 67
seafood *see* fish
seeds
  constipation, treatment for 302
  digestive brew 304
  dried seed arrangements 149
  linseed drink 302
  seed bread 57
  seed mustard 36
  seed remedy for indigestion
    and flatulence 304
  sesame Parmesan biscuits 64, *65*
  sesame pumpkin damper *53*, 54
septic tank activator 157
sewing
  appliquéing 228, *229*
  children's clothes 228–31
  mitring *222*
  patchwork 223–7
  piping *248*
  quilting 223–7
  stitches 222
  table linen 244, *245*, 246–9
shampoos 296, *297*
shaving
  aftershave splash 295
  cut lotion 295
  pre-shave moisturiser 295
  soap, fragrant 295
shell decorations *250*, 252–3
shellfish *see* fish
shelves 142–4
sherry (sabayon sauce), peach
    compote with 84
shortbread fingers, orange 78, *79*
shoulder massage *305*

shower preparations *see* bath
    and shower preparations
skin
  blisters, remedies for 301
  care
    children 306
    men 294–5
    women *see* body/face/
      foot/hand/leg care
  chilblains, remedies for 301
  conditions, remedies/treatments for
    acne 300
    athlete's foot 300–1
    boils 302
    dermatitis and eczema 303
    itching 304–5
    nappy rash 306
    pimples 300
    rashes 306
    spots 300
    warts 307
  corns, removal of 302
  sunburn, treatments for 302
sinusitis, inhalant for 306
sleeplessness, treatments for 304
soap
  almond-rose 285
  fragrant shaving soap 295
soapwort
  face cleanser 287
  shampoo 296
soda bread *53*, 54
soil, feeding 160–1
sorbets
  kiwi fruit 90
  lemon-mint 92
  making 93
  melon and peach 92
  strawberry 90
sourdough 56
Spanakopitakia 46
spices 37–39
spinach
  freezing 95
  Spanakopitakia 46
sponging 106, 118, *119*
spots, treatments for 300
sprains, treatments for 307
spreads 40–41

sprouts, Brussels: freezing 95
squash, freezing 95
stamps, novelty 236–7
steam inhalant, fresh 306
stencilling
  craft 221
  interior decoration 102–3, 107–9,
    118, 120, 122
steps, garden 160, *183*
sterilising *see* bottles: sterilising
stings, treatments for 301
stitches, sewing 222
stocks 50–51
Stollen 81
stomach rumbling, remedy for 304
strawberries
  growing 170–1
  red wine and strawberry cup
    75, 76
  strawberry cream cake *60*, 61
  strawberry facial 290
  strawberry ice poles 91
  strawberry jam 24, *25*
  strawberry sorbet 87, 90
  strawberry yoghurt mask 291
sultana and apple muffins 67
sunburn, treatments for 302
sweetcorn, freezing 95
sweets 70–73
syrup for freezing fruit 96

T

tables
  decorating 117, 244–9
  linen 244, *245*, 246–9
  painting 121
  placemats *245*, 246–9
tags, gift *266*, *267*, 268–9
tapenade 40
tarts, sweet 68
tassels 127–8
  paper 269
tea
  iced 76
  leaves as fertiliser 217
tea tree oil 278, 300, 303
  gentle tea tree ointment 303

teeth
  cashew nut oil 293
  cinnamon mint tooth powder
    292
  minty-fresh toothpaste 292, *293*
  sage 293
  toothache, treatments for 307
tension, treatments for 304
terrines *see* pâtés
throat, sore, treatment for 307
tiles, painting 154–5
tiredness, treatments for 307
toddlers *see* children
toilet cleaner 157
tomatoes
  bottled tomato sauce *33*, 34
  fresh tomato pasta sauce 42
  green tomato chutney 20, *21*
  growing *162–3*, 166
  olive and sun-dried tomato bread
    53, 54
  oven-dried *33*, 34
  pots, in *162–3*, 166
  puttanesca sauce 43
  spicy tomato chutney *21*, 22
  sun-dried tomato pesto 43
  tomato and basil salsa 33
  tomato herb tart 44, *45*
tools
  decorating *101*, 102, 103
  garden *161*, 190, *191*
toothache *see* teeth
tortoiseshell finish 221, 240
toothache, treatments for 307
toothpaste, tooth powder 292, *293*
travel sickness, remedies for 307
trees
  fruit 168–9
  planting 168, 169
  pruning 168, 169, 178
  topiary 176–8
  training 168–9
trellises 185–9
troppo ice blocks 91
Turkish delight *71*, 73

316

U

ulcers, mouth, treatments for 305
upholstering chairs *132*, 134

V

vanilla
  ice cream 88
  pudding 85
veal, ham and pork terrine 48, *49*
vegetables
  chutneys 20-22
  freezing 94-95
  growing 162-3, 165-7
  mixed, freezing 95
  mixed vegetable pickle 16
  pickles 16-19
  pots, in 162, *163*
  salad *162-3*
  stock 51
  see also names of vegetables
vindaloo paste 37

vinegar
  flavoured vinegars 35
  scented vinegar toner 289
vodka
  citrus vodka liqueur 76
  hot Bloody Mary *74*, 76

W

wallpaper borders 116
walls
  borders *103*, 116, 155
  colour 101
  design *102*
  fresco effect 104
  ornaments on *102*
  painting 104-7
  proportions 100
  ragging 105-6
  sponging 106
  stencilling 102-3, *107*, *108*, 109
  texture *100*
walnut and pear bread *56-57*, 58

warts, treatments for 307
washing gel, fabric 157
washing-up liquid 156
water features 161
whisky eggnog *74*, 76
white bread, country 55, *57*
wholemeal seed bread 57
wind, remedies for 304
windows
  disinfectant cleaner 156
  painted glass 125-6
wine, red, and strawberry cup *75*, 76
wirework 161
  garden lights 200-1
  pot stands 206-7
  strawberry hangers 171
  topiary 178
witch hazel infusion for acne
    and pimples 300
woodwork: shelves 142-4

Y

yeast 15
  breads 55-59
  Kugelhopf 63
yoghurt
  frozen chocolate-nut 93
  frozen passion fruit 92
  strawberry yoghurt mask 291

Z

zabaglione, iced 93

Conversion Charts

You may find these conversion charts useful if you find working in metric measurements difficult.
Remember that it is never wise to mix metric and imperial measurements in the same recipe as amounts given are not necessarily
exact equivalents. So if you start in metric, continue in metric throughout the project.

WEIGHT

Metric	Approx imperial	Metric	Approx imperial
5g	⅛oz	425g	15oz
10g	¼oz	450g	1lb
15g	½oz	500g	1lb 2oz
20g	¾oz	550g	1lb 4oz
25g	1oz	600g	1lb 5oz
35g	1¼oz	650g	1lb 7oz
40g	1½oz	675g	1lb 8oz
50g	1¾oz	700g	1lb 9oz
55g	2oz	750g	1lb 10oz
60g	2¼oz	800g	1lb 12oz
70g	2½oz	850g	1lb 14oz
75g	2¾oz	900g	2lb
85g	3oz	950g	2lb 2oz
90g	3¼oz	1kg	2lb 4oz
100g	3½oz	1·2kg	2lb 10oz
115g	4oz	1·25kg	2lb 12oz
125g	4½oz	1·3kg	3lb
140g	5oz	1·5kg	3lb 5oz
150g	5½oz	1·6kg	3lb 8oz
175g	6oz	1·75kg	3lb 13oz
200g	7oz	1·8kg	4lb
215g	7½oz	2kg	4lb 8oz
225g	8oz	2·25kg	5lb
250g	9oz	2·5kg	5lb 8oz
275g	9½oz	2·7kg	6lb
280g	10oz	3kg	6lb 8oz
300g	10½oz	3·5kg	8lb
325g	11½oz	4·5kg	10lb
350g	12oz	5·5kg	12lb
375g	13oz	6kg	14lb
400g	14oz	8·5kg	18lb

VOLUME

Metric	Approx imperial	Metric	Approx imperial
30ml	1fl oz	1.2 litres	2 pints
50ml	2fl oz	1.3 litres	2¼ pints
75ml	2½fl oz	1.4 litres	2½ pints
85ml	3fl oz	1.5 litres	2¾ pints
90ml	3¼fl oz	1.7 litres	3 pints
100ml	3½fl oz	2 litres	3½ pints
125ml	4fl oz	2·5 litres	4½ pints
150ml	5fl oz ¼ pint	2.8 litres	5 pints
175ml	6fl oz	3 litres	5¼ pints
200ml	7fl oz ⅓ pint		
225ml	8fl oz		
250ml	9fl oz		
300ml	10fl oz ½ pint		
330ml	10½fl oz		
350ml	12fl oz		
375ml	13fl oz		
400ml	14fl oz		
425ml	15fl oz ¾ pint		
450ml	16fl oz		
500ml	18fl oz		
600ml	1 pint 20 fl oz		
568ml	1 pint milk		
650ml	1 pint 2fl oz		
700ml	1¼ pint (1pint 5fl oz)		
750ml	1 pint 7fl oz		
800ml	1 pint 9fl oz		
850ml	1 pint 10fl oz		
900ml	1 pint 12fl oz		
1 litre	1¾ pints		

SPOONS

Metric	Imperial
1·25ml	¼ teaspoon
2·5ml	½ teaspoon
5ml	1 teaspoon
10ml	2 teaspoons
15ml	1 tbsp/3 tsp
30ml	2 tablespoons
45ml	3 tablespoons
60ml	4 tablespoons
75ml	5 tablespoons
90ml	6 tablespoons

LINEAR MEASUREMENTS

Metric	Approx imperial	Metric	Approx imperial	Metric	Approx imperial
2mm	1/16in	9.5cm	3¾in	27cm	10¾in
3mm	1/8in	10cm	4in	28cm	11in
5mm	¼in	11cm	4¼in	29cm	11½in
8mm	⅜in	12cm	4½in	30cm	12in
10mm/1cm	½in	13cm	5in	31cm	12½in
15mm	⅝in	14cm	5½in	33cm	13in
2cm	¾in	15cm	6in	34cm	13½in
2·5cm	1in	16cm	6¼in	35cm	14in
3cm	1¼in	17cm	6½in	37cm	14½in
4cm	1½in	18cm	7in	38cm	15in
4·5cm	1¾in	19cm	7½in	39cm	15½in
5cm	2in	20cm	8in	40cm	16in
5·5cm	2¼in	21cm	8¼in	42cm	16½in
6cm	2½in	22cm	8½in	43cm	17in
7cm	2¾in	23cm	9in	44cm	17½in
7·5cm	3in	24cm	9½in	46cm	18in
8cm	3¼in	25cm	10in	48cm	19in
9cm	3½in	26cm	10½in	50cm	20in

TEMPERATURE EQUIVALENTS FOR GAS AND ELECTRIC COOKERS

This table, based on information by British Gas and the Electricity Council, compares oven thermostats marked in °C with those marked in °F, and with gas marks. These are specimen dial markings, not conversions.

°C	°F	Gas mark
110	225	¼
120	250	½
140	275	1
150	300	2
160	325	3
180	350	4
190	375	5
200	400	6
220	425	7
230	450	8
240	475	9

Printing and binding: Brepols Graphic Industries NV,
Turnhout, Belgium
Paper: Townsend Hook Ltd, Snodland, England

040-706-01